CPPR

961   CPPR

David Dorward

was born and educated in Dundee. After graduating MA in English and Philosophy at St Andrews he completed a law degree and training in Dundee. National Service (at NATO HQ in Fontainbleau) was followed by a very brief period in legal practice. In 1959 he joined the administrative staff of his old university, where he remained for 32 years, eventually attaining the position of Secretary. Retirement at age 60 enabled him to indulge to the full his desire to write, and his publications include *Scottish Surnames; Scotland's Place-names; Dundee, Names, People and Places* and *The Glens of Angus*. He and his wife Joy live in retirement in Strathkinness, in sight of their beloved Sidlaws and Grampians.

SCOTTISH
SURNAMES

David Dorward

mercatpress
www.mercatpress.com

First published in 1995 by HarperCollins

This edition published 2003 by Mercat Press Ltd
10 Coates Crescent, Edinburgh EH3 7AL
www.mercatpress.com

ISBN: 184183 0453

Set in Palatino and Korinna at Mercat Press

Printed and bound in Great Britain by
Bell & Bain Ltd, Glasgow

INTRODUCTION

Although Scotland is a small country of less than five million inhabitants, forming part of the United Kingdom of Great Britain and Northern Ireland, there are reckoned to be thirty million persons of Scottish descent scattered over the globe, many of them bearing family or given names from their country of origin. Not surprisingly there is quite a degree of world-wide interest in Scottish names. Despite the numbers involved, the repertoire of names is not large and it is possible to make a study of them which is both systematic and discursive in nature; the small proportion of different surnames (compared say with England and the USA) is due mainly to the nature of Scotland's social structure in mediaeval times, which was feudal in the Lowlands and tribal in the Highlands, and always patriarchal in character.

For the present purpose the Scottishness of a name is to be judged by its current prevalence in this country and not by its historical or linguistic origin. To use other criteria would be to eliminate names such as **Kelly** (thirty-ninth commonest in the land) and to clutter the columns with interesting but obsolete examples like Morville or Muschet. The result is a collection of around one thousand names, reckoned to be the commonest in Scotland. In passing it may be noted that their linguistic origins work out approximately as follows: Anglo-Saxon (which for this purpose includes Scots) 35%; Scottish Gaelic 21%; Irish Gaelic 11%; Norman-French 7%; Norse 4%; other (comprising mainly classical and biblical) 14%. Interestingly and perhaps disappointingly, 'other' contains no names whatever of Italian, Polish, Asian or African origin: they are simply not present in sufficient numbers in the statistical records to justify inclusion.

Personal Names

The Scottish personal name system is common to English and the other Indo-European languages: that is to say, forenames (which in every culture precede surnames by many centuries) come from three main sources: 1. Classical (e.g. Alexander, Hector); 2. Biblical (e.g. David, John); 3. Vernacular (e.g. Lamb– now only found as a surname– and Sven or Swein). The familiar compound Germanic formations popularised by the Norman invaders are as common in Scotland as in England: such names are William (*Wilhelm*– 'will helmet'), Robert (*Hroth beorht*– 'fame bright'), and Henry (*Heinrich*– 'home rule') where each element has a meaning but the total formation is senseless. The 'themes' of these names were usually macho and prestigious, rather like the brand names of cigarettes and motor-cars in our own time. It is the admixture of Norse and Gaelic elements which provides the characteristic Scottish sound of such forenames as Gunn and Ronald, Angus, Douglas, Duncan, Ewan and Lachlan: each of these forenames, and many others besides, became the basis of a surname

The stock of forenames in the mediaeval period was remarkably small; names tended to run in families and had to be perpetuated, and this resulted sometimes in the inconvenience of two siblings sharing the same forename (see **Hutton**, **Rattray**, **Soutar**). In Gaelic-speaking areas the repertoire was varied by invoking the name of a saint. The Celtic world abounded in saints, each of whom had his or her name day, and it was common to name a child according to the saint appropriate to its natal day. In Gaelic-speaking areas this could be accompanied by the use of the prefix *maol* (a devotee, literally a 'tonsured one'); the devotee of St Columba was **Malcolm** and the devotee of Jesus was Malise or Mellish. Even more common was the use of the prefix *gille* (Gaelic for lad or servant) which gives **Gilchrist**, **Gillies** (servant of Jesus), Gilbride (St Bridget), Gilfeather (St Peter), Gilmartin and many others, which later became familiar surnames.

Surnames

Scholars recognise in every culture a 'surname period', i.e. a stage when society becomes too complex to make it possible to identify individuals by given name alone. In England this is reckoned to have taken place as society became stabilised after the Norman Conquest of 1066. There was of course no Norman conquest of Scotland, which remained a sovereign and independent state until the beginning of the 18th century. However, in the early mediaeval period there was little in the way of a fixed boundary between Scotland and England; the Anglian population came as far north as the Forth (and the Cumbrian as far as the Clyde), and the result in these areas was a common name-system. Even more important was the marriage of the Conqueror's son with Malcom Canmore's daughter, and the subsequent peaceful Normanisation of the upper echelons of Scottish society. Beginning in the 12th century there was a large influx of Anglo-Norman settlers into Scotland, a trend encouraged by the early Scottish kings who wished to see the replacement of unruly Celtic chiefs by magnates who spoke a more accessible language. A result of this influx and of the subsequent feudalisation of Lowland Scotland was the emergence of a host of surnames, including those of the great dukedoms and earldoms such as **Hamilton**, **Crawford**, and **Lindsay**; these names became very widespread when adopted in large numbers by vassals and serfs, and later by tenants and retainers of the great families.

In the Gaelic-speaking Highlands, the 'surname period' is of much longer duration, beginning with the origins of the clan system and lasting almost until modern times. Most clans claim to have a historical progenitor belonging to the 12th century, and some Irish ones–such as the O' Neills–can go back a further 200 years. At the other end of the scale, a surname could be created instantly and at will by adding a *Mac* prefix to any existing name, and this process continued until long after the 'surname period' in the Lowlands was over. An 18th-century parish register contains the entry 'Hugh Machuisteanmacuileammacrory alias Mackay', which is a four-generation pedigree containing the information that its referent is the son of Uisdean, grandson of William and great-grandson of Rory. On the adoption of his alias, Hugh's alternative *Mac* names would be abandoned and in some cases lost. Surnames which change with each generation are still a feature of the Icelandic name-system.

The Principal Types of Surname

It is generally recognised that in Western European cultures there were four distinct ways of acquiring a surname. In the Scottish context these are (a) by taking the father's Christian name and using it as a patronymic (e.g. **Davidson**, **MacGregor**); (b) by taking the name of one's occupation (e.g. **Smith** or its Gaelic equivalent **Gow**); (c) by taking a locality name, either specific (e.g. **Ross**, **Sutherland**) or general (e.g. **Wood**, **Hill**); and (d) by receiving a nickname which sticks (e.g. **Brown**, **Little**, **Young**). There is a fifth way, which does not create a surname but adopts an existing one, and the classic case is that of the individual who called himself **MacFarlane** out of admiration for the motif on a biscuit tin.

(a) Patronymics

Scotland has perhaps more than its usual quota of these, and the Lowland names **Thomson**, **Robertson**, **Wilson**, **Anderson**, **Johnson**, **Paterson**, **Watson** and **Henderson** are among the thirty commonest. The Scots language forms its diminutives in a different way from English (for example, preferring the suffix -ie to the suffix -kin—compare Scots 'mannie' with English 'mannikin'). The hypocoristic versions (pet forms) of these patronymics provide a large number of surnames; thus, **Robbie** equates to the English Robinson/Robson and **Dickie** to English Dickson/Dickens.

Mac names are by definition patronymics. They account for no more than twenty percent of Scotland's surnames, even in the Highlands. They however cut across the various classifications and deserve a section to themselves.

(b) Locality Names

While there is a tendency in England for places to be named after people, in Scotland people tend to be named after places. The familiar English formations of Birmingham, Kensington, Nottingham (where the homestead takes its name from the tribal leader) are confined to those southernmost portions of Scotland where the Anglo-Saxon naming system was powerful; elsewhere in Scotland settlement-names are much more likely to be topographical in character. Documentary evidence for Scottish surnames in the mediaeval period is sparse, and we are lucky to have the Ragman Roll of 1296, an instrument of homage which Edward I extracted from all substantial Scottish landholders during his military campaign of that year. The Roll lists around two thousand contemporary nobility, barons, landowners, burgesses and clergy (a thinly-populated Scotland); by no means all those listed have surnames (some are just forenames with territorial designations), but the vast majority of surnames are of the locality-type. This confirms the statement by the late 16th-century historian Hector Boece that in 1061 Malcolm Canmore directed his chief subjects to adopt surnames from their possessions. Boece records such names as **Calder, Lockhart, Gordon, Seton, Galloway, Lauder, Menzies, Meldrum, Shaw, Learmonth, Cargill, Rattray, Dundas, Cockburn, Mar, Abercrombie, Morton** and **Leslie**; not all of these are in fact territorial names, which may indicate that their etymologies were already obscure to a historian writing in the 16th century; however, it may be accepted that there was a directive from above for people of importance to take locality names. Subsequent monarchs imported to Scotland many English nobles whose names and those of their retainers testify to a continental origin: Balliol, Bethune (**Beaton**), **Bruce**, **Colville**, **Fraser**, **Hay**, **Melville** and **Montgomery**, which now sound quintessentially Scottish, are all derived from places in north-western France. Other immigrants at this time brought their English settlement-surnames, and these include **Graham**, **Ramsay** and **Gourlay**. To this list might be added the Scottish locality-names **Murray**, **Ross**, **Forbes** and **Douglas**, which, as surnames, subsequently became famous in Scotland's history.

The common people followed the patrician example, and locality names became frequent, no longer with the implication that the bearer was the owner of the territory from which the name was taken. Some incomers brought the names of their country or state– **Fleming** from Flanders, **Norrie** from Norway, **Bremner** from Brabant, Danskin from Danzig. **Strang** or **Strange** were names that might be given to any stranger. As often as not, a name would have an unspecified location: **Wood** meant a dweller at a wood (any wood); more specifically, **Hislop** came from the hazel valley. Many Gaelic habitational names achieved greater fame as surnames: **Buchanan**, **Urquhart** and **Drummond** are examples. Sometimes it is the place of occupation that is referred to in a surname: **Spence** (cf. Sir Patrick Spens of ballad fame) meant a worker in a larder, and **Milne** is literally 'at the mill'.

(c) Occupational names

As might be expected, names derived from trades and occupations were to be found mainly in the burghs, where English was the dominant language (Gaelic survived much longer in rural areas). These names record a multitude of different trades and functions, some of them very specialised. **Smith** is the commonest name in Scotland, England and the USA. The next most celebrated is

Stewart, from the hereditary post of High Steward of Scotland, and which became the name of the royal dynasty from 1370 to 1714. But as James V rightly observed, 'all Stewarts are na sib [not related] to the king', and there were many humbler sty-wards (hall-keepers) who graced the name.

Most late-mediaeval trades are commemorated in occupational names, and those with a peculiarly Scottish accent include: **Lamont** (law-man), **Lorimer** (harness-maker), **Naismith** (cutler), **Napier** (linen-draper), and **Sillars** (silversmith). Various types of herdsman are recorded in **Hoggarth**, **Shepherd** and **Stoddart**. The obsolete agency-suffix '-ster' acquired contemptuous associations in English–e.g. trickster, punster, gangster–but retains its respectability in the Scottish surnames of **Baxter** (baker), **Brewster** (brewer), **Dempster** (arbiter), **Lister** (dyer), and **Webster** (weaver).

(d) Nicknames

At first sight there is little to distinguish these from a corresponding list of English names: the simple adjectives of colour, size etc. give such names as **Brown** (the second commonest name in Scotland), **Black**, **Gray**, **White**, **Small** and **Young**–none of which sounds particularly Scottish. But in their respective Gaelic versions they appear as **Dunn**, **Duff**, **Glass**, **Bain**, **Begg** and **Ogg**. Two of the most celebrated of Highland names–**Cameron** and **Campbell**– are thought to belong to the nickname class, as do **Forsyth** and **Kennedy**. Another type of nickname is racial in character, and refers to the bearer's ethnic rather than geographical origin. **Scott** is perhaps the most famous of these names; it dates from the time when non-Scottish inhabitants of North Britain (in the form of Britons, Angles and Normans) were still clearly identifiable; and ethnic diversity is further illustrated by the names **Wallace**, **Galbraith** and **Inglis**.

Mac names

No discussion would be complete without an analysis of *Mac* names, of which there are reckoned to be over twelve hundred different examples on record. Very many of these are completely unfamiliar nowadays for reasons which are explained below.

The classic *Mac* name is monogenetic, i.e. has a single point of origin in the common progenitor and founder of the eponymous clan. Originally a clan surname would be used more for the purposes of identification than differentiation: thus, the descendants of the 13th century Eoin mac Griogair ('John, son of Gregor') would band together under the aegis of the clan MacGregor (literally 'children of Gregor's son'). But for day-to-day purposes **McGregor** would give insufficient differentiation, and 'by-names' referring to immediate parentage, occupation, appearance, age, etc., might in time become permanent surnames (see **Gow**, **Ogg**).

Not all *Mac* names indicate a clan affiliation: it was the custom to create ephemeral surnames by adding the Mac prefix to an existing name, and such a process is of frequent occurrence on the fringes of Gaelic-speaking territory, where Lowland first-names had already penetrated in their hypocoristic or pet forms. Examples of these Highland border surnames are **MacFadzean** (son of Paton), **MacRobbie**, **MacWattie** (son of Walter) and **MacGibbon** (son of Gilbert). These are family surnames which happened to become permanent.

Another group of *Mac* names is occupational, where reference is to the son of a person with a particular function. **MacIntyre** is *mac an-t saor*, the son of the carpenter; **MacTaggart** the son of a (lay) priest; **MacPherson** the parson's son and **MacIntosh** the son of the chief. Sometimes the reference is to a person of particular appearance or character–such as **MacGlashan**, son of the grey man; or **MacCall**, son of the warrior; or **MacQuarrie**, son of the proud one.

The Lost *Mac* Names

Only two or three hundred of the recorded *Mac* names are in common currency today, and the reasons are partly linguistic and partly historical. Linguistically, many of these *Mac* names are very unwieldy, and, to non-Gaelic speakers, virtually unpronounceable. Awkward surnames tend to drop out of use, or to be phonetically assimilated to another name or to be translated into the majority language. Someone moving from the Highlands to an anglophone area and whose name was MacComghan was quite likely to modify the spelling of his name to **Cowan** (which sounds much the same); and a MacThoimish might well become plain **Thomson** in similar circumstances.

The historical reasons for the depletion of *Mac* names are equally compelling. Not all members of a Highland clan bore the clan surname: on the contrary, it is known that the clan Cameron, to take a random example, consisted of persons with such names as MacChlerich, Macgillonie, Macildowie, MacOnie, MacOurlie, MacSorley, MacWalrick and MacEantach. When these clansmen left their native glens for the Lowland towns or the colonies they would do one of two things with their cumbersome surnames– they would adopt the clan surname of Cameron or else take a random and neutral name such as Smith or Brown. That partly explains why there are so many Smiths and Browns–and Camerons–in Scotland today.

Spelling of surnames did not become standardised until well into the 19th century. The form 'Mc' is simply a printers' contraction and implies nothing as to the history of the name or the genealogy of its bearer. Similarly it is a matter for individual choice whether or not the stem has a capital letter, although Maclean is surely more correct than **MacLean**. (For the purpose of consistency, the stem of every *Mac* name is given a capital letter in this dictionary except where specific individuals or families are referred to). Many of the early Highland emigrants would be illiterate and would take with them only the sound of their surnames: this accounts for some of the bizarre spellings of Gaelic names found mainly in North America, where MacLeod has appeared as McCloud, and MacLachlan as McGlauflin. Other choice examples are MacCambridge (son of Ambrose), Furguson, Chissim and Urghad.

Immigrant Names

Scotland's population has been continually on the move since the beginning of recorded history, and probably well before. The Picts were originally immigrants, speaking a language about which very little is known; the Strathclyde Britons spoke a variety of P-Celtic akin to Welsh (which is referred to as Brittonic for the purposes of this work); the Scots were 5th-century immigrants from Ireland, speaking a Q-Celtic language which evolved into Gaelic. The Norsemen were more than just hit and run raiders and in fact colonised the northern and western isles for more than three centuries until they were seen off at the Battle of Largs in 1263; although Norse did not survive beyond the mediaeval period as a spoken language in mainland Scotland, it left a vast legacy of personal and place names on the assimilation of the Viking settlements to Gaeldom. English immigration has been a constant factor in Scottish history, and the influence of the Normans, Bretons and Flemings has been mentioned already. But the event which in the modern period has changed the nature of the Scottish populace is the arrival of the Irish in the last century. By far the largest part of Scotland's immigrant population comes from Ireland, beginning in the late 18th century and reaching a flood with the potato famine of the 1840s; the effect was particularly noticeable in Glasgow, where by the 19th century one third of Scotland's population was located. The arrival of these incomers coincided with the onset of the Industrial Revolution and an acute labour shortage. At its peak in the 1850s Irish immigration was reaching many thousands per week, and it was said that at this time the cotton spinners of Scotland were exclusively Irish. The effect was that many Irish surnames became so common in Scotland as to have become naturalised (eg. **Docherty**, **Gallagher**, **Murphy**).

The Highland Scots and the Irish share the same linguistic heritage, as the name **Kennedy** attests. An Irish name such as **Kelly** possesses the additional interesting feature that it is a contraction of O Ceallaigh, meaning 'descendant of war'. The O formation (it should not be followed by an apostrophe) which is so characteristic of Irish onomatology is not indigenous to Scotland but it corresponds to the Gaelic word *ogha* meaning grandson. Ireland also has its own huge crop of MAC names, most of them unfamiliar in Scotland but indistinguishable linguistically from their Scottish Gaelic equivalents.

Pronunciation

People are or should be free to pronounce their names as they wish, and there is no absolutely correct form; but phonetics have made a big difference to the evolution of surnames, and a short survey is in order.

There is some evidence that English speech mechanisms could not cope with the Norman velar (rolled) 'r', and forenames beginning with this letter tended to be pronounced by some of the natives with an initial 'h'. This is thought to be the reason why the pet forms of Richard were Hick and Hickon, that of Robert was Hob, and those of Roger were Hodge and Hodgkins. When these became fixed surnames they took the characteristic English forms of Hicks, Hickson, Hobbes, Hobson, Hodges, Hodgkinson and so on. The Scots have never had any difficulty in rolling an 'r', with the result that we have a profusion of **Ritchies**, **Robertsons** and **Rodgers** (often pronounced Roa-jers, with a growling initial consonant)–names not so common south of the Border.

The Highland diaspora and the decline of spoken Gaelic have resulted in some unsatisfactory anglicisations such as McPartridge ('son of Patrick') and **Mulholland** ('devotee of St Colann') and indeed there is hardly an Irish patronymic which has not escaped massacre. In Gaelic compound-names the stress goes on the qualifying and not the generic term–eg. Portree, 'harbour of the king', and the same goes for surnames such as **Fordyce**. The tendency in anglophone circles to shift the accent has the effect of obscuring the etymology, **Lamont** being a case in point; and to stress the first syllable of such names as **Abernethy** or **Carnegie** is to give oneself a mouthful and to make nonsense of the meaning. Without being fussy or pedantic, it is reasonable to pronounce other people's names as correctly as one knows how.

This dictionary is intended less as a work of reference than as providing material for intelligent and informed browsing. If one's own name is not included, that of one's mother or spouse may well be, and most people of Scots descent will find sufficient signposts to follow.

The dictionary has no bearing on genealogical research or family history; the word clan is used sparingly, the word sept only in an Irish context, and the word tartan hardly at all. Such terms are not useful in connection with onomastics, the scholarly term for the study of names. Scottish onomastics is quite distinctive, not just an English name-system with a northern accent. There are no 'posh' names in Scotland, and Norman blood has been thoroughly diluted by the local supply. No one family is 'older' than any other in Scotland. The royal name of **Stewart**, as the Gaelic saying has it, is the 'race of kings and tinkers' (*cinne nan righ 's nan ceard*), and the Dukes of Argyll were happy to lend their **Campbell** surname to their scruffiest clansmen. At the same time, most Scottish surnames are internationally regarded as highly prestigious, and some have been appropriated by persons who have done them little credit.

It gives no pleasure to demolish popular legends, especially if these are of long standing, but sometimes this is necessary; a case in point is the surname **Turnbull**, concerning which the story persists that a doughty Borderer saved the life of Robert the Bruce by forcibly diverting a bull from molesting the royal person; thereafter, says the 16th-century historian Boece, the king endowed him with great possessions and his lineage to this day is called Turnbull. There are several drawbacks to this theory, one being that the legend is one of the recurring motifs of Celtic mythology and the other that surnames are nearly always acquired in a natural and humdrum way and very rarely as a result of a particular happening, however picturesque or dramatic.

The traditional approach to surname-study has been etymological–attempting to find out what a name or its components mean. This has been done with every entry in the dictionary, sometimes with nugatory results, for the literal meaning of a name is usually of no practical importance whatever; to mistake John White for Tom Brown can never be attributed to colour-blindness. It must also be remembered that even the original bearer of a surname was probably unaware of its lexical meaning: this is particularly the case with locality names, and the first **Douglas** would not know or care that his name meant 'black water', or which was the black water in question. More important than meaning perhaps is the usage-profile of a name, its history, its pronunciation, its distribution and its cognates in other languages. It is this type of miscellaneous information which the dictionary tries to provide; and perhaps to show in the bygoing that a study of our family-name system, as well as reflecting the changing linguistic situation in Scotland from the earliest times, reveals in a remarkably coherent way the essential geographical, historical and social features of the nation.

The Top 100 Surnames in Scotland

The following table from the Registrar General is a recent list of the 100 commonest surnames in Scotland in descending order of frequency.

What the table does not show is that Smith occurs twice as frequently as Miller (itself a name which has edged up four places in a century). Once one reaches the middle of the list the differentials in frequency are markedly narrower, and at the tail-end there is only a single figure gap between Mackie (which the Registrar General does not recognise as the same name as MacKay) and MacCallum.

Not all names in the list are Scottish, as witness the Irish imports Kelly, Gallacher, Murphy and Donnelly. Jones, the commonest surname in Wales and the second in England, only just squeezes onto our list.

1 Smith	17 Taylor	33 Davidson
2 Brown	18 MacKenzie	34 Bell
3 Thomson	19 Ross	35 Simpson
4 MacDonald	20 MacLean	36 Kerr
5 Robertson	21 Paterson	37 Graham
6 Wilson	22 Young	38 White
7 Campbell	23 Mitchell	39 Cameron
8 Stewart	24 Walker	40 Martin
9 Anderson	25 Watson	41 Allan
10 Miller	26 Gray	42 Duncan
11 Johnston	27 MacLeod	43 Fergusson
12 Scott	28 Fraser	44 Grant
13 Clark	29 Henderson	45 Kelly
14 Reid	30 Hamilton	46 Black
15 Murray	31 Morrison	47 Wallace
16 MacKay	32 Hunter	48 Russell

49 MacGregor
50 MacMillan
51 Marshall
52 Gordon
53 Gibson
54 Wood
55 Gallacher
56 Muir
57 Sinclair
58 Milne
59 Kennedy
60 MacFarlane
61 Craig
62 Watt
63 Stevenson
64 Sutherland
65 Munro
66 Dickson

67 Burns
68 MacIntosh
69 MacPherson
70 Murphy
71 Cunningham
72 Wright
73 Ritchie
74 Crawford
75 MacIntyre
76 Douglas
77 Docherty
78 Christie
79 Currie
80 Shaw
81 Hughes
82 Boyd
83 Cook
84 Donnelly

85 Jamieson
86 Boyle
87 MacLachlan
88 Bruce
89 Williamson
90 King
91 Donaldson
92 Fleming
93 Hill
94 Mackie
95 Moore
96 Finlay
97 Murdoch
98 Rae
99 MacCallum
100 Jones

ACKNOWLEDGEMENTS

Some of the material in the Introduction to this Dictionary appeared in *Namenforschung: ein Internationales Handbuch zur allgemeinen und europäischen Onomastik*, published by de Gruyter of Berlin in 1996; a small portion of the text has already appeared in the author's *Scottish Surnames* (Blackwood 1978, reprinted Mercat Press, 1979 & 1992).

Any work on Scottish surnames must owe something to G.F. Black's monumental *The Surnames of Scotland* (New York, 1946); later standard works in a wider field include Cottle, *The Penguin Dictionary of Surnames* (London, 1967); Dunkling and Gosling, *Everyman's Dictionary of First Names* (London, 1983); Reaney, *A Dictionary of British Surnames* (London, 1976); Hanks and Hodges, *A Dictionary of Surnames* (Oxford, 1988); McKinley, *A History of British Surnames* (London, 1990) and MacLysaght, *The Surnames of Ireland* (Shannon, 1969). The insights of these scholars are respectfully acknowledged although not always uncritically followed. The author is also indebted to the staff of the General Register Office of Scotland for help in matters of statistics and regional distribution of surnames. On place-names, W.J. Watson and W.F.H. Nicolaisen have been the unfailing guides.

A

Abbott An occupational name, related to employment in the household of an abbot, or possibly the descendant of a (lay) abbot. A family called Abbott possessed the lands of Edzell in the 12th century. The name is more commonly found in its Gaelic form *mac an aba*, 'son of the abbot' (see **Macnab**); indeed it is probable that in many cases Abbott is a shortened re-translation of Macnab.

Abercrombie A parish-name in Fife, meaning 'mouth of the winding stream'; as often happens, however, the surname has achieved much greater fame than the place-name. Abercrombie of that Ilk (i.e. of Abercrombie) is first recorded in 1296 but the direct line died out in the middle of the 17th century. Andrew Abercromby was provost of Dundee in 1513, and founded the Black Friars monastery there. Dane (Dean) Henry Abercromby was prior of Scone in the 1550s. Sir Ralph Abercromby (1734-1801) fought with great distinction in the French wars and died after the victory of Aboukir Bay; Sir Patrick Abercrombie was a noted town-planner, and author of the 'Greater London Plan' of 1943.

Abernethy *Aber* means 'mouth of' and *Nethy* is a Celtic river-name of uncertain origin. Abernethy is the name of a district in Speyside and of a village near Perth, once visited by William the Conqueror; the village, being of some importance in the middle ages, gave rise to the surname, first found in Fife and Perthshire. Patrick and William Abernethy, kinsmen of the earl of Fife, were responsible for his murder in 1289. The surname spread to Ireland and beyond in the 17th century, and more recently in its variant spelling Abernathy became familiar in the USA through a prominent member of the Civil Rights movement.

Adair Although it has been claimed that this is a Scottish form of **Edgar**, an Irish origin, from O Daire, is much more likely; indeed, the name is probably most familiar through the ballad of Robin Adair, an 18th-century Irishman. Various members of the Adair family had grants of land from the crown in the time of Robert the Bruce; the surname is now most frequent in the west of Scotland.

Adam / Adamson The biblical Adam probably got his name from the Hebrew word *adama*, meaning earth; it was a very popular first name throughout Europe in the mediaeval period. Adam was abbot of Dryburgh in the 1180s, and another Adam held the same position in Melrose. As a surname, Adam is the most usual form in Scotland; alternatives are Adams and Addams, but commoner than either is Adamson, particularly in the Tayside region. Robert Adam (1728—92), the great architect, is the most famous bearer. The Gaelic equivalent is MacAdam, found mainly in the south-west; John Loudon Macadam, the road-builder who gave the word tarmac to the English language, was an Ayrshire man. See also **Aitcheson**, **Aitken**, **Eadie** and **Easson**.

Adie–see **Eadie**

Affleck Lord Auchinleck, the father of James Boswell, took his title from the family estate in Ayrshire. There was a Patrick de Achenlak in Lanark in 1296, but Auchinleck barely survives as a surname in Scotland (although it is remembered as that of a famous Second World War general). The local pronunciation ('Affleck') however gives a familiar if not numerous family name, appearing nowadays mainly in the Borders and Aberdeenshire. There are villages of Affleck in Lanarkshire and near Dundee (probably with the same etymology as Auchinleck–'stone field'); the Angus Afflecks were armour-bearers to the earls of Crawford.

Agnew There are three possible derivations: (i) a nickname based on the late Latin word *agnellus* meaning 'little lamb'; (ii) a place name in Normandy, Agneaux (see Introduction); (iii) an anglicisation of the Irish name *O Gnimh*. Historically, a Norman family settled in Lochnaw in south-east Scotland and were appointed hereditary sheriffs of Galloway in 1363; most Scottish Agnews are therefore likely to be of this lineage.

Aikman The etymology of this name is obscure; an association with oak seems not unlikely. Alisaundre Akeman rendered homage to Edward I of England in 1296. The name was formerly associated with Arbroath Abbey, and although still found in Angus is now commoner in Lothian.

Ainslie A place name, certainly from furth of Scotland, and very possibly identifiable with Annesley in Notts.; (Anglo-Saxon *ansett-leah*–'hermitage-clearing'). Many English locality-names gave rise to Scottish surnames (see Introduction), and Ainslie makes its first appearance with a landowning family in the Borders in the late mediaeval period. John Ainslie, born in Jedburgh in 1745, made one of the first surveys of Scotland. Robert Ainslie was a correspondent of Robert Burns; his descendants became landowners in Aberdeenshire. Andrew Ainslie was a petty criminal who helped Deacon Brodie to steal a silver mace from Edinburgh University.

Airlie When the **Ogilivies**, one of the oldest families in Angus, were ennobled in 1491, they took their title from the local lands of Airlie which they owned. The name became widely familiar through the ballad of the Bonnie Hoose o' Airlie and the nefarious deeds which took place there; but as a surname Airlie is absent from the early records and now virtually restricted to Glasgow.

Aitcheson 'Son of Adie' or of little **Adam**. Aitcheson is found fairly widely throughout Scotland from the 14th century onwards, sometimes in the spelling Acheson, which is the one preferred in America. In 1553 the artist John Acheson travelled to France to take a likeness of Mary Queen of Scots for use in the Scottish coinage. The related English diminutive forms Addison, Atkins and Atkinson are fairly recent introductions to Scotland; the latter is now quite common in Edinburgh.

Aitken A double diminutive of **Adam**. The -kin ending is not typically Scottish, but the name itself is among the 100 commonest Scottish surnames and is rarely found elsewhere.

Alexander From the Greek personal name Alexandros, 'defender of man'. It became a royal name in Scotland in the 12th century with the accession of Malcolm Canmore's son as Alexander I, and was gradually adopted as the typical Scottish forename. In its pet form Sandy it was almost synonymous with a 'Scots laddie'. As a surname it is first recorded in the west of Scotland in the 15th century, and is now prevalent everywhere. A family of Alexanders were landowners in Menstrie in the 16th century, and one of them became earl of Stirling; the earldom failed at about the time of the '45. The Gaelic form of the name is Alastair, hence the surname MacAllister and MacAleister. MacAlexander, once common in the west, is now virtually unknown. The Dundee records for the 1550s contain the name of 'Sir David Alexrson', a contraction for Alexanderson, another obsolete form.

Allardyce Allardice was the name of a barony in the former county of Kincardine; its etymology is obscure, but the second element is probably the Gaelic word *deas* meaning south. Traditionally the Allardices all trace descent from a family which took its name from the barony during the reign of William the Lion (1165—1214). An Allardice heiress married into the family of Barclay of Urie, who took the name of Barclay Allardice, and laid claim to the earldom of Strathearn, Menteith and Airth; no decision having been reached, the titles remain dormant. The name is still to be found mainly in the east of Scotland.

Allan Usually from the ancient Celtic personal name Ailin (*ail* meant a rock in Old Gaelic), although a Germanic derivation is also possible. Alan (in its usual spelling) was very frequent as a first name in Scotland from the Middle Ages onwards. It is also said to have been a popular forename among the Breton followers of William the Conqueror who settled in large numbers in Lincolnshire; thus the prevalence of this name in parts of England. As a surname its variants are Allen, Allison, Callan and MacAllan (Thomas Macalyeane was provost of Edinburgh in 1562). Allen is even commoner in England (and the USA) than in Scotland.

Allison Usually from Ellis, a mediaeval forename and a contraction of Elijah; Ellis and Ellison are very common surnames in England and the USA. The girls' name Alison is a pet form of Alice, but this is unlikely to provide the etymology for the surname: matronymic forms (i.e. deriving from the name of the mother) were virtually unknown among the canny Scots, since the naming of a child in this way might imply that the father was not known. David Aleson owned land at the Shore Head of Dundee in the early 16th century; but the name is now commonest in the Glagow area.

Alloway From a place name which occurs in the various forms Alloway (Ayrshire) and Alloa and Alva (Clackmannanshire) and incorporating the Gaelic elements *all mhagh* 'rocky plain'. The surname was formerly current mainly in Aberdeen, but is now found sparsely throughout Scotland and elsewhere. An alternative derivation of the surname as it occurs south of the border is from the Old English personal name Ethelwig ('noble battle').

Anderson 'Son of Andrew', from the Greek *andros*–'manly'. The cult of St Andrew, introduced into Scotland in the early Middle

Ages, became a focus for nationalism in the 12th and 13th centuries; Andrew consequently became a very popular Christian name in Scotland (it still is), and its derivative Anderson is the ninth commonest Scottish surname. The earlier form of the name was Androsoun, later Andrewson, but by the 15th century had been metathesised into its modern form. John Anderson, a scientist born in Roseneath in 1726, was the founder of Anderson's College, which later became the University of Strathclyde. MacAndrew is the Highland version of the name; as often as not it means 'devotee of Saint Andrew', which is made explicit in the other Gaelic form of the name–Gillanders (literally, 'gillie' or 'servant of Andrew').

Andrew / Andrews–see **Anderson**

Angus From the Celtic personal name Aonghus, consisting of the elements *aon* (one) and *gus* (choice). First documented by Adamnan, the biographer of St Columba, the name occurs in various spellings as that of an early king, and was adopted as the name of a Pictish territory; many centuries later it was re-adopted as the name of a district which used to be the county of Forfarshire and is now part of Tayside region. Some bearers of the surname will have acquired it through the personal name, others perhaps from its earlier locational form. Its Gaelic pronunciation has produced alternative spellings such as Neish, and has led to the mistaken idea that it is equivalent to Aeneas. Hennessey is an Irish version, originally *O h-Aonghusa*. See also **MacInnes**.

Annan Annan is a river-name in Dumfries of great antiquity and unknown etymology; long ago it was also a habitation name in Tayside. The surname, recorded as far back as the 13th century, was found mainly in Angus, Fife and Aberdeenshire. Thomas Annan and his son James were noted photographers in Fife in the last century. Annand is found in the north of England–in such cases probably from the Norse personal name Onund.

Arbuckle From a place in Lanarkshire, possibly deriving from the Gaelic *ard an buachaille* ('herdsman's height'); the stress would be on the 'buck' syllable. There was a John Arnbuckle in Irvine in 1499, and from then on the surname has been sparsely recorded in Glasgow and the west. Some Arbuckles rose to fame in the USA, notably John Arbuckle who was a 19th century philanthropist and sugar refiner; rather less worth mentioning is 'Fatty' Arbuckle, one of the early Hollywood playboys.

Arbuthnot From the Kincardineshire parish of that name. One of the subjects of William the Lion took his name from his estate of Arbuthnott (*aber buadhnet*–'mouth of the healing stream') and the surname was virtually confined to that part of Scotland. It is pronounced with the stress on the second syllable. Dr John Arbuthnot (1667-1735), son of the episcopal manse at Arbuthnot, was physician to Queen Anne and a well-known figure in literary London; he created the figure of John Bull and was a strong advocate for the union of Scotland with England.

Archibald From the Germanic personal name Ercenbald–'noble bold' (see Introduction). It was a favourite forename amongst the earls of Douglas and the chiefs of clan Campbell (usually in a Gaelic mistranslation–see **Gillespie**). Although not specifically Scottish nor very common as a surname, Archibald is found more frequently in Lowland Scotland (especially Lothian) than anywhere else.

Armour An occupational name from armourer, a maker of arms and armour. The name is found throughout Lowland Scotland from the 13th century onwards, with no particular point of origin. Effie Ayrmer lost a pair of sheets in the bleaching at Dundee in 1554. Jean Armour was the long-suffering wife of Robert Burns.

Armstrong A Border surname which originated as a complimentary nickname–'strong in the arm'. The first recorded Armstrong was pardoned for manslaughter in Carlisle in 1235; it is not known whether he was from north or south of the border. The Armstrongs later became a powerful and warlike border clan in Liddesdale and their exploits attained great renown in the border ballads. The name received renewed prominence in the USA in the 20th century first through Louis 'Satchmo' Armstrong and then through Neil Armstrong, the first man on the moon.

Arnott From the locality name Arnot near Kinross, where a family of Arnotts flourished from the 12th century onwards. David Arnott of that Ilk took part in an archery contest between Scotland and England in 1535 (Scotland won). The name spread to many parts of the Lowlands and was well known in Edinburgh in the 15th and 16th centuries. The place name probably derives from the Gaelic *eornach*, meaning 'barley-land', but an English derivation of the surname is also possible, as a diminutive of the Germanic personal name Arnold ('eagle rule').

Atkinson–see **Aitcheson**

Auchinleck–see **Affleck**

Auchterlonie From the lands of Auchterlonie near Forfar. *Auchter* is a common Gaelic place-name element meaning 'top of' and the stem may be *lonaidh* meaning road or path– 'summit of the path'. The landed family of Auchterlonie is recorded in the Ragman Roll of 1296 (see Introduction) although the 'de' prefix remains for another two hundred years–a convenient example of how territorial surnames only gradually became fixed. The name remained localised in the eastern shires until the 17th century and later spread all over Scotland in a variety of spellings, including Ochterlonie. Willie Auchterlonie of St Andrews, golf-club maker and professional to the Royal and Ancient, won the Open in 1893 at the age of twenty-one, using only seven home-made clubs. His descendants are still in the town.

Auld The Scots form of 'old'. In Anglo-Saxon times, Ealda was a common personal name meaning old, and as a surname Auld could be translated as 'son of Ealda'–making it a patronymic rather than a nickname (see Introduction). The surname occurs frequently in Ayrshire from early times; 'Daddy' Auld was the real-life minister of Burns' comic-hypocrite Holy Willie. MacAuld has also been recorded, and in Ireland the name is Oulde. But there appears to be no equivalent English surname deriving from the adjective old, to counterbalance the surname Young which is equally common in both countries.

B

Baikie A surname which comes from a place in Angus (meaning unknown). It is found mainly but infrequently in east Scotland. The Orkney Baikies probably have a different (local) source for their name. William Baikie, doctor of medicine of Edinburgh University, was a distinguished 19th-century naturalist and explorer.

Baillie In Latin, a *baiulus* was a porter or steward; the word passed into Old French as *bailli*, meaning a bailiff. A bailie in local government in Scotland was the equivalent of an alderman. Such is the derivation of the surname Baillie, which is first recorded in Lothian in 1311. A tradition that the family of Balliol changed their name to Baillie because of the unpopularity of the royal bearers of the former name appears to be unfounded, despite the fact that Balliol is now extinct as a surname. The Baillies were Border lairds for many centuries, and the name has always been at its most frequent in the south. Robert Baillie, the Presbyterian divine, left a vivid contemporary account of the events leading up to the Civil War in the 1640s. Joanna Baillie, the 'immortal Joanna' of Sir Walter Scott, was born in Bothwell in Lanarkshire. Dame Isobel Baillie, the greatly beloved soprano of the inter-war years, was the daughter of a baker in Hawick. The forms Bailey and Bayley, of similar derivation, are frequent in England.

Bain The Gaelic adjective *ban*, meaning white or fair-haired, was very common as a nickname but rarely achieved permanence as a surname (compare **White**). When it did, it was not confined to the Highlands, and the first Bain is recorded in Perth in 1324. Alexander Bain from Caithness was a pioneer in telegraphic printing (the forerunner of fax) and the inventor of the electric fire-alarm. Another Alexander Bain was a typical 'lad o' pairts'; leaving school in Aberdeen in 1829 at the age of eleven, he went on to become a crony of Thomas Carlyle and John Stuart Mill, and later professor of Logic at the University of Aberdeen. It is sometimes claimed that the Bains are a branch of the clan Mackay, which is probably no more than to say that there were Bain families in Strathnaver. The English versions of the name such as Bayne, Baines are of different, probably Norman, origin; but see also **MacBean**.

Baird The earliest Scottish recording of the name is that of Richard Bard, in Lanarkshire in the early 13th century. The origin is uncertain, the Gaelic word *bard* having the two distinct meanings of 'enclosure' and 'poet'. The name may even be Flemish; but the legend should be discounted of the king's life having been saved by the killing of a savage boar. Bairds were landowners in the Manor valley in the 16th century; the name was common in Lanarkshire, Stirling and Edinburgh, and spread at an early date to the north east and to Aberdeenshire; in one of his less inspired prophecies, the 13th-century wizard Thomas the Rhymer predicted that 'there shall be an eagle on the craig while there is a Baird in Auchmeddan': there is now neither. The *Dictionary of National Biography* includes several Bairds, all of them Scots, among them General David Baird, hero of Seringapatam and veteran of the Napoleonic wars. The most celebrated bearer of the name must however be John Logie Baird, inventor of television and changer of all our lives, who was born in Helensburgh and educated in Glasgow.

Balfour From the barony in Fife, which was pronounced with the stress on the last syllable; it means 'pasture village', and there are three other occurrences in Scotland. The Balfours were a landed family in Fife from the later middle ages: John Balfour got a grant of the lands of Balgarvy from James II, and his descendants held appointments in the royal household and were later ennobled as the Balfours of Burleigh. At one time there were twenty landed families of Balfours in Fife; one of their most notable representatives was Arthur James Balfour, Conservative statesman and writer and architect of the Balfour Declaration guaranteeing a national home for the Jews in Palestine.

Ballantyne From the lands of Bellenden between Ettrick and Teviot, a place that was the rallying point of the Scotts of Buccleuch and the war-cry of the clan; it may be from the Gaelic *baile an deadhain*–'dean's farmstead'. Robert Bellentyne was abbot of Holyrood from 1484 to 1500. Sir John Bellenden was privy councillor to Mary Queen of Scots, but changed sides because of his implication in the murder of Rizzio. Sir William Bellenden, a devoted royalist, was created Lord Bellenden of Broughton in 1661, and there were many other Bellendens famous as scholars, statesmen and lawyers. The surname seems to have become obsolete in this spelling, but came into prominence in the 19th century with the Kelso firm of publishers, James and John Ballantyne, who were the secret partners of Sir Walter Scott and largely responsible for his financial ruin; their nephew was R. M. Ballantyne, the celebrated author of improving but exciting books for boys.

Ballingall A Kinross name, originally that of a settlement, meaning 'strangers' village' (see **Gall**). The surname became common in Fife; Sir George Ballingall, born 1780, was an alumnus of St Andrews University and a noted military surgeon. The name is now infrequent and seldom found outside Glasgow.

Balneaves The lands of Balneaves in Angus are the source of this uncommon but interesting surname. It is probably from the Gaelic *baile neimh* ('sanctuary village'), although the ending was sometimes Latinised to *nativorum*–'native'. The surname spread to Fife and Atholl, and was that of a famous Protestant Reformer who died in 1579. The Glasgow form Balnave is just as frequent and may come from another forgotten settlement of the same name.

Banks Of general topographical origin, applied to a hillside or riverside dweller. The surname occurs in a charter of 1217 in the Latinised form of *de Riparia*, the scribe having interpreted the word bank in an aquatic sense. In the far north the name may come from the village of Banks near Kirkwall (Old Norse *bakki*–a sea cliff). But since this surname is even commoner in England, a northern origin is unlikely in the absence of other evidence.

Bannerman A hereditary title pertaining to the office of standard-bearer, possibly to the early Scottish kings. There is a charter of 1368 by David II of lands in Aberdeenshire to his physician Donald Bannerman; from then on the name crops up frequently in that area. Lord Bannerman of Kildonan was a prominent Liberal politician, rugby internationalist and enthusiast for the Gaelic language.

Barbour An occupational name, from the Middle English *barbou*, which meant surgeon and dentist as well as hair-stylist. Two brothers of the name were taken prisoner at Dunbar castle in 1296. The name occurs frequently throughout the Lowlands from the 14th century onwards. John Barbour, archdeacon of Aberdeen, was the author of an epic poem (1375) called *The Brus,* celebrating the exploits of King Robert the Bruce and James Douglas in the war of independence. The English spelling of the name, Barber, is less common in Scotland.

Barclay A characteristic example of a Scottish family name which derives from an English place-name–not Berkeley in Gloucester-shire but from the small Somerset village of Berkley ('birch wood'). It occurs very early in Scotland: Walter de Berklai, owner of lands in Galloway and the Mearns, was chamberlain of Scotland in 1165;

another Walter Barclay forfeited his lands in 1306 for supporting the Bruce. The Barclays acquired considerable estates in the shires of Aberdeen and Banff, and were hereditary constables of the latter. A Barclay laird made his fortune in the Thirty Years War and got the lands of Urie near Stonehaven. An astonishing number of Barclays achieved fame in the various spheres of law, theology, medicine and literature, not to speak of the profession of arms: it was Prince Barclay de Tolly who commanded the Russian army which defeated Napoleon in 1812. Barclay's Bank can trace its origin to a grandson of the house of Urie.

Barker A bark-stripper or tanner. Really a Yorkshire name, but it has been found in the Scottish Lowlands from early in the 13th century.

Barnes Much commoner in England, and may sometimes come from Barnes in Surrey, although any unspecified barn in any part of the kingdom could give rise to the surname. There was also a parish of the name Barnes in Aberdeenshire (from Gaelic *bearn*– 'gap'); this may account for some local instances of the surname, which spread to Dundee and the central belt. John Barnis was a chaplain in Dundee in the 1550s, and a Barnes was provost of Glasgow in 1687. George Barnes, born in Dundee in 1859, was one of the first Scottish Labour MPs and a member of the war cabinet in 1917.

Barr A name so peculiar to Scotland that it is omitted from most surname-dictionaries. *Barr* in Gaelic is literally the crop–the top of anything, the head of the corn, the sprouting of the hair, that which requires to be cut. As a place-name element, *barr* (as in Barrhead) means crest or height. The surname may come from the village of Barr in Ayrshire–it is mostly to be found in the west–but may equally well be a general topographical reference like the surname **Hill**. The earliest form is de Barre; and it appears from the records of 16th-century Dundee that Barre, **Barrie** and Barry were virtually interchangeable.

Barrie / Barry There are several possible derivations of this name: in England and France, the origin is the Anglo-Norman word *barri*–a rampart (hence Madame DuBarry); an Irish origin, from a personal name is also possible; and there is a Gaelic word *borrach* meaning hill-grass. But for most of the Barries in Scotland, Ireland and Wales the origin will be as for **Barr**. More specifically, there is a village of Barrie in Angus, and the surname, first recorded in 1360, is still very commonly found in that county. Thomas Barrye, unicorn pursuivant, had his right hand cut off and was banished for forging the Regent's signature in 1590. Self-banishment was the lot of J. M. Barrie, author and dramatist, who was born in Kirriemuir but spent most of his life in fashionable London. Barrie families in Farquharson and Gordon country claimed allegiance to these respective clans.

Batchelor The literal meaning of the word bachelor is a young knight, or novice in arms, and is thought to have come from popular Latin *baccalarius*. Bachelor meaning an unmarried man is a comparatively recent usage, and the surname simply referred to a person at the 'prentice' stage in life. Although not exclusively Scottish, the name was recorded in Haddington in 1296, and later appears with some frequency in Angus, Fife and Perthshire, where it was apparently spelt and pronounced Baisler.

Bates–see **Beattie**

Baxter The Scottish form of baker, the *-ster* suffix having survived longer in Scotland than elsewhere (see Introduction). Reginald Baxtar is recorded in Fife around 1200, and the name occurs with various spellings all over the Lowlands, particularly in Angus, where the Forfar Baxters were supposed to have been bakers at the royal residence. The Baxters of Kincaldrum introduced power-weaving into Dundee, became immensely rich and endowed the city with magnificent benefactions including Baxter Park and the college that was to grow into the University of Dundee. Not all Baxters were Scottish–there was Richard Baxter, the famous English Presbyterian divine–but the name is much commoner here than is its English counterpart Baker.

Beat–see Beattie

Beatson–see Beattie

Beaton Bearers of this name divide into two categories, Lowland and Highland. (i) The original Lowland Beatons appear to have descended from Anglo-Norman settlers (see Introduction) who brought with them the name of their village of origin, Bethune in Pas de Calais. Bethune, the original spelling of the surname, is now relatively uncommon. Beaton is first recorded in Fife in 1165, and is still borne by several landed families in the county. James Beaton. Archbishop of St Andrews, was one of the regents during the minority of James V; his nephew David, Cardinal Archbishop of St Andrews (1494-1546) was murdered in revenge for his condemnation of the reformers; and David's nephew James was the last Roman Catholic archbishop of Glasgow. (ii) The Highland Beatons bore the name Macbeatha or **Macbeth** until the end of the 16th century. As hereditary physicians they were appropriately (but not deliberately) named, for *mac beatha* means 'son of life'. The first to be recorded is Patrick Macbetha of Islay, physician to Robert the Bruce, and for the next two hundred years his kinsmen were official physicians to the Macdonald chiefs, of whom they held lands. The Mull Beatons attended to the medical needs of the Macleans of Duart. One of the Beatons was reportedly sitting on the deck of the *Florida* when it blew up in Tobermory Bay in 1588; miraculously he survived. Another branch of this scholarly family settled in Fraser country; one of them was medical adviser to Lord Lovat before falling from grace for sheep-stealing. The categorisation of the name became confused in the 1550s when a Bethune from Fife settled in Skye and left numerous descendants there, who came to adopt the local spelling.

Beadie / Beedie–see **Beattie**

Beattie A diminutive of Bartholomew ('son of the twin'). Many children were named after this apostle, and other variants are Beedie, Beat, Beatson and Bates (the latter more common in England). The name, first recorded in Berwick on Tweed in 1384, was well known in the Borders. Later it became popular in the Mearns, and it was claimed that at one time or another every farm in Laurencekirk was in the hands of a Beattie. James Beattie (1735-1803), poet of *The Minstrel* fame, was a schoolmaster in Fordoun before becoming professor of Moral Philosophy at the University of Aberdeen.

Begbie From the lands of Begbie near Haddington; the meaning is 'Baggi's farm' (whoever he may have been). The surname has remained highly localised, seldom appearing outside the Edinburgh area.

Begg From the Gaelic adjective *beag* meaning small, in the surname context 'short of stature', and very common as a nickname in the Highlands in the pre-surname period (see Introduction). Beggs are recorded in the early 13th century in Stirlingshire (which at that time would be solidly Gaelic-speaking). The name was also said to have been common in Edinburgh in the 16th and 17th centuries.

Bell Several derivations are possible for this name, which is not exclusively Scottish, but is or was the forty-fifth commonest in the land. Bell could be from the occupation of bell-ringer; or from living near a bell-tower; or from *le bel* meaning beautiful or handsome. John Bell was a notary in St Andrews in 1246. The surname was commonly found in the Borders: 'Bellis' are included in the list of unruly clans in the West March, and they also proliferated in Dumfriesshire.

Bennett Benedict was the patriarch of western monks, and founder of the Benedictine order; his name was greatly revered and widely used as a Christian name from the 12th century. Its Latin meaning is 'blessed', and as a surname it has cognates in most European languages. The earliest documented form in Scotland was Benet (1402); nowadays by far the commonest spelling is with the double 'n' and double 't'. No specific Scottish claims can be made for this name, despite its frequency in Edinburgh from the 17th century onwards.

Bennie / Benzie(s) These surnames, although pronounced in the same way, probably come from different sources. Bennie is a place in Logiealmond near Perth, and is probably a derivative of the Gaelic *beann* meaning peak (see also **Binnie**). Alexander Benne was deacon of the websters (weavers) in Stirling in 1522, and the name became quite common in that area. The Benzies seem to originate on Donside, but the etymology of their name is unknown. James Banyeaucht and John Baynze turn up in the district in the 1500s; two centuries later there appears Robert Benzie, a church elder said to have dabbled in witchcraft. The names, sometimes mutually confused, are now found mainly in Edinburgh and Glasgow.

Berrill–see **Birrell**

Berry There is a tradition (perfectly plausible) that the surname originated in the Berry region of France and was brought to Scotland in the post-Conquest period. Berrys are recorded at an early date in Fife and Angus; Robert Berry and his family suffered severe financial loss when his property was burned in the sacking of Dundee in 1553. A branch migrated to Strathdon and Coldstone in the 17th century; tartan-seekers would have the choice of Forbes or Farquharson. Some of them returned south in the1780s, and there has been a landed family of Berrys in North East Fife for over two centuries. English Berrys probably derive their name from the Anglos-Saxon *byrig*–'at the manor'– and the surname is that of the viscounts Camrose and Kemsley. It may also in some cases be a variant of **Barrie**.

Bertram An Old English personal name, *Beorh-tram*, meaning 'shining raven' (see Introduction), and Scottish only by long association. It is found in many spellings, including Bertie, and was recorded in Inverkeithing as early as 1296. A Walter Bertrahame was provost of Edinburgh in 1482.

Bethune–see **Beaton**

Beveridge Scholars are not agreed as to the derivation: is it from the place-name involving the Old English *befer-ig*–'beaver island', or is it linked to beverage (Old French *bevrage*, from Latin *bibere*, to drink); and is it no more than coincidence that James and John Beverage were fined in 1677 for brewing under-strength beer? The name, whatever its origin, was first recorded in St Andrews in 1302, and subsequently became well-known in Fife. James Beverage attended to the midwifery needs of Mary Queen of Scots, and Alex Baviridge was a monk in Culross about the same time. It is still among the fifty commonest names in Fife.

Binnie Binning is an old barony in West Lothian, and may be derived from the Gaelic *beinnach*, meaning 'hilly'. The surname appears in various guises including Binney, Binning and Binny, but Binnie is most common. William de Binnin was prior of Newbattle in the 13th century, and John Binning is recorded as burgess of Edinburgh in the reign of David II. Sir William Binning was provost of that city in 1675, where the name had then become quite common. It is also found in Aberdeen, Perth and Stirling.

Birrell Almost certainly from the village of Burrell in Yorkshire, and first recorded as a surname in the North Riding in 1282. Burrell, Berrill and Birrell are all versions of the same name; the latter is nowadays by far the commonest form north of the Border. The accent, whatever the spelling, is properly on the first syllable. Birrells are to be found in the Borderland from mediaeval times, and were frequent in 16th-century Glasgow. John Burrel was a goldsmith in Edinburgh in 1578, and Robert Burel was a burgess of that city around the same time. Sir William Burrell (1861-1958) the son of a Glasgow shipowner, spent the latter part of his life as an art collector and in 1946 bequeathed his vast and magnificent collection to the city of Glasgow.

Birse From the village of that name in Aberdeenshire; in early documents it is written as Bras, making the etymology uncertain. Duncan of Birse was a burgess of Aberdeen in the 15th century, and the name crops up frequently in eastern Scotland, where it has remained fairly localised.

Bissett The Old French adjective *bis* meant 'brownish-grey', and was applied to the rock-dove, whose colour it exactly describes: *bisset* was the diminutive form, and gives the French surname Bizet. The Bissetts reputedly came to Scotland as part of William the Lion's attempt to feudalise his kingdom with Anglo-Norman knights (see Introduction); they arrived in Selkirkshire by way of Nottingham before 1200. Henricus Byset was witness to a royal charter of the late 12th century, and his son John obtained a crown grant of lands in the north. The family, by then lords of Aboyne, got into serious trouble in 1242 in a feud with the earls of Atholl, the result of which was exile and excommunication and forfeiture.

Bissetts are among the oldest landed families in Aberdeenshire, where the name still flourishes.

Black A name descriptive of the original bearers' dark hair or swarthy complexion; but confusion has become endemic between the Old English word *blaec* (meaning black) and Old Norse *bleikr* (meaning its opposite of white or pale, as in 'bleach'). The latter also gives the surname **Blake**, but without standardised spelling or knowledge of pronunciation it is impossible to separate the Blakes from the Blacks. Only when a contemporary scribe helpfully latinises the name to *niger* can a Black be safely identified. (Blackie and Blaikie are almost as common and equally confused). Blacks appear all over the Lowlands from the 12th century onwards, particularly in Edinburgh, St Andrews and Prestwick. The name is very often an English rendering of a Gaelic patronymic, usually of **Macildowie** (*mac gille dhuibh*–'son of the black lad') and many Blacks of Highland origin have claimed membership of the clan Lamont. Black is not exclusively a Scottish name, although of the ten Blacks listed in the *Dictionary of National Biography* no fewer than seven are Scots.

Blackie–see **Black**

Blaikie–see **Black**

Blair The word *blar* is a common Gaelic place-name element, meaning field (usually of battle), and Blair Atholl is only one of many examples. The surname is of multiple origin, but the first recorded bearer is Stephen Blare who lived in Angus in the late 12th century. William de Blaar was chaplain to Sir William Wallace when he was governor of Scotland; Brice Blair of Ayrshire forfeited his lands to Edward I in 1306. Other Blairs have won fame as physicians, bankers, lawyers, divines, soldiers, authors and party-leaders. Robert Blair was the gloomy poet of *The Grave*, a work which enjoyed great esteem in the mid 1700s and was a precursor of the Romantic movement in English poetry.

Blake Not a distinctively Scottish name, although frequent enough throughout the Lowlands since the late mediaeval period, especially in Edinburgh. The English Blakes are mainly to be found in the southern counties, and the poet Blake was a Londoner. (See also **Black**).

Blyth A settlement name from Lauderdale, originally a barony and more recently a farm. William de Blyth of Chirnside did homage to Edward I in 1296, and the name later turns up in Perth, Dundee and Aberdeen. Blyth was apparently a common name among the Border gypsies. The English version can be either from the town of Blyth in Northumberland, or a variant of Bligh, meaning blithe.

Boag There are many spellings, including Book, Boak, Buack, Boik and Boyack, and the reference may be to a now-forgotten settlement-name, possibly involving the Scots word *baulk*, meaning an unploughed ridge of turf, hence a boundary. The surname was widespread in the Lowlands, without ever being frequent, and was found in Orkney in the 16th century.

Boath An Angus name, from Both, meaning hut or bothy (compare Gaelic *buth* and Scots *booth*). Hugh de Boath is said to have acquired the lands of Panbride near Carnoustie as a reward for his services to David II at the battle of Dupplin in 1332; it is recorded that as part of the benefaction he also received the hand of the Panbride heiress in marriage.

Bolton The name of a settlement in East Lothian. William fiz Geoffray de Boultone did homage to Edward I in 1296, and a century later a Scot named Robert of Bolton was released from prison in Colchester. But most bearers of the name will have originated in the city of Bolton ('house-settlement') in Lancashire.

Bonnar From the French *de bon aire*, literally 'well-bred' but now meaning gracious or debonair. Spelling variants are Bonar (almost as common) and Bonner. The name is first found in Aberdeen in the 13th century. William Boner was constable of Kinghorn in 1328, Roger Bonere was a burgess of Aberdeen in 1342, and John Bonere owned a ship which was wrecked in 1388. Dane (Dean) John Bonar appears in the Dundee records for 1554. The Reverend James Bonnar was an educational pioneer in Perth in the mid-18th century. There were many Bonars in Fife, and at one time no fewer than 37 branches of the landed family were recorded. Bonar is also an Irish surname, of obscure origin.

Bonthrone A Fife name, recorded there from the 17th century onwards, but with no earlier records and an unknown etymology. There was a Thomas Bonthron in Letham in 1617, and a William Bunthorne in Dysart in 1640. Bontrones and Bontrams are recorded in Edinburgh in the 17th century. Where, one asks, did W.S. Gilbert find the name Bunthorne for his opera *Patience*, since it occurs in none of the English reference books?

Borland The board-land was that which supplied the laird's table, and there are many places called Bor(e)land, notably in the shires of Dumfries, Ayr, Galloway, Fife and Perth, together with Borlum on Loch Ness. This victualling arrangement does not seem to have applied south of the Border, so that Borland is a distinctively Scottish surname. It is first recorded in Ayrshire in 1513, but is not localised in its distribution.

Borthwick Anglo-Saxon *burh wic*, meaning 'fort village'; it might just as easily have been called Castleton. The barony of Borthwick was originally in Roberton parish in Roxburgh. Thomas de Borthwic is recorded in 1368; his son William obtained lands in Midlothian which he then named after his original possessions, and the family built Borthwick castle which is visible from the

23

A68. The surname quickly spread to Edinburgh and beyond, and the Aberdeen records have a William Borthwyk as baillie and Patrick Borthwik as burgess at the end of the 14th century. Peter Borthwick, born in the parish of that name, became a Tory politician and later editor of the *Morning Post*.

Boswell From Beuzeville in Seine-Maritime. Not all the Boswells who came over in the Anglo-Norman influx (see Introduction) ended up in Scotland, but a Roger de Bosvil is recorded in the 13th century as a landowner in Fife. The surname, never frequent, became famous in the 18th century as that of a very noteworthy family of lawyers and literati. Alexander Boswell graced the Scottish bench as Lord Auchinleck; his son James was the celebrated biographer of Dr Johnson; his grandson, Sir James Boswell, was an antiquary and poet; and several collaterals distinguished themselves in the law.

Bowden From Bowden in Roxburghshire, where it appears that the tenants of Kelso monastery took their surname from the barony. The name, originally Botheldene 'house in the valley', is usually pronounced to rhyme with Cowden. The surname is however much commoner south of the Border, since there are many places in England (eighteeen in Devon alone) which are called Bowden (pronounced 'boaden') and usually meaning bow-shaped or curved hill.

Bowie From the Gaelic word *buidhe* meaning yellow or fair-haired. The name is Highland in origin–Bowies were found in Jura and South Uist– but spread all over the rest of Scotland from the 15th century onwards. A family of Bowies appeared in Strathspey, and were adherents of the Grants. The name was said to be very popular in Stirling and Dunblane in the 17th and 18th centuries.

Bowman The name is commoner outside Scotland, and, with its meaning of 'archer', has cognates in many languages. It is however well established here; a Gregory Bowman appeared in Aberdeen in 1333, and several others are recorded in Glasgow in the 16th century.

Boyce Originally the French *du bois* ('from the wood'); it occurs frequently in mediaeval charters as de Bosco or del Bois. Two individuals of the name de Boys and one of Boyes are mentioned in the Ragman Roll of 1296. The number of spelling variants of this name is astonishing: Boyst turns up in Cupar in 1521, and five persons called Boist are in Dunblane a century later; the Boys of Panbride were an old landed family in Angus, and the historian Hector Boece, who was born in Dundee's Overgate around 1465, was probably of the same stock. The name is now most often found in Glasgow. See also **Buist**.

Boyd The generally-accepted derivation is from the Gaelic *Boid*, literally 'of Bute'. The first Boyds are recorded in Ayrshire in 1205, and one of them distinguished himself at the battle of Largs in 1263. It was a Boyd who, by kidnapping the young James III, became effective governor of Scotland during the royal minority, and the descendants of this Boyd became earls of Kilmarnock; the 4th earl was beheaded for his part in the '45 rebellion, and the earldom was temporarily forfeit. Another Boyd, of Wigton descent, emigrated to Australia in 1841 and gave his name to a town in New South Wales. Boyd has always been a West-of-Scotland name, although it went to Ulster with the Scots settlers, and also flourished in Edinburgh at about the same time. It is still among the hundred commonest names in Scotland.

Boyle From Bieville near Caen; the name was brought to Scotland in the mediaeval period as part of the importation of Anglo-Norman knights (see Introduction). The de Boyvilles were castellans of the castles of Dumfries, Wigton and Kirkcudbright, and the name of Boyle was for long confined to that part of the country, where it was apparently pronounced 'bow'. David Boyle of Kelburne became

1st earl of Glasgow in 1703, was one of the commissioners of the union between England and Scotland, and was active on the government side during the rising of 1715. Boyle is now among the 100 commonest Scottish surnames and widespread in the Lowlands. The Irish Boyles, also of Anglo-Norman stock, achieved some distinction as earls of Orrery, Cork, Burlington and Shannon, barons Marston and Carleton and viscounts Blessington. The physicist Robert Boyle was of the Cork family. The Irish Boyles, twice as common as the Scots, were however not all of Norman stock: there was a native surname *O Baoghill*, derived from an Irish personal name, and anglicised to Boyle, and a number of these must have swelled the ranks of the Scottish Boyles.

Bradley From the Old English words *brad leah*, meaning 'broad clearing'. There are dozens of English settlement-names of this type, so it is likely that most Scottish Bradleys are imports.There is however a William de Bradeleye mentioned in 1296 as being resident in Scotland, and it is quite possible that he took his surname form the lands of Braidlie near Hawick. It is also claimed that Bradley can in some cases be an English substitute for the Gaelic personal name *O Brolachain*, which was at one time current in Argyll.

Brady An Old English origin has been claimed, from the adjective *brad* and the noun *eage*–'broad-eye', or with the eyes set wide apart; but a more likely derivation is from the Irish personal name O Bradaigh. The name occurs in Dundee and Edinburgh in the 15th century. Brady, the Moors murderer, was born in Glasgow. The name, not all that common in Scotland, is even rarer elsewhere.

Braid From the lands on the south side of Edinburgh, comprising the Braid ('broad') Hills, Plewlands and Bavelaw. Sir Henry de Brade, sheriff of Edinburgh in the reign of William the Lion, is mentioned in a royal act as one of the twelve Scottish knights appointed to meet with their English counterparts for the purpose of settling border regulations. The lands of Braid remained in the same family for another two hundred years; the surname also stayed localised to an unusual degree, although it later became common in Fife and is found in the Kirk Session records of St Andrews from the 15th century onwards. A 19th-century graduate of Edinburgh University, Dr James Braid, experimented with mesmerism and coined the term hypnotism. Another James Braid, the Fife-born golfer, won the Open five times.

Brand An English personal name from the Germanic element *brand*, meaning sword (as in Hildebrand). Thomas Brand was a burgess in mediaeval Edinburgh, and the name occurs frequently in the register of marriages for the parish of Edinburgh for the years 1595 to 1760. There was also a castle Brand in Angus belonging to a family of that name, which is still a familiar one in the county.

Bremner The older form of the name–Brebner–gives the clue to its meaning, viz. a native of Brabant, a duchy in the Netherlands. There was considerable trading activity between the Low Countries and the ports on Scotland's eastern seaboard from mediaeval times onwards, and permanent settlement was not uncommon. The name was synonymous with 'weaver' in the early trades organisations of Dundee. Bremners were frequent in most parts of Scotland; variant spellings include Brymer and (in England) Brabham. Brabazon, not native to Scotland, is from the same root.

Brewster This name is not necessarily Scottish although the -ster suffix is characteristic–see Introduction; it is commoner here than is its English counterpart Brewer, which is what the name means. Thomas le Breuester of Lanarkshire appears in the Ragman Roll of 1296, and Robert Brouster was burgess of Glasgow in 1487. Sir David Brewster (1781-1868), the natural philosopher, was Principal successively of the Universities of St Andrews and Edinburgh.

Brockie A diminutive of the Scots word *brock*, a badger, probably in origin an uncomplimentary nickname. Gilbert Broky was 'chantour' of Brechin in 1411. The name, now scattered, was once common in the shires of Aberdeen and Moray.

Brodie From the lands of Brodie on the Moray Firth. The place name has been derived form the Gaelic adjective *brothach* , which in a topographical context would mean something like muddy. When Michael de Brothie received from Robert the Bruce a charter for his properties in Moray, it was not for services rendered but as heir to his father Malcolm, Thane of Brodie, one of the descendants of the old Pictish aristocracy of Scotland. The loss by fire of the Brodie castle muniments in the the Civil War of 1645 however makes the early history of this family somewhat obscure. Alexander Brodie of Brodie was a zealous Presbyterian who played his part in the mutilation of the nearby Elgin cathedral and later tried to force his uncompromising beliefs on Charles II. The surname spread beyond Moray, and crops up in Edinburgh from 1599 onwards. An unworthy bearer of the ancient name was William Brodie, a respected deacon councillor of Edinburgh by day and an accomplished burglar by night: this Jekyll-Hyde prototype was hanged for his misdemeanours in 1788.

Brough An English place-name, found in Yorkshire, Derbyshire and other areas; it comes from the Old English word *burh* meaning fort. Most Broughs are in Scotland by recent immigration, but the surname is also native to Orkney where it derives from the corresponding Old Norse word *borg*. It turns up in Perthshire in the 17th century and later appears in the Edinburgh Marriage Register.

Brown One of the commonest surnames in Scotland, England and the USA, and having cognates in every European language. It refers to the colour of the original bearer's hair or complexion or clothing; but one must wonder how it was ever a sufficiently distinctive description to be worth perpetuating in a surname. Indeed attempts have been made to derive it from the Germanic personal name Brun (as in Brunnhilde). In Scotland the name obviously has many points of origin, and has never been localised; although recorded with great frequency from the 13th century its bearers appear to have no connection one with another. In more recent times Brown was one of the many neutral names adopted by clansmen who wanted to be rid of their cumbersome or politically incorrect Gaelic patronymics, and John Brown, Queen Victoria's favourite gillie, is thought to have been a case in point.

Bruce From a place in Normandy, almost certainly Brix near Cherbourg, but possibly Le Brus in Calvados. The first Robert de Brus crossed the Channel with William the Conqueror and fought at Hastings; the second Robert Bruce accompanied David I to claim his Scottish throne. Six generations later this family, by now long established in Annandale, produced in the Robert the Bruce the man who was to make himself the ruler of an independent Scotland. The royal Bruce line died out fifty years after the battle of Bannockburn in 1314, but its offshoots (probably all descendants of the original de Brus) were granted lands in Clackmannan and Fife. The senior branch of the family was elevated to the earldom of Elgin, and there are three other Bruce peerages. Thousands of ordinary Bruces all over Scotland would, as vassals, have taken their name from the landowner; and Bruce is now among the hundred commonest Scottish surnames and one of the best known all over the world.

the Old English *hurne tun* meaning 'stream

Borderland, where it first appears in Scottish records. There is however a village of Brunton near Cupar in Fife, which may account for some local occurrences of the surname.

Bryce / Bryson From Bricius, a 5th-century saint who succeeded St Martin as bishop of Tours. The name came to England with the Norman Conquest, and appears in Scottish records at the end of the 12th century. Richard Brice, burgess and alderman of Stirling, rendered homage in 1296, and a family called Bris was in the service of the earls of Cassilis in the 16th century. The name flourished in Stirlingshire and Lennox, while its derivative Bryson was once common in Strathclyde.

Bryden A Border surname, which occurs in the Ragman Roll (see Introduction) and also figures frequently in the Flodden Roll of the burgesses of Selkirk in 1513. The origin may be Briddon in Leicestersire or Bredon in Worcestershire, both meaning 'fort-hill'.

Buchan The name of a district in Aberdeenshire, derived possibly from the Brittonic *bwch*, meaning cow. Ricardus de Buchan, clerk of the bishopric of Aberdeen, and William de Buchan, who was a local landowner, are recorded in 1281 as the first bearers of the surname, which initially was confined to the north east of Scotland (where it is still commonest). In the 17th century the kinsmen and dependents of the Erskine earls of Buchan apparently took the Buchan surname; one of them, Thomas Buchan, was a Jacobite general at the time of the Glorious Revolution and another, Peter Buchan, was a noted collector of Scottish ballads in the 19th century. John Buchan, one of the most successful authors of his day, was a Borderer both by descent and by inclinaton; he took the title of Lord Tweedsmuir on his elevation to the peerage.

Buick This is the Scots version of the English surname Bewick, which comes from the Old English *beo wic* ('bee-farm') and is the name of several places in Northumberland and Yorkshire. The Bewick family of wood-engravers were from Newcastle; and the Scottish Buicks may have been early immigrants who changed the spelling of their English name on settling here. David Buick, born in Arbroath in 1854, was taken to the USA at the age of two, worked on a farm and later as a plumbing wholesaler, built his first car in 1903 and founded the Buick Motor Company; but like many who make the journey from rags to riches he had a return ticket.

Buist A Fife surname, and still found mainly in the Kingdom. A Buist family firm of jute barons was well known in Dundee in the last century, where the name is still pronounced 'bist'. Another Dundonian Buist became editor of the *Bombay Times* in 1839. The name is thought to be a variant of **Boyce**.

Burgess The modern form of an older word *burgis*, which meant inhabitant (usually freeman) of a town. In Scotland, burgage-holding involved an obligation to contribute to the defence of the became common here as elsewhere; it was at one time among the top fifty names in the USA. Edmund Burke, the celebrated statesman, orator and political theorist, was born in Dublin in 1729; his only apparent Scottish connection is his rectorship of the University of Glasgow. Regrettably, the best-known Scottish representative is William Burke, an Irish navvy who became involved in the body-snatching trade and was hanged in Edinburgh in 1829 with few to mourn his departure.

Burness–see **Burns**

Burnett A variant of the Germanic personal name *Beornheard*, which means 'bear-hard' (see Introduction); it was popular in Normandy and came to these islands with the Conquest. The Scottish pronunciation of the surname, with its stress on the first syllable, acts as a reminder of its relationship to the forename Bernard. Roger Burnard was a Border landowner about 1200; Alexander Burnard or Burnet was a retainer of Robert the Bruce and was rewarded with grants of land in the forest of Drum and barony of Kincardine, where the name became thoroughly naturalised. A later Alexander Burnet was archbishop of St Andrews in the1690s. Gilbert Burnet, an Aberdeen family and a staunch Whig and scheming prelate, was rewarded with the bishopric of Salisbury in 1689 or services to William and Mary. Perhaps the quaintest was James Burnett, Lord Monboddo, judge and pioneer anthropologist who scandalised Dr Johnson and anticipated Darwin in maintaining that his speechless but flute-playing orang-outang represented the 'infantine state of our species'.

Burns The Anglo-Saxon word *burn* is extraordinarily pervasive in Scottish place-nomenclature, and has given rise to many surnames, all with the same general meaning of 'stream-dweller'. In its singular form of Burn it is found in the south west of Scotland in the 13th and 14th centuries, but is now very rare, no doubt because of assimilation to the name of the national bard. The father of the poet came from Kincardineshire and spelt his name Burness (it is still current there). In 1786 the brothers Robert and Gilbert decided to adopt the spelling Burns, probably because they disliked the mispronunciation 'bur-ness', with its misplaced stress on the last syllable. Another pair of Burns brothers, James and George, were Glasgow shipowners who pioneered steam navigation in the 1830s, and founded what was to be the Cunard line.

Burnside A common place-name in Scotland and Ulster, but not in England; as a surname it is distinctively Scottish. John Burnesyid was recorded in Brechin in 1511, and the name becomes quite common in Edinburgh from the next century onward. John Burnesyde was MP for Culross in 1650.

Burrell–see **Birrell**

Butchart An occupational name for a butcher or slaughterer, ultimately from the Old French *bouc*, meaning a ram. An alternative

33

is from the Old French *bouchard* (literally a 'corker'). The terminal 't' is an analogical formation as in **Lamont** and **Stewart**. The name was found in Angus and Perthshire in the 15th and 16th centuries, and was associated with the Abbey of Coupar-Angus about that time. Anne Butchart was 'scurgit' for theft in Dundee in 1523. Slightly later the name also appears in the Edinburgh Marriage Register, sometimes as Bouchart, Boutcher, Boutchart and Butchard.

Butler Really an English and Irish name, and particularly common in America. The original meaning of butler (from Late Latin *buticula*, a bottle) was wine-steward, and it became a hereditary office of great importance in the Middle Ages. A Norman knight accompanied Henry II on his invasion of Ireland, and was made chief butler of Ireland (the word had acquired the meaning of 'overlord'). This Butler's descendants became earls and later dukes of Ormonde, one of the most powerful families in Ireland over a period of 400 years. Butlers appear in the Scottish records in the 12th century, and three of them figure in the Ragman Roll (see Introduction); but the name has never been as common in Scotland as elsewhere, and most Scottish Butlers are likely to be of English or Irish stock.

C

Cadell–see **Calder**

Cadenhead Reference is to the head waters of the Caddon burn in Selkirkshire (cf. the better-known Caddonfoot). The surname appears to have migrated to Aberdeenshire in the 16th century, and is still most commonly to be found there.

Caird From the Gaelic word *ceard*, meaning craftsman or tinker, an occupation not ranking very high in Gaeldom's social scale. Gilfolan Kerd was accused of piracy in 1275, and Adam Kerde of the parish of Fyvie was excommunicated in 1382. Jane Card was a blaspheming and slanderous gossip in 16th-century Dundee. Sir James Caird was a well-known 19th-century agriculturalist and author. The Caird Hall in Dundee is named after a jute-manufacturing family who were also noted local benefactors. The brothers Edward and John Caird (philosopher and theologian respectively) were leading figures in Glasgow University in the late Victorian era; down the Clyde were the Greenock shipbuilders Caird and Company.

Cairney Usually a contracted form of *MacCearnaigh*, son of Cearnach, a personal name which means 'victorious one'. The surname is virtually restricted to the Glasgow area, which may indicate an Irish provenance; and indeed it is common in Ireland, sometimes in the spelling Kearney. But the name was also found in Galloway at an early date, and a version of it was native to Perthshire, deriving from the lands of Cardeny near Dunkeld.

Cairns Most often from the lands of Cairns in Mid-Calder, Midlothian, although any place where stones are piled into cairns is a possible origin. The name occurs frequently in Lothian records in the later 14th century, particularly in church circles, and became very common throughout Lowland Scotland. David Cairns, born in Roxburgh in 1872, was one of the leading churchmen of his time. Cairns is now to be found mainly in the greater Glasgow area.

Calder There are many places in Scotland so-called, and also some in Cumbria, Lancashire and Yorkshire, with various etymologies: the Scottish one involves the Brittonic words *caled* meaning hard and *dwfr* meaning water, and a familiar variant is Cawdor. The surname is first recorded in Scotland in the late 12th century, when Hugh de Kaledouer witnessed a charter by William the Lion at Montrose. The name was said to have been common in Caithness in the 17th century, in the spelling Caldell; and Cadell is another variant. Baron Ritchie-Calder of Balmashanner near Forfar was famous in the post-war years for the popularisation of scientific knowledge.

Calderwood From the lands of Calderwood in Lanarkshire. The surname is said for some reason to have been common in Dalkeith in the 17th century, but nowadays it is almost exclusively a Glasgow name.

Caldwell The name of several places, including one each in Warwickshire, North Yorkshire and Worcester; but most Scottish bearers will be named after the lands of Caldwell ('cold spring') in Renfrewshire. The surname was common in Edinburgh in the 17th century, where it is still to be found; but it is at its most frequent in Glasgow.

Callaghan An anglicised version of the Irish name *O Ceallachain*, 'descendant of Ceallach'; he was a 10th-century king of Munster, but the meaning of his name is doubtful. Callaghans were and are very numerous in Co Cork; in Scotland the name (not a native one), is mainly to be found in the Glasgow area.

Callan–see **Allan**

Callander There are several places in Scotland with this name–the Perthshire one is best-known but was in fact borrowed by a local laird from its homonym near Falkirk; the etymology is doubtful. Richard Callender was constable of Stirling Castle in 1282, and the name has remained surprisingly localised in the Central region.

Calvert–see **Herd**

Cameron Traditionally, from two Gaelic words *cam sron* meaning 'crooked nose'; but it is likely that these terms were used in the toponymic and not facial sense. The earliest form of the name is Cambron, and the persistence of the medial 'b' in the written records points to a derivation from the lands of Camberone (now Cameron parish) in Fife. The early documentation certainly indicates a Lowland origin; John Cameron of Baledgarno in the Carse of Gowrie was forfeit to Edward I in 1306, and later in the century Hugh Cambrun was sheriff of Forfar and John Cambron was sheriff of Perth. It is not until over a hundred years later that Camerons appear in Lochaber, the traditional seat of the clan. The clan Cameron played a distinguished part in Highland history, both as staunch supporters of the House of Stewart and subsequently as providers of a Highland regiment for the British army. Nor must the Lowland Camerons be forgotten: Richard Cameron, the Covenanter, was a Fifer in whose honour the Cameronian regiment was raised. Cameron comes into the top thirty Scottish surnames.

Campbell Unlike **Cameron,** this surname genuinely appears to have its origin in the facial peculiarity of its progenitor, traditionally one Gillespic O Duithne, who flourished at the beginning of the 13th century. Campbell comes from two Gaelic words, *cam* meaning crooked and *beul* meaning mouth; the attempted derivation *de Campo Belli* is absurd–Latin was not much spoken in Lorne and Argyll which is the clan's homeland. The Campbells were either far-sighted or fortunate in their alliances. Rewarded for their support of Robert the Bruce, they used their increasing power to oppose the MacDonald Lordship of the Isles; they contrived to be on the winning side in the Civil wars and Jacobite risings of the 17th and 18th centuries, and consequently suffered less than others from the destruction of clan power in the the mid -18th century. By Victoria's reign there were no fewer than forty Campbell estates in Scotland, amounting to almost 1,250,000 acres of land. Most of it was owned by the Duke of Argyll, but there were large acreages in Perthshire, Stirlingshire, Ayrshire and at Cawdor in Nairnshire. It should be no surprise that Campbell is the commonest Gaelic surname in Scotland today; and, in the west, the third commonest of all names.

Candlish A Wigtownshire name, a contraction of MacCandlish ('son of Cuindlis'–an Irish personal name). It is relatively uncommon in either version.

Canning–see **Cannon**

Cannon Although apparently native to the south-west of Scotland, and recorded there in the 16th century, the wide currency of this name in the Glasgow area is probably due to the fact that its real home is in Connaught, and that it came over in the 19th-century wave of Irish immigration. Cannon is an anglicisation of O Canain, a personal name derived from *cana*, a wolf-cub. It also appears in Ireland in the form Canning.

Cant Probably a metonymic occupational name for a cantor or singer, or a nickame for a spontaneous songster. Cants are first recorded in the late 14th century in Fife, whither by tradition they emigrated from the Low Countries as dealers in cloth. The name appears frequently in Edinburgh in the two succeeding centuries, but has become largely confined to Tayside. Elene Cant, a Dundee 'wifie' of the 1550s, was 'stroublit' (vexed) by her slandering neighbour, Agnes Thomson. Andrew Cant, the covenanting leader and chaplain to the Scots army in 1640, was a courageous advocate of monarchy during the Cromwell regime; his son Andrew was principal of Edinburgh University from 1675-85. The great philosopher Immanuel Kant is thought to have had an Edinburgh grandfather.

Cardno From the settlement of that name near Fraserburgh, Aberdeenshire, meaning 'copse-place'. The surname is highly localised and scarcely found outside Buchan.

Cardus–see **Carruthers**

Carey Not often found outside the Glasgow area, where however it is quite common, Carey is almost always an anglicisation of the Irish name O Ciardha, a personal name incorporating the Gaelic word *ciar* which means dark. It is not recorded in Scotland before the modern period.

Cargill From the lands in East Perthshire, whose name contains the Brittonic word *caer*–'fort'; both the place-name and the surname should have the stress on the second syllable. Thomas Cargill was appointed master of the Grammar School of Aberdeen in 1580, and the name is subsequently recorded widely in the eastern half of the country. Donald Cargill, a covenanting preacher born in Rattray, was condemned to death for high treason in 1681. It is said that one hundred and fifty years ago, in the Angus fishing village of Auchmithie, one third of the population bore the surname of Cargill, and it is still very common among fisherfolk.

Carlin–see **Carroll**

Carmichael From the place-name Carmichael ('Michael's fort') in Lanarkshire; the stress is on the second syllable, and the 'ch' is pronounced as in 'loch'. Recorded as a territorial designation from the 1220s, it achieved surname status about two hundred years later; a George Carmichael was elected bishop of Glasgow in 1482. Sir James Carmichael was created Lord Carmichael in 1647, and earl of Hyndford in 1701; the peerage has been dormant since 1817. The name is common in Glasgow and Edinburgh.

Carnegie This surname (pronounced with the accent on the second syllable) is now more resonant than the place-name from which it comes–that of a former barony in the county of Angus and derived from the Gaelic *cathair an eige*–'fort at the gap'. The lands of Carnegie were acquired in the 14th century by a family called de Balinhard; the family took the Carnegie surname, and later became earls of Southesk. James, the 5th earl, was present at the raising of the Jacobite standard in 1715, and is reputed to be the hero of the song *The Piper o' Dundee*. The surname attained international celebrity in the person of Andrew Carnegie, the steel millionaire turned philanthropist, whose benefactions grace many towns in his native Scotland.

Carney / Carnie From the Irish personal name *Catharnach*, meaning 'warlike'. The Irish Carneys claim descent from Tadhg O Catharnaigh who died in 1084 and who was also known as *An Sionnach* (the fox); the name was often anglicised to Fox. Some of the Scottish Carnies may have taken their name from the place near Skene in Aberdeenshire, where the surname is first recorded in the 14th century.

Carr Although recorded in central Scotland from the 15th century onwards, Carr is mostly a North-of-England name, and originates with several settlements there; it comes from an Old Norse word meaning alternatively 'marsh' or 'brushwood'. It is also frequently found in Ireland, where it can derive from O Carra (descendant of Carra, meaning 'spear') or from a saint called Cathair. In the early Border records however all Kers are written Car, and inevitably there is great confusion between the two names: the commoner Scottish form is **Kerr**.

Carradice–see **Carruthers**

Carrick The name of the Carrick district of Ayrshire comes from the Brittonic *carreg* , later Gaelic *carraig*–' a rock'. A Duncan Karryc was recorded in Lennox in the 13th century, and a Beatrix Carrik turns up in Glasgow in 1554; but otherwise the name is sparse and found mainly in the south-west.

Carrigan–see **Corrigan**

Carubbers–see **Carruthers**

Caruth–see **Carruthers**

Carruthers A place-name near Ecclefechan in Dumfries, from the Brittonic word *caer* ('fort') and the personal name Ruther (possibly the kingly name of Rydderch). In the 13th century the stewardship of Annandale was held by a family of this name on a hereditary basis under the Bruces; two centuries later the Carruthers were included in the roll of unruly clans in the West Marches. The name was locally pronounced Cridders, and is now mainly found in Glasgow and Edinburgh. The similar forms of Carradice, Cruddas, Cardus, Carrubbers and Caruth, are not in fact related but derive from other place-names embodying the word *caer*.

Carson The etymology is uncertain, but the 13th century records show 'de Carsan', which would indicate a territorial origin. There was a landed family of Carsons in Galloway which ended in the direct line in the reign of James IV, and the name was prominent in Dumfries and Kirkcudbright for several generations. The surname became very frequent in Northern Ireland, and appears to have migrated back to Scotland in recent years.

Carstairs From the place of that name in Lanarkshire, originally Casteltarres ('Tarres's castle'). William Carstares (1649-1715), a Glasgow-born clergyman, was friend and adviser on Scottish affairs to William of Orange; he became principal of Edinburgh University, and was four times moderator of the Church of Scotland. The surname is now found mainly in the Tayside area, but has never been very common.

Carswell *Carse* in Scots means 'low alluvial land along the banks of a river', and the surname probably comes from an (unidentifiable) place-name incorporating this word. Carsewell ('cress-well') in Buckinghamshire is another possible but less likely source. The surname is mainly to be found in Glasgow and Dundee.

Casey Widely distributed in Eire, this surname is a recent importation into Scotland. It is from the Irish personal name *Cathasach*, which means watchful or vigilant. It has become quite common in Glasgow and Edinburgh.

Caskie Usually an abbreviation of MacCaskie, a Galloway name now found most often in Glasgow. For etymolgy, see **MacAskill**.

Cassels Originally applied to anyone living near or working at a castle; more particularly, it may come from one of a number of place-names involving the word castle, such as Cassilis in Kirkmichael parish, Ayrshire. It is not recorded in Scotland before the 17th century, when it began to appear in Lanarkshire; it is still mainly to be found in the west.

Cassidy An Irish name, originally *O Caiside*, which means 'curly-haired'. The Cassidys were a scholarly family from Fermanagh who acted as physicians to the Maguires. They must have emigrated to Glasgow in large numbers in the last century, for the name although missing from the earlier records is nowadays quite common there.

Cattanach Literally, 'belonging to the clan Chattan'. The Celtic tribes took their names from animals, and the Catti ('cats') were described by Tacitus as being even more fierce than the other Gauls; centuries later a loose confederation of clans comprising MacIntoshes, Macphersons, Macgillivrays and Farquharsons adopted the tribal name. The surname Cattanach originated in upper Deeside and Donside, part of the traditional clan Chattan territory, and is still to be found there. It also migrated south, and James Catnach of the Seven Dials was a well-known London bookseller in the early 1800s, purveying penny chapbooks, ballads and broadsides.

Cavanagh An Irish surname, not found in the Scottish records until modern times, but now fairly common in Glasgow and Edinburgh. It comes from the personal name *Caomhanach*, meaning a follower of Caomhan, which was the name of no fewer than fifteen saints in the Irish calendar. Caomhan itself is from the Gaelic word *caomh* meaning gentle or kind. The Cavanaghs claim descent from the ancient kings of Leinster.

Chalmers The Scottish version of Chambers, it means a chamber-attendant or chamberlain. The 'l' indicates that the vowel which precedes it is long, giving the old pronunciation 'chaumers'. During the reign of William the Lion it is recorded in the scribal Latin form of *de Camera*; when the name comes to figure in the Ragman Roll of 1296 it is often Frenchified as *de la Chaumbre*. Alexander of Chamour was 'forspekar for the comownis and merchandis' of Aberdeen in 1461, and another Alexander Chaumir was elected serjeant in the same city a few years later. Gilbert Chaumere (the terminal 's' is a late development) had a safe-conduct into England about the same time. James Chalmers, inventor in the 1830s of the adhesive postage-stamp, came from Arbroath. Thomas Chalmers, born in Anstruther and a graduate of St Andrews, pioneered the movement which led to the Disruption of the Scottish established church in 1843 and to the formation of the Free Church.

Chambers Although not so frequently found in Scotland as its alternative version, **Chalmers**, this name has many distinguished Scots bearers, including William and Robert Chambers, sons of a Peebles cotton manufacturer, who founded *Chambers's Journal* in 1832 and completed the *Encyclopedia* in 1868. Sir William Chambers, son of a Scottish merchant in Stockholm, was the the architect who designed Somerset House in the Strand.

Chapman An occupational name, meaning a merchant or trader, from the Old English word *ceap* signifying barter or bargain. The surname is first recorded in Dundee in 1296 in connection with an enquiry into the death of Ralph Chapman. William Chapman was prior of Aberdeen in 1327, and Hugh Chaypman was bailie of Stirling in 1387. Walter Chepman, merchant burgess in Edinburgh, was granted a patent by James IV to establish the first printing press in Scotland. The surname, widely distributed throughout Scotland, is just as common south of the Border.

Charles Charles (which just means man–cf. Scots *carl*) was rarely found in these islands before the end of the 16th century, by which time the 'surname period' (see Introduction) was over. The forename Charles came to Scotland in the train of the Stuarts, who had strong ties with France, and it makes few surnames either here or anywhere else; significantly it does not figure in any common *Mac* name, MacKerlies being very rare birds indeed. But Charles does appear as a surname in Aberdeenshire in 1569, and in Orkney in the following century.

Cheyne One of the many naturalised French names that have become part of the Scottish scene. Quesnay in Normandy comes from the word *chene*, and means oak-plantation; a family from this location was transplanted to Buckinghamshire, and moved north around 1200 in the reign of William the Lion. Reginald Cheyne was appointed chamberlain of Scotland in 1267; his successor, another Reginald, figures in the Ragman Roll of 1296 as lord of Duffus and Inverugie in Buchan, a third Reginald was a signatory of the Declaration of Arbroath in 1320, while a kinsman, Henry Cheyne, was bishop of Aberdeen around the same time and is said to have built Balgownie Bridge there. The family fame continued with James Cheyne, a 16th-century Aberdeen philosopher and mathematician, and George Cheyne (1671-1743) an Edinburgh physician and advocate of vegetariansm. Meanwhile, the original Buckingham stock had flourished and, in the person of Charles Cheyne of Chesham Bois, became viscounts Newhaven in 1681; the title became extinct in 1738.

Chisholm From Chisholme near Hawick, thought originally to be 'cheese-holm', a meadow used for dairy farming. During the process of feudalisation it became a barony, and the name of Alexander of Chisholm appears in the records in 1249. A few years later John de Chesehelme is mentioned in a bull of Pope Alexander IV. By the middle of the 14th century, Sir Robert Chisholm had succeeded to the hereditary post of constable of Castle Urquhart on Loch Ness; his kinsmen and followers established themselves in the area, and the Chisholms by an advantageous marriage became lairds of Cannich and Strathglass and chiefs of a Highland clan, whose members would take the Chisholm name. Having become converted to Protestantism, the clan was officially non-Jacobite, and escaped the post-Culloden reprisals only to suffer the evictions of the following decades. The Border Chisholms continued as a landed family until the end of the last century, and the name is as frequent there as in the north.

Christie Christian, a favourite forename in France, was introduced to this country after 1066. In its diminutive form of Christie it became very popular in Scotland, particularly in Fife where it eventually achieved the status of a surname. John Chrysty was a burgess of Newburgh in 1457, and the name spread all over the Lowlands; although there were landed Christie families in Montrose and Kildrummy the name cannot be identifed with any particular area. Willliam Christie, shoemaker and dean of the Cordiners of Glasgow in the early 18th century, built up a vast business which latterly looked after the footwear of the entire British army. Christison used to be a Glenesk name; and the form MacChristie has been recorded in Galloway. Chrystal was another form, and **Gilchrist** was sometimes shortened to Christie.

Chrystal–see **Christie**

Clacher–see **Mason**

Clark In the early Middle Ages any literate person could style himself *clericus,* a word which is appended to signatures in countless documents of the period. The Ragman Roll of 1296 contains the names of nine persons calling themselves Clark, but these probably did not become surnames. Later the word appears as Le Clerc, but the transition from a designation to a surname was gradual. The term clerk (which also meant secretary, scribe, scholar or cleric) had passed into Gaelic as *cleireach* which survives only in the Irish forms of Cleary and MacCleary, said to be among the earliest hereditary surnames in that country. By the 15th century the name Clark had spread widely, and today it is the fourteenth commonest surname in Scotland. Among the most noted bearers were Sir John Clerk of Penicuik, advocate, antiquarian, musician (he studied under Corelli) and commissioner for the Union of 1707, and his son John who was a noted writer and artist; the Clerk Maxwells, of whom the great physicist was one, were of the same stock. The name is also common in England, sometimes in the spelling Clarke.

Cleary / Clearey–see **Clark**, **MacCleary**

Cleland There is a place near Motherwell called Clelland ('clay land'), and a Lanarkshire family styled itself Cleland of that Ilk. John Cleland, creator of Fanny Hill and other bawdy characters, was of Scots parentage. The name may also be a contraction of **MacLellan**.

Clement From the Latin *clemens* ('merciful'), the name of a saint who was a disciple of the apostle Paul. Clement was also the name of a number of early popes, and it became a popular Christian name. The first recorded appearance in Scotland is with Clement, elected bishop of Dunblane in 1233. A William Clement was involved in the burning of Dumbarton in 1487. The name is quite commonly found in Glasgow and Edinburgh, often with the terminal 's' indicating 'son of'.

Cochrane From lands near Paisley; the etymology is obscure, but possibly incorporates the Brittonic word *coch*, meaning red. The Ragman Roll includes the name of one William de Coughran, and it recurs frequently in royal charters in the following two centuries. Robert Cochrane, the architect who built the Great Hall of Stirling Castle, was a favourite of James III, and was created earl of Mar; the ennoblement was temporary however, for Cochrane (a clipper of the coinage) fell foul of his peers and was hanged on Lauder Bridge in 1481. The family of Cochrane of that Ilk ended in 1600 with an heiress, whose husband Alexander Blair assumed the surname and arms of Cochrane; their son was created 1st earl of

Dundonald. The 10th earl, Thomas Cochrane (1775-1860) was a naval commander and adventurer whose exploits included the liberation of Chile from Spanish rule; he later commanded the Greek navy. The name is now very common throughout the Scottish Lowlands, especially Tayside. Some **MacEacherns** from Kintyre may have changed their name to Cochrane, despite there being no semantic connection whatever between the two names. It is also said that among the Scots Guards in the service of France the name appeared as Colqueran.

Cockburn The name appears as a territorial designation around 1250, in the person of John de Kockburn in Collessie in Fife; reference is to a place in Berwickshire, now pronounced 'co-burn'. The etymology is probably 'gowk (cuckoo) stream', although the source of the place-name Cockburnspath is undoubtedly the Old Norse personal name Kolbrand. The surname was–and is–most commonly to be found in the Borders and Lothian. The Cokburnes of Henderland were a freebooting Border family. John Cockburn of Ormiston was an 18th-century agricultural improver; Alison Cockburn, his contemporary, was a friend of Sir Walter Scott, and composed a version of *The Flouers of the Forest*; Henry Cockburn, Lord Cockburn, was judge, politician, author and zealous Whig; and Sir George Cockburn was the admiral who conveyed Napoleon to St Helena.

Cole Basically a south-of-England name, not recorded in Scotland before modern times: its frequent occurrence in Glasgow (the haven for most 19th-century immigration) suggests that it comes here by way of Ireland, where it is very widespread, and is the family name of the earls of Enniskillen. The Irish version is usually a contraction of MacCool, which in turn comes from *Mac Giolla Chomhghaill*, 'son of the servant of Comhgall', the name of an early

Irish saint. Coles who consider themselves to be of English origin can however derive their name from a diminutive of **Nicholas**.

Coleman This name poses some of the problems of **Cole**. Coleman is really a Kent name, and normally just means 'collier'. But there is an alternative Celtic source, viz., the Irish personal name Colman, which is a diminutive of Columba, the name of the 6th-century missionary who converted the Picts (or some of them) to Christianity. Coleman has affinities with the name **Malcolm**; it is recorded in Edinburgh in 1482, and is now surprisingly widespread in Scotland, particularly in Glasgow, which became the home of so many names of Gaelic origin.

Collie The Gaelic word *coille* (pronounced 'coll-ye') means 'copse', and figures in countless place-names. It is probably the source of the surname also, which occurs mainly in Aberdeenshire. Thomas de Colley of Kildrummy on Donside figures in the Ragman Roll of 1296 (see Introduction), and Willam Coly was a burgess of Aberdeen in 1436. A derivative is Collison, said to have been one of the chief surnames in Aberdeenshire in the 18th century.

Collins A common English surname, and a double diminutive of **Nicholas**. It is even commoner in Ireland, where it is or was among the thirty most popular surnames. The Irish derive it from the personal name Coilean (which means a whelp or pupppy). Collins is not recorded in Scotland before modern times, but is now quite frequent because of the influx of English and Irish bearers of the name–probably mainly the latter, since most Scottish Collinses are to be found in the west. William Collins, born in Eastwood in 1789, was a weaver turned bookseller who founded the Glasgow publishing firm.

Collison–see **Collie**

Colquhoun This Gaelic name (pronounced 'ca-hoon', with the stress on the second syllable) comes from the lands of Colquhoun in Dunbartonshire; the derivation is probably *cuil cumhann–* 'narrow corner'. The lands were acquired in the 13th century by Umfridus de Kilpatrick, whose family took the Colquhoun surname from them; the name appears in various spellings in the records of the 13th and 14th centuries. Around 1350 Sir Robert Colquhoun married a local heiress and became lord of Colquhoun and Luss on Loch Lomondside, where his descendants still reside. Another Colquhoun, who lived in the 16th century and was a cannon-founder by trade, emigrated to Sweden and left distinguished descendants there with names such as Cahun, Caun, Gaun, Gahn and Kharun. In America it often appears as Cahoun, which was the name of a vice-president of the USA; occasionally it is apparently used as an anglicisation of Cohen.

Coltart–see **Herd**

Colville From Colleville near Bayeux. The first recorded Scottish bearer is Philip de Colevillle who possessed baronies in Roxburghshire and was a hostage for William the Lion under the Treaty of Falaise in 1174. Philip's son Thomas, who died in 1219, was lord of Oxnam and Ochiltree. The surname appears regularly in the records of Lothian and the Borders for the late mediaeval period; Colvilles were famous in Fife and Kinross in the 16th and 17th centuries as lawyers, churchmen and writers. The name often became in the vernacular Colvin (in the same way that Melville became Melvin); however, Sir Sidney Colvin had no known Scottish connection other than his friendship with Robert Louis Stevenson.

Comrie The Perthshire village of Comrie derives from the Gaelic *comraidh–*'meeting of the waters', as do other places with the same name. Some MacGregors are said to have settled in Comrie and adopted the village surname in preference to their own sensitive patronymic (see **MacGregor**). Nowadays the surname is found in Glasgow, but only sparsely in Perthshire.

Connelly / Connolly An Irish name, whose Scots bearers are mainly to be found in the large cities. It comes from *Conghalach*, a personal name meaning 'valiant one'.

Conner / Connor From the Irish personal name *Conchobar*, apparently meaning 'high will'. O Connor is the ninth commonest name in Ireland, and that of six distinct and important septs, one of whom descends from the last High King of Ireland; in Scotland it usually loses its O prefix (which means 'descendant of' and requires no apostrophe).

Cook An occupational name with cognates in every Germanic language, and among the fifty commonest surnames in England. The terminal 'e' is reckoned to be an affectation. In its Latinate form *Cocus* (not that anyone actually called himself that) the name is frequent in the early Scottish records: 'Willelmus Cocus', who received a toft (homestead), 'John Cocus de Balcasky and Richard Cocus of Abircrumby' were charter witnesses in 1260; a dozen years later Richard Cook's name appears in the vernacular form as a janitor at Dunfermline Abbey. Andro Kuk was banished from Dundee for heresy in 1521. These examples are all in east Scotland, but the name Cook was so widespread as to defy placement

Cooper The cooper's trade, as maker and repairer of wooden vessels such as barrels, tubs and buckets, was one of the most important in mediaeval times, and gives rise to surnames in many languages; the noun is preserved in 'chicken coop'. In the 13th century there is a record of one Alanus Cuparius ('Alan the Cooper') but this ephemeral designation may not have become a permanent surname. Two different points of origin are the place-names Cupar, county town of Fife, and Coupar Angus. The spellings Coupar and Cowper are also found; the poet William Cowper was of Fife ancestry. Thomas Cooper, who died in 1953, was the virtual embodiment of the Law of Scotland: he was judge, legal scholar and historian, Lord Justice General and Lord President of the Court of Session. Common in all parts of Scotland, the name was at one time among the thirty most popular in England.

Copeland From the Old Norse *kaufland*, meaning 'bought land' as distinct from inherited land, the word gives the place-names Copeland in Cumbria and Coupland in Northumbria. John de Coupland is remembered as the hero of the battle of Nevill's Cross in 1346, but it is not known how and when the name came to Scotland. It is recorded in Orkney in 1455 and in Shetland fifty years later, and became quite common in Aberdeen.

Corbett A nickname from the French word *corbeau* meaning crow or raven, and very popular with the Normans. The first Scottish Corbet came via Shropshire and settled in Teviotdale in the early 12th century, as a vassal of the earl of Dunbar. The family became landowners in the Borders, but the direct line expired in 1241. A Robert Corbet owned some land at Gamrie which he gave to Kinloss abbey in 1227; three other families of the name rendered homage in 1296 for their lands near Roxburgh. The name subsequently became common throughout Scotland, usually with the double 't' spelling.

Cordiner A cordwainer was a maker of shoes from goatskin leather which came from Cordoba; the cordiners were elected into a fraternity in Edinburgh in July 1349. Thomas Cordoner was admitted burgess of Aberdeen in 1442, and Robert Cordoner held lands in Kintore at the same time. Although recorded elsewhere, and as far north as Caithness, the name is primarily an Aberdeen one.

Cormack–s e e **MacCormack**

Cosgrove The English Cosgroves derive their name from a place in Northamptonshire, where Cos is an Anglo-Saxon personal name. But in Scotland Cosgrove is much more likely to come from the Celtic name *Coscrach* which means 'victorious one'. O Coscraigh was a common name in Ireland, and came to Aberdeenshire in the time of St Columba; it appears in the 16th and 17th century records in the spellings Coskroch, Cokrie and MacCroskie. Cosgroves are found all over Scotland, but never in large numbers.

Costello A reduction of the Irish name *Mac Oisdealbhaigh*, and correctly pronounced with the accent on the first syllable. Oisdealbh was one of the sons of Gilbert de Nangle, a Norman who settled in Ireland after the Conquest: the barony of Costello in Co Mayo is named after him. The name is not recorded in Scotland before modern times, and now mainly in the Glasgow area.

Coull From the place of that name in Aberdeenshire; *cul* is a familiar Gaelic place-name element meaning 'back', which is possibly the derivation of the surname. Recorded as a territorial designation in the early 12th century, it subsequently appears as a surname in the records of Glasgow and Fife. Coull was a traditional name among fisherfolk, very common in such places as Cullen and Ferryden in days gone by, and still to be found mainly in the eastern half of Scotland.

Coulter From the Gaelic words *cul tir*, meaning 'back land', a common place-name, exemplified in Lanark and in two places near Aberdeen. Richard of Culter was sheriff of Lanark in the early 13th century; Andrew de Cultyr held lands in Aberdeen in 1281. The name is now mainly to be found in Glasgow and Edinburgh.

Couper–see **Cooper**

Coutts From the village of Cults near Aberdeen; it is probably from the Gaelic term *cuillt* meaning 'nook, corner', a familiar place-name element. Richard de Cotis was a landowner in Elgin in 1343;

John and Donald de Cowtis were implicated in the murder of one of the Ogilvys of Angus in 1392. A family of Coutts obtained a Crown charter in 1433 of the lands of Auchtercoul. Another family of the name settled in Montrose in the 1570s; William Coutts became provost of the town, and it was one of his descendants, Thomas Coutts (1735-1822), who founded the London banking firm. Several Coutts families are found in Edinburgh in the 16th and 17th centuries, and John Coutts was provost of the city in 1742; the name has however remained surprisingly localised in its area of origin.

Cowan A Lowland surname which is thought to be a transliteration of one of several Celtic names; there are no Cowans in the records before about 1560. Candidates are the Irish patronymic *O Comhdhain* (pronounced Cowan), and the Gaelic patronymic *Mac gille chomghain* (usually shortened to MacCowan); the etymologies are uncertain. Cowan's Hospital in Stirling was founded in 1639 by John Cowan, a merchant in the town. With such diverse origins, the surname has no particular location within Scotland.

Cowie Traditionally from the old barony of Cowie in Kincardineshire; Herbert de Cowy is mentioned in a charter of 1394. Cowie may also be a variant of Cowe (a personal name recorded in Musselburgh as early as 1359) or of **Collie**. John Cowy was a burgess of Aberdeen in 1505, and Janet Cowie was arraigned for witchcraft in Elgin in 1646. The name was so common in Buckie that there were at one time no fewer than twenty-five George Cowies in the village; Cowies were also well-known in Newburgh in Fife, where the pronunciation was apparently 'coo-ie'.

Cox An English or Irish name which arrived in Scotland in fairly recent times. The English version may be a nickname with the general meaning of cocky or cock-a-hoop, but it may equally well be a pet form of **Cook**. In Ireland, where the name is also common, it is a translation of the name Coiligh, from the Gaelic *coileach* meaning cockerel. James Cox, a native of Lochee (once the Irish suburb of Dundee), took over his father's linen manufacturing business, and with his three brothers founded the partnership which in 1840 became Cox Brothers, the largest jute firm in the world; it continued through five generations, employed thousands of women, and is part of Dundee's social history.

Crabbe / Craib In England this name derives usually from the apple, but in Scotland it is of Flemish origin and refers to the crustacean. John Crab was a Flemish engineer who was rewarded by Robert the Bruce with a grant of lands in Aberdeenshire in recognition of his devastating efficiency at the siege of Berwick in 1319. Another John Crab, possibly his son, became a burgess of Aberdeen and was appointed to treat for the ransom of David II. Alexander Crabbe became an operative in a Dundee flax mill in the 1830s at the age of four and a half. The name cannot now be assigned to any particular locality.

Craig The name, with its variants Craik and Craigie, originally applied to someone who came from one of the several places so called, or who lived near a crag. Three different families in the 15th century styled themselves Craig of that Ilk (i.e. of Craig). Johannes de Crag, burgess of Aberdeen, had a charter of land at Rubislaw in 1358, and the family occupied Craigston Castle at Kildrummy for two hundred and fifty years. Master Richarde of Crag was vicar of St Mary's, Dundee in the 1550s; Reche Crag, a Dundee baxter, was accused of selling bread under weight in 1521. John Craig, a St Andrews University divine, was imprisoned for adopting Protestant tenets, sentenced to death by the Inquisition, escaped to become a colleague of John Knox, and saw the Reformation through; James Craig, an 18th-century architect, published designs for laying out Edinburgh's New Town; other Craigs were famous in the legal profession. Craig is among the sixty commonest names in Scotland, but is comparatively little known elsewhere.

Cram / Cramb–see Crombie

Cranston From the barony of that name in Midlothian; it embodies the personal name Cran (which comes from the bird, as does the mechanical crane) and was current in the shires of Banff, Aberdeen and Inverness in the 1300s. Thomas de Cranstoun, provost of Edinburgh, was ambassador of James II in 1449; Thomas Cranstoun was knighted in the 1450s and one of his descendants was raised to the peerage with the title of Lord Cranstoun; the peerage became extinct in the last century. Other branches of the kindred were notorious Border reivers; but Kate Cranston presided over Victorian Glasgow's most select tearooms, some of whose decorative interiors were designed by Charles Rennie Mackintosh.

Crawford There were several habitations so-called (originally 'crow ford') in England and Scotland; the surname can come from any one of them, but most Scots will take their name from the barony of Crawford in upper Clydesdale. By 1296 there were three separate Crawford families who did homage to Edward I for their lands in Ayrshire. Around this time the Crawford genes were transmitted in an interesting way by the marriage of two heiresses, one to a Lindsay who was the ancestor of the earls of Crawford and the other to the father of William Wallace. In their own right the Crawfords played a leading part in the turbulent history of their country. Thomas Crawford of Jordanhill was a member of the household of Mary Queen of Scots and was active in investigating the murder of her husband Darnley ; he captured Dumbarton Castle with 150 men in 1571, received the surrender of Edinburgh Castle two years later, and was rewarded with a grant of the lands of Dalry. The senior branch of the family, the Crawfords of Kilburnie, received a baronetcy in 1781. The name is now eightieth in the order of frequency of surnames in Scotland.

Crichton From the old barony of Crichton, south of Edinburgh. *Crioch* is Gaelic for boundary, and *toun* is the old Scots word for homestead. Turstan de Crectune was a witness to David I's charter to Holyrood around 1128, and the name occurs frequently in late mediaeval documents, in no less than twenty-four different spellings, including Kreittoun (1328) and Greythorn (1429). By the late 1500s, the Crichtons of Eliock were coming into prominence; Robert Crichton was Lord Advocate and later a judge; his son Sir Robert had a troubled career and forfeited his property, while his brother James ('the Admirable Crichton') ended a brilliant career of scholarship by being killed in a brawl in Mantua in 1585. Another branch of the family were styled lords of Sanquhar; the 6th Baron, Robert Crichton, was an assassin who was paid out with his own coin in Great Palace Yard in 1612; nevertheless the family became earls of Dumfries under James I in 1633. Crighton is a rarer spelling.

Crockett In England (where it is less common) this name is thought to come from *croquet*, meaning a curl; in Scotland it may be either from a lost place-name or a contraction of the Galloway name MacRiocaird ('son of Richard'). Two Crocketts appear in the Ragman Roll of 1296, both landowners in Lanarkshire. The wild frontiersman, Davy Crockett, was very probably of Scots descent; and there is no doubt about the origin of S. R. Crockett, the once popular novelist who wrote about genteel life in Dumfriesshire in the 19th century.

Croll Mainly to be found in the Mearns and Tayside, Croll almost certainly comes from a place-name: but that of Crieul in Seine-Inférieure is perhaps a somewhat far-fetched suggestion. Bertram de Criolle is recorded in the 1250s , but this is still a designation rather than a surname. There was an Alexander Criole in Fettercairn in 1539, another in Keithock a few years later, and a number were recorded in Brechin in the following century. Jonkyn Croil was a tailor in Dundee in 1560. James Croll, a typical 'lad o' pairts', was born in 1821, apprenticed as a wheelwright, joined the Geological Survey and taught himself museology and cartography; he eventually became a Fellow of the Royal Society and published standard texts on physical geology.

Crombie A place-name which incorporates the Gaelic word *crom* meaning crooked (see also **Abercrombie**). There are several examples in eastern Scotland, each of which could have produced a surname. The most likely is Crombie in the parish of Auchterless in Aberdeenshire, but there is another in Torryburn. Robert Crumbie was a chaplain in Brechin in the mid-15th .century; nowadays the name is found all over the country.

Crosbie / Crosby The name means a settlement by a cross, or even crossroads, and it occurs in several places in the south of Scotland; it is also found in northern England (in Cumbria alone there are four Crosbys), so it cannot be claimed that Crosbie is mainly a Scottish surname. Frequently found as a territorial designation in the pre-surname period, it emerged at an early stage as a fairly common surname in the shires of Wigton and Dumfries. A family of Crosbies are said to have been followers of Robert the Bruce. Andrew Crosbie, advocate, was a friend of Boswell and Johnson and is reputed to be the original of Councillor Pleydell in *Guy Mannering*. The name was also taken over by the Irish (see **Cross**).

Cross A name with cognates in most European languages, it was applied to someone who lived near a cross, or possibly carried a cross in a religious procession (but cross meaning 'peevish' is a modern usage). John Cruche was a burgess of Edinburgh in 1567 and James Corss was a mathematician in the same city a century later. In Ireland there is or was a surname Mac an Chrosain (*crosain* means a poet, and the MacCrossans were bards to the O Mores); the name was sometimes shortened to Crossan (a common name in Glasgow) or mistranslated to Cross or even **Crosbie**.

Crow / Crowe This can be a nickname from the bird, referring to any of its several characteristics. The name is recorded in Dunblane in 1470, and is now common in every district of Lowland Scotland. Another possible derivation of the name is from the Irish patronymic *Mac Conchradha*, which was simplified (a little) to MacEnchroe and (a lot) to Crowe. The terminal 'e' is not a final deciding factor, but can be an indication of Irish origin. James Crow (1800-1859) was born in Scotland and benefited his fellow men by effecting vast improvements in the methods of producing whisky; he founded the distilling industry of Kentucky.

Cruddas–see **Carruthers**

Cruden Almost exclusively an Aberdeenshire name, it comes from the district of Cruden in Buchan, which in turn took its name from the river; the etymology is uncertain. Thomas Croudane was a burgess of Aberdeen in the mid 15th century. The best-known bearer is Alexander Cruden who became a bookseller in London and in 1737 produced a monumental concordance of the Old and New Testaments; not surprisingly perhaps, he became subject to periodic fits of insanity, believing that he had a divine mission to reform the nation's morals.

Cruickshank It means 'bent leg', not necessarily implying bow-leggedness in the bearer, for the term might be taken in the toponymic sense, and refer to an unidentified place-name (see **Shanks**). John Crokeshank was a burgess of Haddington, whose name appears in the Ragman Roll of 1296; Cristinus and John

Crukshank were burgesses of Aberdeen in the 15th century, and there are many references in contemporary documents to others of the name, which soon became numerous all over Scotland. The famous caricaturist George Cruikshank, who illustrated some of the early works of Dickens, was of Scottish ancestry.

Cullen From Cullen in Banffshire; the name derives from the Gaelic word *cuilan*, meaning a little nook. It is recorded in the 14th and 15th centuries as a territorial designation, prefixed by a 'de'; towards the end of this period there appears the name (without the 'de') of one Andrew Colleyn, merchant in Aberdeen. William Cullen, MD Glas., whose long life spanned most of the 18th century, was the foremost physician of his time, and his son Robert, Lord Cullen, was a judge and legal reformer. Despite its north-east origin, the name is now found mainly in Glasgow, and it may be that some of the Glasgow Cullens are from Ireland; the Irish version of the name is a contraction of *Mac Cuillin* (whose stem comes from a personal name meaning 'holly'); Cullen has also been recorded in Ireland as a variant of **Collins**.

Cumming Almost certainly from the Normandy town of Comines. In its earlier form of Comyn it is found in eastern England in the 12th and 13th centuries, brought there by immigrants, and it reached Scotland with the family of Wilhelmus Comyn, who was appointed chancellor to David I. His successors, by making advantageous marriages, first with the granddaughter of King Donald Ban and second with the heiress of Buchan, became one of the greatest families of Scotland and one with a double claim to the throne; this claim was effectively negated with the murder of the Red Comyn by Robert the Bruce in 1306, and the power of the Comyns began to decline. The senior branch of the clan however acquired the lands of Altyre in Moray, and later the property of Gordonstoun. The Cumming-Gordons retain the clan-lands and the chiefship. Cumming is a name which is found all over Scotland; Cummings tends to be the English form.

Cunningham The name of a district in Ayrshire, originally *Cunegan* (the 'ham' ending is the work of an anglophile scribe). A Norman adventurer was given the manor of Cunningham in the 12th century, and adopted as a surname the name of his property. The family established themselves as supporters of the Crown and were duly rewarded with further grants of land; they acquired by marriage the lands of Glencairn, and by the 15th century had been ennobled as earls of Glencairn. Alexander, the 5th earl, principal promoter of the Reformation in Scotland, was fanatical in his destruction of Catholic relics. James, the 14th earl, was a friend and patron of Robert Burns: the poet named his fourth (legitimate) son James Glencairn Burns. The name Cunningham spread to all parts of Scotland from the 1400s onwards, (in at least twenty different spellings), and is now among the seventy most frequent in the land.

Curran An anglicised version of the Irish patronymic O Corraidhin (*corran* means a point). Currans were recorded in mediaeval times in the shires of Ayr and Wigton, but most bearers of the name will be of more recent Irish provenance.

Currie The Gaelic word *coire*, meaning 'cauldron', is a familiar place-name element which figures in the name Corrie in Dumfriesshire, Arran and elsewhere (but not Currie in Midlothian, which is a different word). Another Gaelic word *currach*, meaning bog or fen, is an alternative derivation. From such a source come the frequent references to the name Currie in the early charters. But there is another and intriguing derivation: a celebrated family of Clanranald bards which flourished from the 1400s to the 1700s had the Gaelic patronymic

Mac Mhuirich; this never gave rise to a common surname, but being pronounced 'mac-oorie' it was often anglicised to Currie. It would be pleasing to think that this ancient bardic name resurfaced in a new form. Whatever its origin, the name Currie became very common in all parts of the country–achieving 79th place in the 1950s. James Currie was friend, editor and biographer of Burns; Finlay Currie, the Scottish actor, was born in Edinburgh in 1856.

Cuthbert A compound Teutonic name (see Introduction) whose components *cuth* and *beorht* mean respectively 'famous' and 'bright'. Cuthbert was the name of a 7th-century saint who was the subject of a cult in mediaeval times, especially in the north of England and southern Scotland; his name is commemorated in Kirkcudbright. A family named Cuthbert settled in Inverness in the early 15th century; the name is well-documented in eastern Scotland during the same period. Its derivative Cuthbertson has a similar origin and distribution.

Cuthill There is a place in East Lothian near Prestonpans called Cuthill, and this provides an obvious derivation for the surname (though not pronounced 'cut-hill'). But the real origin is probably the Gaelic word *comhdail*, a meeting or assembly, and there are other settlements with a similar name. Thomas and George Cuthill are recorded in 1536, and the name was current in Stirling in the 18th century. It is now to be found mainly in the Tayside area.

D

Dalgarno From the lands of Dalgarnock in Dumfriesshire, meaning 'field of the noisy stream' (in Gaelic, *dal gairneag*). Among the early records is the name of John de Dalgarnock, who was prior of Lesmahagow in 1348; but the name has been associated with Aberdeenshire since the 13th century, and is still largely to be found in that area. Johannes de Dalgarnok was a burgess of Aberdeen in the 1330s, and another man of the same name was an Arbroath burgess at the same time. George Dalgarno, a 17th century Aberdeen philosopher, tried, in anticipation of Leibniz, to formulate a philosophical language.

Dalgleish From the lands of that name near Selkirk, with the meaning 'green field' (Gaelic *dal glas*). The bearers of the name seem to have established a reputation as disturbers of the peace in the Borders, and one John Dalglese was hanged in 1510 for acting 'art and part' in the burning of Branxholm and Ancrum. George Dalgleish, servant of the earl of Bothwell, suffered a similar fate (plus quartering) for involvement in the murder of Darnley. More law-abiding kindred established themselves in Fife and Perthshire; but the name remains most frequent in Lothian.

Dallas Dallas is a place near Forres, established over a thousand years before its namesake in Texas. The name is probably the Old Gaelic *Dallais*–'at the meadow'. The lands of Dolays Mykel ('greater Dallas') were granted by William the Lion to an Englishman named William of Ripley; it is very likely that he went native and took the Dallas designation, which eventually became a surname. William Dolasse appears as a procurator in Brechin in 1435, and Henry Dolas in Arbroath a few years later. In 1513 Henry

Dallas of Cantray, who had married a Mackintosh, joined with his wife's kinsmen in the hership (raid) of Petty near Inverness; the Mackintosh connection seems to have endured, for there were Dallases serving in the Mackintosh regiment at Culloden more than two hundred years later.

Dalrymple A place in Ayrshire, from the Gaelic *dal cruim poll*– 'field of the crooked stream'. The barony of the name was held in 1371 by Malcolm and Hew de Dalrympill, and a descendant of one or other in 1429 acquired the estate of Stair in Ayrshire. The first Viscount Stair was the author of the famous *Institutes,* a codification of the law of Scotland. It was his son, Sir John Dalrymple, Master of Stair, who in 1692 made the preliminary arrangements for the Massacre of Glencoe; created an earl in 1703, he did little to enchance his posthumous reputation by his part in preparing the Act of Union of 1707 and securing its passage through the Scottish parliament.

Daly Originally *O Dalaigh* , 'descendant of Dalach', a personal name embodying the Gaelic word *dail* , meaning meeting or assembly. Dalach was an Irish chief, 10th in descent from Niall of the Nine Hostages. The surname Daly is nowadays found mainly in Glasgow (the result of Irish immigration in the 1840s) but there was a contingent in Dundee, often using the spelling Dailly.

Dalziel / Dalyell The name of a place in the Clyde valley, recorded in 1200 as Dalyell and Daleel. It comes from the Gaelic *dail ghil*– 'at the white field', and 'dal-yell' represents the correct pronunciation; 'de-yell' is also acceptable. Hugh de Dalyhel was sheriff of Lanark in 1288; Thomas de Dalielle was obliged to submit to Edward I of England in 1296. The head of the family was ennobled as earl of Carnwath in 1639. General Tam Dalyell was commander-in-chief of the royal forces in Scotland between 1666 and 1685; his savage repression of the Covenanters won him the nickname of 'the Muscovy beast who ... roasted men'; he was an ancestor and namesake of the milder-mannered MP of our own time. Sir John Graham Dalyell wrote *The Darker Superstitions of Scotland* (1835).

Daniel / Daniels Daniel ('God is my judge') was an Old Testament prophet who interpreted the writing on the wall for Nebuchadnezzar and was thrown into the lions' den for his pains. His adherence to his faith throughout it all won him great popular acclaim, and Daniel became a favourite given-name in most European cultures, and not only among Jews. It duly reached Scotland, and eventually became a surname; Walter Daniel had a safe conduct to England in 1424, and John Dangzell is recorded in Dunfermline in 1562. It has never been very frequent here, but is found in some quantity in the larger cities.

Darling This name means what it says; it comes from the Old English *deorling*, 'beloved one'. Used as a forename until at least the 14th century, it appears first as a surname in the person of Waldevus Darling, who witnessed a charter in Roxburgh in 1338. John and Andrew Derling were burgesses of Edinburgh in 1381; more than 500 years later another Darling was Lord Provost of Edinburgh, to which city the name is now virtually confined.

Darroch The name of a place near Falkirk, from the Gaelic word *darach*, meaning oakwood. John Darach was a bailie of Stirling in 1406, and Mariote Darach was nurse to the infant daughter of James II in the 1460s. James Darrow was a notary public in St Andrews in 1482. It is said that a number of Darrochs migrated to Islay and Jura in late mediaeval times and became adherents of the MacDonalds.

Davidson David was a royal name in Scotland as well as in Judea and was one of the Christian names widely employed at the font.

The embryonic surnames of *fiz Dauid* and *filius Davidi* appear frequently in the records up to the 14th century, but the first genuine surname is that of Robert Davidson, provost of Aberdeen, who was killed at the battle of Harlaw in 1411. Although mainly a Lowland surname, there was a Highland clan of Davidsons in Badenoch, so given to sanguinary feuding that they became virtually extinct in the Middle Ages. The Roxburgh Davidsons formed themselves into a Border clan in the 16th and 17th centuries. Thomas Davidson was master of the Sang Scule in Aberdeen in the 1680s In common speech, David was frequently contracted to Davie or Daw, and this gives the additional patronymics **Davie**, Davison and **Dawson**.

Davie See **Davidson**. Meg Davie is recorded in Aberdeen in 1408; Jonet Davie was a scold who was fined for her bad habit in 1669. The name is commoner in the eastern half of the country. A derivative of the name is Davison: Adam Davyson, merchant and burgess of Edinburgh, had a safe conduct into England in 1360. Davies, fifth commonest surname in England and even more so in Wales, makes only an occasional and latish appearance in the Scottish records.

Dawson Daw was once a familiar contraction of David, and Dawson is now a very frequent name, especially in the Aberdeen area. John Daweson was in the service of the earl of Douglas in 1405; Duncan Dalsoun was coalman to the king in 1531; and there were Dawsons in Auchtermuchty at about the same time. Some of the Badenoch **Davidson**s are thought to have changed to Dawson.

Day Sometimes a pet form of David, or a rendering of the Gaelic form *Daidh*; perhaps also from the Old English personal name *Daeg*. There have been Deys in Banffshire from earliest times, and they are probably from the first of these two sources: the names

Day and Dey are still most commonly found in the north-east. It may well be however that the west-of-Scotland Deys are of different origin, for there is an old Irish name *O Diaghaidh*, often anglicised to O Dee or Dey, both very common in Ireland.

Deacon / Deakin A deacon was a church dignitary, and was normally celibate; in Scots usage, however, a deacon was also the master of an incorporated company or trade, and the surname in both its spellings usually comes from the latter source; the reference can also be to the servant of such an official. Walter Dekne, a burgess of Perth, had a safe conduct into England in 1291. Nowadays the surname is at its most common in the Glasgow area.

Dean In the Highlands a valley is called a glen; in the Lowlands the more normal term was den, from Old English *denu*. Dean is a common place-name element in the Lowlands: there is a village called Dean in Edinburgh and another near Kilmarnock. The surname in its singular form is usually from this source (but see also **Deans**). John Dene was a burgess of Irvine in 1499 and the name has been common in Ayrshire since the 1500s.

Deans A dean was originally in charge of ten persons (Low Latin *decanus*), then head of a chapter of canons in a cathedral or of a faculty in a university. The surname obviously becomes confused with **Dean**, but Deans has been very frequent in Scotland from the 16th century onwards, originally in the form Deinis or Deins. John Deanness, a slater to trade, was a burgess of Glasgow in 1588; the name was and is common in the Borders.

Deas From the Gaelic word *deas* (pronounced 'jes' and meaning south), a common place-name element occurring in such names as **Fordyce**. Dyce itself is near Aberdeen, and gave rise to the local surnames Dyes, Dys and Dyce. James Dais was recorded in

Dundee in 1611, Andrew Daes was a stabler in Edinburgh in 1627, and James Daes was minister of Earlston church in 1643. In its modern spelling of Deas the name is found sparsely all over Scotland.

Delaney A continental origin has been claimed, on the grounds that there are many place-names in Normandy which seem to fit. But the surname is very numerous in Ireland, and a local origin is much more likely, in the Irish personal name Dubhshlaine (made up of the elements *dubh* meaning black and *slan* meaning defiance). Alternatively, the suffix may be from the river Slaney. Most Scottish Delaneys are to be found in Glasgow.

Dempsey O Diomasaigh was one of the few Irish chiefs who defeated Strongbow in battle; his successors rose to great prominence as Irish patriots, until they met ruin as a result of their loyalty to James II. The name means 'descendant of the proud one' and was very frequent in Ireland. It is not recorded in Scotland until modern times, and now mainly in Glasgow.

Dempster Under the feudal system of heritable jurisdiction, which persisted in Scotland until 1747, a laird was empowered to have certain offences within his territory tried by his dempster. This office (from the word 'deem' or judge) tended to become hereditary and as usual produced a surname. Andrew Dempster who lived at Menmuir in Angus around 1350 seems to bave been hereditary dempster to the abbot of Arbroath. Two who went astray were Alexander and William Dempster, described as 'broken men', who assisted the MacDonalds of Glencoe in a raid on Moray in 1602. The Dempsters of Dunnichen were an Angus family who achieved fame in the 18th century as agriculturalists.

Denholm The name of two places, one in Roxburghshire and another in Dumfriesshire, with its origin in the Old English words *dene holme* , meaning 'valley meadow'. Guy de Denholm did homage for his Roxburgh lands in 1296, and the name was subsequently common in Lanarkshire. It is now encountered mainly in Edinburgh. There is also a place called Denholme in West Yorkshire with the same meaning which gives rise to an English surname.

Dennison Dennis has been a popular forename since the time of the decapitation of St Denis, bishop of Paris (a.d. 272). So, on the face of it, Dennison means 'son of Dennis'. But Dennis could also be a version of 'Danish'; and in Scotland a strong influence has been the barony (now suburb) of Denniston, which has its origin in 'Daniels toun' and produced a surname as early as the 1300s; Robert Denniestoun or Danielston was admitted as a freeman of the Incorporation of Goldsmiths in Edinburgh in 1547.

Deuchars–see **Dewar**

Devine The original form of this Irish surname is O Daimhan and its derivation is *damhan*, a fawn; it also appears in the form Devane. Mainly a Glasgow name, with a presence in Edinburgh, it is not recorded in Scotland before the 1850s.

Devlin The O Doibhlins were a leading Ulster sept; the name was sometimes simplified to Dolan. Dobhlin is a personal name of uncertain origin, possibly from *dobhail* meaning unlucky. Most Scottish Devlins are now located in Greater Glasgow.

Dewar In Gaelic *deoradh* means a pilgrim or stranger and was also the term for someone who had custody of the relics of a saint: a Perthshire family of this name were for centuries custodians of the crozier-head of St Fillan. There are two places called Dewar in Midlothian (possibly of similar origin) which would provide local surnames: Thomas and Peires de Deware did homage to Edward I of England in 1296. Dewar is the family name of the barons

Forteviot, and has become almost synonymous in Perth with the manufacture of whisky; the city has benefited greatly from the philanthropic endeavours of its Dewar sons. Dewar also gave rise to a *Mac* name: the Skye family of *Mac gille dheoradha* ('son of the Dewar's lad'), simplified their surname to *MacLeora*, sometimes spelt **MacClure**. The variant spelling Deuchars is not uncommon.

Dey–see **Day**

Dick / Dickie Although found in every part of Britain, the surname Dick is particularly numerous in Scotland. It is of course a diminutive of Richard. John Dic is recorded in Ayr in 1490, and Wille Dic was deacon of the 'bakstaris' (bakers) of Stirling a generation later. Sir William Dick, Provost of Edinburgh, and one of the richest Scots of all time, used up his immense fortune in financing the armies of the Covenant; his destitution was completed by a fine imposed on him by Parliament for his unwise support of the Stuarts. Sir Alexander Dick, who lived in the city a century later, was a well known physician and correspondent of Dr Johnson. The double diminutive, Dickie, is hardly less common: it is recorded in Glasgow in 1504, and David Dickie was a burgher of Montrose in the following century.

Dickson The commonest of the Richard derivatives in Scotland (see **Richardson**): Richards, Dixon, Hicks and Higgins 'mean' the same as Dickson, but are forms far more widely found in England. The poet Barbour, in his epic on Robert the Bruce, tells of one Thomas Dicson who was the faithful follower of the Douglas in the capture of Castle Douglas on Palm Sunday 1307. The name appears in Aberdeen, Edinburgh and Inverness from the 15th century onwards, and is now common everywhere. William Dickson was a 19th-century authority on the law of evidence. In the early 1900s two Dickson brothers of Montrose made vast sums of money on emigrating to Sweden, where the surname still flourishes.

Dingwall The place-name Dingwall in Easter Ross is a reminder that the Viking parliament met there; Old Norse *thing vollr* means 'assembly-field'. Dingwall appears as a territorial designation in 1342, but does not emerge as a surname proper for another 200 years, when the records show Thomas Dingwall as a burgess of Aberdeen. A 16th-century bearer of the name, Sir John Dingwall, judge and provost of Trinity College, is said to have had a pretentious Edinburgh residence which he styled Dingwall Castle: it occupied a site near the present Register House, and was the subject of unpleasing comment from George Buchanan and John Knox.

Divers A Donegal name, an adaptation of the patronymic O Duibhidir, which is probably from the Gaelic *dubh odhar* ('black, drab'). The name, with its variant O Dwyer, is seldom found outside Glasgow.

Doak The Glasgow version of **Doig**

Dobbie / Dobie / Dobson Bob is today a familiar rhyming diminutive of Robert; in the 'surname period' (see Introduction) Dob was the usual pet name, and produced the surnames Dobbie, Dobie, Dobson and a few others. Thomas Doby was a feuar in Peebles around 1470, and the name is recorded all over the Lowlands. John Dobysoun was a burgess of Lanark in 1429; John Dobsoun lived in Kelso around 1560, and John Dobsone was in Selkirk a century later.

Docherty From the patronymic O Dochartaigh, which in turn derives from the Gaelic adjective *dochartach* meaning something like 'unlucky'. Although Docherty does not appear in Scotland until recent times, it now in its various spellings occupies eighty-seventh place in order of frequency and is the second commonest Irish surname in Scotland after Murphy. It is found mainly in Glasgow and Edinburgh.

Dodds Mainly an Edinburgh name, maybe from the lands of Doddis in Berwickshire. Alexander Dodys, servant to Patrick Dunbarre, had a safe conduct into England in 1425. John Doddis was prior of the Black Freres in Dundee in the 16th century. Another family of Dodds are said to have flourished in Golspie for centuries. The name emigrated to France and is still found there. A William Dodd of Inverkeithing is recorded in 1296, but this is thought to be an entirely different name, commoner in England but of obscure origin.

Doig 'Servant of Cadoc', a Cambro-British saint; the name was found in areas where he was venerated–Kilmadock in Menteith for example means Cadoc's church, and St Maddoes in Gowrie was named for the saint. Alexander Doge was vicar of Dunnichen in Angus in 1372, and so were some of his descendants. Alexander Dog was canon of Inchmahome in Menteith in 1491, and the name continues to crop up in that district. Besse Dog was a slanderous gossip in Dundee in the 1520s; Captain James Dog became provost of that city after attempting to repel an English invasion of 1547. There was a family of Doigs in Brechin from the early 1500s, and Dr David Doig was the rector of Stirling Grammar School whom Burns met on his Highland tour. The name is now commonest in Tayside, particularly around Dundee. In Ulster, whither it migrated, it sometimes becomes Davock or Doak. The Welsh equivalent is Cadogan.

Dolan From the Irish patronymic O Dubhshlain, which comprises the Gaelic words *dubh slan*–'black challenge'. There has been some confusion with the names **Devlin** and **Delaney**.

Donnachie The clan Donnachie, better known nowadays as Robertson of Atholl, was named after a warrior called Donnnchadh

Reamhar, who lived at the time of Robert the Bruce and whose name in English would be Duncan the Stout. So the surname means literally 'of the line of **Duncan**'.

Donald Donald is a forename of great antiquity and is first recorded in a Roman inscription of a.d. 20 as being that of an ancient British prince. In Gaelic the name is Domhnall (the 'mh' being silent) and comes from an older Celtic form *dubno val dos* meaning 'world mighty ruler, prince'. It is still very popular as a forename, and has cognates in Welsh and Breton. As a surname with a MAC prefix it did indeed become world mighty (see **MacDonald**), but in its original form it is recorded in the Book of Deer in 1100; it turns up again in Kinross in 1328, Aberdeen in 1395 and in the Borders a century later. It is now widespread.

Donaldson The popularity of **Donald** as a forename has produced several patronymics besides **MacDonald.** One of these is Donaldson, which may sometimes be a literal translation of MacDonald but as often as not will have been borne by the son of an unrecorded Lowland Donald. The name occurs early, long before the decline of the Gaelic language; Henry Donaldson was one of the garrison of Edinburgh castle in 1339, and Donaldsons were an important family in Strathdee in the 1520s. The name turns up in the records frequently in the following two centuries– usually in the Lowlands–and although not so common as MacDonald it is still among the hundred top Scottish surnames. It is conspicuous in Edinburgh through the achievements of James Donaldson (1751-1830) who founded the hospital which bears his name, and who also left large sums for the maintenance and education of poor children.

Donnelly Having nothing in common with the two preceding names, Donnelly is an attempt at the Irish patronymic *O*

Donnghaile, which comprises two Gaelic words *donn* (brown) and *gal* (valour). Ballydonnelly in Co Antrim is named after the sept, some of whose members rose to fame in the United States. Not found in Scotland until recently.

Donoghue / Donohue Originally *O Donnchadha,* this is an Irish version of **Duncan**. The name originated in Co Cork, and migrated to Kerry. Some of its bearers gained renown in the 18th century as mercenary soldiers: Juan O'Donogu (1751-1821) was the last Spanish ruler of Mexico.

Doran An anglicised version of O Deoradhain, an Irish patronymic based on a diminutive of the Gaelic word *deoradh*, meaning a pilgrim, and figuring in the name **Dewar**. It is found in Kirkcudbright in 1685, but the fact that it is now almost confined to Glasgow suggests that the Dorans came from Ireland in the 19th century.

Dorward The office of door-ward to the king was both honourable and hereditary, and in mediaeval Scotland it subsisted in the powerful family of de Lundin who migrated from Tayside to Aberdeenshire in pursuit of their (spurious) claim, through marriage, to the earldom of Mar. The de Lundins, having obtained large tracts of land in the Dee valley, adopted the occupational rather than a territorial surname. A member of the family, Sir Alan Durward, rose to prominence and was regent of the kingdom during the minority of Alexander III in 1250. Thereafter the family seems to have fallen into obscurity; but there were lesser doors to be warded than those of the king's palace, and most Dorwards assume descent from the relevant functionaries at the abbey of Arbroath, in which district the name is still to be found in large numbers.

Dougall–see **MacDougall**

Douglas A place-name before it became a surname, Douglas now has its widest currency as a male Christian name. It comes from the Gaelic *dubh glais* meaning black water, a descriptive term frequently met in Scottish topography. Douglas was unknown as a forename until the 16th century, and even then as often as not it was a girl's name. The first member of the family on record is William de Douglas in the 12th century, and there were four main branches of the family in mediaeval times: (i) the Black Douglases of Douglasdale, the most famous of whom was Sir James Douglas who attempted to take the Bruce's heart to the Holy Land for burial; (ii) the Douglas earls of Morton in Dumfriesshire; (iii) the Red Douglas earls of Angus; and (iv) the Drumlanrig branch who became marquesses of Queensberry. 'None durst strive against a Douglas' was the 16th-century saying when the dynasty was at the height of its power, and the history of mediaeval Scotland is inseparably bound up with the rise and fall of the various branches of the noble house of Douglas. As for the ordinary Douglases, who would be called after their laird, theirs is the eighty-second commonest name in the land.

Dow A variant of **Duff,** common in Aberdeenshire, where it was pronounced 'doo'.

Dowie Probably an abbreviation of **MacIldowie**–originally *mac gille dhuibh*–'son of the black lad'. Dowies are first recorded, in Dunblane, in the 1660s, but the Macildowie record goes right back to the 12th century, to a hermit on Iona. A Nigel Mackegilduf was in Carrick in the reign of Alexander II; other versions of the name appear in Beauly, Lochaber and Edinburgh.

Downie The possible sources for this name all indicate the earlier pronunciation 'doonie'. The Irish patronymic *O Dunadhaigh* means 'fortress-keeper', and gives rise to Downie in Ireland. *O Duibhne*, legendary founder of the clan Campbell, is mentioned in the 11th century Book of Deer. Back in Scotland there was a barony of Downie or Duny in Monikie parish near Dundee (involving the word *dun*–'hill or fortress') which gave the common local surname of Downie. The name occurs sparsely in the early records (in Arbroath, Dundee, Aberdeen and Glasgow) but its present distribution is too wide to say whether any individual Downie is of Scottish or Irish origin.

Doyle The Irish version of **Dougall**.

Drever An Orkney name, second commonest on the island, from *drivar* , the Norse equivalent of 'driver', i.e. one in charge of horses or oxen. John and Brandy Dravar are recorded in 1492, and Nicholas Dravar was in Kirkwall fifty years later. Jonet Drever was tried for witchcraft in Orkney in 1615. Drevers are now fairly numerous all over the north east of Scotland.

Drummond The Gaelic word for back or spine or ridge is *druim*, plural *dromannan*, and this gives several place-names, including Drymen in Stirlingshire. Malcolm Beg, so-called from his small size, married a daughter of the earl of Lennox, and his descendants took their surname from the lands of Drymen. The family acquired by marriage the estates of Stobhall and Cargill, and the clan's centre of gravity moved to eastern Perthshire, where it remains still. Numerous cadet branches have occupied lands ranging from Glenartney in the west, through Strathearn to the fringes of the city of Perth; and Drummonds are still thick on the ground in these parts. The clan were always arch-royalists, supporters in turn of Robert the Bruce, Mary Queen of Scots, Montrose and the Old and Young Chevaliers. The chief became earl of Perth, and the title was elevated into a short-lived Jacobite dukedom. Lord John Drummond held the rank of lieutenant-general in the Prince's army in 1745. The Drummond lands were forfeited thereafter but restored in 1784, and a Drummond, earl of Perth, still lives in the ancient mansion of Stobhall.

Dryburgh From the lands of Dryburgh in the Borders. Peter de Dribur is in the 13th-century records, but this would be a designation rather than a surname. The records are very sparse and there is not much mention of the name until 1626 when Helen Dryburgh is accused of witchcraft. The surname, while not very frequent, is still mostly found near its place of origin.

Dryden Although this could be a Scottish settlement-name as found in Midlothian and Selkirk (and meaning 'dry den'), Dryden is really a north of England surname, from some unidentified place in Cumbria or Northumberland. Drydens must have moved north at an early stage, for the name appears in the records in 1296, as a territorial designation rather than a surname. Laurence Dridane held a tenement in Stirling in 1481; the name remains more common in the southern half of Scotland.

Drysdale The place-name Dryfesdale in Annandale is pronounced Drysdale, and comes from a Norse word *drifa* meaning sleet or driving snow. The surname, first recorded in 1499, was also originally written Dryfesdale. Thomas Dryisdaill, the Islay herald, was a burgess of Aberdeen in the early 1600s. John Drysdale, an Edinburgh divine, was minister of the Tron Church in the 1760s and a friend of Adam Smith. Dan Drysdale, born in Kippen, was a sturdy full-back who captained the Scottish XV on eleven occasions between the wars. Now mainly an Edinburgh name.

Duff The Gaelic word *dubh*, meaning black, is a pervasive element in Scottish names; it is the basis of Duff, a name which goes back to the 10th century, when Duff, king of Alba was killed at Forres. Dunkan Duf is recorded in Kintyre in 1292, and another family of Duffs appear in Aberdeen at the end of the next century. It was a later family of Duffs who were ennobled in the 1700s, first in the Irish and later in the Scottish peerage; a descendant was created Duke of Fife in 1889 when he married the daughter of Edward

VII; Duff House was one of their many residences, and the village of MacDuff was named by them (see also **MacDuff**). Alexander Duff, born in Pitlochry, was a famous missionary in India in the last century. Duffy is an Irish verson of the name; but Duffie is usually a shortened version of **MacPhee**. See also **Dow**.

Duffus From the lands of the same name in Morayshire, meaning 'at the black place' (Gaelic, *dubhais*). The name appears as a territorial designation from the early 13th century in the person of Arkembaldus de Duffus, followed by David of Dufis in Inverculin a century later. By the 1480s it attains the status of a proper surname, when David Dufus appears in the records as a burgess of Aberdeen. The name is still mainly to be found in that county.

Duguid A well-known Aberdeen surname, of unknown origin, and locally pronounced 'jookit'. The first recorded Duguid was a messenger in Aberdeen called Robert Doget, and lived at the beginning of the 14th century. At the same time there is recorded an Adam Doghete in St Andrews, and in 1382 John Dogude of Perth went to Prussia in the king's service. The name continues to appear (in fifteen different spellings) in various places, but is always commonest in Aberdeen.

Dunbar *Dun* means a fort in Gaelic and *barr* is a summit, and the place-name (in East Lothian) is pronounced with the stress on the second syllable; so is the surname. A descendant of Gospatrick, earl of Northumberland, received the lands of Dunbar in a grant from King Malcolm III; the family were later elevated to the earldoms of Dunbar and March, but were deprived of both by James I when they had become so powerful as to be a threat to the royal authority. The best-known of the family was William Dunbar, the great Renaissance poet who was a courtier of James IV and who is said to have died at Flodden.

Almost as famous in their time were the two Gavin Dunbars (uncle and nephew) of Aberdeen who pursued scholarly lives in the turbulent era of the 17th century.

Duncan Duncan comes from two Gaelic words *donn* (brown) and *cath* (warrior). Donnchad, 11th abbot of Iona, died in 717; a later Duncan was abbot of Dunkeld, and another was an ill-fated king in the 11th century; Donchadus was the name of an earl of Fife in 1150. These of course were all forenames, but by the 1360s, John Dunhan had been recorded in Berwick-on-Tweed, and the surname was soon found all over the Lowlands, with innumerable points of origin; nowadays it is the twenty-fifth commonest in the country. Perhaps the most famous bearer is Admiral Viscount Duncan of Camperdown, born near Dundee, who achieved a spectacular victory in a naval battle in the wars against Revolutionary France. Two Andrew Duncans, father and son, were leading physicians and professors in 19th century Edinburgh; and it was a minister called Henry Duncan who founded the first savings bank in 1810. Donoghue and MacDonagh are Irish forms; Duncanson is also found in Scotland.

Dundas Dundas (accent on the second syllable) is a place near Edinburgh, and probably means 'south fort' (Gaelic *dun deas*). The lands were owned in the 12th century by a descendent of Gospatrick, earl of March; his grandson Helias de Dundas is the first recorded bearer of the name (around 1200). His descendants, who later styled themselves Dundas of that Ilk, retained their lands until well in the 19th century. Another branch of the family are recorded as holding lands in Linlithgow district in 1296, and John de Dundas acquired the barony of Fingask in Perthshire in 1364. There is not much Dundas history for another 300 years, until Sir James Dundas was elevated to the peerage as Lord Arniston and suffered penalties for refusing to renounce the Covenant. The family really achieved fame in the person of Henry Dundas, 1st Viscount Melville, nicknamed 'Harry the Ninth' and 'the Uncrowned King of Scotland'; he and his son were virtual rulers of the land and in the dispiriting period between the '45 and the French Revolution.

Dunlop The stress in this Ayrshire place name comes on the second syllable; the meaning is thought to be 'muddy fort' (Gaelic *dun laib*). Dominus Willelmus de Dunlop is recorded in Ayrshire in 1260, and Neel Fitz Robert de Dullope a generation later (these were mere territorial designations, not yet surnames). A family styled themselves Dunlop of that Ilk in 1496, and the surname became quite common in the west of Scotland. A Dunlop lieutenant-general won fame at the battle of Seringapatam; another family were well known as professors and principals of Glasgow University; but the most famous was John Boyd Dunlop, a veterinary surgeon who made his name a household word with the perfection of the pneumatic tyre in the 1880s.

Dunn There are several possible points of origin: (i) from the lands of Dun ('fort'), near Montrose in Angus; this accounts for the frequency of the name in the eastern half of the country; Adam de Dun was Dean of Moray in the 1250s; John Dun was a property-owner in Edinburgh in the 1460s. (ii) the Gaelic word *donn* meaning brown, which was a common nickname in the Highlands and which became a surname in its own right, sometimes with the spelling Don; Thomas Dun, who was hanged at Elgin in 1296 for stealing books and vestments from the church may have been one of the 'brown' Dunns. (iii) a Middle English word *dunn* meaning dark or swarthy gave rise to the form Dunne, once the twenty-seventh commonest surname in Ireland.

Dunnett From the place in Caithness, which means 'headland hill'. Gilbert Dynnocht was vicar of Durness in the mid-16th century;

Matthew and George Dunnett were apprehended as rebels in 1670. The name is still found in Caithness and Orkney, but has also migrated southwards in large numbers, mainly to Edinburgh.

Dunsmore / Dunsmuir From a forgotten Fife estate called Dundemore, whose etymology is unknown. Patrick de Dundemer of Fife gave homage to Edward I in 1296. The name is said to have migrated to Antrim in the 17th century, and thence to the USA where it became established as Dinsmore. There are still Dunsmores in Glasgow but not many left in Fife.

Durie Durie comes from the Gaelic *dobharach*, and means something like 'little stream'; it occurs in several place-names, at least two of them in Fife. Duncan de Durry is recorded in the late 13th century, and John Dury was a cleric in St Andrews in 1464. Walter Doray turns up in Coupar Angus 1500 and Andrew Dure in nearby Newtyle in 1519. Andrew Durie was bishop of Galloway and abbot of Melrose in the late 16th century; his brother George, abbot of Dunfermline and archdeacon of St Andrews, tried to avenge the murder of his uncle the Cardinal Archbishop Beaton; Durie's son John was a noted Scottish Jesuit. Other Fife Duries were strong on the Protestant side: John Durie was a Presbyterian minister and supporter of John Knox, and his son and grandson were zealous reformers.

Durward–see **Dorward**

Duthie A contraction of the Gaelic patronymic *Mac gille Dubhthaigh*, 'son of the servant of St Duthac', who was the patron saint of Tain. Marjory Duthe is recorded in Orkney in 1492, and there were seven of the name in Dunblane a century later. Duthies are still to be found most commonly in the north east.

Dyce From a parish in Aberdeenshire. The surname is the same as Deas and belonged to several Aberdeen burgess families: John de Diss is recorded there in 1467. Alexander Dyce (1798—1869) was a noted Shakespearean scholar; his cousin William was a painter of Highland landscapes and one of the founders of the pre-Raphaelite school.

Dyes–see **Deas**

E

Eadie A double diminutive of Adam, common in Aberdeen and Edinburgh in the 17th century, and now fairly widespread. William Ade of Inverkeithing figures in the Ragman Roll of 1296, and Andreas Ade is recorded in Edinburgh fifty years later; James Adie represented Perth in the Scottish Parliament in 1596, and William Ady was one of the regents of Marischal College in 1644. Eadie and Adie are the modern forms, but the name also appears in the spelling Eddie, which is particularly popular in the north east.

Easson Another derivative of Adam. The tradition is that an Atholl man whose father's name was Adam called himself Ayson or Easson; and various families named Ayson are recorded as owning lands in Strathtay in the late 15th century. The surname became common in Stirling and Dunblane in the following century, and it turned up in Caithness about the same time. John Easson was member for the burgh of St Andrews in the Scottish Parliament in 1681.

Easton This means 'east farmstead' and occurs in very many contexts in Scotland and England; specific examples are in Peeblesshire and near Bathgate. The surname is sparsely recorded and is now to be found mainly in Edinburgh.

Eddie–see **Eadie**

Edgar An Anglo-Saxon personal name Eadgar whose components mean 'prosperity' and 'spear' (see Introduction). Eadgar was the name of the anglophile son of Malcolm Canmore and his English Queen Margaret; no doubt the forename thus acquired a certain cachet in the early 12th century. A family named Edgar held lands in Berwickshire of the earls of Dunbar, and another were landowners in Nithsdale in the reign of William the Lion (c.1200). Richard Edgar of Wedderlie, owner of the castle of Sanquhar, was a witness at the second marriage of Robert I, and there were other landed families of the name in the south west.

Edmiston / Edmundstone Both names mean 'Edmund's farm' (see Edmonds) and the origin is a place near Edinburgh. Henry de Edmundistun was witness to a charter around 1200; and the name, never very common, migrated in the 1560s to Shetland, where two centuries later it was that of a distinguished family of surgeons, writers and naturalists. Patrick Edmonstone of Newton was a Stirling laird whose Jacobite activities led to a charge of high treason which was found not proven in 1708. Not the same as Edmundson, which is a Yorkshire/Lancashire name.

Edmonds Edmond/Edmund is an Anglo-Saxon personal name meaning 'prosperity protection' (which sounds like an insurance company, but see Introduction); it owed its popularity in England to the East Anglian king, St Edmund the Martyr (d. 869). Aedmund was the name of David I's chamberlain; the surname does not appear until the 17th century, when William Edmen was recorded as a bailie of Stirling and Janet Edmont as an Edinburgh housewife.

Edward / Edwards Similar in meaning to Edmund (see **Edmonds**), Edward enjoyed great popularity in England and Wales: Edward (the Confessor) preceded George as the patron saint of England, and Edward was among the 20 commonest surnames in that country; it was even commoner in Wales. Some of this popularity rubbed off on Scotland, where Edward quickly became a family name, particularly common in the lower Tay valley. There was a Watty Edward in Angus in 1504, and an Andreas Edwaird in Perth in 1550. An Angus family of the name produced three gifted clergymen, all born-again Jacobites and all deprived of their living in 1689; one of them turned his remarkable talents to architecture, and designed Brechin castle. In the Angus regiment commanded by Lord Ogilvie of Airlie in the '45 there were eleven soldiers with the surname (the commonest in the muster-roll after Ogilvie). The terminal 's' is a relatively late development here.

Egan An Irish name, a shortened form of MacEgan, often found as Keegan. It was originally *Mac Aodhagain*, meaning 'son of little Aodh', and associated with MacKay. It is probably a fairly recent importation from Ireland, and is found mainly in Glasgow and Edinburgh.

Elder The reference is not to a tree but to the senior of two persons with the same name. Elder is not a notably Scottish name, but has a fairly long history here; John Eldar of Corstorphine was recorded as a burgess of Edinburgh in 1423; another John Elder denounced Cardinal Beaton and assured Henry VIII that the Highland clans would rise in his support if he were to invade Scotland; a third John Elder (at a much later date) was a noted maritime engineer and shipbuilder in Glasgow. Thomas Elder, an energetic Lord Provost of Edinburgh, quelled riots unaided, commanded the Royal Edinburgh Volunteers and was appointed postmaster general for Scotland in 1795.

Eliot A surname with no fewer than seventy different spellings, ranging from 'Allat' to 'Ellwood'; it probably derives from the Middle English forename Elyat, Old English Aelfwald ('elf-ruler'). Eliot was a particularly common forename in the Borders, but seems to have almost dropped out of use as such when it became a surname in the 15th century. Robert Elwald of Redhaugh, Roxburgh, captain of Hermitage castle, was squire to the earl of Angus in the 1450s and chief of a Border clan; a more senior branch were the Elliots of Stobs, whose chief was raised to a baronetcy in the 18th century. The Elliots of Minto produced the poetess who wrote *The Flowers of the Forest* and the earl of Minto who became Governor-General of India in 1807. Eliot is not however exclusively of Border provenance, for it is also an Angus place-name which gave rise to a local surname; and T.S. Eliot is of undisputed English descent.

Ellis A vernacular form of the name Elias or Elijah ('Jehovah is God'), popular in the middle ages because of the many saints who were named after the prophet. Joon Heles was burgess of Dundee in 1482, and David Elleis was keeper of the parish kirk of Aberdeen in 1565. An Ellis family of English origin is said to have given its name to Elieston in West Lothian and in its diminutive form, the name can give Elliot (see **Eliot**). 'Son of Ellis' sometimes became Allison; and in Wales 'son of Ellis' (ap Ellis) became Bellis.

Elmslie / Emslie Of English origin, but with a thoroughly Scottish pedigree, the name signifies a clearing in an elm wood; like **Lindsay** it probably refers to one of many English place-names of this type. Robert de Elmleghe or de Elmsly figures in the Ragman Roll of 1296 as a landowner in Aberdeenshire, and William de Elmysley is recorded in Aberdeen in the 1330s. James Emslie of Loanhead was the first of the granite quarrymasters, whose line began in the mid-18th century. Elmslie (the first 'l' is silent) and Emslie are still very much Aberdeen names.

Elphinstone A place in Midlothian called Elphinstone, first recorded in the 12th century, is the source of the surname (it means 'Alpin's toun' or farmstead). Two lairds of the name, both from Berwickshire, feature in the Ragman Roll of 1296. John de Elphinstone married the heiress of Airth in Stirlingshire and acquired the lands which formed the barony of Elphinstone. From this branch of the family came the ill-fated earls of Balmerino, whose misplaced loyalties were construed as treason, often with fatal results. The northern branch of the family achieved more:

William Elphinstone (1431-1514), bishop of Aberdeen and founder of the University, was Lord High Chancellor of Scotland; he was responsible for the introduction of printing into Scotland, and his death is said to have been hastened by the news of the defeat at Flodden. A later generation of Elphinstones won fame as 19th-century governors of India. The name is now uncommon even in the Aberdeen district.

Elrick The name of several places in the north east, it means a deer-trap, i.e. a defile into which deer were driven. As a surname, its history belongs exclusively to Aberdeenshire, and that is where it is still to be found. Three persons of the name of Elrick appear in the Sheriff Court books for Aberdeen in the early 1500s; John Elrik was witness in an Aberdeen witch trial in 1597.

English–see **Inglis**

Erskine The surname derives from the place near Glasgow, and possibly means 'green ascent'. Henry de Erskyn is mentioned in a charter of Alexander II, and Johan de Irskyn figures in the Ragman Roll of 1296. Sir Robert of Erskine, Chamberlain of Scotland under Robert II, founded several Erskine dynasties: his grandson acquired the earldom of Mar, and a younger brother founded the house of Dun near Montrose. A later descendant married into the earldom of Buchan, and a cadet branch acquired the title of Lord Cardross. The best known of the Erskine nobles is the 6th earl of Mar, the 'Bobbing John' of the Jacobite Rising of 1715, whose undoubted talents did not include military strategy. Erskines also made their mark on Scotland's later history–Mary Erskine, born in Clackmannanshire in 1629, pioneer of girls' education; Ebenezer Erskine who founded the Scottish Secession Church in 1740; Charles Erskine who was Lord Justice Clerk in 1748; John Erskine of Carnock, author of the *Institutes of the Law of Scotland* ; and Thomas Erskine who became Lord Chancellor in

1806. The name has taken some odd forms: an Areskin of Pittodrie was provost of Aberdeen in 1638; in France it appeared as Hasquin and Assequin, although Voltaire preferred the spelling Hareskins.

Esplin A corruption of Absalom ('father of peace'). Thomas Esplane is recorded in Aberdeenshire in 1500, and John Esplane was a burgess of Stirling in 1564. Grisel Hespline consorted with witches in Perth in the following century. The name is still found in the Dundee area, but sparsely elsewhere.

Eunson 'Son of **Ewan**' and an anglicised form of **MacEwan**. Johan Ewynsone was a Perthshire laird who figures in the Ragman Roll of 1296, and another John Ewinson is recorded in Perthshire in the1460s. By the next century the name is appearing sparsely all over Scotland. In Orkney and Shetland the surname may be from Old Norse Jonsson. The alternative spellings of Ewanson and Ewenson are now almost unknown.

Evans Although among the ten commonest in England and Wales, Evans as a surname is unknown in Scotland until modern times. It means 'son of Evan', a Welsh form of John, and corresponds to **Jones**. Evan was not uncommon in Scotland as a forename, a variant of **Ewan**; and in 1695 the equivalent of a private member's bill was passed to allow Evan MacGregor, merchant in Edinburgh, to retain his clan surname on condition that his children became Evansons. The condition was ineffective, for Evansons are no longer to be found.

Ewan / Ewen An Anglicised form of the Celtic name *Eogann*, now acknowledged to be a Gaelic derivative from the Latin form of the Greek *Eugenius* meaning 'well-born' (and having no connection with Hugh or with yew trees). Ewan is recorded very early as a forename, and has retained its popularity as such to the present time. Douenaldus Ewain is recorded in 1165, which is early for an established surname. It is nowadays numerous throughout Scotland, but particularly so in the Aberdeen area. Ewing is a characteristically Irish form of the name, now commonest in Glasgow, and it is reasonable to assume that many Scottish Ewings may be of Irish origin.

Ewart A place called Ewart near Wooler in Northumberland, meaning 'river enclosure' (Old English *ea worth*), is thought to be the origin of the surname. The tradition is that a Northumbrian family of the name moved north to Roxburghshire and then migrated to Galloway; the surname first appears there in the late 16th century. Andrew Ewart was treasurer of Kirkcudbright in 1583, and Nigel Ewart turns up in Annandale in 1607 At the battle of Waterloo, Ensign Ewart, while a sergeant in the Royal North British [*sic*] Dragoons, captured the standard of the French 45th regiment, from which the eagle badge later worn by the Royal Scots Greys was derived.

Ewing–see **Ewan**

F

Fagan An Irish patronymic, usually from *O Faodhagain*, which is a personal name of doubtful origin, possibly Norman; it can also be rendered into English as Fegan. Fagan is not recorded in Scotland until modern times, and is rarely to be found outside Glasgow.

Fairbairn A nickname, also found in the North of England, which probably means what it says, as do the English Fairchild and the Shetland **Goodlad**. Robert Frebern is recorded in Lothian and Fife in the 12th century, and his descendants established themselves in Ayrshire. Stephen Fairburn, a burgess of Berwick on Tweed, was in charge of the commissariat of Arbroath Abbey in the 1320s; James Forbrayne was a burgess freeman of Glasgow in the 16th century. Nowadays mainly to be found in Edinburgh and district.

Fairgrieve The origin is unknown, but it is almost certainly native to Scotland; it may represent a lost place-name, probably in the Lothians or Borders, for the surname is virtually confined to that area. Thomas Feirgrive is recorded in Bentmylne in 1658, and Gideon Fairgrieve in Melrose a few years later.

Fairley / Fairlie From the town on the Firth of Clyde near Largs, probably 'fair lea', a fine fallow field. A family, whose name by tradition was Ross, were given the lands of Fairlie by Robert I, and changed their surname to Fairlie. William de Fairlie was granted a pardon by Edward III of England in 1385 for alleged war-crimes. William Fayrley was a burgess of Edinburgh in the same century; he seems to have played an important part in the capture of Edinburgh Castle from the English in 1342, and it was from his line (the Fairlies of Braid) that John Knox later took a bride.

Fairnie–see Fearn

Fairweather Usually taken to be a nickname for a person of sunny disposition, on analogy with the English surname Merryweather. John Phairwedder was a landowner in Perth in the the mid-15th century; Christopher Farewether was serjeant of Linlithgow in 1472; and Valter Farwedder was presbyter of Dunkeld a century later. The name Fairweather is and always has been strongly localised in Angus, and constantly recurs in the Commissariat Record of Brechin between 1576 and 1800.

Falconer This is the usual Scottish spelling of the name: Faulkner is commoner in England. The name appears frequently in the early Scottish records as an occupational designation; William the falconer lived at Marytown near Laurencekirk in the 14th Century; although he no doubt kept and trained falcons for hunting, he may have had a different surname, for his estate was known as Halkerstoun (see **Haxton**), but his descendants were called Falkoner. Robert le Faukener appears in the Ragman Roll as a Mearns landowner; Heliscus Faucuner was a burgess of Montrose in 1350 and Andreas Fawconer is recorded in Elgin a few years later. The American novelist William Faulkner was descended from a Scots settler from Inverness called Falconer.

Farmer In mediaeval times the term meant a tax collector, whose cut of the proceeds was a fixed sum (*firmus*); it was not until the 17th century that it was applied to the cultivation of land. Robert Fermarius is recorded in Peebles in 1262, Alan Fermour in St Andrews in 1391, Andrew Fermour in Perth in 1458, and Edmond Fermorar in Dundee in 1557: that gives an indication of the early distribution of the name, which is now fairly evenly spread all over Scotland.

Farquhar / Farquharson From the Gaelic personal name *Fearchar* which means 'very dear one'; it was a popular Celtic forename and is recorded (in some bizarre spellings) all over mediaeval Scotland. As a surname it was never very frequent, except in its various patronymic forms such as MacFarquhar, MacKerchar, MacErchar and Kerracher. Chiefly however, it appears in the form of Farquharson: a 14th century warrior named Fearcher Shaw, himself related to the MacIntosh chiefs, founded a dynasty who settled in Mar and took the name Farquharson. Their progeny flourished on the braes of Angus and Mar where the name is still found in large numbers. Particularly notable are the Farquharsons of Invercauld and formerly of Balmoral, which latter property they sold to Queen Victoria. There were other Farquhars in different parts of Scotland who founded their own dynasties, and the name is recorded in southwest Scotland in the 14th century, and somewhat later in Orkney; but Angus and Aberdeenshire are still the places where Farquharsons are thickest on the ground.

Faulds Fauld is the Scots form of 'fold', as in 'sheepfold', and figures in many place names, notably in the counties of Ayr, Renfrew and Lanark. Arthur Fauldis was recorded in Glasgow in 1536, and Archibald Faulds a century later. Robert Fauls, who appears in the 1670s, was a carrier of baggage; and Robert Fauls lived in Buittle about the same time. Henry Faulds, an Ayrshire man, pioneered the use of fingerprinting in crime-detection in the late 19th century.

Fearn The Gaelic word for alder (*fearna*) gives several place names in Scotland, notably one in Ross and one in Angus. Sir Andrew Fearne was a chaplain of the cathedral church of Dornoch in 1512; Robert Fearne was curate of Golspie in 1546; and a family styling themselves Fern of that Ilk were followers of the earls of Ross. The Angus records show Peter de Fearne as witness of the charter of foundation of the Maison-Dieu at Brechin; John Fern was a burgess of Perth in 1432, and the name occurs in Dundee and St

Andrews in the following two centuries. A third 'alder' place name is Fernie in north-east Fife. William de Ferny was a juror on an inquest in Fife in 1390, and William Ferny of that Ilk was chamberlain of the county in the 1560s. English Ferns have a different origin for their name–*viz.* 'bracken'.

Fenton A common place name (meaning 'marsh-settlement') and by no means confined to Scotland. Native Fentons have several possible points of origin. Fenton Hill in Angus indicates an early settlement of that name; John de Fenton was sheriff of Forfar in 1261, and there is a tradition of landed families of Fentons in the country until the mid 15th century. There was also a barony of Fenton in East Lothian, held by the lords of Dirleton; the name of Sir William de Fentone figures in the Ragman Roll of 1296, and William and John Fenton were punished by Edward I for supporting Robert the Bruce.

Fenwick A place name meaning 'fen-farm', and occurring in Northumberland, West Yorkshire and Ayrshire. Nicholaus Fynwyk was provost of Ayr in 1313; but the name is more frequent in the east, and the Border Fenwicks are thought to have come north in the mediaeval period–'five hundred Fenwicks in a flock', as the old ballad has it–and on the occasion of the raid of the Reidswire turned out for the English side.

Fergusson The first recorded settlement of Gaelic-speaking Scots from Ireland was made about the year 500 by one Fergus Mor, who has sometimes been hailed as the founder of Scotland's monarchy. There is no clan Fergusson derived from him, however. What happened was that the personal name Fergus (it means 'super-choice') acquired great popularity and prestige in both Scotland and Ireland, and many families of completely different origin took the surname Fergusson. Perhaps the best-known is the Ayrshire family whose ancestors were awarded the lands of

Kilkerran by Robert I. Fergussons were and are found all over Scotland: Adam Ferguson, the 18th century philosopher was born in Logierait of a landed Perthshire family, fought at Fontenoy and retired to St Andrews; the poet Robert Fergusson, of Aberdeen ancestry, died in the Edinburgh asylum in 1774 at the age of twenty-four. J. D. Fergusson, the colourist painter, was born in Perthshire in 1874. Fergus itself is quite rare as a surname, and is usually contracted to Ferris, but the Gaelic version of MacKerras is familiar.

Ferrie–see **Ferrier**

Ferrier Ferrier is an occupational name which is also found in the north of England. It usually means a farrier or blacksmith, and frequently appears in the early records as an occupational designation; one Robertus Ferrarius (a blacksmith), owned land near Newbattle in the 12th century. The name can also mean a ferryman, and there is a recorded instance in the 16th century of a family of Ferriers who owned the Ferrylands in Cardross and plied their trade across the Clyde. The name became established in Angus at an early date as that of a landed family. Susan Ferrier was a friend of Sir Walter Scott, and herself a good novelist. Ferrie and Ferry are different, and usually come from the Irish patronymic *O Fearadhaigh*, while Ferries is a variant of **Fergus**.

Ferris–see **Fergus**

Fettes / Fiddes Fiddes, the name of two baronies in the shires of Aberdeen and Kincardine, was formerly known as Futhos or Fothes (possibly embodying the Gaelic *fothair* 'a slope'). Edmund de Fotheis and Aeuin, his son, are recorded in the early 13th century; later in the same century, the family received from the Earl of Buchan a charter to the whole lands of Fothes. The surname was adopted by the tenantry and soon spread: Jhone Fethy was master of the Sang Schules in Dundee, Aberdeen and Edinburgh successively, in the 15th century, and was a distinguished composer; Lowrens Fettas is recorded in Brecin around the same time, and John Fettas appears in Fife in 1521; by the following century the name has appeared in Aberdeenshire, and in the Cabrach in the spelling Fiddes (now the usual modern form). The name is still prevalent in its place of origin; and it was a Laurencekirk man, William Fettes, whose grandson migrated to Edinburgh and founded the college which bears his name.

Finlay / Finlayson From the Gaeilc personal name Fionnlagh– originally *fionn laoch* or 'fair hero'. It was very popular as a forename, more often than not with an intrusive 'd', giving *Findlay*. As a surname, it has many different points of origin; Andrew Fyndlai was chaplain of Brechin in 1426, and Robert Finlaw is recorded in Leith fifty years later; John Phinlaw appears in Fife and John Findlo in Montrose, both in the 1630s. The patronymic Finlayson in fact occurs earlier: Brice Fynlawesone was a Stirlingshire laird whose name figures in the Ragman Roll of 1296; and Duncan Finlayson appears in Banff in 1342. By the 15th century there are Finlaysons all over the Lowlands, and *MacKinlay* (the Gaelic equivalent) begins to appear in the Glenlyon and Balquhidder areas of Perthshire. MacKinlays also spread to Ireland, and William McKinley, 25th President of the USA, was descended from an Ulster Scot. Finlay and its variants are among the hundred most frequent surnames in Scotland.

Finnie / Finney This name is at its most common in the Aberdeen area but is found all over, including England and Ireland. It can be a diminutive of Finn, one of the oldest English personal names (and itself a recognised surname). Or it can be a variant of *Fionn*, the Gaelic version of Fingal. Perhaps more often it is a version of the Irish patronymic Feeney. Spellings and locations do not give much of a clue: John Fynne and David Fynie are both recorded in Aberdeen at the beginning of the 16th century; John Fynne is in Glasgow and John Finny in Brechin in the 1560s; Thomas Fynnie and Margaret Phinne are citizens of Edinburgh a century later. John Finnie, a Midlothian farmer who was the first to discover the importance of chemicals in agricultural practice, was the founder in 1842 of the Agricultural Chemical Association of Scotland.

Finnigan Seldom found outside Glasgow, Finnigan is a fairly recent import. It is however very widespread and numerous in Ireland. It comes from the patronymic *O Fionnagain* and means 'descendant of the fair-haired one'.

Firth Not necessarily a native Scottish name, although it has been familiar in Lanarkshire and the Borders since the early 17th century. It usually comes from an Old English word meaning woodland or scrub, and indeed there is a place of the name in Roxburghshire. It is also recorded in Orkney, where it comes from the parish of Firth (cf. Modern Norwegian *fjord*).

Fisher A surname with equivalents in practically every language, it is very frequent in Glasgow and Edinburgh and arrived there in large numbers as a result of trade and commerce; also it is or was the thirty-fifth commonest surname in the USA. Michael Fysser was a bailie of Perth in 1334; Donald Fyschear was in Atholl a century later; Andro Fischar was in Lanark around the same time and Thomas Fyschear was a bailie of Edinburgh in the 1600s. The Gaelic equivalent of the name–*mac an iasgar* or Macinescar, frequently recorded in the *Black Book of Taymouth*–became obsolete in that form and was translated as Fisher.

Flanagan An Irish patronymic, originally *O Flannagain*, which incorporates the Gaelic word *flann*, meaning ruddy. The Flanagans were an important Connaught clan; when some of them came to Scotland in the 1840s they settled mainly in Glasgow and Edinburgh.

Fleming Among the more welcome incomers to Scotland in the mediaeval period were the men from Flanders–the Flemings. Traders in wool, they formed a colony in the upper Clyde valley and became a useful component in the Anglo-Norman polity which ran Scotland during the reign of David I (who himself had married a Flemish princess). Robert Fleming, courtier and architect of the marriage of the Maid of Norway to the son of Edward I, threw in his lot with the Bruce faction; he was rewarded with a grant of the lands of Lenzie and Cumbernauld; his descendants became successively Lords Fleming and Earls of Wigtown. A large number of the Flemish immigrants actually took the name Fleming; nowadays it is among the hundred commonest names here, to be found in quantity in every area save Aberdeen. Sir Alexander Fleming, discoverer of penicillin, was an Ayrshire man, and Ian Fleming, creator of James Bond, was of Scots descent. Of humbler status than either was James Fleming, the last institutional jester in Scotland, who was the author of the celebrated quip: 'I'm the Laird o' Udny's fule–wha's fule are ye?'

Fletcher A *fléchier* in Old French was an arrow-maker, and as an occupational name Fletcher was known throughout Britain. The trade was as common in the Highlands as elsewhere, and the word was borrowed into Gaelic as *fleisdear*, giving the surname *Mac an Fhleistear* which was re-rendered into English as Fletcher. The Fletchers of Glenlyon were hereditary suppliers of arrows to the MacGregors. There is however a completely different trade which can give rise to the surname, and that is flesher (still a common name for butcher in Scotland). It is probable that the John Flechyr who lived in Roxburgh in the 1300s was an arrowsmith, as was

Baty Flessor, his contemporary in Ayr; but in the 16th century Fleshers were common in Dundee and by then it had become impossible to separate the names derived from the two callings. Andrew Fletcher of Saltoun was the patriotic Scot whose violent opposition to the Union of 1707 is still remembered; so is his wise opinion that a nation's ballads are more important than its laws.

Flett Among the dozen commonest names in Orkney; it is thought to derive from the place name Flett (meaning a strip of field) in the neighbouring Shetland archipelago; alternatively it may come from the Old Norse personal name *Flotjr* meaning swift or speedy (hence the English adjective 'fleet'). The names of Kolbein Flaet, Ioni Blatto and Mawnus Flatt appear in the 15th century records relating to Kirkwall, with a diversity of spelling which should not be surprising. The name spread, but not usually very far, and Fletts are now probably most numberous in the Aberdeen area. Sir John Flett was Director of the Geological Survey.

Flockhart The earlier from of this name was Flucker, which has caused puzzlement. A clue may possibly be found in the fact that the Nethergait of Dundee in mediaeval times was known as the Flukergait–the road taken by men fishing for flukes, a species of flatfish relating to the turbot and of some commercial importance; a fluker or flucker was therefore a fisherman. If this theory is correct–and they still fish for flukes in the Tay–then it explains why Flokers, Flukers and Flukars were common in fishing communities, particularly those of Fife and Newhaven near Edinburgh. The earliest citation of the name is John Fflocker in Fife in 1275, and four hundred years later there were still Flookers in St Andrews. Alternatively Flockhart may be a form of the personal name *Folkard* ('folk-hard') with the 'l' and the 'o' transposed. Whatever is origin, the name would gradually evolve into its present form, possibly gaining strength by its similarity in sound to **Lockhart**.

Florence From the forename Florentius, a 3rd century Christian martyr. It became popular in Norman times, making an early appearance in Scotland in the person of William I's nephew, the bishop-elect of Glasgow. It was almost invariably masculine, and means 'flourishing'; there is no connection, other than semantic, with the city of the name. Master Florence Wilson of Moray was one of the foremost Latin scholars in Europe in the 16th century. As a surname, Florence was late to appear in the records, but was current in Aberdeen in the 18th century; it is still to be found there in plenty.

Flynn From an Irish patronymic, *O Floinn*, meaning 'ruddy'–see **Flanagan**. The name Flynn·is widespread in Ireland and particularly common in Cork, Connaught and Ulster. It is now very numerous all over Lowland Scotland.

Foley This Irish patronymic was originally *O Foghladha*; the word *foghlaidh* in Irish Gaelic means a marauder or pirate, and the clan came from South Munster. In Scotland, Foleys are to be found mainly in Glasgow and Edinburgh.

Forbes From the lands of Forbes in Aberdeenshire; the Old Gaelic term *forba-ais* means 'at the land or place', and indicates the disyllabic nature of the name–all too often lost in the modern pronunciation of 'Fawbs'. (Tom Forbes who enlisted in the French army in the 18th century had his name phonetically registered as 'Fort Bays'). Forbes was and is the name of a well-known Aberdeenshire clan, who had held lands in Strathdon long before they were erected into a barony in 1271. Alexander Forbes was raised to the peerage by James I in 1445, and his descendants acquired large tracts of land in various parts of the north east (including half of the earldom of Mar); they formed other dynastic branches of the clan, including Pitsligo, Culloden, Craigievar and Monymusk. Robert Forbes, episcopalian bishop of Ross and Caithness, was arrested for Jacobite activities early in 1745 and missed all the action; however he compiled a massive dossier of the rebellion which he published under the title of *The Lyon in Mourning*; it remains a valuable source-book for historians.

Ford With the meaning a stream-crossing-place, Ford is the name of several settlements in Scotland, and the surname has many points of origin. Thomas de Furd was a presbyter in the diocese of St Andrews in 1406; Adam Furde had the lands of Burncastle at the end of that century; George Fuird was a butcher in Inverness in the 1600s and Isobel Foorde lived in Moneydie in the 1680s. The name is to be found in England and America in even greater numbers than here.

Fordyce A place near Banff, it means 'south slope' (Old Gaelic *fothair deas*), and the accent is firmly on the second syllable. The surname is recorded in Aberdeenshire in the 16th century, and it remains at its commonest in that area. Although not a clan, the Fordyces would turn out in support of the Forbeses in the days of clan warfare. In the more enlightened 18th century, there was a family of Fordyce in Aberdeen which provides a classic example of the Scottish success story: Fordyce *père* was provost of the city; the elder son David became professor of Moral Philosophy at Marischal College; the second son James was a presbyterian divine who could count Dr Johnson among his intimates; his nephew Sir William was a famous physician; only the youngest brother Alexander let the side down–after becoming a highly successful banker in London, he absconded with the funds, after which the bank stopped payment, causing a panic of national proportions.

Forrest In the mediaeval period the word forest meant, as well as a wood, a tract of ground set aside for the royal pastime of hunting, and might well be treeless–as is the Forest of Reay to this day. It was a labour-intensive concern, and produced a large number of surnames. Forrest was the name given to someone who lived or worked at a forest; two Douglas tenants in Dumfriesshire are recorded in the 14th century as 'de Forest', and the name continued to be documented all over the Lowlands, the 'de' shortly to be dropped. William Forrest and Robert Forest had safe conduct to England in the 1450s; but no such protection was afforded to Henry Forrest, a Benedictine friar who was burned at the stake at St Andrews for his reforming principles in 1533.

Forrester See **Forrest**. Archebaldus Forrester appears in Lesmahagow as early as 1164; the name recurs in Dumfries and Stirlingshire in the next century, and John le Forester figures in the Ragman Roll of 1296 as a Berwickshire landowner. Adam Forrester was chief alderman of Edinburgh in 1373 and later acquired the manor of Corstorphine; a descendant was created Lord Forrester of Corstorphine in 1633, but the title was later subsumed under the United Kingdom peerage. The Forresters of Garden were a prominent family in Stirlingshire for two centuries, much given to neighbourly feuding. Jonet Froster appears in Dundee in 1521. Forster is a contraction of the name, found most often in the north of England, but Fosters have been recorded in Glasgow since the 1480s and are still quite numerous all over Scotland.

Forster–see **Forrester**

Forsyth A Gaelic personal name, with the stress on the second syllable despite the baneful influence of *The Forsyte Saga*. The popular etymology is *fear sithe* ('man of peace')–but this is somewhat doubtful. Osbert filius Forsyth displays the patronymic in Sauchie in 1308, and it recurs frequently as a forename up until the 16th century. But oftener it is a territorial designation, even although there is no known place-name which fits. Thomas de Forsith was canon and prebendary of Glasgow in the 1480s and William de Fersith was a bailie of Edinburgh in the following century, and there are several other 'de Forsythes' who cannot be located in any particular place. Alexander Forsyth, an Aberdeenshire man, combined in an unusual way the professions of clergyman and inventor of firearm mechanisms; he patriotically refused Napoleon's offer of £20,000 for the secret of his percussion cap.

Foster–see Forrester

Fotheringham Originally Fotheringhay, the name of an estate in Northamptonshire, famous as the location of the prison of Mary Queen of Scots. The name, which later acquired the characteristically English sufix '-ingham', means 'foddering place' or grazing, and the estate was held by the Scottish royal family in the 12th century as part of the honour of Huntingdon. When the Earl of Huntingdon assumed his *alter ego* of King David II and returned to Scotland in 1357 he looked kindly upon his former English neighbours; Henry de Fodringhay was in due course given land near Dundee, and his collaterals and descendants acquired further territories in Angus and around. Thomas Fothringhame was provost of Dundee in 1454; the estate of Fotheringham near Forfar is still in the family. The name travelled to other parts of Scotland, including Orkney, and is now common in Glasgow as well as in Angus.

Foulis / Fowlis A name which is distinctively Scottish, but never became very frequent; it comes from the Gaelic word *foghlais* ('sub-stream or rivulet') which produced at least half a dozen place-names (usually in the Fowlis spelling). William de Foulis was vicar of St Ninian's, Stirling in 1295, and Alan de Foulis was a canon of St Andrews ten years later. Alexander Foulis was parliamentary commissioner for Linlithgow in the 15th century. Sir James Foulis, private secretary to James I, was the first of a well-known family of Scottish judges. In the 18th century there were several generations of Faulls (later Foulis) who were booksellers in

Glasgow. David Foulis was a physician and composer of talent who flourished in Edinburgh in the same period. But Fowles is a southern name with avian connections–see **Fowler**.

Fowler The trade of bird-catcher produced surnames in many languages; Fowler is mainly a southern-English name, but is recorded in Scotland as an occupational designation from earliest times. The first documented bearer is John Fowler in Berwick-on-Tweed in 1370; Gilbert Fouler was sheriff of Edinburgh around the same time; William Fowler, an Edinburgh merchant of the 1550s, gave his name to Fowler's (later Anchor) Close in the High Street. Thereafter the name is found in large numbers in Glasgow, the Borders and Aberdeen.

Fox A nickname from the animal, and can refer to colouring, cunning or rapacity. A William Fox lived in Kelso in the 1560s and there was another of the name in Brechin a century later. Always much commoner in England, it is now however quite numerous in Glasgow. The indigenous word for fox is **Tod**.

Frame The origin is in some doubt; Frames are recorded in Campsie and Lanark in the 15th century, Arthur Frame is in the Glasgow records in the 1550s, and Daniel Frame in Edinburgh a century later. Despite this evidence, the name is most familiar in Ulster, where it is thought to involve the Old English word *fremde* meaning 'stranger'; and it may well be that the name itself is of Irish provenance.

Francis / Franks–see **French**

Fraser The oldest recorded forms of this Norman name are de Fresel, de Friselle and de Freseliere–all convincingly French– but the meaning is unknown, and it is difficult to identify a place in France that it might have come from; the depiction of the strawberry plant (*fraisier*), later adopted as the clan's armorial device, is a pun on the surname. What is certain is that a Norman knight named Frisel brought the name to Scotland as part of the feudalisation which took place in the 12th century; one of his kinsmen, Sir Simon Frisel, known as 'the Scottish patriot' was strong in support of Wallace, and the family was awarded lands in Buchan; in the 13th century the Frasers also owned the greater part of Tweedsmuir. By a series of advantageous marriages the family acquired further territories in Ross-shire and were raised to the peerage in the person of the first Lord Lovat. In time the Frasers became a genuine Gaelic-speaking clan with an established dynastic kindred and a realistic feeling of blood-relationship between chief and clansman. Most Highland Frasers could claim kinship with the Lovat family or its cadet branches; and the name, while frequent throughout the country, is still among the six most common in the Inverness area.

Freeman Usually a south-of-England name; but it was recorded in Peebles as early as 1296 when Jacob Freman acknowledged Edward I as his feudal overlord; William Freeman was a peasant at Coldingham priory a little later. It means what it says (the opposite of serf) and is now found in Edinburgh and Glasgow, sometimes as Freedman.

French The early records contain a Latinate designation–not yet a surname–of *Francus*, meaning 'from France'; it evolved into a group of surnames including French and Frank. The latter may have come north with the Bruces of Annandale, and the name Franke is recorded in Moffat in the 13th century. Six individuals of that name appear in the Ragman Roll of 1296, three of them in the shire of Roxburgh, two in Edinburgh and one in Fife. But even at this stage the name was becoming interchangeable with Franciscus, which basically means the same but refers to the saint of Assisi. It was a William Francis who guided Randolph up the rock of Edinburgh Castle in 1315. Nicholas Franch was curate of parish church of Stirling in 1475, and the name France was common in 17th century Dunblane. French is well-known in Ireland, and may have made its way over to this country; this is certainly the commonest form of the name in Scotland, with Francis as runner-up; Franks is much less often found. See also **Rankine**.

Frew Until Kincardine Bridge was opened in the 1930s, the lowest public crossing-point on the River Forth (apart from Stirling Bridge) was at the Fords of Frew. The place (which may come from a Brittonic word meaning current or stream) became of some strategic importance, and the name appears widely in the records as a surname from the 16th century onwards. But a 19th century influx of Frews from Ulster has contributed to the popularity of the name in Glasgow; the Irish Frews get theirs from *Freowine*, an Old English personal name.

Frisel / Frizzel Unusual versions of **Fraser**.

Fyall–see **MacPhail**

Fyfe / Fyffe These surnames come from the county (now region) of Fife, which in mediaeval times was an earldom and in the dark ages was an independent province (*Fib*); by tradition this was a Pictish royal name. The surname is widespread rather than frequent, and belongs to no particular area.

G

Gaffney An Irish patronymic, originally *O Gamhna* or 'descendant of Gamhain', a personal name meaning 'calf' or 'stirk'. The name is widespread in Scotland, but of recent appearance.

Gair The Gaelic adjective *gearr* means 'short', as in Gairloch, and the surname Gair or *Gear* means short in stature. Mac Iain Ghiorr was a famous pirate in Gaelic song and legend; in real life the family of Gair of Nigg have been prominent for many centuries in an entirely benevolent way. The name was recorded in Skye and Wester Ross in the 16th century, and later around Inverness.

Galbraith Society in mediaeval Scotland was just as multi-racial as it is now, and before the days of political correctness it was common to use nicknames which indicated ethnic origin. One such is Galbraith, which means literally 'stranger-Briton'–a reference to an inhabitant of the British kingdom of Strathclyde who remained there after the Gaelic invasions from Ireland around AD 500. The earliest recorded bearer is Gillescop Galbrath, who lived in Lennox in the 13th century and whose descendants were granted land there. Other Galbraiths at this time were harpers in Galloway. Hugh de Galbrath was provost of Aberdeen in the 1340s, and the name later turns up in Angus. Robert Galbraith, a Lord of Session was murdered in 1543; James Galbraith was deacon of the tailors in Edinburgh's Canongate in 1554.

Gall The sense of oppression felt by the Highlanders at the hands of their more powerful neighbours was summed up in the Gaelic phrase *mi-run mor nan Gall*, which means 'the great hatred of the strangers'; these were mainly English-speaking Lowlanders, which is the sense of the surname Gall, with its variants *Gauld* and Gauldie. There was a John Gal recorded in Perth in 1334, and the name has ever since been familiar in that area. In early times the name was often spelled and pronounced *Gaw*; a William Gaw lived in Glasgow in the 1390s, and this spelling is still found three hundred years later. A northern version, Gallie, refers to the people of Caithness–in Gaelic *gallaich*. Galls are now mainly to be found in the Dundee and Aberdeen areas–but see also **Galt**.

Gallacher Twenty years ago this was among the sixty most frequent surname in Scotland–it now seems to have slipped out of the top hundred, possibly because alternative spellings (there are reckoned to be twenty-three of them) have messed up the statistics. Gallagher is the commonest version in its native Ireland, where it is in the 1st XV of surnames. *O Gallchobhair* (to give the original form) means 'descendant of Gallchobar', a personal name comprising the words *gall* ('stranger') and *cabhair* ('help'). Most Scottish Gallachers are in the Glasgow area, but the name has been well established all over the country for a century.

Galletly–s e e **Gellatly**

Galloway In the early historical period various provinces of Scotland took their name from the tribes which inhabited them: the *Gall Ghaidhil*–'stranger-Gaels' or 'foreign Scots'–were probably free-booting Norse-Hebridean settlers, and gave their name to the district known as Galloway, which was earlier a much larger area comprising Renfrew, Ayr and Dumfries. Galloway occurs frequently in the records as a territorial designation from the 13th century, but does not emerge as a recognisable surname until two hundred years later; John Galway was a shipmaster in Lanarkshire; Sande Gallowey was involved in a *tuilzie* (brawl) in Lanark in 1488; and from the 1600s the name is found all over Scotland. Nowadays it mainly belongs to Glasgow and Edinburgh.

Galt Originally a nickname, from Old Norse *goltr*, a boar. William Galt was a bailie of Perth in 1367, and John and Alexander Galt were burgesses of Aberdeen a century later. The name has strong Ayrshire associations: Samuel Gault was one of the early Scots settlers in New Hampshire, and the novelist John Galt, a native of Irvine, founded the town of Guelph in Ontario, where he served for a time on a British government commission. Ocasionally the name may be a variant of **Gall**, in a spelling now more familiar in the west of Scotland. A reduced form *Gatt* is not uncommon in the north-east.

Gamble–see **Gemmell**

Garden / Gardener / Gardiner Gardiner (the most usual spelling) is an occupational name, referring to the fruit and vegetable trade rather than to the cultivation of flowers. A Nicholas Gardener is recorded in 1329, and Robert Gardner was a notary in Dunblane in 1426. An Edinburgh family named Gairdner produced some notable physicians in the 18th century. Garden is now a very common name in the Aberdeen area, but surprisingly does not appear in the early records. Francis Garden, Lord Gardenstone, an 18th-century agricultural improver was the founder of the village of Laurencekirk, and Garden was also the name of a family of Jacobite professors in Aberdeen. Mary Garden, the Aberdeenshire soprano, created the part of Mélisande in Debussy's only opera.

Gardyne A name with a long and well-documented history in Scotland, although by no means frequent outside Angus; it comes from the lands of Gardyne near Forfar, and its etymology is no doubt similar to that of **Garden**. Indeed in the early records the two names are virtually interchangeable, along with their French equivalent of **Jardine**.

Garioch From the district of Garioch ('rough place') in Aberdeenshire; it appears in the records as a territorial designation from 1264. By 1475 it had become a surname, when William Gariach was admitted as a burgess of Aberdeen. The name continues to be found, but not in abundance, in the north-east. Other forms of the name are *Geary*, *Gerrie* and *Gerry*.

Garrett See **Gerrard**. John Garrot was a burgess of Glasgow in 1600.

Garrow An Aberdeenshire version of **Garvie**. Johannes Garrow and Donald Gerrow are recorded in the Dee valley in the 1520s.

Garvey / Garvie The Gaelic adjective *garbh* means 'rough, brawny', and the Celtic personal name Gairbhith, also found in Ireland, has this sense. John Garwy was a shepherd in Cluny near Dunkeld in the 17th century, and the name has always been frequent in Perthshire and Angus. The name may sometimes however be from a northern French form of Gervaise–see **Jarvie**.

Gauld An Aberdeen version of **Gall**.

Gavin Sir Gawain was the legendary nephew of King Arthur and brother of Mordred, their father being king of Lothian. The name seems to be of Brittonic origin (perhaps from *gwallt-avwyn*, ' bright hair') and became associated with Galloway, of which an early chronicler makes him king. It later achieved some fame as the Christian name of the Renaissance poet Gawin Douglas, and has soared in popularity in recent years. As a surname, Gavin is still commonest in the West of Scotland, where it was first associated with the bands of gypsies that roamed the Border in the mediaeval period.

Gear–see **Gair**

Geary–see **Garioch**

Geddes A place near Nairn, of doubtful etymology but possibly from the Gaelic *gead ais*–'at the rigs'; the pronunciation preserves its di-syllabic origin. The surname has been most commonly found in the North East, although there were offshoots elsewhere from earliest times. Alexander Geddes was a cleric in Glasgow in the mid-15th century, and Matthew Geddes, vicar of Tibbermore, was chaplain and secretary to Gawin Douglas, bishop of Dunkeld; Matthew Geddes was a canon of Aberdeen about the same time. There was a Jenny Geddes in Edinburgh in the 1630s, but alas no real evidence to support the tradition that, when the prayer-book was introduced to the kirk of St Giles, she flung her stool at the preacher with the cry 'Wha daur speak mass in my lug?' John Geddes was a friend of Robert Burns; and his brother Bishop Alexander Geddes was a noted scholar and poet. But the best-known Geddes was Sir Patrick, town-planner, sociologist and a human ecologist ahead of his time, who founded the Edinburgh Social Union in 1885 and was largely responsible for the regeneration of the Old Town.

Gellatly This is a familiar enough surname in Dundee, Perth and Angus, although scarcely anywhere else; its variants of Galletly (Scottish), Golightly (English) and Galloghly (Irish) are also current. Golightly means 'go lithely' and was possibly a nickname applied to a messenger; Galloghly is a reduction of the Irish patronymic *Mac an gall-aglach* ('son of the *galloglass* or 'foreign warrior-youth'. Gellatly may be from either or these, or alternatively from a lost habitaion-name. The oldest spelling in Scotland is to be found in the name of Henry Galythly, bastard son of William the Lion, and grandfather of the Patric Galythly who was a claimant to the Scottish throne in 1291. In the same century, Henry Golithely or Galighly was recorded in the Ragman Roll as a landowner in Angus.

Gemmell From Old Norse *gamall*, meaning 'old', but which folk-etymology has confused with **Gamble**. Gemmell was once common in Ayrshire as a forename; its earliest recorded appearance as a surname is in Roxburghshire in the person of Hugh Gamyl, who held lands there in the late 14th century. Gabriel Gymmil was a cordiner in Edinburgh two hundred years later. Now found mainly in Glasgow and to a lesser extent in Edinburgh.

George Originally a Greek name, and that of the mythical patron saint of England; but George was never much in vogue at the font in Scotland in the Middle Ages–nor indeed since. George did however have a certain currency as a surname in Ayrshire in the 15th and 16th centuries, and is now reasonably frequent, but without diminutives and variants. Georgeson is not native to Scotland, and is uncommon here (it may indeed be Old Norse *Sigurtsson*). Even more oddly, there is no *Mac* form, the few MacGeorges being really mis-spellings of MacDewar (see **Dewar**).

Gerrard A Germanic compound (see Introduction) whose constituents mean 'spear' and 'brave'. Introduced to Britain by the Normans, it appeared in Scotland in the 12th century as the name of the abbot of Dryburgh; it takes another 400 years for it to emerge as a surname in Aberdeenshire, where it is still to be found in quantity. In its alternative spelling of Garrett it is not unknown in Glasgow; but Garrity is a different name, being a simplified version of the Irish patronymic *Mag Oireachtaigh*.

Gerrie / Gerry–s e e **Garioch**

Gibb / Gibbon Diminutives of **Gilbert**. A David Gyb lived in Cupar in the 1520s, a Robert Gib in Linlithgow a century later; the name is now common everywhere but particularly in the Glasgow area. The Reverend Adam Gib, a fervent 18th-century Protestant, had the ironic nickname of 'Pope Gib'. Gibbon was a popular Christian name in Scotland from the 15th century, and duly made its appearance as a surname; it also produced the patronymic

MacGibbon, which was once common in Perthshire and is still to be found in large numbers in Glasgow. Gibbonson figures frequently in the early records, mainly in Perthshire, but has now been swallowed up by **Gibson**. The characteristic English forms of Gibbs and Gibbons are relatively rare in Scotland (although James Gibbs, architect and designer of St Martins in the Fields, was born in Aberdeen in 1682).

Gibson The commonest derivative of **Gilbert** and among the top fifty Scottish surnames; see also **Gibb / Gibbon**. Johun Gibsoun surrendered the castle of Rothesay in 1335; Thomas Gibbeson broke his parole in 1358; Thome Gibson was a landowner in Dumfries in the 15th century; and John Gibsoun was chamberlain of Glasgow at the same time. The Gibson family of Durie in Fife, one of whom produced in 1690 the earliest collection of Scottish legal decisions, held their estates for nearly 300 years from 1500; and there are still many Gibsons around Leven. Provost Walter Gibson, younger son of a Lanarkshire laird, was apprenticed to malt-making and, by dint of defying the Navigation Acts and sailing his ships under the English flag, became the richest merchant in Glasgow in the 1680s.

Gifford Usually taken to be a nickname–from the Old French *giffard*, meaning 'chubby-cheeked' (cf. *Kiefer*, the German word for a jaw); there is however a place in Normandy which may fit. The Giffards or Giffords were a Norman family who obtained large land-holdings in England after the Conquest. Some members came north, and in 1186 William the Lion granted a charter confirming Sir Hugh Gifford in his estates at Yester in East Lothian; the village of Yester was subsequently known as Gifford. In 1250 Alexander III gave support to a proposed expedition to the Holy Land by Richard 'called Giffard'. Although the name reached other parts of Scotland (Andreas Giffard was a bailie of Aberdeen in 1408) it never became frequent, and Gifford is still associated mainly with

East Lothian. It is also the name of a prestigious lectureship in natural theology, founded by Lord Gifford, a 19th-century Edinburgh judge. An English cognate is Jefford.

Gilbert A Norman personal name comprising the elements *gisil* ('hostage') and *berht* ('bright')–see Introduction. It quickly became confused with the Celtic name Gilbride ('servant of St Bridget')–with which it has no linguistic connection–and so enjoyed an accidental popularity in several Highland families. The forename Gilbert was common in the south-west in the 14th century (much later it was the name of the younger brother of Robert Burns) and it began to achieve surname status in Glasgow and Edinburgh in the mid-16th century. But it never became nearly as frequent as its derivatives **Gibb**, **Gibbon** and **Gibson**.

Gilchrist In Gaelic *Gille Chriosd* means 'servant of Christ', and Gilchrist was a favourite Christian name in the Highlands. As such, it produced the inevitable *Mac* name, and there are still some MacGilchrists around. Gilchristson was also common, but was later absorbed by **Christie**. Patrick Gilcristes, a landowner in Stirling, and Kilschyn Gilcrist, a Perthshire laird, both appear in the Ragman Roll of 1296 (see Introduction).

Gilfillan *Gille Fhaolain* is 'servant of St Fillan', and Gilfillan was a common Christian name in Gaeldom. It appears as a surname in the 16th century in the person of Ewin Gilfillane, a murderer who eventually suffered the fate of his victims. Of better standing were a family of preachers, the most famous of whom was George Gilfillan, who inspired the citizens of Dundee with his oratory in the mid-Victorian period.

Gill Gilli was an Old Norse name, no doubt derived from the familiar place-name element *gil* meaning 'ravine'. Gill, the modern surname from this source, is to be found mainly in the Aberdeen area, which would be puzzling were it not for a local tradition which maintains that the Gills came from Cumberland, where they owned lands which were named after them, viz. Gillsland. This is entirely plausible; and if it fails to account for the Perth Gills and Peeblesshire Gills and Gyles, one can add that *ghyll* is a north of England word for ravine or glen, which also produced surnames on both sides of the Border.

Gillan / Gillen / Gillon Probably from Gaelic *giullan*, a diminutive form of *gille*, meaning 'lad' or 'servant' (see Introduction). Its surname-derivatives are very sparsely recorded in the Scottish historical records, and now found mainly in Glasgow.

Gillanders–s e e **Anderson**

Gillespie Gillespie, like **Kennedy,** is of dual nationality–Scottish and Irish–reflecting the common language of the two countries during the 'surname period'. *Gille easbuig* means 'servant of the bishop' and was a popular Christian name from the 12th century. For some obscure reason it has been accepted as a 'translation' of the Germanic name Archibald–which it certainly is not. In Ireland it was the surname of septs in the counties of Donegal and Down; in Scotland it is found mainly in Glasgow, and the ethnic origin of its bearers must be a question of genealogy and not linguistics. Transplanted to England the name became Gilhespy. There were two Scottish Gillespie brothers in the 17th century, both graduates of St Andrews, the one a divine and the other a historian; the latter (an anti-royalist) was deprived of his offices at the Restoration. A century later, James Gillespie, a prosperous Edinburgh snuff-merchant, founded a hospital and left valuable educational endowments for his native city.

Gillies In Gaelic, *Gille Iosa*–'Servant of Jesus'; this is a well-documented Christian name from the early 12th century, replacing

Malise which means the same (see Introduction). Gillies begins to emerge as a surname in the 1300s, and became quite common in Badenoch and the Hebrides. It is now well distributed throughout Scotland and beyond. Gillies was the name of a talented famiy who flourished early in the last century: Adam, Lord Gillies was a judge, his brother John was historiographer royal for Scotland, and their niece Margaret was a competent painter. Sir William Gillies, RSA, was an Edinburgh artist whose Scottish landscapes are among the best of the 20th century.

Gilmour / Gilmore *Gille Moire* means 'servant of (the Virgin) Mary', and was a popular font name in the mediaeval period. It achieves surname status in the Borders in the 1300s, but gives rise to no familiar MAC form, possibly because Gaelic had by this time already retreated north of the Highland line.

Gilroy Usually a contraction of **Macilroy**. Ewen Gilry is recorded in Drumelzier in 1331, but Gilroy is not associated with any particular area. (Gilruth is a name from the same stable, tending to be found more in the Highlands). In Ireland the name appears as Kilroy.

Gilzean Originally pronounced 'Gill Ian'–see **MacLean**.

Gladstone *Gled* in Scots is a kite or hawk, and Gledstanes was a settlement (now a farm) near Biggar in Lanarkshire. Gledstanes was a territorial designation for a hundred and fifty years before it became a surname; and Gledstanes of that Ilk was a well-known Lanarkshire family. Harbert Gladstanis was a well-doing notary in Dundee in the 1560s. George Gladstanes, who died in 1615, was the complete St Andrews man: a graduate of the University, he became its principal, as well as being archbishop of its diocese and a privy councillor. It was Sir John Gladstone of Lanarkshire who anglicised the name; he was the father of the celebrated statesman and premier, William Ewart Gladstone. The surname, never very frequent, is now found mostly in Edinburgh.

Glasgow First recorded in 1116 as Glasgu, a burgh on the Clyde. The etymology has been debated for many years, but the current theory is that Glasgow comprises the Brittonic words *glas* ('grey/green') and *cau* ('hollows'). The designation 'de Glasgow' was current in the records until the late 15th century, when it quietly attains permanency as a surname: the first (inauspicious) example seems to be Alan Glasgw, who was named as the unfortunate victim in a murder trial in 1494. The currency of the surname would originally be *outside* the city; and even now there are many more Glasgows in Edinburgh than in Glasgow. (There is no family-name 'Edinburgh', doubtless because the town was not so called until after the 'surname period'–see Introduction).

Glass The Gaelic adjective *glas* is a common place-name element meaning 'blue/grey' (see **Glasgow**), and it is also a component of many personal names: the forename Glas and the surname MacGlashan are examples. Glass as a surname in Scotland is from such a source. The Glasses were landowning families in Bute in the 16th century, and the name crops up frequently in the diocese of Dunblane over the next two hundred years. The Rev John Glass, minister of Tealing in the 1700s was the founder of a religious sect known as the Glassites. In England, however, where the name is not uncommon, a derivation from the trade of glazier or glassblower is generally accepted.

Glen / Glenn / Glennie Glen and Glenn are common surnames, particularly in Glasgow, and the supposition is that they referred to a glen-dweller (unspecified). Glennie is an Aberdeenshire name, borne by many generations of farming folk in Dee- and Don-side; there is a firm tradition that the name comes from Gleney near Braemar, although the accentuation of the place-name ('glen eye') seems to refute this. Possibly the Gaelic dative form *aig a' glinne* provides the answer. A William Gleny is recorded in Aberdeen in the 1390s; a Robert Glynn was a burgess of the city in 1554, and there have been thousands of Glennies in the locality since then– including James Glenie, born in 1750, who combined the sciences of mathematics and gunnery.

Glendinning From a place in Dumfriesshire, originally Glendonwyne ('valley of the white fort'). It appears regularly in the records as a territorial designation, and there were 'Glendonwyns of that Ilk' until the late 18th century. In 1504 Bartholomew Glendunwyne had his goods stolen; by the end of the century the Glenduningis were named among the unruly clans of the West March; John Glendinning was outlawed and his lands forfeited because he supported Montrose in 1645. Most Glendinnings now lead less colourful lives in the big cities.

Glover Neither the name nor the trade is particularly Scottish, but there have been Glovers in this country from the earliest times–at least since the 13th century, when Simon Glover of Perth was obliged to do homage to the English king. Sir Walter Scott, always careful in these matters, chose the name Catherine Glover for his heroine in *The Fair Maid of Perth*, explaining that this was the trade of her artisan father.

Gold Gold is a very potent word, whether as a noun denoting the commodity itself or as an adjective describing its colour or quality. The name can come from either, but usually refers to the colour of hair or to the wealth of the bearer. In addition, there is an Old English personal name Golda (from the same source) which became a patronymic in Scotland as well as in England. Adam Gold was a bailiff of Montrose whose name appears in the Ragman Roll of 1296; Gould is a variant, current in Angus and Perthshire from the 16th century, and Goold is also found. The diminutive form Goldie belongs mainly to Ayrshire and Lanarkshire. Gowdie was a name for the treasurer of an incorporated trade (short for *gowd-maister*). Gowdie and Goudie are Edinburgh spellings which appear in 1598; Isobel Gowdie was burnt as a witch there, having resumed human form after appearing to her accusers variously as a hare and a crow.

Good Usually from the Old English personal name Goda, meaning 'good' or a contraction of one of the many compound names containing this word–e.g. **Goodwin**. Thomas Gude is recorded in Ayrshire in 1533; John Gwid was a mason in Pollock, and John Gud was a tenement-holder in Glasgow, all about the same time. The name belongs to no particular locality, and is just as common in England.

Goodall Possibly from a settlement in Yorkshire, but more likely an occupational name referring to a brewer of 'good ale'; despite its English origin it reached Scotland at a very early date, being recorded in 1290 in Kelso. John Guidall was in Dysart and Thomas Goodall was in Perth in the 1540s; thereafter the name is widespread in the Lowlands, and even turns up in Orkney.

Goodfellow To be interpreted literally, in the sense of 'good companion'. John Gudefalow was a presbyter and notary public in St Andrews in 1469. Later the name is recorded in Angus, Lanarkshire and Edinburgh, and is now to be found almost anywhere.

Goodlad A Shetland name, now found sparsely throughout Scotland. The 'lad' element may originally have meant a servant.

Goodwin Originally a forename, from the Old English words *goda wine*–'good friend'. The bishop of St Andrews had two servants called Goodwin in the 1120s, but the name itself has no specific Scottish connection. It appears as a surname in the early 15th century in the person of Thomas Goodwyn or Gudewyne who was a brother of the order of St John of Jerusalem. In Scotland it is now to be found mainly in the Glasgow area.

Gordon Sir Adam of Gordon (a place in Berwickshire) was rewarded by Robert the Bruce with the lordship of Strathbogie, and the family acquired additional estates in the north east in the wake of the departed Comyns, becoming lords of Badenoch. The weakness of central government in the early Middle Ages made it important to have strong men in the regions, and what the Campbells were to the south-west Highlands, the Gordons were to the north-east. An earldom (of Huntly), followed by a marquessate and finally a dukedom, were the rewards of this family's not always disinterested service. Another branch, the Gordons of Haddo, became earls of Aberdeen. The Gordons are notable as being a dynastic family rather than a tribal clan; although all-powerful in the north it was as landowners and not as patriarchal chiefs that they drew their strength. The 1st Earl of Huntly is said to have laid the foundations of his 'clan' by rewarding all who took the name Gordon with a gift of meal; thus certain of his followers were called the 'Bow' o' Meal' Gordons to distinguish them from the true stock. Possibly as an indirect result, Gordon now almost makes the fifty top surnames in Scotland.

Gormley From the Irish patronymic *O Gormghaile* , meaning 'descendant of Gormghal', a personal name whose derivation is ambiguous. There were at one time Gormleys in Argyll, but the name is not really indigenous to Scotland, and most of the present Glasgow Gormleys will be of Irish stock.

Gorrie Usually a contraction of *MacGoraidh* ('son of Godfrey', in its Norse form), it appears sometimes as MacGorrie or MacGorry; the *Mac* version is still current in Ireland. The Skye MacGorries were descended from a MacDonald Lord of the Isles who died in 1380, and Gorrie is still reckoned to be a MacDonald name. The

Cowal branch are the progeny of Godfrey, the Red Baron (floruit 1430). A family of MacGorries settled in Glenalmond in the mid-16th century, which probably accounts for the large number of Gorries who once lived in Perthshire.

Goudie–see **Gold**

Gough The original home is Wales and the earlier form of the name is Coch, Welsh for 'red' (see **Cochrane**). The tradition is that a family of this name settled in Co. Waterford in the 13th century and later branched out to Dublin. Some Goughs no doubt re-emigrated to Scotland at the time of the potato famines; and the name is now most commonly found in Glasgow. Alternatively, Gough was a familiar name on the English-Welsh border, and may have travelled north to Scotland. It can also be a variant of **Gow**.

Gould–see **Gold**

Gourlay In the early records, Gourlay is always prefixed by 'de'; so the origin is almost certainly a place-name, as yet unidentified but possibly in Normandy or Picardy. The titles 'de Gurlay' and 'de Gurley' are recorded in Angus in the mid-13th century; the brothers Hugh and William Gurle were removed from the king of Scotland's council in 1255. The Ragman Roll of 1296 contains the names of several Gourlay lairds in the Lothians and Roxburghshire. There were Gourlays lairds of Kincraig in Fife for over six hundred years. Robert Gourlay was provost of Stirling in 1330, and John Gourlaw was a monk at Arbroath half a century later. Normand Gourlay of Dundee was hanged and burned for heresy in 1522.

Govan Derived from the lands of Govan in Lanarkshire, and now almost confined to that county. There was however at one time an important landowning family of Govans in Peeblesshire which died out in the early 19th century.

Gove A version of **Gow**, found mainly in Aberdeen, with outliers in Tayside. Colin Gove was constable of Tarradale in 1278.

Gow The Highland version of **Smith**: *gobha* is the Gaelic word for blacksmith, and the surname Gow is very often a contraction of *Mac a' ghobhainn*–'son of the smith' (see **MacGowan**). Blacksmiths (they were also armourers) were in evidence throughout Gaeldom, so there is no particular location or clan affiliation for the name Gow, although it was very common in Perth and Dunblane in the 1600s and 1700s. Niel Gow, born near Dunkeld in 1727, was the most famous fiddler and songwriter of his day in Scotland, and his sons carried on the tradition. The Irish form is **Gough**.

Gowan / Gowans Versions either of **Gow** or **Govan**. See also **MacGowan**.

Gowdie–see **Gold**

Grace / Gracie–see **Grassie**

Graham Of pure Anglo-Saxon origin, the name comes from an English manor (thought to be Grantham, which was spelt Graham in the Domesday Book–legends about Grimm's Dyke are now discounted). William de Graham accompanied David I to Scotland on his return from England; through marriage with a Highland heiress, the Grahams acquired a power base in Perthshire and the family rose to great prominence in the Wars of Independence; they were unjustly deprived of the earldom of Strathearn in the early 15th century. The Grahams were not a Highland clan but a Lowland family, with numerous branches in Menteith, Drymen, the Borders and Angus. They were militarily inclined, and two of them–Montrose and Claverhouse (both of them staunch supporters of the Royalist cause in the 17th century)–have taken their place in Scotland's Valhalla. James Graham, 3rd Duke of Montrose, was responsible as a Member of Parliament for legislation in 1782 to repeal the infamous Act of 1747 which rendered it a criminal offence to wear Highland dress. R.B.Cunninghame-Graham was the anarchic son of a Menteith laird whose political prominence in the 1920s has been eclipsed by his literary fame. The romantic but incorrect spelling Graeme was introduced by the scholar George Buchanan in the 16th century.

Grainger A grange (Latin *granagium*–'granary') was the farm steading where the monks stored the produce for the nearby monastery, and the person in charge was the granger. This word first appeared as an occupational designation, sometimes in the Latinised form of *graneter* (there was a John Graneter in Inverness in 1430). As a permanent surname, however, Grainger is of very ancient usage in Scotland, Hugh Granger having been recorded in Paisley as early as the 1180s. The name (not exclusively Scottish) is now found mainly in the Glasgow area.

Grant This nickname (meaning 'of great stature') started life in Normandy, and the family motto of *Tenons ferme* predates by several centuries the more familiar *Stand fast*. The tag Le Grand was applied to a Nottinghamshire property-owner who acquired lands in Strathspey in the 13th century. From these not untypical beginnings the great clan Grant arose, with branches in Glenmoriston and Aberdeenshire. The Grant lands in the Spey valley were elevated into a regality after the Glorious Revolution of 1688, and Sir Ludovic Grant of Freuchie built the model village known today as Grantown-on-Spey. Intermarriage with the daughter of the Ogilvie earl of Seafield brought that title into the family, and there were three other Grant baronetcies. The Grants are a typical case of a clan which got a foothold in the Highlands through marriage-settlement or other legal means and extended their possessions by the sword. Feudalism reverted to tribalism in a surprisingly short time, and the clan memory took no account of its non-Celtic origin. Most Scottish Grants will probably have had their origin in Strathspey as tenants of their incomer-landlord; although having no real kinship with him, they would take his surname and claim his chiefly protection. Most of them would have not the slightest idea of the latent grandeur of the name.

Grassick / Grassie The Gaelic word *greusaiche* means 'shoemaker'; Lowland tongues refashioned it into the various forms of Grass, Grassick, Grassie, Grace, Gracie and several others–Grassie is probably the nearest phonetic approximation to the Gaelic, while the Grace/Gracie spelling tends to be commoner in the west of Scotland. John Grass or Cordonar (see **Cordiner**) was in Crathie in 1539, Donald Grasycht in Lochalsh in 1548, and John Graissie in Buchlyvie in 1632. Gracie is the name of the tallest man in the UK; over seven feet, he inherited the title from his brother who died in 1993. In Lowland Scots the equivalent name would be **Soutar**, which was taken by some emigrant Highland shoemakers.

Gray The twenty-eighth surname in order of frequency in Scotland, and much commoner in this spelling than in that of 'Grey'. The meaning is the same however, and the adjective would refer to hair colouring, complexion, or clothing (although probably not personality). But there is no disputing the claim of the landed family of Gray to have come from a place of the name in Calvados in Normandy. Hugo de Gray appeared in Fife in the early 13th century; a hundred years later Sir Andrew Gray, in reward for his support of Robert the Bruce, received large grants of land in the Carse of Gowrie; a descendant was created a lord of Parliament in 1485, and the family were prominent lairds in east Perthshire until the 20th century. A third possible source of this common name is as a literal translation of the Gaelic *glas* or of its offshoot **Glass**.

Green Unlikely to have its origin as a nickname, unless the reference were to the dress or immaturity of its bearer; much more likely is a reference to abode by a village green or some such place. Green used to be among the top twenty surnames in England: in Scotland it does not even make the first hundred. It appears early as a territorial designation; 'Roger of the Green', a Roxburgh laird, did homage to the English king in 1296; John Grene was chancellor of Moray in the mid 15th century. The name never belonged to any particular locality, and its frequency in present-day Scotland is partly due to English penetration.

Gregory From the Latin *gregorius,* Greek *gregorein* meaning 'watchful'; it was the personal name of at least two saints and sixteen Popes. The surname Gregory, absent from the early Scottish records, is from the same source, very often through its Gaelic version *Griogair*; indeed in Scotland Gregory can be a substitute for **MacGregor**, having made its appearance after 1603 when the clan name was proscribed. John Gregorie was minister of Drumoak in 1635, and the name was well-known in Aberdeenshire. There was a quite remarkable dynasty of Gregorys from that shire, beginning with David, a physician and inventor who was born in 1627, and his brother James, the famous mathematician and astronomer, ranging through scholarly sons and medical nephews, producing Gregory's Mixture in the bygoing, and ending with Sir William who was governor of Ceylon in the 1870s.

Gregg / Greig A contraction of **Gregory**, but not necessarily with the clan MacGregor connection, Greig was at one time common in Fife in assorted spellings: Walter Greg was recorded there in the early 13th century. Patrick Grige was a burgess of Aberdeen in 1488. William Gregg was hanged at Tyburn in 1798 for treasonable dealings with the the French. The Norwegian Griegs are descended from John Grig of Fraserburgh whose son settled in Bergen in the late 18th century: Edvard Grieg, the composer, is of this stock.

Grier / Grierson Thought to be a contraction of **Gregor** or an anglicising of **MacGregor**. The family of Grierson of Lag in Dumfriesshire claimed descent from Gilbert, son of Malcolm MacGregor, who died in 1374; he in his day was known alternatively as MacGregor or Gregorson, but by 1400 his successors were called Grierson and were granted lands by the earl of March in that name. A later laird of Lag, Sir Robert Grierson, was a perfervid Jacobite and the original of Sir Walter Scott's Redgauntlet. John Grierson was a prior of St Andrews and principal of King's College, Aberdeen in the 16th century; Sir Herbert Grierson, writer and scholar, was born in Lerwick in 1866; John Grierson, maker of documentary films, was from Stirlingshire. Grierson is nowadays quite a familiar name in Tayside.

Grieve From the Middle English word *greve*, meaning steward or manager. It was until recently standard usage for the second-in-command of a farm, although it had grander beginnings, being the term for a royal official who played a major part in the feudal and urban structure of Scotland; it is cognate with *Graf* (the German term for Count). Johan Grieve was a Berwickshire landowner whose name appears in the Ragman Roll of 1296; Johannes Grefe, who lived in Fyvie, Aberdeenshire was excommunicated in 1382. Grieston Tower in Traquair is named after a family of Grieves who lived there in the 1400s.

Griffen / Griffin–see **Griffiths**

Griffiths From the Old Welsh personal name *Gruffydd*, of uncertain etymology. Although there are some Griffiths in Scotland, the usual form of the name here is Griffen. Robertus Griffin held land in

Newtyle in Angus before 1226, and there was a William Griffin in Morayshire in 1233. But most Scottish Griffens are to be found in the area of Greater Glasgow, and will derive their name from the Irish patronymic *O Griobha* , a personal name referring to the griffin or gryphon.

Grigor–see **Gregory**, **MacGregor**

Grimmond A Perthshire surname, a contraction of **MacCrimmon**. The late Lord Grimond was born in St Andrews, of Dundee antecedents, where the name was prominent in the Jute trade.

Guild In most mediaeval Scottish towns, the merchant venturers organised themselves into a group known as the guild brethren, with an elected Dean to execute common policy and a chaplain to look after their spiritual needs. From the early 15th century the Guildry operated under a charter of incorporation from the Town Council, and assumed an importance which it retains in some degree until modern times. In common usage, Guild referred to the member and Guildry to the organisation. Alexander Guild is recorded in Stirling in the 1420s, and a century later Thomas Gulde was a monk of Newbattle in Midlothian. Andro Guld of Dundee was in trouble in 1550 for selling a cow which yielded insufficient milk. The name was quite common in Angus and Perthshire from the 15th century onwards; nowadays it is mainly found in Dundee. Strangely, it does not appear in dictionaries of English surnames.

Gunn From the personal name, or from a short form of one of the compound Norse names (e.g.Gunnhildr) of which the first element is *Gunnr* (meaning 'battle'); our word 'gun' is supposed to be from the same source. The clan ocupied a position in the northern Highlands uncomfortably reminiscent of that of the MacGregors to the south: set about by powerful enemies–the earls of

Sutherland and Caithness on the one side, the MacKays on the other–the Gunns had a continual struggle for survival throughout the Middle Ages. The Highland clearances of the early 19th century finally deprived them of their ancient territories, and those members of the clan who did not emigrate were forced to eke out a living in the coastal villages. Yet Gunn is still among the top twenty surnames in the Highland region, and its fame has been enhanced by Neil M. Gunn, son of a Caithness skipper and one of the great modern Scottish novelists.

Guthrie From the hamlet near Forfar, a version of the Gaelic *gaothairach* , meaning 'windy place'. Sir David Guthrie of Guthrie was armour-bearer to King James III, as well as being lord treasurer of Scotland and sheriff of Forfar; branches of his family flourished around Arbroath and Dundee. The name spread: David Goithry was burgess of Aberdeen in the 1460s and James Gotthra was miller at Eyemouth in 1581. Henry Guthrie, a graduate of St Andrews, was bishop of Dunkeld in the 17th century. A separate family had meanwhile appeared in the south-west, spelling their name Gotray or Gotrey; John Guttraw assaulted his younger brother to the effusion of blood in Stichill in 1659. Thomas Guthrie, the apostle of the ragged schools, was born in Brechin in 1803 and became a famous preacher and philanthropist in Edinburgh; his descendant Sir Tyrone Guthrie was equally well known in the very different world of the theatre.

H

Hadden A variant of **Haldane**. Silvester Hadden is recorded in Angus in 1514, Adam Haddane in Dolphinton in 1679, and Alexander Hadden in Edinburgh a little later. A family of Haddens was well-known in Aberdeenshire, where the name is still most frequent.

Haddock–see **Haddow**

Haddow From 'half-davach'. A davach was an old Scottish land-measurement, and a half-davach would be equivalent to a smallish field; Haddo in Aberdeenshire is a corruption of this ancient term. The surname Haddow is probably from the same source although it is commoner in Edinburgh and Glasgow than in the north-east; Haddock is another version. Alanus de Haldawach was excommunicated in 1382; Archibald Haddow was recorded in Lanark in the early 17th century.

Haggart A contraction of **MacTaggart**. John Haggart lived in Perth at the end of the 16th century, and the name was common in this area (particularly around Caputh and Dunkeld) for many years. It is still very much a Tayside name.

Haggarty / Haggerty / Hegarty From the Irish patronymic *O hEigcertaigh* , which incorporates a word meaning 'unjust'; this Ulster surname, absent from the older Scottish records, is commonly found in Glasgow, with some examples in the Edinburgh area.

Haig The Scottish Border family of Haig gets its name from La Hague, in Manche in Normandy, whence it was brought by one Petrus del Hage in the 12th century. Peter Haig of Bemersyde in the 1270s paid a rent (in the form of salmon) to the convent of Melrose; the Haigs held their Bemersyde lands until 1867, and in 1921 a grateful nation repurchased the estate for Field Marshal Earl Haig. As a surname Haig belongs to the group Hague and Hay, all ultimately deriving from the Old Norse word *hagi*, an enclosure, and cognate with our word hedge. Most Haigs and Hagues are in the Edinburgh area–but see also **Hay**.

Hain / Hainey–see **Heaney**

Hair / Hare From the Irish patronymic *O hAichir*, meaning descendant of Aichear–'the fierce one'; unlike most Irish names however it is recorded in Scotland at an early date. William Hare was a burgess of Edinburgh in 1366; but his much later namesake, the accomplice of William Burke in the body-snatching trade, was a recent Irish immigrant. Patrick Ahaire was a bailie of Ayr in the early 15th century, and Christine Hare lived in Irvine a hundred years later. The name is now found mainly in Glasgow and Edinburgh, more commonly in the spelling Hair; Hare is next, with Haire well behind.

Halcro / Halcrow The lands of Halcro in South Ronaldsay in turn took their name from Halcro in Caithness; the origin is probably Norse but the meaning is unclear. David Haucrow lived in South Ronaldsay at the end of the 15th century; Sir Nycoll Haucro or Halkraye was parson of Orphir a hundred years later. A reference in 1640 to Hew Halcro 'of that Ilk' probably implies the ownership of an Orkney estate. Halcrows are still virtually confined to the northern isles, but not in very large numbers.

Haldane From the Old Norse personal name *Halfdanr*–'half-Dane', a reference to somebody of mixed parentage. The other half is not necessarily Scottish, since the name also occurs south of the Border, but the Haldanes of Gleneagles have been a powerful

Perthshire family since the 13th century, when Aylmer de Haldane was obliged to submit to Edward I. This remarkable family in more recent years produced Robert Haldane and his brother J.A. (both religious writers, born in the 1760s); grandsons R.B. Haldane, the Victorian statesman, lawyer and philosopher, and John Scott Haldane, the physiologist and philosopher; granddaughter Elizabeth, Liberal politician and scholar; great-grandson J.B.S., the famous geneticist; and Naomi Mitchison (*née* Haldane) the writer. Another Haldane laird, of Keiller near Dundee, was killed at the battle of Pinkie Cleugh in 1547.

Halkett Although never frequent, this name has a long and well-documented history in Scotland. It probably comes either from Halkhead in Renfrewshire or Hawkwood in Lanarkshire, but the twenty-nine different recorded spellings do not determine the matter. The name is recorded thrice in the 13th century–in the persons of Sir Henry Hakette and Richard Haket in Dumfries and Sir Walter Haket in Ayrshire, and a few further sightings occur in the latter county. From the 1350s the Halketts of Pitfirrane come into prominence, and henceforth the name is strongly associated with Fife. John Halket was in Dysart in the mid-16th century, and Robert Holkat in Culross. A century later there was at least one Halkhead family in Dysart. Elizabeth Halket, Lady Wardlaw, born in 1677 was the reputed authoress of the ballads *Hardyknute* and *Sir Patrick Spens* ; and Hugh Halkett, born in Musselburgh in 1783, became a Hanoverian soldier with the title Baron von Halkett.

Hall A locality name, given to someone living or working at the 'big hoose'. As a surname it is much commoner in England (where there were more hall-employees) but its recorded history in Scotland dates from the 1370s, when Thomas Hall was surgeon to Robert II; he obtained a grant of land in Renfrewshire, which his descendants retained for two hundred years. Henry Hall, a strong supporter of the Covenant, was one of the leaders at Drumclog and Bothwell Bridge; David Hall of Edinburgh emigrated to the USA and became a partner in Benjamin Franklin's printing business. The name was recorded frequently in Glasgow, but nowadays is more common in the Edinburgh area.

Halley Possible derivations abound: it may be a habitation name from some such place as Hailey ('hay-field clearing', occurring in Bucks, Herts and Oxon.), and this is no doubt where Edmund Halley the astronomer got his name; or it may come from from Halley in Deerness in Orkney (Thomas Halle was a tacksman or tenant there in the early 16th century). But the surname is commonest in Dundee and Glasgow, cities which were host to large numbers of Irish immigrants, and this perhaps makes more likely the derivation from the patronymic *O hAille*, which means 'descendant of Aille', a personal name of unknown origin.

Halliday A nickname for someone born on a *haly* or holy day, of which the early calendars contained not a few. Thom Haliday was the nephew of Sir William Wallace; Adam de Halide was a juror on an inquest in St Andrews in 1303; the Hallidays of Hoddam were a once prominent family in Dumfries, where the name is still familiar.

Hamill From the village of Haineville or Henneville in Manche, Normandy. The name of William de Hameville or Heyneuille appears in Annandale at the end of the 12th century (probably not yet as a hereditary surname); at the same time Walter de Hamule settled in Lothian on obtaining a grant of land from William the Lion. In 1452 Robert de Hommyl got a charter in confirmation of lands already held by him in Roughwood in Ayrshire. The name occurs frequently in Glasgow from then on; the Ayrshire family migrated to Ireland, where the name became and still is current; no doubt some Hamills returned to Glasgow, the place mainly associated with the name.

Hamilton *Hamel dun* means 'crooked hill' in Old English, and Hambledon is a place name found in Hampshire, Surrey and Dorset, with the variants Hambleton and Hambleden in other English counties. Walter fitz Gilbert de Hameldone, whatever his place of origin, owned properties in Renfrew during the Wars of Independence; for his services to the Bruce he was duly rewarded with the Comyn lands in Lanarkshire, which in turn were named after him–now the modern town of Hamilton. As a result of marriage into the royal line in 1474 the 2nd Lord Hamilton was created Earl of Arran; the next earl became Marquess of Hamilton, and the 3rd Marquess became the 1st Duke of Hamilton. This noble family played a central if not always reputable part in the history of Scotland. Its offshoots however were most notable: Patrick Hamilton, martyred for his Protestant beliefs in St Andrews in 1528; Sir James Hamilton, Renaissance architect and designer of the palaces of Linlithgow and Falkland; and the grandson of the 3rd Duke who climbed Vesuvius twenty-two times and married Emma, beloved of Lord Nelson. But the many Hamiltons here and elsewhere, who would not claim descent from the ducal family or any of its aristocratic branches, probably derive their name from the Lanarkshire estate rather than the original 'crooked hill'.

Hanlin / Hanlon From the Irish patronymic *O hAnluain*, a personal name which appears to incorporate the word *luan* meaning 'champion'. The Hanlons, an Ulster sept not recorded in Scotland until recent times, are now fairly frequent in the Glasgow area.

Hannah / Hannay From a Scottish patronymic *O hAnnaidh*– unusual because it is one of the very few native 'O' names (see Introduction). It means 'descendant of Annach', a personal name whose meaning is obscure. Gilbert de Hannethe was a Wigton laird whose name figures in the Ragman Roll of 1296. John Hanay appears in Glasgow in 1477 and Robert Ahannay in Wigton a few years later; but the Wigton family were by tradition ruined in a feud with the Murrays of Broughton. James Hannay was the preacher whose reading of the liturgy in St Giles Kirk in Edinburgh in 1637 was by tradition interrupted by the aerial arrival of a three-legged stool (see **Geddes**). The name became established in Ulster, and may have migrated back to Glasgow, where it is now very commonly found.

Harcus / Harkess / Herkes From the lands of Harcarse (meaning unknown) in Berwickshire. Adam of Harcarres was elected abbot of Newbattle in 1216, transferring to Melrose three years later. Three Berwickshire landowners of the name appear in the Ragman Roll of 1296, as does Alisaundre de Harcars of Fife. Sir Robert Harcars was sheriff of Perth in the early 14th century, and Alexander de Harcars was sheriff of Forfar at the same time. The name continues to occur frequently in the Lowland records, and was taken to Orkney in the 16th century, where it appears in the characteristic forms of Harcus, Arcus and Orcas.

Hardie / Hardy From an Old French word *hardi* , meaning bold or brave. William Hardy was a Lanarkshire landowner who had to submit to Edward I; there was an Alexander Hardy in Arbroath in the early 16th century, and a William Hardy in Orkney at the same time. Hardie is the usual spelling of the name in Scotland nowadays. James Keir Hardie (1856-1915), a Lanarkshire miner, was the virtual creator of the British Labour movement. The Aberdeenshire Hardies are said to have been originally **MacHardy**s.

Harkness The place to which this name refers has never been identified, but the surname was for long associated with Annandale and Nithsdale; nowadays it is found mainly in Glasgow and Edinburgh. It may even be a corruption of Harcarse—see **Harkess**—and a form Hardkneys is found in the late mediaeval period. James Harkness of Locherben was responsible for the rescue of some Covenanters from the royal troops in the Enterkin in 1684, and his brother Thomas was next year hanged in the Grassmarket of Edinburgh for complicity in the same affair. Alexander Harkness was a schoolmaster in Dumfries in the early 1800s; his family prospered in Limerick. Edward Stephen Harkness, an American millionaire who was of the Dumfries descent, was a major benefactor of St Andrews University in the 1920s, and founder of the Pilgrim Trust.

Harper The harper was a hereditary musical retainer in the households of many great families, especially in the Highlands; the tradition persisted until well into the 18th century, with Roderick Morison (*an Clarsar Dall*–'the blind harper' of the MacLeods) and Murdoch MacDonald, who served the MacLeans of Coll. In non-Gaelic-speaking parts the occupational designation became the surname, and there are several Harpers from Edinburgh, Lanark, Ayr and Berwick who figure in the Ragman Roll of 1296. See also **MacWhirter**, which was sometimes translated as Harper.

Harrison This surname, meaning 'son of Harry', is or was among the thirty commonest in England and the USA. Although much rarer north of the Border, it has a long Scottish pedigree; Sir Laurence Harrrison or Herryson was recorded here in 1497, and fifty years later James Harryson was a strong advocate of union with England.

Harrower An occupational name from the process of raking, and for some reason uncommon in England. William Harrower or Herward was keeper of the royal moor and warren in Crail in the reign of David II (late 14th century). Robert Harrower was a burgess of Perth in the 1440s and John Harwar was vicar of Cortachy in Angus at the same time. The name became well-known in Fife in the 16th century, and is now fairly widespread. (The surname Harrow, however, must be a recent importation, and comes from the town in Middlesex; the place name derives from the Old English *hearg*, meaning 'shrine').

Hart / Harte There are three possible derivations of this surname: in ascending order of probability they are (i) a nickname from the animal; (ii) a habitation name from the manor of Hert in Durham; (iii) from the Irish patronymic *O hAirt* ('descendant of Arthur'). In any given case it is impossible to decide on linguistic evidence alone. Henry Hart was a burgess of Lanark in 1296; Michael Hart received a charter of the lands of Braxfield a generation later; and Nichol Hart was accused of acting art and part in the murder of Cardinal Beaton in St Andrews in 1546. Around the same time a notable Edinburgh family named Heart included a burgess, a printer and a member of parliament. The name is common in the two large cities.

Hartley Principally a Northern English surname, it means 'stag glade'. The name apparently fled north of the Border when Andrew de Hardela of Westmoreland was executed for treason in the late 13th century. It is widespread in Scotland, but never became of frequent occurrence.

Harvey / Harvie From a Breton personal name Haervie, whose component parts are *haer* and *vy* and which mean 'battle' and 'worthy' (see Introduction). The name was introduced to England at the time of the Conquest, and became very frequent; it is the family name of the marquess of Bristol. Hervey was the name of one of William the Lion's marshals; he was granted lands in East Lothian. John Hervy was a wine-taster and bailie of Aberdeen around 1400 and John Hervi was a juror in Edinburgh a few years later. The name–now commoner in the spelling Harvey–is widespread, with a good showing in Dumfries and Galloway.

Hastie It means what it says, and must originally have been applied to a quick or even a rash person; strangely, it is seldom found in England. Robert and John Hasty are recorded in Midlothian in the 1370s, and Thom Haste a hundred years later; in the following century the name of Henricus Hastyis crops up in Edinburgh and that of Thomas Hastie in Beauly. According to tradition, a family of Hasties were the hereditary pipers of Jedburgh for nearly three hundred years; and there were a number of Hasties in Lanarkshire in the 17th and 18th centuries. The present day distribution of the name has not changed much.

Hastings This name has an exclusive quality: it comes from the place in Sussex where King Harold failed to repel the invaders in 1066, and was the surname of a very important family who later became earls of Huntingdon. A branch migrated to Scotland in the reign of William the Lion and obtained a grant of land at Dun near Montrose. Johanne de Hastinge was sheriff and forester of the Mearns in 1178; a descendant married into the Scottish royal family, and as earl of Menteith unsuccessfully claimed the throne in 1290. Meanwhile, other offshoots had acquired estates in Perthshire and Berwickshire and married with noble families (including that of Atholl). But the family never fulfilled its potential in Scotland, and the surname, although frequent enough to justify inclusion, is now restricted more or less to Glasgow and Edinburgh.

Hawthorn Hawthorn (from Old English *haga* 'hedge' and *thorn* 'thorn') occurs in many place-names south of the Border; the Scottish surname is thought to have come from Hawthorn in Co. Durham. It first made its appearance in the south west, initially in Galloway and then in Wigton, where a family of Hawthorns were landowners from the 15th century. Margaret Hathorn was in Carstairs in 1602, James Hauthorne in Stranraer in 1628, and

Esther Halthorn in Kirkcudbright a century later. The name is still commonly to be found in the south-west.

Haxton The older form was Hackston, which itself was a contraction of Halkerstoun ('hawksman's farm'), a place in the Mearns held by the king's falconer. Johan de Haukerstone was a Lothian landowner whose name appears in the Ragman Roll of 1296; the name was said to have been common in Edinburgh in the 15th and 16th centuries, and William Haikston was a tailor there in the 1680s. David Hackston of Rathillet was a Covenanting Fife laird who was executed in 1680 for his part in the murder of Archbishop James Sharp on Magus Muir near St. Andrews. Haxton (to give the name its modern spelling) is now mainly to be found in the Glasgow area.

Hay From one of several places in Normandy which involve the words La Haye; (*haie* means hedge or stockade, and dried grass does not come into it). The first of the name in Scotland was William de la Haye; he came from the village of the name in La Manche, was butler to William the Lion and obtained lands in Errol in the Carse of Gowrie at the end of the 12th century. The family rose rapidly in importance, becoming lords of Errol and Lord High Constables of Scotland. Other branches became earls of Kinnoull and marquesses of Tweeddale. Meanwhile the un-ennobled Hays also flourished, producing a distinguished family of jurists in the 16th and 17th centuries, and multiplying until in the 1950s their name became the eighty-second most common in Scotland; although it has now lost that position the name is still very frequent in the Aberdeen area, with strong representation in Tayside also.

Hayes This has no genealogical connection with the preceding name; its origin is either English (from one of the many places in that country called Hayes, notably Middlesex), or from the very popular Irish patronymic *O hAodha* , 'descendant of Aodh' (see **MacKay)**. Hayes is found principally in the Glasgow area, and the latter derivation is the more likely.

Healey / Healy There are two Irish patronymics from which this surname may come: (i) *O hEalaigthe* , a Munster name which means 'descendant of the ingenious one'; (ii) *O hEilidhe* from Connaught, which means 'descendant of the claimant'. Both are pronounced approximately as Healey, and it is scarcely surprising that the bearers who emigrated to Glasgow in large numbers chose this simplified version.

Heaney Eanna was an Irish saint whose name enjoyed some popularity although its meaning is uncertain; as a patronymic it became *O hEanna*, and was anglicised to Heaney. Most Scottish Heaneys are to be found in Glasgow .

Heggie Possibly a corruption of *MacEdamh*, 'son of Adam', the 'c' of 'mac' having become the dominant sound, as was quite common (see **Keddie)**. But more acceptable is a derivation from St. Fechin, whose name is the basis of Lesmahagow. Donald Hegy was a piper who helped the English to incinerate Dunoon in 1546, but was graciously pardoned by Mary Queen of Scots. There was a Patrick Hegy in Perthshire in 1567, and James Heagie was a merchant burgess of Stirling in the early 1600s; Janet Heggie lived in Fife about the same time, and there were three generations of Heggies employed in Carron ironworks.

Henderson A patronymic from the given name Henry; its older form was Henryson, but the intrusive 'd' proved easier on the tongue, and the modern spelling now prevails. Never a clan in any sense of the word, the Hendersons formed a number of unconnected families who lived in different parts of Scotland. It is possible to recognise three main branches: (i) Henderson of

Fordell in Fife, whose earlier name was Henryson and who came originally from Dumfriesshire; William Henrison was chamberlain of Lochmaben Castle in the late 14th century. The poet Robert Henryson was a clerical schoolmaster attached to Dunfermline Abbbey in the 15th century; and Alexander Henderson, the Covenanter, was born in Fife around 1583. (ii) In the far north a chieftain of the clan Gunn had a younger son Henry who founded a family of MacHendries or Hendersons who settled in the lowlands of Caithness. (iii) A branch of the original Glencoe stock which claimed descent from Henry, son of the Pictish King Nechtan, styled themselves MacEanruig or MacKendrick, which was later translated into Henderson. There are of course many other Hendersons who originate with some unsung Henry: the surname is among the top thirty in Scotland, and the distribution very wide.

Hendry / Henry Henry was originally a Germanic personal name consisting of the elements *heim reich* ('home power'–see Introduction). It has always been a popular forename in this country, the vernacular form of Harry not having caught on as it did in England; the intrusive 'd' however is characteristically Scottish (see **Henderson**). As a surname, Henry and Hendry first became frequent in Ayrshire and Fife; it is now fairly evenly distributed, in both spellings, and Hendrie is also not unknown.

Hepburn Hepburn and Hebburn are places in Northumberland and Durham respectively, from the Old English *heope burna*–'wild-rose stream'. Tradition has it that Adam de Hepburne, a prisoner of the earl of March, was granted the lands of Traprain and North Hailes in return for saving the earl from a savage horse: whatever the truth, the Hepburns became very extensive landowners in Lothian and the Borders. The Hepburns of Hailes were ennobled as earls of Bothwell in 1488; John Hepburn, a younger brother of the 1st earl, was prior of St Andrews and founded St Leonards College there in 1512; the 4th earl was the doubtful champion and legal husband of Mary Queen of Scots; the 5th earl was accused of witchcraft; both died in exile and with them the earldom. Sir John Hepburn (1598-1636), born in East Lothian and educated at St Andrews, was founder of the Royal Scots Regiment.

Herbert A popular first name with the Normans, it was originally *heri berht*–'army-bright'–a typically Teutonic formation (see Introduction). Herbert is the family name of the earls of Pembroke, Montgomery, Caernarvon and Powis, as well as that of two barons, a great philosopher and an even greater poet. In Scotland it was neither so frequent nor quite so distinguished. Herbert, abbot of Kelso, was appointed bishop of Glasgow in 1147, and Herbert was Lord of Kinneil in West Lothian about the same time; it is not found as a surname until the 16th century, when Archibald Herbertson appears in the records as a burgess of Glasgow. Robert Herbertsoune was a notary public in Edinburgh; Peggy Herbison was a diligent Labour politician of the old school.

Herd / Hird In older usage, 'herd' meant the herdsman rather than the flock; and in the days when hedges were few and fences non-existent the only way to protect the 'bestial' was to employ someone to do it. The herdsman's function was a vital one, and it has produced a wide range of surnames of which Herd and Hird are the least specialised: others are **Shepherd**, Coward (cowherd), Calvert (calf-herd), Coltart (colt-herd) and **Hoggarth**. The surnames Hird and Herd are recorded in Arbroath in the 14th century, and became quite frequent in the east coast counties. David Herd, born in Marykirk in the Mearns, was a song-collector in the time of Robert Burns. The modern distribution of these names has hardly changed.

Heriot / Herriot Very well-known as the name of George Heriot (1563-1624), jeweller and personal treasurer to James VI, and founder of Heriot's Hospital in Edinburgh. The Scottish surname derives from the Lothian village, whose name comes from the Old English words *here gatu* , meaning 'military equipment'. Heriot was a territorial designation for three hundred years before it became a surname: in the 16th century a William Heryot appears in the records of Haddington, and thereafter the name becomes quite frequent, particularly in Edinburgh and the Lothians. In England the surname is less common, and is a diminutive of Henry or Harry.

Heron / Herron A rare English surname which was originally brought by a Northumberland family who migrated to the Stewartry in south-west Scotland in the 11th century. It probably started life as a nickname, from a fancied resemblance to the bird. Robert Heyrun is recorded in the Borders in the late 13th century, and Roger Heron appears in Berwickshire a generation later. The name turns up in Aberdeen and Glasgow in the 16th and 17th centuries, and later in Edinburgh. Herons however became quite numerous in Glasgow in the 19th century, which suggests an alternative Irish origin for the name.

Hewitt / Hewitson These surnames belong to a group which derive from the forename Hugh–see also **Houston**, **Howat**, **Howie**, and **Hughes**. Hewitt is a diminutive and Hewitson a patronymic, the Gaelic equivalent being MacHugh. There was a Meg Huet in Aberdeen in 1408, but the next sighting is not for two hundred and fifty years, when the name of Alisoune Hewat turns up in Cockburnspath along with five others. The names (far commoner than Howat or Howatson) are now found mainly in Glasgow and Edinburgh.

Higgins A common surname in England, where it is taken to be a rhyming diminutive of Richard (along with Hicks and Dixon and several others–see Introduction). In Scotland however it is much more often an Irish import, from one or other of two patronymics, both loosely rendered into English as O Higgins: the first is *O hUiggin* which means 'descendant of Vikings', and the second is *O hAodhagain* ('descendant of little Aodh'–see **MacKay**). The fact that most Scottish Higginses are to be found in the Glasgow area perhaps tends to confirm the Irish provenance.

Hill / Hills These are very common English surnames, not often specific as to place of origin. In Scotland also they occur from the 13th to the 15th century as territorial designations, without it being disclosed which hill the bearer came from or lived beside. The surname had became common all over the Lowlands by the 17th century. George Hill was Principal of St Mary's College in the University of St Andrews at the end of the 18th century, and although he was a distinguished scholar it is scarcely credible that the five other professors of his name and lineage who were on the Senate at this time were appointed for the best reasons. David Octavius Hill, born in Perth, was a 19th-century landscape and portrait painter, and the first to apply photographic techniques to his art–and vice versa.

Hind / Hynd The latter version used to be commoner, but the English spellings of Hind, Hinde and Hinds, have overtaken it in recent years. The name comes from the Middle English *hine*, a 'hind' or 'peasant', and the earliest references are to be found in Glasgow, where the name still prevails. David Hynde was a burgess there in the 15th century, and about that time many other examples were recorded in the west as well as in Fife.

Hislop / Hyslop A Scottish name which has its English counterparts in Haslip, Haslop and Haslup; all have the same meaning of 'at the hazel hope (or valley)'. Alexander Heselihope was recorded in Edinburgh in 1425, and there was a William Heslihope who was vicar of Cortachy in Angus at the same time. Stephen de

Heslyhope was a notary in Glasgow a little later, and Thos Hislop was recorded in Renfrewshire in 1525. Joseph Hislop, who died at a great age in Fife comparatively recently, was a distinguished operatic tenor who unfortunately found little outlet for his talents in his native Scotland.

Hobbs / Hobson These common English surnames are very seldom found in the Scottish records until the modern period, for reasons which are explained in the Introduction. Hob as a pet form of Robert was not unknown in Scotland (Edward I derisively referred to Robert the Bruce as 'King Hobbe'), and Hab sometimes substituted for Rab in the west, but such rhyming diminutives are an English characteristic. The few Hobbs, Hobbeses and Hobsons who live in Scotland are most likely of southern origin.

Hodge / Hodges / Hodgson A rhyming diminutive of Roger (see **Rodger**). Not very common in Scotland, but well documented from an early date. There was a Laurence Hoige in Glasgow in the mid-16th century; Mariota Hodge was a housewife and Thomas Hodge a burgess, both of Edinburgh, in the 1620s. The genitive form Hodges occurs sparingly–Thomas Hodgis was a merchant in Glasgow in the 15th century–and Hodgson does not appear until modern times. Hodgkin is represented by one Alexander Hogekin in Lothian in 1583; but the double diminutive patronymic Hodgkinson is very rare in Scotland.

Hoggan / Huggan These names occur mainly in the large Scottish cities, but not with great frequency, and are pet forms of Hugh–see **Hughes**. Andrew Hoggan lived in Dunblane in the 1680s, John Hogine was in Angus in the following century, and William Hoggan was provost of Lochmaben around the same time. Hagan is an Irish name which is also a Hugh-derivative; but Hogan is a reduction of *O hOgain*–'descendant of the young one'.

Hogarth / Hoggarth / Hoggard Literally 'hog herd'–the keeper of the swine; but in Scotland *hogg* means a young sheep–so the name is equivalent to **Shepherd**. A Henry Hoggart was recorded in the Borders in 1525, and somewhat later there was a Robert Hoghyrd in Dunfermline. Charles Dickens married into a Hogarth family which originally hailed from Edinburgh, where the name is still mainly to be found.

Hogg In England this is usually taken to be a reference to swine, either in the occupational sense of swineherd or an uncomplimentary nickname. Malmer Hoge is recorded in Lennox in 1294; and the names of Henry Hogg and John Hogg figure in the Ragman Roll two years later as Border landowners. The name has always been associated with Edinburgh and the Borders: a family of Hoggs were influential city burgesses in the 14th century; and James Hogg, the Ettrick Shepherd, has now attained a literary eminence denied him in his lifetime. John Hogg, porter at St Andrews University in the late 18th century and beloved mentor to students, was celebrated in a poem by Robert Fergusson.

Holland The name sometimes derives from the Old English terms *holh land* , meaning 'hollow land'. There are eight English villages so-called, and various settlements in Scotland also bore the name: Richard Holande, who was vicar of Ronaldsay in 1467 took his name from a place in the locality. Thomas de Holande was a chaplain in Dundee around the same time, and his contemporary Andrew Holand was vicar of Airlie. There were several of the name in Ayrshire in the 15th century. But the most likely source for the numerous Glasgow Hollands is the Irish patronymic **Mulholland**, abbreviated in Co. Limerick to Holland. The name can also be a reduction of the Irish name Holohan, which is the likely origin of the word hooligan. Whatever the provenance, there is no Dutch connection.

Holmes A very common name in the northern half of England: it comes from the Old Norse word *holm* meaning 'island in a river'. In Scotland it usually has a specific derivation from the lands of Holmes near Dundonald in Ayrshire; Joannes Homys is recorded in Ayr in 1460. There was a James Hoomes in Inverness in 1668. Most Scottish Holmes are now in the big cities, and their names are probably of English origin.

Home–see **Hume**

Honey / Honeyman Occupational surnames from beekeeping or honey-selling, an important concern in the days before sugar was available commercially. The names are strongly localised in Fife, specifically between Falkland and St Andrews. Willam and Johne Hwnymane lived in Cupar in the 1520s, Alexander Huinman was in Dunfermline in 1555, and Robert Huineman was minister of Dysart a century later. John Honey, a student, rescued five men single-handed from a wrecked ship in St Andrews bay on New Year's day 1800.

Hood From the Old English personal name Huda, whose meaning was probably related to head-covering. The name of Robert Hude or Hod is recorded in 1255; Robertus Hud of Leith and Robert Hod of Aberdeen belong to the same century. In Angus there occur the names of David Hude or Huyd and John Hude, vicar of Abernyte, both in the 15th century; Michael Hud was recorded in Kelso in 1567. Thomas Hood, poet and punster, spent his early-19th-century childhood in Dundee.

Hope The Middle English word *hop* meant a small valley, and 'hope' was a common place-name element in southern Scotland. As a surname it belongs both there and in the north of England. John Hope, a Peeblesshire landowner, did homage to Edward I in 1296; and there was a Thomas Hope in Edinburgh in 1478. John de Hope accompanied Madeleine de Valois, wife of James V, to Edinburgh in 1537; his descendants were created earls of Hopetoun and marquesses of Linlithgow. John Hope, the 1st marquess, became Governor General of Australia in 1900 and his son was viceroy and Governor General of India from 1936 to 1943. Thomas Hope of Rankeillor in Fife was an 'improving' 18th century landlord. The surname is still found mainly in Edinburgh and the Borders.

Hopkins / Hopkinson 'Son of little Hob', a pet form of Robert (see **Hobbs**), common in England and Wales, but comparatively rare in Scotland. Matthew Hopkin was a miller in the early 17th century; some years later the name of John Habkine was recorded in Ayr and that of William Hebkine in Campbelltown.

Horne Not a specifically Scottish name, but well documented here from an early date. A horn, because of its shape, is very prevalent in the imagery of most languages and cultures in the mediaeval period: the term could be applied to a mountain peak or to the bend in a river, and only later did it refer to an instrument or utensil. Horn became a place-name element in England, as in Hornsea; and such is no doubt the source of the surname in southern Scotland. John Horn was a 13th-century Borderer, and Alan Horne was recorded in Lochmaben in 1328; thereafter the name is found all over the Lowlands.

Horsburgh The name means 'horse brook', and there were lands near Innerleithen which were so called. Symon de Horsbroc figures in the Melrose abbey records in the early 1300s, and the name is frequently to be found there in the next century . William de Horsebroch was a Glasgow man; and in 1440 Robert Horsbruk was prior of St Andrews. These examples apart, the name was strongly localised in the Borders, as it still is. Florence Horsbrugh, MP for Dundee during the war years, became in 1953 the first Tory woman cabinet minister.

Hosey / Hosie No tidy etymology is possible for this name, very Scottish but never very common. It turns up in a variety of places and spellings, by far the oldest on record being Hose, a family who claimed to come from Houssaye in Normandy, and who possessed the manor of Craigie in Kyle in the 12th century; however, this particular family later appear to have adopted a new surname from their property. The name also appeared in the far north, with '-son' attached: the Shetland name Hoseason is thought to be a version of 'son of Aassi' (a Norse form of Oswald). Inevitably the name came to be popularly associated with the biblical Hosea. Hosies (the commonest spelling) are now scattered all over Scotland.

Hossack / Hossick A name of obscure origin, long established in Inverness, where an Alexander Hossack was recorded in 1508. A Cromarty family of Hossacks in the 17th century were popularly credited with unusual powers of prophecy. The name later turns up in Aberdeenshire, but is now sparse and scattered.

Houston 'Hugh's settlement' is the name of a place near Glasgow, and there were many Houston families in the district in the 15th and 16th centuries; the various spellings include Hawystoun, Howstoun, Hawstoun and Hawestoun. Houston is still remembered in Glasgow as the name of a mercantile family who helped to lay the foundations of Scotland's industrial economy in the 18th century. (Houston in Texas was called after the descendants of an Ulster Scots family who emigrated to Philadelphia at that time; given the etymology of the name, the Texan pronunciation is quite logical). The name apparently migrated to Ross-shire, where it is still to be found; but the Caithness Houstons were originally Ogstons.

Howat / Howitt / Howatson This group comprises another of the Hugh-derivatives–see **Howie** and **Hughes**. Howat started off as a personal name, the mediaeval equivalent of 'Hughie'. Robert

Howat was a cleric in Aberdeen in 1469, and the name still enjoys a continuity in that city. Glasgow is its other home, starting with James Howatt in the 17th century. The form Howatson has a similar distribution and almost as long a pedigree.

Howden Howden is a place near Kelso, from the Old English *holh* ('hollow') and *dene* ('valley'). It is frequently recorded in the pre-surname period as a territorial designation, and appears three times in the Ragman Roll of 1296 as the name of landowners in the shires of Edinburgh and Roxburgh. William Hauldyn was a bailie in Lanark in 1328; from this time onwards the name sometimes becomes confused with **Haldane**. The English Howdens originate in Yorkshire.

Howie / Howieson The second commonest group of the Hugh-derivatives–see **Howat** and **Hughes**. There was a Joyhnne Howy who was accused of an Ayrshire murder in 1526; William Howie, his contemporary in Brechin, was more law-abiding. Robert Howie was the first Principal of Marischal College before he moved to St Andrews in the late 16th century. Howieson is found in Edinburgh as early as 1450; there was a John Howison in Aberdeen early in the next century and a Nicholas Howyson in Kelso. Both forms of the name were and are common all over the Lowlands. Howe is different–it comes from an English place-name, and is not recorded in Scotland before the modern era.

Hudson The derivation is usually the Old English personal name *Huda*–see **Hood**. But Hudson–which is much commoner in England than here–can also be yet another version of Hugh (cf. **Hutcheon**). James Hudson was in Kelso in the 15th century and two more of the name occur there in the 16th, with later sightings in the Borders and Perthshire.

Huggan A Hugh-derivative, akin to **Hoggan**. There were Huggons in Fife in the 16th century, and Agnes Hugan was recorded in

Lauder in 1628; Janet Huggin is found in Bute a generation later, and David Hugin turns up in Aberdeen around the same time– an indication of the present distribution of this name.

Hughes Hugh was a very popular forename, introduced to these shores by the Normans; it comes from *hugu*, a Germanic word meaning 'heart' or 'mind' (and appears in many compound names such as Howard and Hubert). Hugh also spawned large number of surnames–see **Hewitt**, **Hoggan**, **Houston**, **Howat**, **Howie**, **Huggan** and **Hutcheson**. Hughes ('son of Hugh') was at one time among the top twenty English and Welsh surnames, and now takes 69th place in Scotland. But it does not occur in the old Scottish records (the only 15th century citations being Hugosoun and Hughson); the reason for its absence may be that for centuries Hugh was accepted as the English equivalent of the Celtic name Aodh (see **MacKay**), although there is no connection between the two words as to either origin or meaning. The Irish patronymic *O hAodha* was rendered into English as Hughes, as were other versions of the name Aodh; so some Scots of the name Hughes may well be disguised MacKays or MacCoys.

Hume Interchangeable with Home until the 19th century; David Hume (1711-76) the great philosopher who was born in Edinburgh of Berwickshire parents, changed the spelling of his name in protest against its mispronunciation as 'home', although his brother John retained the Home spelling. The name is of territorial origin, from the lands of Home in Berwickshire (Old Norse *holmr*, meaning island or water meadow). William of Home and Geffrai de Home were two 13th century Border lairds, and Alexander de Hume turns up in Annnandale in the 1400s. Alexander and David Hume were conservators of the truce between Scotland and England in 1451; Wiliam Hoom was a merchant burgess of Glasgow in the 1660s. The 6th Lord Home accompanied James I on his translation to London, and was created 1st earl of Home; his descendant the 14th earl renounced his title in 1963 to become Prime Minister. John Home (unconnected with the noble family but a distant cousin of the philosopher) was a Lowland Jacobite who was taken prisoner at the Battle of Falkirk in 1746 and imprisoned in Doune Castle; he wrote a history of the Rising and a play entitled *Douglas*, so successful in its day as to prompt comparison with Shakespeare. Joseph Hume, the radical politician, was born in Montrose in 1777.

Humphreys / Humphries The given-name Humphrey is a typical Germanic compound (see Introduction), whose parts mean 'bear-cub' and 'peace'. In the early records the aspirate is usually missing: Andreas Vmfray was cantor of the church of Dunkeld in 1374; Andrew Umphray was a burgess and notary in Perth in the mid 15th century and William Umfra was a burgess of Aberdeen at the same time. Sir William Vmfray was chaplain of Dornoch in the next century and Thomas Vmphray was a burgess of Elgin in the 1590s. Umphray is still current in Shetland, but Humphrey and Humphreys, the usual spellings, are mainly found in Glasgow.

Hunt / Hunter The hunt was an important part of the economy in the Middle Ages, and 'hunter' occurs very frequently in the early records from Beauly to the Borders as an occupational designation. A Norman family of Hunters settled in Ayrshire in the 13th century, and gave their name to Hunterston; another family were of Polmood. Three Hunter landowners in Paisley appear in the Ragman Roll of 1296. Maurice Hunter was provost of Stirling in 1327 and Aymon Hunter was burgess of Cullen at the same time. Agnes and Tebe Hunter fell out over the ownership of a kirtle in Dundee in 1521. The brothers William and John Hunter were respectively an anatomist and a surgeon in Glasgow in the 18th century, and the Hunterian museum was originally formed to house their collections. Hunter is much commoner than Hunt, and ranks thirty-seventh in the commonest Scottish surnames.

Hutcheon / Hutchinson / Hutchison Hugh-derivatives all–see **Hughes**, **Howat**, and **Howie**. An old French form of Hugh was *Huchon*, which in Scots was mispronounced as Hutcheon; this gives the very common group of surnames under this heading, to which must be added the Gaelic version of MacCutcheon. Hutcheson is associated with Glasgow, because of the benefactions of the brothers George and Thomas who in 1639-41 founded the hospital (later school) which bears their name. An earlier example is James Huchonsone who lived in Glasgow in the mid-15th century; and John Huchonson was a burgess of Ayr at the same time. The name was common all over the Lowlands and made its appearance in Inverness in 1624.

Hutton From the Old English *hoh tun*, meaning 'promontory settlement', a place-name which appears in Dumfries and Berwickshire (and much more commonly in England as 'Houghton'). Symon de Hotun was recorded in Lanarkshire in 1263, and John Hudton was abbot of Coupar Angus in 1460. Two brothers in Dundee in the 1550s shared the name John Hutone– a not uncommon phenomenon which reflects the high infant mortality rate of the time as well as the limited repertoire of baptismal names (see Introduction). In the 17th century the name occurs in Stirling, Kirkcudbright, Dundee and Fife; some Huttons migrated from Cumberland to Ireland at that time, and no doubt a few of them came to Scotland two hundred years later. John Hutton, originally a herd lad at Caerlaverock, became physician to William and Mary and Queen Anne, and member of Parliament for Dumfries. James Hutton, the Edinburgh geologist, originated the theory of the geological cycle.

I

Imlach / Imlay An Aberdeenshire surname of uncertain origin, possibly a variant of **Imrie** but more likely from a lost settlement name in the north east. Thomas Imlach was a burgess of Aberdeen in 1440, and others of the name appear in the city records for the time. Agnes Imlay was burnt for witchcraft there in 1597. Robert Emlach was in Aberchirder early in the 17th century, and there was at the same time a Thomas Imloch in Nigg and a George Imlach in Keith. John Imlach, born in Aberdeen in 1799, wrote *Gin I were whaur Gadie Rins*. The name, even in its more usual spelling of Imlay, is still scarcely known outside the shire.

Imrie / Imray From the Germanic personal name Amalric whose components mean 'work' and 'rule'–see Introduction; it came via Anglo-Norman, and its cognate in England is Amery, a name unknown here. Emeric (he had no known surname) was a Lombard from Flanders who appeared in Berwick in 1329; Ade Emry was burgess of Dunblane in 1424; Walter and Thomas Ymery were in Stirlingshire in the 16th century, and James Immerie was in Dunfermline at the same time. In the 17th century it went through a phase of being spelt Imbrie; John Imbrie was a burgess of Glasgow in 1611. The name is now widespread, and possibly commonest in the Edinburgh area.

Inch / Inches / Insch This group of surnames derives from the Gaelic word *innis* (see **Innes**) which is a familiar place-name element both on its own (e.g. Insch in Aberdeenshire) and in combination with another noun (as in Inchcape). The name of John del Inche, burgess of Inverkeithing, appears in the Ragman Roll of 1296; John de Inche was in Montrose in the 1430s, Thomas Inche in Banff and William de Inche in Tullibody at the beginning of the next century. Duncan Insche turns up in Culross in 1652, and George Inch in Edinburgh in the 1730s. It is highly unlikely that the surnames of these persons had any common point of origin.

Inglis This is the northern and Scottish form of 'English', and could originally have been a nickname applied to an incomer from south of the Border. The term Inglis appears in the records from 1153 until about 1400 as a national identity tag, and is not found in the records as a hereditary surname until the name of John Inglis appears in Aberdeen in 1402. There were many bearers in Scotland from earliest times: several landowners designated 'Inglis' figure in the Ragman Roll of 1296–three from Lanarkshire, one from Perthshire, one from Kintyre and one from Dumfries. Thomas Ynglis appears in Edinburgh in 1449 and James Ynglis in Glasgow around the same time; and Master Alexander Lenglis was archdeacon of St Andrews in 1564. Elsie Inglis founded a maternity hospital in Edinburgh, where her name is still a household word. The name is also common in Glasgow; naturally it was never widely current in England.

Ingram From an old Germanic personal name Ingelramn whose suffix means 'raven' (see Introduction). Its first appearance in Scotland is in pre-surname days: Hyngelrom was at Newbattle around 1142, and Engelram was successively rector of Peebles and archdeacon of Glasgow until he became Malcolm IV's chancellor. John Ingeram was in Arbroath in 1330, and William Ingelram was chaplain of Stirling in the 1470s. An 18th-century Glasgow provost called Archibald Ingram made a fortune trading with the Americas and the West Indies. Ingram tends now to be regarded as an Aberdeenshire name.

Inkster Inkster is a place in Orkney, from Old Norse *eng setr* (farm-meadow'). William Inkseter and Huchon Inksettir are recorded in

Orkney in 1492, and Magnus Ingsittir was in Orphir in the 1570s. The name is heavily localised in the northern isles, with only a few strays in Aberdeen.

Innes The Gaelic noun *innis* has the related meanings of island, riverside-meadow, haugh, resting-place, green spot and milking place; it provides the name of the barony of Innes on the Moray Firth. The first of the line was Berowald, a Flemish adventurer who was granted lands by Malcolm IV in 1160, confirmed in a charter of 1226 in favour of his grandson. The family of Innes were a powerful influence for good and evil in that part of Scotland for the next five centuries. The bad deeds of the family include the usual ones of murder, witchcraft and rebellion; the good (and there remains a considerable credit balance) include the rebuilding of Elgin Cathedral after its sacking by the Wolf of Badenoch in 1390 (work that was to be undone at the Reformation). There followed much later a period of intensive historical research carried out by the Innes family, culminating in the *Innes Review* and the scholarly labours of Cosmo Innes (born in Durris, 1798). There were numerous cadet branches of the family, and a considerable tenantry who would have adopted the surname, with the result that the name Innes still proliferates in that part of Scotland between Spey and Lossie where it originated.

Ireland There were vast numbers of Irish immigrants to Scotland in the 19th century, and they brought their surnames with them. But in pre-surname days a settler from across the Irish sea would be recorded as 'de Ireland'; Patrick de Ireland, accused of housebreaking in Forfar, was hanged in 1296. David de Ireland was one of the Scots prisoners taken at Dunbar Castle in the same year. Robert de Irland was a Stirlingshire landowner who was obliged to submit to Edward I in 1296. John Ireland, born in St Andrews in 1440, was a philosopher and theologian. (By this time, the 'de' disappears from the records, and Ireland has become a hereditary surname). James Ireland, an adulterer, took his place on the stool of repentance in Blairgowrie in 1649–for the twenty-fourth time. The name is commonest in those towns where Irish settlement was concentrated–in Glasgow and Dundee (and, incidentally Liverpool). But the Orkney Irlands are different: their name came from Old Norse *eyrar land* 'gravel beach', although some of them adopted the Ireland spelling.

Irons An Angus name, not very common but still familiar in Dundee. It is thought to come from Airaines in Normandy. The name of David Yrnis or Irnys is recorded in 1485; William Irnis was in Arbroath in 1506. Sir James Irnis was a notary in Perth in 1546; Eufamie Yrnis was in Dundee a generation later, and Elizabeth Irons turns up in Meigle in the 1690s.

Ironside In Scotland the reference is not usually to a mail-clad warrior but to the familiar Gaelic river-name *earn*, which is to be found in many locations besides Strathearn: there are examples in Ironside in New Deer in Aberdeenshire, and Earnside in Moray. The name was always commonest in the north east: Magi Irynsyd was banished from Aberdeen in 1570; around the same time Patrick Irnesyde was allowed to remain in the city; James Irnesyde of Foveran was accused in 1627 of being an idle and masterless man. Edmund Yrinsyde of Drumcarrow, who lived in the 13th century, seems to be an exception to the rule; his name probably reflects the traditional English usage.

Irvine / Irving These two surnames are one and the same, from the place in Ayrshire (which itself is derived from the Brittonic *ir afon*– ' g reen water'). Robert de Hirewine is recorded in Dumfries in 1226, Robert de Iruwyn in St Andrews a few years later; John de Herwyne was in Buittle and Gilchrist Herwynd was in Morton, both in 1376. The Irvines of Drum in Aberdeenshire were the most important landed family of the name; their progenitor, William de Irwyn, was granted the barony by Robert I in 1324. Sir Alexander Irvine of Drum, an ardent Royalist, was sheriff of Aberdeen in the mid 17th century; his son Alexander was outlawed and imprisoned for his Royalist loyalties in 1644-45, and his kinsman Robert died in the Civil War. Sir James Irvine, a noted chemist and Principal of St Andrews University until his death in 1952, was of Ayrshire stock. The name has been widespread in Scotland since the late mediaeval period, and at some stage migrated to Ireland: there is an Irvine castle in Fermanagh built by a Scottish Irvine.

Isbister A Shetland place-name meaning 'estuary farm', which has become a common surname in the northern isles. Robert Ysbuster of Harray on Orkney is the first recorded bearer. Malkon Eysbuster was bailie of Harray in 1607, and Huchoun and Adam Isbister were recorded in Kirkwall about the same time. There are a few expatriate Isbisters in the Lowland cities, but the vast majority are still to be found in Orkney and Shetland.

Izzatt / Izzet This surname has several spellings but only one correct pronunciation: 'iz-it'. It comes from Ysolde or Iseult (Welsh Essylt), legendary wife of King Mark of Cornwall and lover of Tristan. Earl Gilbert of Strathearn married an Iseult from a local Norman family in c. 1210, which may be the reason for its having become naturalised in Scotland; it also has cognates in England (Izzard) and in Ireland (Izod). Alexander Ezat is recorded in Culross in 1569; Thomas Essat was a messenger in Kilwinning in 1579, and there was another family called Easet in Kirkcudbright about the same time. George Ezat was a burgess of Glasgow in the 1630s and the name is said to have been quite common around the Firth of Forth in the 17th and 18th centuries.

J

Jack Usually taken to be a pet form of John, through the intermediate form of Jankin or Jenkin; but just as often it will be a diminutive of James, via the Latin *Jacobus* and the French *Jacques*. As a forename, Jack was never as common here as it was in England, with the consequence that **Jackson** is less frequent also. But the surname Jack is and has been very common since at least the 15th century: Wil Jak was tenant of the mill of Keithock in Angus in 1473; Duncan Jak is recorded in Dundee a little later, and there was a Gilbert Jak in Uddingston and a John Jak in Glasgow at the same time. Robert Jack, merchant and burgess of Dundee, was hanged in 1567 for currency offences; ten years later a ship belonging to Andro Jaik of Aberdeen was lost with all hands.

Jackson In mediaeval Scotland, 'son of Jack' was quite likely to mean 'son of James' (see **Jack**), and the surname **Jameson** is at least as common as Jackson. William Jacson was burgess of Aberdeen in 1409; a generation later another William Jaksone was burgess of Glasgow. Ranald Jakson was in Angus in 1479, and in the same year David Jaksone was summoned to answer charges of treason there. Although not numerous before modern times, the surname was widespread in the Lowlands; but there are many thousands of English Jacksons, and not a few have settled here.

Jacob / Jacobson Of identical origin with **James**. Most bearers of the name in Scotland will probably be city-dwellers of Jewish or East European extraction; nevertheless the name has a long history in this country, and the records show an Alan Jacob and a William Jacob who were burgesses of Dundee in 1321 and 1348 respectively.

Jaffrey–see **Jeffrey**

James The Authorised Version of the Bible gives the name Jacob to the twin brother of Esau, and the name James to two of the apostles; the result has been to separate two names which are etymologically identical. As a surname James is very common in England and Wales (in 1853 it occupied thirty-fifth place), and it was fairly popular in Ireland, often as a reduction of Fitzjames or MacJames. In Scotland, although popular as a forename of members of the House of Stewart and other commoner mortals, it did not become a frequent surname until modern times. Jamie, a pet form, early became established as a surname in Aberdeen; and Robert Jamie was burgess of Linlithgow in 1623. Neither surname attained such frequency as **Jameson**.

Jameson / Jamieson Son either of James or Jamie (Jimmy is a later formation). A family named Jamieson held the office of crowners of Bute from the beginning of the 14th century for at least 300 years; Alexander Jemison had a safe conduct to trade with England in 1445; William Jamison was a tenant of Pollock in 1472; John Jamyson was a burgess of Aberdeen in 1465; John Jamezing was involved in the murder of the earl of Caithness in 1539; and William Jamesoune was responsible for repairs to the quay of Aberdeen in 1550. The most famous of them all, Glasgow-born John Jamieson (1759—1838), antiquary and philologist and compiler of the *Etymological Dictionary of the Scottish Language*, is silent about his own name. George Jamesone was a noted painter of the 17th century and the earliest Scottish portraitist. The eponymous leader of the Jameson Raid which precipitated the Boer War was born in Edinburgh in 1853.

Japp This surname belongs to a group which includes Jappy, Jopp and Jupp, and derives from the forename Job. Although never a very popular name, Job was current in mediaeval times; in most cases reference is to the biblical Job, or to one of his well-known characteristics, but there are other Middle English versions of the name with an unconnected source. John Jape was a skinner, and burgess of Glasgow in 1584; Alexander Jaip was a feltmaker in Edinburgh in 1672, and Walter Japp was in Fordell in 1699. Jappy is a diminutive which appears sporadically in one or two fishing villages in Banffshire, especially Buckie, about the 17th century– sometimes to the exclusion of all other names. Jopp has a longer history: Robert Jop was burgess of Perth in 1353, John Joip was a tenant of the earl of Huntly in the 1600s and there was a burgess family of Jopps in Aberdeen in the late 18th century. Provost Jopp conferred on Dr Johnson the freedom of the city of Aberdeen on 23 August 1773. The form Jobson appears late on the scene, and never became common.

Jardine From the Old French equivalent of 'garden', the name can be metonymic, meaning a gardener, or someone who lives at a garden. It appears in the records of the 12th century as a territorial designation ('de Jardin') both in connection with the Abbey of Arbroath and in the west of Scotland. John Jardin or Jarding of Applegarth appears in 1476, and William Jarden in Buittle in 1684. There was a family of Jardines who were lairds in Perthshire and Dumfries, and the name is still in the top twenty in the south-west. See also **Gardyne**.

Jarvie / Jarvis Jarvis is a Central French version of the Norman name Gervase ('spear'), and Jarvie is its diminutive. Thom Jarva is recorded in Stirling in 1547; Edward Jarvey in Powis in 1633; and Robert Jarvie in Peebles and John Jervie in Falkirk, both in 1689. The surname is not exclusively Scottish; indeed it was an English Jarvis whose colleagues, after he had been hanged, named his hackney horses 'jarveys' in memory of him. See also **Garvie.**

Jeffrey / Jeffries / Jaffray From the English forename Geoffrey, of which the second syllable is Germanic *frithu* ('peace'); the first syllable may mean 'pledge'. The name appears first in the Scottish records in the form 'le fiz Geffray', and two Peebles burgesses so designated appear in the Ragman Roll of 1296. Nothing is known of this 'Geffray', but he was probably an Anglo-Norman retainer of one of the early Scottish kings. The characteristic form of the name in Scotland is Jaffray, and this is the spelling of the surname as it first appears in the Borders in the 1500s in the person of John Jaffray; John Jofra is recorded in Brechin in 1552, and William Joffra in Linlithgow in 1586. Grissell Jaffray was tried in 1669 for witchcraft, found guilty and conemned to death. Francis Jeffrey, Lord Jeffrey (1773—1850) was a Whig, judge, critic, founder and editor of the *Edinburgh Review* and friend of Charles Dickens. The name in this spelling is usual in Edinburgh, although Aberdeen tends to retain the older form.

Jenkins Jenkin is a double diminutive of John. Although usually associated with Wales, the surname is probably Flemish in origin, and certainly has a long association with Scotland. It is found as far north as Morayshire in the 16th century, and John Jenkin was a bailie of Glasgow in 1584; David Jonkene was recorded in Angus in the 1600s, and Bartholomew Junkyne was a bailie in Aberdeen at the same time. The terminal possessive 's' ('son of') is modern, and indicates southern origin or influence.

Jessamine / Jessiman Probably from the town of Jesmond in Northumberland (meaning, oddly, 'Ouse mouth'). John Jesseman and William Jessieman are recorded in the lordship of Huntly in the 1600s. James Jessiman was in Aberdeenshire in 1654, John Jessiman in Moray in 1710, and Ann Jessamin in Aberdeen in the 1770s.

Johnson Johnson is the tenth commonest name in England and Wales; it never achieved anything like the same frequency in Scotland (but **Johnston** is a different matter). Wautier Jonessone of Berwickshire was compelled to do homage to Edward I in 1296; William Jonessone is recorded in Aberdeen in 1368, and Thomas Jonsoun was a burgess of Ayr in 1508. The Caithness Johnsons are said to be descendants of John, third son of a chief of clan Gunn; and it is possible that others are disguised MacIans, although that name was never common outside Glencoe.

Johnston / Johnstone In mediaeval times the city of Perth was known as St John's Toun or St Johnston, and many of its natives took their name from it. Indeed when the clan Gregor was proscribed some Perth MacGregors are said to have renounced their 'unhappie name' and assumed that of Johnston. There were many other 'touns' belonging to someone called John which would give rise to surnames: for example, the Border family of Johnstone took their name from the lands of Johnstone in Dumfries. They were ennobled as earls of Annandale; William the 3rd earl was a strong opponent of the Union of 1707. Prior to that another Annandale Johnstone, Lord Warriston, had brought fame to the name by drawing up the National Covenant of 1637; although his ultimate fate was the hangman's noose, his son became Secretary of State for Scotland and led an inquiry into the Glencoe massacre. A completely different family of Johnstones had lands in Strathspey in the 17th century, while another took their name from the lands of Johnstonburn in Humbie in East Lothian. Johnston was the name of a 19th-century Edinburgh family of geographers. Tom Johnston, Labour statesman and Secretary of State during the war years, was chairman of the Hydro Board.

Jolly This surname has to be taken at its face value, but bearers who find it difficult to maintain the necessary degree of jollity when teased about it may have recourse to the Old French *jolif* meaning gay or handsome. Alan Joyly is recorded in Kincardineshire in 1492; James Joly was in Dalry in 1541, Janet

Jolly in Leslie in 1646, and Robert Jollie in Edinburgh in 1677. The name is widespread without ever having been frequent.

Jones The commonest name in Wales, and the second in England, Jones means 'son of Jon', or John. The surname is completely absent from the historical records of Scotland, which indicates that the thousands of present-day Scottish Joneses are fairly recent imports.

Jordan Jordan, originally a river name from Palestine, became a favourite baptismal name in Europe from association with John the Baptist. Recorded as a forename in Scotland in the 12th century, it emerges as a surname with Magister William Jordanus in Aberdeen in the following century. The name may have attracted analogical formations from other languages, and of the many Jordans in Scotland some could originally be Irish *MacSiurtains* or MacJordans. The name is most frequent in Glasgow.

Joss A variant of **Joyce**. William Joos was chaplain to Robert III in 1402; Thomas Joce was bailie of Inverkeithing in 1359; William Joss was tenant of Westhall, Aberdeenshire in 1513; and the name was to become that of a landed family in Banffshire in the 18th century. It still belongs very much to the north-east.

Joyce Originally a male forename, Joyce was only occasionally borne by women in mediaeval times. It derives from the French personal name Josse, which in turn is from *Jodoc* ('little lord'), a Breton saint of the ninth century. As a surname it became very common in Ireland where it was introduced by the Normans in the 12th century. Outside Ireland, it is found mainly in Glasgow.

Jupp–see **Japp**

K

Kane From the Irish patronymic *O Cathain*, a personal name embodying the word *cath* meaning battle. The O Kanes were a leading sept in Ulster up to the time of the Plantation (the attempt by James VI in 1609 to colonise the province with Lowland subjects). The Ulstermen repaid the compliment one hundred and fifty years later, when Kanes and others settled in large numbers in Glasgow and central Scotland. The name is often confused with **Kean**.

Kavanagh– s e e **Cavanagh**

Kay Several English and Welsh origins are possible, but for most Scots bearers of the name it will be a reduction of **MacKay**, originally with the same vowel-sound. The name was recorded all over Scotland from the 14th century, in at least nine different spellings. John Kay started his career as a barber in Dalkeith, then became a fashionable miniaturist and caricaturist in Edinburgh, taking likenesses of Adam Smith and most of his leading Scots contemporaries. The spelling Keay is fairly common in Perthshire, and Caie was not unknown.

Kean / Keen This surname does not appear in the early Scottish records. John Kene was a writer to the signet in Edinburgh in 1609; James Kewne and Barbara Kewn were in Borgue in the1680s; and Mary Keand was in Kirkcudbright around the same time. The name was taken to be a contraction of MacKean, which itself is a corruption of MacIan ('son of John'). But the MacIans were never very thick on the ground, and a much more likely source is the Irish name Keane, from *O Cein* ('descendant of Cian'), or even **Kane**.

Keay–s e e **Kay**

Keddie A contraction of MacKeddie, which was originally *MacAdaidh* or 'son of Adie'; the equivalent Lowland name is **Aitchison**. The name of John Kady is recorded in Dysart in 1577, and that of Margaret Keddie in Roberton in 1623; Alexander Kadie was a tailor in Edinburgh and James Keadie was a hatmaker in the city, all at about the same time. James Keddie was bewitched in Wemyss later in the century, and Donald Kedde was apprehended as a rebel in Caithness. The name is found all over Scotland; and in Dundee it sometimes appears as Kiddie.

Keiller / Keillor From a river-name in Angus (cf Inverkeilor); the etymology is the same as **Calder.** The Ragman Roll of 1296 (see Introduction) contains the names of Dunkan del Celer, burgess of Perth, and Ranulph de Kelor of Kildrummy in Mar. John de Kelore, who lived in the late 14th century, was apparently the last member of the landed Keiller family in Angus, although the name is still commonest in that area. It became very familiar through the art of James Keiller and his successors, of Dundee, who perfected Great-aunt Margaret's marmalade recipe and whose confections are famous the world over.

Keir Keir is a place-name which comes from the Gaelic *cathair* or Brittonic *caer* meaning 'fort'; there are several examples, but the most likely source of the surname is Keir in Stirlingshire. Andrew del Keir, a landownder in that area, was obliged to do homage to Edward I in 1296; William Keir was a burgess of Stirling, and John Kere and Mariota his wife had a grant of land in Aberdeen, all in the 1360s. Thomas Kar was deacon of craft in Stirling in the late 16th century, and Thomas Kere was the equivalent of burgh chamberlain of Forfar at the same time. Sir David Lindsay Keir, constitutional historian and Master of Balliol, was educated in

Glasgow, at the Academy and University. As will be obvious from the variety of spellings, Keir must have often been confused with **Kerr**; and there is also a Gaelic adjective *ciar* ('dark') which could sometimes have been the origin of the name Keir.

Keith As a place-name, Keith probably derives from the Brittonic word *coed* meaning 'wood'; there are places in Banffshire and East Lothian which could have produced the surname, although Keiths have always been more numerous in the north-east. In the 12th century records Keith appears with great frequency as a territorial designation, and emerges as a hereditary surname two hundred years later. Sir Robert Keith, Great Marischal of Scotland (i.e. in charge of the royal horses), who had received a grant of land from King John Balliol, led the Scottish cavalry at Bannockburn, and died at the Battle of Durham in 1346. A descendant who had been ennobled as Lord Keith was created Earl Marischal in 1456; there were ten Earl Marischals in direct line until 1715, when the failure of the Jacobite Rising ended the Keith family fortunes. George Keith, the 4th earl, was a great statesman in his day and founded Marischal college in 1593; his namesake, George, the 9th earl, commanded the Jacobite cavalry at Sheriffmuir and was the architect of the abortive rising of 1719. His younger brother, who had also been 'out' in '15 and '19, was made a Field Marshal by Frederick the Great and was killed in the Seven Years War.

Kelly Kelly is today among the forty commonest Scottish surnames (and in the 1st XV for Strathclyde); in the late mediaeval period it was quite rare. The explanation lies in the fact that Kelly is also the second commonest surname in Ireland: the vast majority of Scottish Kellys are of Irish stock. Not all, however, for there are lands of Kellie in Fife and Angus (the name comes from the Gaelic *coille*, meaning a wood) and some bearers of the name will have originated in these places: for example, a John de Kelly was abbot of Arbroath in 1373; David Cille was abbot of Cambuskenneth in the 1450s and James Kelle was a notary public in St Andrews in 1526. Edward Kellie, a Scot, was appointed director of music to Charles I in 1629. William Kelly, mill manager in New Lanark in the 1790s, was a pioneer in the technology of the cotton industry. The Irish version of the name is from *O Ceallaigh*, meaning 'descendant of war'. The spelling is no guide (Kelly is a hundred times commoner than Kellie), since both Scots and Irish had a blithe disregard for how they wrote their names.

Kelman From a place in Aberdeenshire (*caol monadh*–'narrow hill'), where the surname is still most commonly found. William and James Kelman were burgesses of Aberdeen in the 1590s; a little later an Alexander Kelman was recorded in Dundee.

Kemp An Ango-Saxon word *kemp* meant warrior or champion, and in more recent memory there was a Scots verb 'to kemp' meaning to strive. The German title *Mein Kampf* ('my struggle') will come to mind; and all these words come ultimately from the Latin *campus*, 'battlefield'. So the surname Kemp means 'warrior', and although not particularly Scottish it has a long history in this country. William Kemp was a burgess of Edinburgh in 1423, and Donald Kemp was one in Dingwall in the 1560s; Andro Kemp was 'maister of the sang scule in Sanctandros' in the late 16th century. The name also became quite common in Ireland. George Meikle Kemp had a varied career as shepherd, carpenter's apprentice, millwright and architect; he designed the Scott Monument in Edinburgh.

Kennedy The Kennedys were the dominant family in south-west Scotland at a time when that part of the country was Gaelic-speaking. The name itself is thoroughly Celtic: *ceann eitigh* means 'grim-headed'. When first recorded the name is always preceded by *Mac*, which confirms that Kennedy was originally a forename (but unconnected with Kenneth). The Irish Kennedys claimed descent from King Brian Boru; the Scottish line originated with one Gilbert, a descendant of the Celtic lords of Galloway, and owner of the lands of Dunure in Ayrshire. The Kennedys of Dunure succeeded to the lands of Carrick, and after a royal marriage were elevated to the peerage as Lords Kennedy. A brother of the first Lord Kennedy, James Kennedy, bishop of St Andrews and Chancellor of the University, was one of the most notable statesmen of his time; his college in St Andrews still flourishes. The 3rd Lord Kennedy was created Earl of Cassilis four years before he died at Flodden; the family later built the splendid castle of Culzean. There were also dozens of untitled Kennedy families, initially in the south west, and later all over; Duncan Kennedy was provost of Aberdeen as early as 1320, and landed families of the name appeared in that shire. The Morayshire Kennedys are an offshoot of a Janet Kennedy who obtained possession of the earldom of Moray about this time. The name no doubt became even more frequent with the influx of Irish Kennedys in the 1850s; it is now around fiftieth in Scotland.

Kenny / Kenney–see **MacKenzie**

Kent Kent was the name of a place in the Shropshire estates of Walter fitz Alan (see **Stewart**), and the surname appeared in Scotland (at Innerwick, East Lothian) as early as the 1150s, probably in the retinue of David I. Robert de Kent was a Lanarkshire landowner whose name figures in the Ragman Roll of 1296. A William de Kent was a burgess of Aberdeen in 1408; another was in Fife in the 1570s, and Robert Kent was a burgess of Burntisland in 1612. But some Kents will have taken their name from the English county.

Kerr Kerr (the Scots form of **Carr**) is a locality name, although there is no such place in the Scottish gazetteers nowadays. The

Roxburgh branch of the family spelt their name Ker, while the Lothian branch was Kerr. There were numerous other offshoots in the Borders, two of whom (of Ferniehiurst and Cessford respectively) vied for the appointment of Warden of the Middle March (a lucrative border-policeman post) until they were united by marriage in 1631. From the union derive the earldom and marquessate of Lothian and the earldom and dukedom of Roxburgh. There grew up a legend that the Kerrs were left-handed, and built their spiral staircases with a left hand thread for better defence by southpaw swordsmen; a derivation of the name Kerr (from the Gaelic *cearr* meaning 'left' or 'wrong') has been devised as evidence, but there is nothing in history, etymology or even common sense to support this notion.

Kerracher–see **Farquhar**

Kerrigan One of a small group of Irish names, including Kieran, which embodies the Gaelic word *ciar* , which means 'dusky'–see also **Keir**. Kerrigan is therefore 'little dark one'; the name is mainly found in Glasgow, but not before the 1850s.

Kettle / Kettles Kettil was a Scandinavian personal name, brought to these shores by the Norsemen at an early enough date to give several place-names both in England and Scotland. It means 'cauldron' and probably refers to a topographical feature rather than a domestic implement–as does the equivalent Gaelic loan-word *coire* or 'corrie'–a hollow cauldron-like place. Ketill was the name of a 12th-century burgess of Perth; James filius Ketel was in Fife in the 1250s; Gelis Kettill was recorded in Shetland in 1576, and there was a James Kettle in Atholl in 1689. The name is common in Fife and Angus, almost always with the terminal 's' (which denotes 'son of'), but it is not predominantly Scottish.

Keyes–see **Keay**

Kidd A nickname from kid, a young goat, presumably with reference to nimbleness. Kidd was a very common name in Arbroath and Dundee, and appears repeatedly in the burgh records from the 15th century onwards. The first to be recorded is 'Robertus Kyd de Dunde' in 1357; Sande Kid and Thome Kyd attended an inquest at Forfar in 1450; John and Nychol Kyd appear in Brechin in the same year. Cristiane Kydde owned land at Longforgan in the 1470s, and Alexander Kyd was in Aberdeen around the same time. The name soon spread all over Scotland and beyond. William Kidd, born in Greenock, was supplied by the authorities with a privateer to help to suppress piracy but was hanged for that same offence in 1701.

Kiddie–see **Keddie**

Kieran–see **Kerrigan**

Kiernan–see **Tierney**

Kilgour The Gaelic word for goat, *gobhar*, turns up in innumerable place-names as 'gour' or 'gower'. The surname Kilgour comes from a place in Fife; pronounced with the stress on the second syllable, it is relatively common in that county as well as in Aberdeen. Thomas Kilgour was chaplain in the palace of Falkland in the 1560s; Henry Kilgor was in Dysart about the same time. Aberdeen examples include John Kilgour in 1540 and another John Kilgour, sacristan of the cathedral church there in 1607.

Kilpatrick It means literally 'cell or church of Patrick' and is basically the same as Kirkpatrick with which it was frequently confused. There are several places called Kilpatrick–in Bute, Dunbarton and Dumfries–which could have given rise to the surname. The records contain the name of Stevene de Kilpatrick, a Dumfries laird who had to do homage to Edward I in 1296. Nigel Kilpatrick was a Scots p.o.w. in Kenilworth Castle in 1302. Thomas de Kilpatryk lived in Wigton in the 1460s, as did Marion Kilpatrick two hundred and fifty years later; the Dunbarton lot included John Kylpatryk in 1495 and Thomas Kilpatrick in 1669. There is however an Irish patronymic *mac giolla Phadraig* ('son of the devotee of St Patrick') which produced another batch of Kilpatricks, and there is evidence that some of them may have settled in the west of Scotland in the 19th century.

King A nickname, either from a kingly manner or from the part played in a pageant. 'Robertus dictus King', who lived in the Garioch in Aberdeenshire in the 1240s, made a bequest to the prior and convent of St Andrews; and King was the name of several landed families in the shire in the 15th century. James King entered the Swedish service and fought valiantly in the Thirty Years War; recalled to England he was created Lord Eythan (Ythan) in 1642 and commanded the Royalist centre at Marston Moor: the title died with him. There is a tradition that some proscribed MacGregors adopted this surname; and it was also common in Ireland as a pseudo-translation of several unmanageable Irish names involving the word *righ* ('king'). Although King comes ninetieth in the list of commonest Scottish surnames, it is more than twice as frequent south of the Border.

Kinghorn This place-name appears first as Kyngorn; the etymology is obscure, but the Gaelic *ceann gronn* ('at the end of the marsh') is a possibility. As a surname, it must have started off in Fife, and was that of the king's secretary, Adam de Kyngorn, who lived in the 1200s. William de Kyngorn was constable of Edinburgh in 1292; and two clerics, one from Linlithgow and the other from Inverness, were obliged to submit to Edward I in 1296. By the mid 15th century the name appears all over Scoland, and it visited the continent in the early 1500s in the person of Alexander Kinghorn who was physician to the King of Denmark. It is now mostly found in Edinburgh.

Kinloch On the face of it the word means 'at the head of the loch', and there are several places in Perthshire and Fife which would give rise to the surname. But the early citations of the surname suggest rather Kindallachan, 'head of the fields or meadows', the name of a hamlet in Strathtay. William de Kyndelloche figures in the Ragman Roll of 1296; and Sir John Kyndeloch was chaplain at the Hospital of St John of Jerusalem in 1438. The Kinlochs were an important Angus family at the period of the Reformation; three hundred years later they also interested themselves in parliamentary reform; in between times, however, they risked losing all in the Jacobite rebellions. William Kinloch, probably a Dundonian, was a 17th century composer of music for the virginals, as well as being a secret agent of Mary Queen of Scots in her captivity.

Kinnaird Richard, a retainer of William the Lion, was granted lands in the Carse of Gowrie in the late 12th century, and as was customary took a surname from his estate–Kinnaird (from the Gaelic *ceann aird*, meaning 'head of the height'). A baron Kinnaird swore fealty to Edward I in 1296, and Rauf de Kinnaird appears in the Ragman Roll as 'du Counte de Perth'. A descendant was created Lord Kinnaird of Inchture in 1682, and the family was strongly Royalist in sympathy. A Kinnaird laird of Culbin in Moray lost his estate in an unusual way–it was buried through drifting sand.

Kinnear In the reign of Malcolm IV (1153-65) a family of Norman origin was established in the north of Fife as vassals of the priory of St Andrews; the head of the family took his surname from the lands of Kinnear (probably Gaelic *ceann iar*–'west headland') now represented on the map only by a farm name. By 1296 Sir John de Kyner was important enough to have his name incuded in the Ragman Roll (see Introduction). Henry Kinnear of that Ilk was appointed commendator of Balmerino Abbey in 1574, and by this time the family had the lucrative monopoly of ferry crossings of the Tay at what is now Newport. George Kinnear was an Edinburgh banker in the early 19th century whose lovely wife was painted by Raeburn. The name, now found all over Scotland, may tend to be confused with **Kinnaird**.

Kirk The name means 'living near or working in a church' and has very many points of origin; it may even occasionally have referred to a foundling baby discovered near a kirk. Sir Patrick Kyrk is recorded in Perth in 1456, and Andrew Kyrk in Arbroath in 1459. Alexander Kirk was a bailie of St Andrews in 1520, and James Kirk was in Inveraray in 1608. The Reverend Robert Kirk, minister of Balquhidder and Aberfoyle, was a Gaelic scholar and author of a celebrated book, published in 1691, which claimed first-hand acquaintance with elves, fauns and fairies.

Kirkland Another way of referring to 'glebe', the land attached to a parish church; there are many places so-called in the north of England and south of Scotland. John de Kyrkeland was recorded in Kelso in 1280, and William de Kyrkland was a burgess of Glasgow in 1424, where most Scottish Kirklands were and are to be found.

Kirkpatrick The name of a number of places in south Scotland; but the point of origin of the surname can be located in Annandale, where Roger de Kirkpatrick held lands of ancestors of Robert the Bruce. John de Kirkepatrike was a Dumfries laird who was obliged to do homage to Edward I in 1296. It was Roger de Kirkpatric who in popular history stabbed Comyn in 1306 in order to 'mak siccar' of his death. The Kirkpatricks of Garvald in East Lothian were another important branch of this family. Kirkpatrick is among the twenty-five commonest names in the Dumfries and Galloway region. See also **Kilpatrick**.

Kirkwood A common place-name in non-Gaelic speaking Scotland with an obvious meaning. John Kirkwood is recorded in Stirling in 1476; Alexander Kirkwood was implicated in a murder in 1526; John Kirkwood lived in Ayr in the early 16th century. James Kirkwood (1650—1708) was dismissed his post of master at Linlithgow Grammar school for refusing to compromise his religious principles. David Kirkwood, 1st baron Bearsden, was an engineer and Red Clydesider at the beginning of the present century.

Knight A personal name before the Norman Conquest, it comes from the Anglo-Saxon word *cniht*–boy, youth or serving-lad. As a surname it may have had that meaning, or was perhaps applied to someone in the service of a knightly family, or may even have been a nickname given to the person who played the knight in a pageant. It is not an exclusively Scottish name, but has a long history here: Robert dictus Kneght was a burgess of Arbroath in the 1330s; John Knycht was canon of Brechin a century later; Gilbert Knight was dismissed by the bishop of Brechin from the headmastership of Dundee Grammar School in 1434.

Knowles Knoll comes from an Old English word meaning hillock–in Scots, *knowe*–and the surname Knowles means 'living at the knoll'. The Gaelic equivalent is *cnoc*, giving **Knox**, and at one time the surnames Knowles and Knox were more or less interchangeable: there was a family called Knows or Knollis in the parish of Deer in Aberdeenshire, who were later known as Knox. John Knowis was a burgess of Aberdeen in the 1460s, and John Knollis was in Linlithgow in 1549. In the form Knollys, the name is more familiar in England.

Knox For the derivation, see **Knowles**. Knock is the name of a place near Greenock in Renfrewshire, and there is a tradition that Adam, son of Uchtred, was granted lands there in the 13th century, from which he took a surname. Hugo Cnox is recorded in Aberdour in 1272, and William de Knock was in Paisley in 1280. William Knocks and John Knoks lived in Cunningham in the 1660s. John Knox, the great and much-maligned reformer, was educated at Haddington school and Glasgow University; his son and grandson were also leading Presbyterian divines; a later descendant, Alexander Knox who died in 1831, was an advocate of Catholic emancipation. Robert Knox, the celebrated anatomist and purchaser of snatched bodies, was educated at Edinburgh High School and University. The name is now widespread in Scotland.

Kyle Kyle is the name of the district in Ayrshire where the birth of Robert Burns took place in 1759; it derives from the name of a 5th-century dynasty called Coel (the reputed origin of Old King Cole). Elsewhere Kyle is a rendering of the Gaelic word *caol* meaning straits (as in Kyles of Bute). Walter of Kyle was around in 1424, and Margaret Kyle lived in Glasgow at the same time. George Kyle was a burgess of Edinburgh a century later, while John and Thomas Kile had the same status in Irvine. The name was taken to Derry at the time of the Ulster Plantation (1609), and some Irish Kyles may well have re-settled in Glasgow in the 1850s.

L

Lafferty A drastic adaptation of the patronymic *O Fhlaithbeartaigh*, which incorporates the Irish Gaelic words *flaith* ('prince') and *beartach* ('valiant'). Sometimes spelled Flaherty and sometimes Laverty, the name is nowadays very frequent in Glasgow, but is in fact a recent importation from Ulster.

Laidlaw The name of William of Lodelawe figures in the Ragman Roll of 1296, as that of an Ettrick laird who was obliged to do homage to Edward I of England. Originally a place-name of uncertain origin, Laidlaw became a frequent surname in the eastern Borderland, particularly Selkirk, where it is still commonly to be found. William Ladlaw of Newton was charged in 1650 with concealing a horse from the English; John Laidlaw was recorded in Lauder in the 1670s and Thomas Laidlaw in Peebles at the same time; and there were several landed families of Laidlaws in the Borders in the 17th and 18th centuries. Will Laidlaw was the steward, amanuensis and faithful friend of Sir Walter Scott.

Laing A version of the name **Lang**, than which it is however much more common; the pronunciation is 'lay-ing', and another version is Leng, the comparative form of the adjective. So Laing in fact probably means 'taller'. Thomas Laing was recorded in Dumfries in 1357; Thomas Layng was a notary in Edinburgh in 1461; John Layng, rector of Newlands in 1472, became treasurer to James III and Bishop of Glasgow. Archibald Layng was a priest and notary in St Andrews in 1502. Two Orkney brothers, Malcolm and Samuel Laing, were noted historians; and R.D. Laing, born early last century in Glasgow of working-class parents, was the author of *The Divided Self* and other anti-psychiatric works.

Laird As a common noun, *laird* is the Scots equivalent of lord, but in normal usage it indicates something less grand than a peer of the realm. As a surname, Laird probably meant simply a landowner, of no great consequence. Roger Lawird or Lauird is recorded in Berwick in 1257; Thomas le louerd is listed in the Ragman Roll of 1296 as a Peeblesshire landowner; Thomas Laird appears in Glasgow in 1552, and David Laird was in Foveran twenty years later. McGregor Laird of Greenock was a famous 19th-century explorer and merchant; and the name gained wider currency as that of a partner in a shipping line.

Lamb An Old English personal name, perhaps connected with lamb-rearing, or perhaps referring to the gentleness of the bearer. There was an Adam Lamb in Roxburgh in 1288; another of the name appears as a Berwickshire laird in the Ragman Roll of 1296. In the 14th century it crops up in such diverse places as Thornhill, Inverness, Edinburgh and Aberdeen. William Lambe was a merchant in 16th-century Edinburgh; Andrew Lambe was another who built for himself a splendid mansion in Leith. The name became very common all over the Lowlands.

Lambert A Germanic personal name incorporating the elements *land* and *beorht* ('bright'), the whole having no coherent meaning, as explained in the Introduction. St Lambert was bishop of Maastricht in 700, and the name (greatly revered by immigrant weavers from Flanders) duly made its appearance in England, and later in Scotland, as a Christian name. By 1296 a Flemish settler is recorded in the Ragman Roll as a Fife landowner, and the name then becomes current (but never very common) throughout the Lowlands. It also went to Ireland, where it became the family name of the earls of Cavan.

Lambie The only thing to be said in favour of the attempt to derive this name from the French *'l'ami'* is that it shows the accepted pronunciation. In fact Lambie is a pet form of **Lamb**. Lambie as a surname was said to be native to Angus, and indeed it has always been familiar there and in Perthshire. Henry Lambi is recorded in Dundee in 1291; and Gilbert and John Lamby appear in St Andrews in the early 1300s. The name was current in Brechin and Montrose later in the same century; and it was an Andrew Lamby who was implicated in the murder of Rizzio in 1565.

Lamond / Lamont The second spelling is now the more common; so alas is the mispronunciation 'La Mont' (which hints at a French or Italian origin, quite impossible in either language). If the stress is correctly placed on the first syllable, the meaning ('law-man', 'law-giver') becomes clear; the final consonant is only there for phonetic convenience (and is absent from such versions of the name as Lemmon). Lamont and Lamond in fact come from Old Norse *logmadr*, which passed into Gaelic as *laomainn*. Mac Clymont is from the same source. The progenitor of the clan Lamont was of the royal house of Dalriada and in the early Middle Ages the clan held large tracts of land in Argyll. An inscription in the ancient churchyard of Kilmun refers to 'the great MacLamond of all Cowal'. But the Royalist Lamonts fell foul of the Whig Campbells and after a particularly bloody massacre in 1646 'all Cowal' became the domain of the latter clan. The Lamonds however diversified: some of them settled in Mar, and a Braemar lad (born in 1805) became professor of Astronomy in Munich (known there as Johan von Lamont). Frederick Lamond, pianist and the last pupil of Liszt, was born and brought up in Glasgow; he died in 1948.

Lang The Scottish equivalent of the English surname Long; it would be applied to anyone of more than normal stature. William Lange was a Berwickshire laird whose name figures in the Ragman Roll of 1296; Adam Lang was recorded in Aberdeen in 1341; Walter Lang was a burgess of Edinburgh in the 1380s, and Willelmus

Lange appears in Aberdeen at the same time. The name has tended to be associated with south Scotland and the Borders, and there were several families of the name in Selkirk in the 17th century. From that town came Andrew Lang, the writer, anthropologist and folklorist. Cosmo Lang, the Aberdeenshire loon who became Archbishop of Canterbury and guided his sovereign through the abdication crisis, was born in Fyvie in 1864.

Langlands From an estate ('long lands') in Peeblesshire, owned by a family which took its surname from the property, and which died out as late as 1894. The surname crops up frequently in Border records from the 14th to the 17th centuries, and is still common in the area.

Latta / Latto A survival of an earlier name, Lawtie, which comes from a place-name whose location and etymology are uncertain. Wiliam and Adam Lathis appear in Ayr in the 1470s, and the surname occurs frequently in the records in the 15th and 16th centuries. Adam Lawte turns up in Coldingham in 1525 and John Lawta in Haddington a little later. James Lawtie was a member of the Scots parliament for Cullen in 1628, and James Lawtie was minister at Chirnside in 1695. Not until the 18th century does the name take on its modern form, with James Lata who appears in Kilbarchan in 1709. Latto seems to be the version favoured in the north east. The name although never very common is characteristically Scottish.

Laughlan / Loughlin–see **MacLachlan**

Lauder From the Berwickshire river name, which is of unknown etymology. William de Lawedre was sheriff of Perthshire in the late 13th century. Robert and Edward Lawedre were merchants and burgesses of Edinburgh in the 1420s, and Sir Alexander Lauder of Blyth was provost of Edinburgh in 1505; another family of

Lauders seem to have been owners of the Bass Rock from an early date. James Lauder, an intimate of Mary Queen of Scots, instructed the young James VI in music. Sir Thomas Dick Lauder was a Lothian man whose novels, unreadable today, had considerable vogue in Victorian times. Robert Scott Lauder, the painter, was born in Edinburgh in 1803; Sir Harry Lauder, the comic Scot, first saw the light in Portobello in 1864.

Laurenson 'Son of **Lawrence**'. John Laurentii (a Latinised transcription) was vicar of Collessie in 1443, and Andro Loranstoun's name is recorded fifty years later. Arthur Laurenson occurs in Shetland in the 19th century.

Laurie A diminutive of **Lawrence**, and a less common spelling of **Lawrie**.

Lavery From the Irish patronymic *O Labhraidha* (pronounced approximately as 'Lavray'); it means 'descendant of the spokesman', sometimes appears in Glasgow as Lowry, but is not found in Scotland until relatively recently.

Law There are three quite different sources, none of them with any legal connection, but now indistinguishable. (i) *Law* is the Lowland Scots word for hill, and occurs in innumerable place-names. Early citations of the surname clearly refer to a place: Robert de Lawe had a safe conduct through England in 1428, and James of Law is recorded in Prestwick sixty years later. (ii) A diminutive of **Lawrence**. (iii) A version of **Low**. Law was a common surname in Glasgow in the 16th century. John Law of Lauriston, born in Edinburgh in 1671, was a financier turned gambler and speculator; he became a French citizen and was appointed Comptroller-General of Finance for France. Robert Laws (of Livingstonia), a pioneer missionary from Aberdeen, was born in 1851; and Andrew Bonar Law, Prime Minister from 1922–23, was brought up in Glasgow.

Lawrence The personal name Lawrence originally meant someone from Laurentium, a town in Italy derived from *laurus*, a laurel. Lawrence was also the name of a 3rd-century saint who enjoyed a popular European cult, and the name has cognates in many languages. It is recorded as a forename in Scotland in the 12th century, and appears as a surname about a hundred years later. Richard Laurens was a landholder in Biggar who was obliged to submit to Edward I of England in 1296; John Lourens was a burgess of Aberdeen in 1541; and John Laurance was a notary in Duns in 1663. Lawrence was never especially a Scottish surname, but it appears for some reason to have its chief location in the Aberdeen area.

Lawrie A diminutive of **Lawrence** which is recorded in no fewer than twelve different spellings in the old records. If an Irish origin is indicated, it can be a version of **Lavery**.

Lawson 'Son of Lawrence', through the diminutive **Law**. Richard Lawson was a canon of St Giles in 1370 and John Lawson was in Linton around the same time; Ady Lawson and John Lauson were in Aberdeen in the early 15th century; Richard Lawson was town clerk of Edinburgh in 1482; a contemporary namesake was Lord Justice Clerk of Scotland, and it is the wife of Sir Richard who is commemorated in the name Lady Lawson's Wynd. Lawson is also a common North of England surname.

Leach–s e e **Leitch**

Leadbetter Not a very common surname, which is hardly surprising since it comes from the specialised occupation of beating lead–for utensils or roof-sheeting. Thomas Ledbeter was provost of Linlithgow in 1328; five hundred years later there was an Alexander Leadbetter who was a merchant in Kelso. There are a few in Edinburgh, but not many.

Learmonth This Border surname comes from the lands of Learmonth in Berwickshire. Alexander Leyremonthe was clerk of works of the town and castle of Berwick in 1434; Jacobus Lermonth was a notary in Glasgow twenty years later. The Learmonth family built the castle of Dairsie in Fife, now restored and inhabited again after centuries of dilapidation: Sir James Learmonth was master of the household of James V, and provost of St Andrews in the mid-16th century. There were also landed families of Learmonths in Kelso and Crail. The Russian novelist and poet Lermontov was a descendant of a 17th-century Scots emigrant who had become a mercenary in the Polish army. Now found mainly in Edinburgh.

Leask An obsolete place-name, which was near Slains in Aberdeenshire, is the origin of this surname. Lask is recorded as a territorial designation in the mid-14th century; Umfra Lask is described as 'of that Ilk' (i.e. of Lask). The name migrated to Orkney, and it is nowadays proportionately more frequent there than anywhere else.

Leckie The name of a former barony in Gargunnock, Stirlingshire, it comes from the Gaelic *leacach*, meaning 'flat-stoned' . Murdoch Leckie flourished around the mid-14th century; David Lekky was denounced as a rebel in 1537; Janet Laiky is recorded in Glenisla in 1599 and Euphemia Laikie turns up in Brechin a century later. Some Leckie families who settled in Donegal and Derry in the 1650s claimed to be members of the clan MacGregor. The name cannot now be said to have any particular location in Scotland.

Ledingham Interestingly, this name is an analogical formation on the lines of English ones like Birmingham and Nottingham (where *ing* means 'tribe' and *ham* means 'homestead'). In fact Ledingham originates in Aberdeenshire, and probably comes from the Gaelic word *leideagan*, meaning 'outlying fields'; the surname survived as Ledigan and Ledikin in Mar until the 17th century. George Ledinghame was recorded in Auchinlik, Aberdeenshire, in 1574; John Liddinghame was in Chapeltown in 1603, and George Ledingham was in Gartly in 1798. It is still very much a north-east surname, uncommon elsewhere.

Lee At one time among the fifty commonest surnames in England; so some Scots bearers may be ultimately of English origin. *Lea* or *leigh* can mean a pasture or a forest clearing, and both of these are frequent English place-name elements. The earliest mentions of the surname in Scotland also indicate that Lee is a place: Alan de Leia is recorded in the 12th century, and Phelippe de la Laye figures in the Ragman Roll of 1296. Jenny Lee, Baroness Lee of Ashridge, wife of Aneurin Bevan and Britain's first Arts Minister, was born in Lochgelly of a mining family in 1904. But note that Lees is usually **Gillies**.

Legg / Legge Usually a nickname, from the lower limb; it might have arisen because of length of leg or some such characteristic. Legge is the family name of the earls of Dartmouth, and it has been known in Scotland since at least the 16th century. William Leg was recorded in Newmyll in 1588, Margaret Leg in Stracathro in 1627, and about the same time Patrick Legg was branded as a known thief. James Legge, the distinguished Sinologist, was born in Huntly in 1815. It is in Banffshire that the name is mainly recorded, and it is still common in that area, usually in the spelling Legge.

Leggat Persons who can give their occupation as that of legate have never been very numerous; in some cases the surname may have been bestowed in connection with a play or pageant, and in others Leggat will be a version of a given name such as Leodgard. Whatever the origin, the name has been continually recorded in Scotland since the early 15th century, when an accountant called Adam Legat appeared in the books in Stirling in 1406. Walter and John Legat had safe conducts to England a few years later, and a

Thomas Legat was recorded in Tain in 1477. In the following century, Laurence Legat turns up in Irvine, and Archibald Legate was a burgess freeman of Glasgow. The name is not associated with any particular part of Scotland, and indeed is not exclusively Scottish.

Leighton From various places in England so called (the name means 'leek-farm'). Lathune is recorded in Renfrewshire in the 12th century as a territorial designation; William de Leghtone swore fealty to Edward I at Kinghorn in 1291. Leighton appears in Angus in the 13th century, where it later became the name of several important landed families. Henry Lichtoun was bishop of Moray and Aberdeen successively in the 15th century, and built a great part of Aberdeen cathedral. Alexander Leighton of Usan near Montrose, a 16th-century physician and divine who was a graduate of St Andrews, was condemned by the court of the Star Chamber but later released. His son, Sir Elisha Leighton, was Charles II's secretary for English affairs in Scotland in the 1650s.

Leiper From the Old English word *leap*, meaning 'basket'; Leiper probably refers to the trade of basket-maker and in Scotland at least has nothing to do with leprosy (leper was rendered as 'lipper'). Johannes Leaper was a burgess of Edinburgh in 1189; Walter Lippre turns up in Turriff in 1272; Patrick Leper appears in Edinburgh in 1368 and Andrew Lepar in Aberdeen in 1487; Alan Leppar and Adam Leppayr were recorded in Prestwick a generation later. This gives some idea of the distribution of the name in the early modern period, and the variety of spellings. Nowadays the name is mainly found in the Aberdeen area, sometimes in the spelling Leaper.

Leishman The name, pronounced 'leesh-man', is of unknown origin, but may be related to **Leitch**. Thomas Lescheman was a burgess of Glasgow in the mid 15th century, and a William

Leischman flourished in Kelso about the same time. Margret Leischman was the victim of a savage assault in Dundee in 1553; the name pops up in Lanark and Stirling about this time, and was reputed to have been very frequent in the Falkirk area. William Leechman was principal of Glasgow University in the 18th century; Sir William Leishman, a Glasgow-born bacteriologist, gave his name to a stain for blood and protozoa.

Leitch The Old English word *laece* meant 'doctor', and the word sometimes appears in the early records as an alternative to *medicus*. Leech (doctor) and leech (the aquatic blood-sucker *Hirudinea*) were originally two different words, which were assimilated by popular etymology. Henry Leche appears in Glasgow in 1325, and William le Leche was a burgess of Aberdeen shortly thereafter. John Leach was a canon of Glasgow in the 1360s. Ferchard Leche had a grant of lands in Assynt in 1386. It is not known if any of these were physicians, but it is believed that a family of the name in Logiealmond practised as doctors. John Leich was banned from the kirk in Dundee in 1521 for a year and a day, for 'stroublance (annoyance) of the priest'. The surname was also current in Menteith and in Brechin in the 16th century. Leitch is the usual modern spelling.

Leith From a Brittonic word equivalent to the Welsh *llaith* meaning wet; the port of Edinburgh takes its name from the river whose estuary it occupies. A family called Leith, who held the barony of Restalrig, were burgesses of Edinburgh in the mediaeval period, and gave their name to Leith Wynd. An offshoot of the family, William of Lethe, was a burgess of Aberdeen and a member of parliament in the 1350s. The name later occurs with great frequency in the records of Aberdeen, in which city it is still principally to be found.

Lemon / Lemmon / Limand This group of surnames has nothing whatever to do with the citrus fruit, but is almost always a version of **Lamont**. Limond and Limand are versions to be found in the south west of Scotland. However,the English name Lemon is from an old word *leman* meaning sweetheart.

Lennie The lands of Leny near Callander were awarded to Alan and Margaret of Lany by Alexander II, and the name appears as a territorial designation from the 13th century; it comes from a Celtic river-name of debatable origin. John de Lanyn of Perth figures in the Ragman Roll of 1296. John de Lany was constable of Tarbet in 1325; Robert of Lany was provost of the church of St Andrews in the early 15th century; Donald Lany turns up in Atholl in 1455, and Bartilino Lanye in Edinburgh half a century later. The Orkney Lennies or Linays may however derive their name from the local settlement of Leinay.

Lennon This name is usually thought to be Irish, as was its most celebrated bearer (although he was of more recent Merseyside origin). It was originally O Leannain, 'descendant of Leannan', a name which means 'lover'–see **Lemon**. Occasionally, however, Lennon can be a contraction of **MacLennan**, and may even be a pet form of **Leonard**.

Lennox The ancient name of a district near Dumbarton occupying a strategic position between Highlands and Lowlands. Thought to come from the Gaelic *leamhanach*, meaning 'elm-place', it was the name of one of the great Celtic earldoms of pre-feudal Scotland and achieved fame if not respectability in 1675 when the illegitimate son of Charles II and the Duchess of Portsmouth was created Duke of Lennox at the age of three. Ordinary folk however had taken surnames from the district as early as the 15th century: John de Lennox is recorded in Glasgow in 1428; William Levinax (an unelided form of the Gaelic) was in Kirkcudbright in 1508, and Donald Levenax of Ayrshire was accused of murder a few years later. George Lennox was a bailie in the service of the earls of Cassilis at Glenluce in the 1540s. A Scots merchant named Robert Lenox emigrated to New York in 1784, and his son founded the Lenox Library there.

Leonard Although much more frequent as a given-name (which is how it originated) Leonard is a familiar enough surname, especially in the Glasgow area. It is a reduction of *leon-hard* or 'lion-hardy'–that is, bold as a lion. St Leonard was a popular saint in mediaeval times, the protector of such various groups as peasants, horses and prisoners. Leonard was also common in Ireland as an anglicisation of various unwieldy patronymics.

Leslie Originally the name of a barony in Aberdeenshire, first recorded in the 12th century as Lesslyn; the origin and meaning are obscure. The town of Leslie in Fife is thought to derive its name from the Aberdeenshire one. The surname may come from either source, but is still stronger in the north; the first recorded bearer is a Fleming called Malcolm who was granted the Aberdeenshire lands in the 12th century; Sir Norman de Lechelyn, an Aberdeen laird, was forced to do homage to Edward I in 1296. The family married into the Scottish royal house, and George Leslie was created earl of Rothes in 1457. The fourth earl was father of Norman Leslie, chief participant in the murder of Cardinal Beaton in 1641; John Leslie, son of the 6th earl, became Lord Chancellor of Scotland in 1667 and two years later was created Duke of Rothes. The family had split into two branches, both of which produced distinguished soldiers: Alexander Leslie, later 1st earl of Leven, was commander of the Covenanting army in Scotland, and David Leslie (no relation, but also a Fifer) was his lieutenant general. The use of the name as a forename (male—Leslie, female—Lesley) is of fairly recent origin.

Lewis Despite its Hebridean echoes, this name is not by origin Scottish; it comes from the Norman personal name, Latinized as

Ludovicus, which itself derives from a Germanic name comprising the elements *hlud* 'fame' and *wig* 'warrior' (see Introduction). This became Clovis and Louis in France, while in German-speaking countries it developed into Ludwig. It became immensely popular as a forename in Wales, perhaps by analogy with Llewellyn, and eventually came to be among the most frequent surnames there and in England. Most Scottish Lewises will probably be imports from the south, although a Celtic origin in the personal name *Lugaidh* ('brightness') cannot be ruled out.

Liddell Occurs in several places in England and south Scotland, most notably in Roxburghshire; the name means 'loud dale', and should therefore be pronounced with the accent on the first syllable. It appears as a territorial designation in the person of Galfridus Liddal in Roxburgh in 1266. After the 14th century it seems to have migrated to Aberdeenshire; Nicholas Lyddal was provost of Aberdeen in 1327; John of Lydel was a merchant there a generation later, and William de Lydell was sheriff of the burgh at the same time. In England Liddell is the family name of the barons Ravensworth; in Scotland it is still celebrated as that of the Olympic athlete Eric Liddell, who was born in China of Scots missionary parents and who died in Japanese captivity during the war.

Lilley / Lillie The name Lilley was first recorded in Scotland in 1296, when two Peebles landowners, Wautier and Thomas Lillock or Lilley were obliged to do homage to Edward I of England. Thereafter it appears regularly in the Borders; nowadays it is as common in Glasgow as anywhere. It probably comes from a place-name–e.g. Lilley in Hertfordshire ('flax-field')–although a nearer source could no doubt be found.

Limand–see **Lemon**

Lindsay Lindsey means Lincoln's Island, and was an administrative district in that English shire. The first of the name in Scotland was Sir Walter de Lindeseya, whose father had accompanied David I on his return north to Scotland early in the 12th century, and whose family settled in Lothian and Upper Clydeside. The name Lindsay–albeit with 200 different recorded spellings–subsequently became one of the most notable in Scottish history. The family fell heir to the lands of Crawford; Sir David Lindsay of Crawford and the Byres became one of the Regents of Scotland and perished in 1268 on a Crusade. A subsequent Sir David Lindsay was created earl of Crawford in 1398. Another branch of the family, the Crawford-Lindsays acquired lands in Glenesk in Angus; while yet another produced Sir David Lindsay of the Mount in Fife whose play *Ane Satyr of the Thrie Estaites* retains its popularity as an excoriation of the corrupt society of pre-Reformation times. A.D. Lindsay, Glasgow-born philosopher and educationalist, was Master of Balliol and Vice-Chancellor of Oxford, and founded Keele University.

Linklater An Orkney place-name, from the Old Norse *lyng klettr*– 'heather rock', recorded as a surname in the northern isles from the 15th century onwards. Although still commonest there, the name migrated south at an early stage: Clinclatter was the name of a Kirkcaldy skipper in the 1680s, and Peter Linklater was a quartermaster on the *Bounty* in 1789, supporting Captain Bligh during the mutiny. Eric Linklater, of Orcadian parentage and educated in Aberdeen, was a prolific and accomplished novelist during the immediate post-war period.

Linton Linton is found as a place-name all over the United Kingdom, with a variety of derivations; Scottish places so called are to be found in Peebles, Roxburgh and East Lothian, and involve the Gaelic word *linne* meaning 'pool'. Other Linton settlements can derive from lint (flax), or from the river Lyne (Brittonic *hlynn*–'a torrent'); and all are possible origins of the surname. There were two Lothian lairds of the name who figure in the Ragman Roll of 1296; Thomas Lyntoun was provost of Aberdeen around 1340; James de Lintoune was a bailie in Edinburgh in the 15th century, and John Linton appears in Kirkcudbright in 1677. Most Scottish Lintons are nowadays to be found in the Edinburgh area.

Lister The Old Norse verb *litta* meant 'to dye', and a *litster* was a dyer. The name is still to be found in St Andrews in its original form of Litster. It is recorded as an occupational designation in the 13th century, and two landowners of the name from Berwick and Edinburgh figure in the Ragman Roll of 1296. John Litster was the first professor of Canon Law at St Andrews University in 1410, and the name appears sporadically all over the Lowlands. Latter-day Listers may be of this descent, or may be incomers from England where the name was also current. Alternatively the name might sometimes be an anglicisation of *Mac an Fhleistear* (see **Fletcher**) or a contraction of MacAllester (see **Alexander**). The name is evenly spread thoroughout Scotland.

Lithgow A contraction of Linlithgow, a town in mid-Scotland, whose origin is the Brittonic *llyn llaith cau*–'pool of the damp hollow'. The surname dates from at least the 15th century, when the names of Robert Lithcw and William Lithqw were recorded, the latter in Scone; in the following century James Lithgo turns up in Dundee. William Lithgow of Lanark was a noted 17th century travel-writer. The surname is now little found outside the Edinburgh area.

Litster–see **Lister**

Little Not really a Scottish name, Little is found mainly in the north of England. But its recorded history in this country dates back to the 14th century, when John Litill appears in Lanark and Martin Litill in Aberdour; and the clan of Littles who traditionally occupied the lower part of Eskdale were one of the unruly elements in the western March. The name is still among the top ten in Dumfries and Galloway. Clemens Little made a bequest to Edinburgh University in 1580 which was the foundation of its library. The surname means what it says, and has its equivalent in other languages, including Gaelic (see **Begg**).

Littlejohn Originally a nickname employed to distinguish between two persons of the name of John, it has its opposite in the surname Meiklejohn. Littlejohn is quite common in the Aberdeen area, whereas Meiklejohn occurs, more sparsely, in Fife.

Livingston / Livingstone From a place, now a New Town, in Lothian, meaning 'Levin's toun'; Levin in turn is from an Old English name *Leofwine*, meaning 'dear companion'. Sir William Livingston was granted the barony of Callender by David II in 1346, and his descendants acquired the earldoms of Linlithgow and Callender; these were forfeited after the Jacobite rebellion of 1715. Another branch of the family was represented in the Ragman Roll of 1296 by Sir Archibald de Levingestoun; yet another produced James of Leyffingstoun who was Chamberlain of Scotland in 1456. In the reign of Charles I one of the titled Livingstons was granted certain hereditary rights in Argyll, and some of his adherents formed themselves into a clan with the name of MacDonleavy or **MacLeay**. The MacLeays assumed the laird's name, adding a terminal 'e', and one of them, David Livingstone, the African explorer and missionary, gave it an international currency. An earlier emigrant, Robert Livingston, left Scotland in 1673 and his family became hugely influential in the USA during the colonial period.

Lobban A Moray surname which may come from the Gaelic *laban* or *lopan*, 'muddy place', although a persistent tradition derives it from *loban*, a peat-basket. (The progenitor of the tribe was said to be a MacLennan who hid under such a receptacle). Sir Charles Lowbane is recorded in Strathnairn in 1542, and William Lobane in Inverness a little later; John Loban was tenant of the Marquess of Huntly in 1600. Two wayward contemporaries were Robert Lobein from Deer, 'an idle and masterless man', and Jonat Lobane, accused of a murder in Inverness. The name is still seldom found away from the north-east.

Lochhead An English-language equivalent of **Kinloch**, it originally referred to someone from the top-end of the lake. (But illogically Kinloch Rannoch is at the *bottom* end). The name appears first in the Ragman Roll of 1296, when Gilbert de Lakenheued of Lanarkshire and Wautier de Lagenheuede of Aberdeenshire were forced to submit to Edward I. Thereafter the name is found most commonly in the south-west; James Locheid was a burgess and guild brother of Glasgow in 1626; much later the name became a household word in the city in connection with furnishing and latterly with funerals.

Locke There is nothing particularly Scottish about this name, which can be either a metonymic term for a locksmith, or a lock-keeper, or a curly-haired person. John Lock of Roxurghshire figures in the Ragman Roll of 1296; another John Lock was a professor in St Andrews University in 1464, and later became rector of Finavon and canon of Brechin. Sande Loke was a tailor in Dundee in the 1560s. The name was quite common in the Glasgow area from then onwards.

Lockhart A typical Germanic compound personal name (see Introduction); its components mean 'bolt' and 'hard', and its French form is *Locard*. The tradition is that two soldiers known as Stephen and Simon Locard settled in Scotland in the 12th century and acquired great wealth and influence, giving their names to the settlements of Stevenston, Simonston and Craiglockhart. Historically, the name of Maucolum Lockare of Ayrshire figures in the Ragman Roll of 1296, and the surname also turns up in Kelso about the same time. George Lokert, logician and theologian, was appointed rector of St Andrews University in 1522; he later became Dean of Glasgow. George Lockhart, laird of Carnwath and staunch opponent of the Union of 1707, was a Tory politician in the reign of Queen Anne; he was killed in a duel in 1731. His brother Philip was a noted Jacobite who was taken prisoner and shot after the battle of Preston in 1715. John Gibson Lockhart conducted battles of a literary sort; editor of the (Tory) *Quarterly Review* and known as 'The Scorpion', he married the elder daughter of Sir Walter Scott and became the Shirra's first biographer.

Logan / Logie / Loggie All of these come from the Gaelic word *lag* meaning ' a hollow', with its derivatives *lagan* ('little hollow') and *lagach* ('place of hollows'), giving rise to a variety of place-names, and at a very early stage to surnames. Robert Logan is recorded in Dryburgh in 1204, Adam de Logan in Gowrie in 1226, and Thurbrand de Logan in Cunningham in 1272. The Ragman Roll of 1296 contains no less than four landowners of the name, from Montrose, Dumfries, Lanark and Wigtown. John Logan was clerk of the royal kitchen in the 1320s, and Donald Logan was 'reader in the Irish [Gaelic] tongue' in Sutherland in 1569. Logans were a landed family in Angus for many centuries, and the last of the lairds died unmarried in 1802. The Logies have almost as long a history; Wauter de Logy was a Fife laird who submitted to Edward I in 1296; Sir John of Logy conspired against Robert the Bruce; Phillip de Logy appears in Dundee in 1321, and Alexander Logy was a burgess of Aberdeen in 1457. Gawin Logie, Principal of St Leonard's College, St Andrews, was an early exponent of the Reformed doctrine. Loggie is a variant of Logie; but Logue is Irish.

Long The southern form of **Lang** and **Laing**; it nevertheless appears very early in the Scottish records. The Latinised name of *Johannes Longus* is recorded in Soutra in the late 12th century; Adam Long appears in Dumfries c. 1259; Gregory le Long was a burgess of Dundee in 1268, and William Long turns up in Dryburgh in the 1350s. The name cannot be assigned to any one place.

Longmuir There are at least two places so-called, one near Ayr and the the other near Kirkintilloch, and the surname comes from one or other; the meaning is of course 'long moor'. Elice de la Longmore and Robert de Langemore were Lothian lairds who figured in the Ragman Roll of 1296, as did Johan de Langemore from Ayrshire. John Langmour was a presbyter in Dalkeith in 1477, and Henry Langmuir was a burgess of Renfrew in the 1570s.

Lorimer A lorimer was a maker or seller of spurs or other bits of harness. The word comes from the Latin *lorum*, meaning 'strap'; the name has had long Scottish associations, starting with Hugh Lorimarius who was granted land near Perth by William the Lion. It was found in Midlothian in the 15th century, later in Stirling and Dumfries, and was very common in Broughty Ferry when it was a fishing community and not a suburb of Dundee. James Lorimer, born in Aberdalgie near Perth in 1818, was the first of a notable Scots family; a jurist himself, he became Professor of Public Law at Edinburgh University; his elder son was a famous painter and another son was Sir Robert Lorimer, famous for his neo-mediaeval work, architect of the Scottish National War Memorial in Edinburgh Castle and the Thistle Chapel in St Giles; a grandson, Hew Lorimer, was a noted sculptor who died in 1993.

Louden / Loudon / Lowden Usually from Loudun in Ayrshire (Old Celtic *Lugudunon*–'fort of Lugus'). The lands of Loudoun were granted by charter to one James, son of Lamb, in the late 12th century; he took his surname from his property as was common practice. James' daughter Margaret married Reginald de Crawford, sheriff of Ayr, whose family duly got the inheritance. John de Lowden was vicar of Kilpatrick in 1418, and Nicholas de Lowdon was in Irvine at the same time. The non-Ayrshire Loudens bear a name which, found originally in Fife, appears as a variant of the word Lothian.

Love Probably a nickname from the Old French word *louve*, meaning 'she-wolf'; this is perhaps corroborated by the first Scottish recording of the name which is in the Latinised form of Walter Lupus ('wolf')–he was a Dundee burgess of the 13th century. But the name may also have been from the term of endearment. There was a Thomas Lufe in Glasgow in the 1430s, and a Jhone Luyff there a generation later. William Lufe and Ranald Lufe were put to the horn as rebels in 1534; and John Lufe was burgh chamberlain of Renfrew in 1567. Lovie is the Northeastern version of the name; in the Banffshire village of of Whitehills, there were at one time eighteen families called Lovie.

Low / Lowe Possible derivations: (i) a contraction of **Lowrie**; and indeed the old pronunciation of Low (to rhyme with cow) is still occasionally heard. (ii) a version of **Love**; and (iii)–perhaps the most obvious–a nickname indicating shortness of stature. Whatever its source, the name has always been common all over Scotland, and belongs to no particular area. Nicholas Loue was recorded in Scone in 1331, William Low in Angus in 1473; in the 1580s Robert Low is found in Fife and John and Robert Low in Brechin.

Lowrie A diminutive of **Lawrence**, and a variant of **Laurie**. Gilbert Lowrie appears in Coldingham in 1497, and David and Robert Lowrie in Irvine in the 1520s; Thomas Loure is found in Doune in 1540 and Joseph Lowrye in Lenzie a century later.

Lowson Usually taken to be a variant of **Lawson**; it was formerly spelt Louson and is still frequently pronounced to rhyme with advowson, so perhaps there is also a connection with **Low**. A Lowson was a burgess of Aberdeen in the early 1400s, and Fynlay Lowson was in Coupar Angus at the same time. A century later Andrew Lousone was recorded in Aberdeen, while Hugh Louson was a prisoner of war in England. The young John Lowson sought legal protection from a scheming uncle in Dundee in 1521. The name is still common in Angus.

Lucas / Luke The original reference was to 'the man from Lucania'. Both forms gained great popularity as Christian names through the third evangelist, and both gave rise to surnames. In Scotland they were sometimes familiarised as Luckie and MacCluckie, while Lucas was popular in Ireland. There were persons of the surname Luke in Berwickshire in the 15th century, and later in Glasgow. Henry Louk appears in Linlithgow in 1530; John Luke or Louk was burgh chamberlain of Rutherglen in the 1560s. William Luck or Luik was a member of the Scots parliament for Forfar in the mid 17th century.

Lumsden A place in Coldingham parish, Berwickshire, named after some unknown person whose given name was Lumb. Lumsden appears in the records as a territorial designation from the 12th century onwards, and Adam and Roger de Lummesdene figure in the Ragman Roll of 1296 as men of substance in Berwickshire. Offshoots of these families acquired lands in Fife and Aberdeenshire in the 14th century, but the name (with its variant Lumsdaine) is still principally associated with the south of Scotland. Some bearers of the name apparently joined the Scots Guards in France, and the muster rolls contain bizarre spellings such as Alomesden and Le Musten.

Lundie There are several places so called, in Angus, Perthshire and Fife, and the name probably comes from an old Gaelic word *lon* meaning marsh. Malcolm of Lundie, a 13th-century Angus laird, was appointed to be the king's door-ward and adopted a surname from his occupation (see **Dorward**), but no doubt some of his kin stuck with the name Lundie. William Lundie of that Ilk, who lived in the late 15th century, was of the Fife stock and indeed was sheriff of the county; the name recurs frequently in the Fife records. Robert Lundy fled Dundee in 1644 in fear of the onslaught of Montrose's army and was fined for his cowardice. The name is now mostly found in the Glasgow area.

Lyall An Old Norse personal name Liulfr, embodying the word *ulfr* ('wolf'), was anglicised to Lyall and became quite common as a surname. There was a John Liel or Lyel in Brechin in the 1420s, and a William Lyell in Edinburgh at the same time. Andrew Liolle was treasurer of Aberdeen in 1468, and Alexander Liel was a burgess there a bit later. Sir Charles Lyell, a founder of modern scientific geology, was born near Kirriemuir in 1797. The name has to be distinguished from **Lyle**.

Lyle Usually a variant of the English name Lisle, referring to any island-dweller or to someone from Lille (*l'île*) in France. Several Northumbrian knights settled in Scotland in the 12th century and used the territorial designation *'de Insula'*; John de Ille of Berwickshire and Richard de Isle of Lothian both figure in the Ragman Roll of 1296. Sir Robert Lyle was created Lord Lyle around 1436; his issue became extensive landowners in Central Scotland, but the peerage became extinct in the 16th century. John Lile of Stoneypath was charged with assisting thieves in 1530; William Leill is recorded in Stirlingshire in 1691.

Lynch An Irish name which took root in Glasgow in the 20th century and flourished. Benny Lynch, born in the city in 1913, became world flyweight titleist in 1935; the name is now found all over Scotland. It is a version of the patronymic *O Loingsigh*, which means 'descendant of the mariner' and comes from Galway.

Lynn The Gaelic word *linne* (meaning pool or channel, not waterfall) is the basis of very many Scottish place-names, and is a possible source of the surname Lynn. An Ayrshire family of the name appears in the early records; and William and Richard de Lynn were well-doing burgesses of Perth in the 13th century. The most usual source however must be the Irish patronymic *MacFhloinn* ('son of the ruddy one'), shortened to Flynn and assimilated to Lynn. Most Scottish Lynns (and Flynns) are to be found in the areas of Irish immigration.

Lyon / Lyons From Lyons in Eure in Normandy (Celtic *Lugudunon* –see **Louden**). The earliest records of the name here are to be found in Restenneth near Forfar in 1321 in the persons of Johannes filius Leonis and Hugo filius Leonis. Twenty years later John Lyon had a charter of the lands of Forteviot and Forgandenny near Perth. Sir John Lyon, chamberlain of Scotland in the late 14th century, was granted lands at Glamis by Robert II; one of his descendants was created earl of Kinghorn in 1606, the title later being changed to Kinghorn and Strathmore, and the family name to Bowes-Lyon. Queen Elizabeth the Queen Mother was a daughter of the 14th earl of Strathmore. There is a tradition that some of the Glamis tenantry followed the clannish practice of adopting the laird's surname. Robert Lyon, a local Episcopal clergyman, became chaplain to Lord Ogilvie's regiment in the '45 and was executed for treason in 1746. The name was also very common in Ireland.

MAC

MacAdam–see **Adam**

MacAleer–see **MacLure**

MacAllan–see **Allan**

MacAllister–see **Alexander**

MacAndrew–see **Anderson**

MacAlpine 'Son of Alpein', a Gaulish forename, cognate with the Welsh Elphin, and the name of several Pictish kings. The son of one of them, known as Kenneth MacAlpin, became the first sovereign of the united kingdom of Picts and Scots, the forerunner of the modern kingdom of Scotland. According to a tradition mentioned (and possibly invented) by Sir Walter Scott, the Clan Alpine comprised MacGregors, Grants, MacKinnons, Mac-Quarries, MacNabs and MacAulays, but there is little historical evidence of the MacAlpines ever forming a coherent clan. A John MacAlpyne is recorded in Perthshire in 1260, and another of the same name was prior of the Dominicans in Perth before becoming one of the Scottish reformers in the 1530s; the name has always been most commonly found in Stirlingshire and Lennox, although it was an Islay schoolmaster, Neil MacAlpine, who in 1832 compiled the well-thumbed Gaelic dictionary. Sir Robert McAlpine, a Lanarkshire man, made a name and a fortune for himself as a builder around the turn of the 20th century.

MacAnally / MacInally / MacNally The Gaelic is *mac an fhailghigh*, meaning 'son of the frail or feeble man'. The Scottish MacInallys were said to be an offshoot of the MacFarlanes in Dumbartonshire; but the name has always been much commoner in Ireland.

MacArdle In Gaelic, *Ardghail*, meaning 'of high valour'. This is an Irish clan, a branch of the MacMahons, and the name is not recorded in Scotland until modern times.

MacArthur Arthur was the name of the legendary hero of British resistance to the Anglo-Saxon conquerors, and from whom the clan fancifully claims descent. In historical times, the MacArthurs were all-powerful in Lorne, and were made hereditary keepers of the castle of Dunstaffnage by Robert the Bruce. James I however decided that they required to be checked; the chief was beheaded and the estates forfeited, and the Campbells succeeded them as strong-arm men in the West Highlands. Nonetheless the MacArthurs continue to figure in the records as hereditary pipers to the MacDonalds of the Isles. Later representatives have kept the name shining: General Arthur MacArthur, of Scottish parentage, became Lieutenant-General of the USA in 1906, and his son General Douglas MacArthur was one of the greatest military commanders of modern times.

MacAskill Asketill was an Old Norse personal name, meaning something like 'sacrificial vessel of the Gods', and was frequently shortened to Askill, or Ascaidh in its Gaelic spelling. MacAskills and Maccaskills, originally from the north-west, are now found mainly in Glasgow. MacCaskie and Caskie were usually Galloway names, now rather rare.

MacAteer The Irish spelling of **MacIntyre**, although there is not necessarily any kinship with the Scottish clan.

MacAulay A conflation of two different names, now hopelessly confused and not to be distinguished on linguistic evidence alone. (i) from the Irish personal name *Amhalghadh* (pronounced Aulay); MacAulays are found in Lennox in 1285, and the name figures in the Ragman Roll a decade later (see Introduction); Sir Aulay

MacAulay of Ardencaple was a vassal of the Earl of Lennox and appears to have retained his lands until the late 18th century. (ii) from the Norse name Olafr, which came to the Hebrides by way of the Viking invaders (Ullapool means 'Olaf's place'). The early history of the Hebridean MacAulays is unknown, and the earliest reference to the clan is not until the 17th century, when they were active in the Montrose campaigns. John MacAulay, who died in 1789, was a Hebridean pastor and father of Zachary, the noted philanthropist and slave-trade abolitionist, and of Aulay, writer and preacher. Zachary's son was Thomas Babington Macaulay, first Baron Macaulay, Whig historian and one of the first of the great anglicised Highlanders.

MacAuslan This means 'Son of Absolom' and was the original patronymic of the clan **Buchanan**. Absolom, son of MacBed, was a 13th-century churchman from the Loch Lomond area, and those of his kinsmen who retained the MacAuslan surname formed a small Dunbartonshire clan, some of whom seem to have enjoyed the designation 'of Buchanan', and in the 16th century embraced the **Buchanan** surname and followed its banner. The remaining MacAuslans led a precarious existence as a neighbour of the Campbells; in the 17th century some of them took the part of the proscribed MacGregors, with dire results. The surname is now mostly to be found in the Glasgow area.

MacAvoy–see **MacKelvie**

MacBain / MacBean These names can be derived from the Celtic saint Beathan, whose name comes from the Gaelic word *beatha* meaning life, and thus connects with the forename **MacBeth**. Or either name could be a contraction of *mac ghille bhan*–'son of the fair lad' (see **Bain**). Historically the MacBeans (pronounced Macbain) were a small Highland clan with strong Jacobite sympathies, probably following the banner of the clan MacIntosh and performing deeds of hopeless valour at Culloden. A more peaceable clansman, Alexander MacBean, was one of the compilers of Dr Samuel Johnson's dictionary.

MacBeath / MacBeth Macbeth is the older form, and was a celebrated royal forename. The Gaelic words *mac beatha* mean literally 'son of life', and by extension 'religious person' or 'one of the chosen'. The historical Macbeth, who lived from 1005 to 1057, was mormaer (thane) of Moray and became king of Scots after killing Duncan in battle (Shakespeare was not writing history). As a surname, MacBeath is the commoner spelling, but the aspirated forms of MacVeigh, MacVey and MacVie are most usually found. This is a family and not a clan name, and was to be found all over Gaeldom, including Ireland; in many cases it was later anglicised to **Beaton**.

MacBrayne In Gaelic, *Mac a Bhriuthainn*–'son of the judge'. This was a hereditary office in parts of the Highlands and islands, and the original MacBraynes would have regarded themselves as part of the service sector rather than as a separate clan. Angus Macbreochane is recorded in Islay in 1503, and the name was scattered around the south west Highlands. It is now rather uncommon, but celebrated as that of a contractor who was perceived as having a monopoly of transport in the area; an irreverent parody of the 24th psalm (metrical version) was current seventy years ago– 'The earth belongs unto the Lord/ And all that it contains;/ Except of course the Western Isles,/ For they are D. MacBrayne's'.

MacBride Usually a contraction of *mac ghille Brighde*–'son of the servant of Bridget', who was the 6th-century abbess of Kildare and both virgin and saint. John McGilbride was captain of Bute from 1370—75; and the archdeacon of the Isles in 1476 was one Makkilbreid. Although MacBride is an old name in Arran, it is commonest in Ireland, and most Scottish MacBrides probably came across in the 19th century.

MacCabe Scots-Irish, from the personal name Caba, which apparently relates to the wearing of a cape. The name first appeared in the Hebrides, its bearers traditionally of Norse origin; MacCabes however turn up in Ireland in 1320 as galloglasses or freebooting soldiers. The name is mentioned in the 16th-century Book of the Dean of Lismore as being a rarity in the Highlands, although there was a John McKape who was taken prisoner in Dundee's campaign in 1689. The wide currency of the name in 20th-century Scotland is probably due to Irish immigration, for the name had become common in the midland counties of Ireland by the late mediaeval period.

MacCafferty An Irish surname, from the Gaelic *mac each mharcaigh*, and meaning 'son of the horse-rider'. The name is not recorded in Scotland before the present century, but has for long been common in Donegal and Derry.

MacCaig 'Son of Taig', a personal name meaning poet or philosopher. Usually found in Ayrshire and Galloway, it occasionally turned up in south west Argyll; and it was in Oban that an eccentric bearer of the name built what is known as McCaig's folly. It also appears in the shortened form of Keague, which is an Ulster name. In the late 17th century, Teague was a nickname for an Irishman (preceding 'Paddy' and 'Mick'); it is the same word as Taig.

MacCall 'Son of Cathal', a Celtic personal name meaning 'wager of war'; MacCall is a more frequent rendering of MacKail and MacHale, but it is not to be confused with **MacColl**. Although of Gaelic origin, MacCall appears first in the Lowlands before 1500, particularly in Ayrshire and Dumfries.

MacCance–see **MacInnes**

MacCallum Calum was and is a popular Christian name in Gaelic-speaking circles; its earlier form was Colm, and is the same as that of St Columba; it appears in a different form in **Malcolm**. Although overtaken in the power struggle by the clan Campbell, the MacCallums were made hereditary constables of Craignish castle in the 15th century. Another branch received a charter to the lands of Poltalloch, still held by MacCallums, although at one point the name was assimilated to Malcolm for reasons which are by no means clear. Gilbert MacCalme was a merchant in Ayr in 1632, and Iain M'Callum was murdered at Dunaverty in 1647. Although still common in Argyllshire, MacCallum has recently lost its place in the top hundred Scottish surnames.

MacCann From the Irish personal name Cana, meaning a wolf-cub; alternative forms are MacCana and McGann. The MacCanns were lords of Clanbrassil, a district of Co Armagh on the southern shore of Lough Neagh; the name is still common in the area, although the power of the clan declined at the end of the Middle Ages; it was no doubt brought to Scotland in the 19th century.

MacCarthy An anglicised form of the Gaelic *Mac Carthaigh*, meaning 'loving'. This familiar surname is not recorded in Scotland until quite recently; it is however the commonest *Mac* name in Ireland, and its bearers have been prominent in that country's history from earliest times.

MacCartney 'Son of Artaine', a personal name with the same root as **MacArthur**; MacArtney was a common surname in the Stewartry from the early 16th century onwards. Gilbert McCartnay is recorded in Galloway in 1529, and there was a Thomas McCartney in Wigtownshire about the same time. The Macartneys of Auchinleck were an old Ayrshire family, who established branches in the counties of Antrim, Down and Armagh; the surname is still very common in Ireland, where it is sometimes abbreviated to Carton.

MacChristie–see **Christie**

MacClure Usually from the Gaelic *mac gille Uidhir*–'son of Odhar's servant'. MacClures were found in large numbers in Galloway and the south west, and three of them (all with different spellings) are recorded in 1526 as followers of the earl of Cassilis, and all on a murder charge. A woman of the name from Galloway was sent to the plantations in 1684: her name had become corrupted to McWhore. A more deserving Ayrshire man, William MacClure (1763–1840) became known as the Father of American Geology. There were also Hebridean MacClures whose name probably has a different sourc e – *mac gille Dheoradha*–'son of the pilgrim's servant' (see **Dewar**).

MacCluskey / MacCluskie An Irish name, an anglicised form of *Mac Bloscaidhe*, from the personal name Bloscadh whose root is apparently *blosc* meaning loud-voiced. The MacCluskeys were a sept of the O Kanes of Ulster, and the name makes only a relatively recent appearance in Scotland.

MacClymont–see **Lamond**

MacColl The son of Coll, a Celtic personal name and that of one of the semi-legendary kings of Ireland and progenitor of the MacDonalds. Coll has always been a favourite MacDonald forename, and it is thought that the MacColls were originally an offshoot of that clan. Alasdair Mac Colla, a son of Coll Ciotach MacDonald, was commander of the Highland and Irish forces in the Montrose campaigns of 1644-5, and attained fame as one of the greatest of Celtic warriors. A number of MacColls settled around Appin and Ballachulish, and followed the banner of the Stewarts of Appin in 1745-6. Eoghan MacColla was a 19th century bard who emigrated to Canada in 1849 but retained enough regard for his native land to publish the magnificent collection called *Clarsach nam Beann*.

MacComb / MacCombie / MacOmie / MacOmish–see **MacTavish**

MacConnell In Scotland this is usually a variant of **MacDonald**, and found mainly in the south west, where Gaelic spelling was more than usually erratic. There are however Irish MacConnells, from the personal name Conall, of uncertain origin; some of these MacConnells may have arrived in Scotland in the last century.

MacConnachie From the Gaelic patronymic *mac Dhonnchaidh*, son of **Duncan**. MacConnachie is, like many another, a name belonging to several families rather than to a single clan. MacConnachies are found in Bute in the early 16th century, almost to the exclusion of any other surnames; others proliferate among the Campbells around Loch Awe and other parts of Argyll; and some adherents of the Robertsons of Struan in Perthshire took the name of Donachie or MacConnachie (see **Robertson**). There are at least eighteen reputable ways of spelling this surname, not counting howlers such as M'Onoghuy.

MacCormack The personal name Cormac was very popular throughout Gaeldom (it comes from *corb mac*, meaning 'charioteer'); MacCormack is a surname with many points of origin, and often of no great antiquity. Because of the fame and charisma of the tenor John Count MacCormack (1885-1945) the name has come to be predominantly associated with Ireland, but its Scottish credentials are unassailable (even though the spelling as often as not is MacCormick); the first Scottish bearer of the name on record is Gillecrist mac Cormaic in Aberdeenshire in 1132.

MacCracken–see **MacNaughton**

MacCraw–see **MacRae**

MacCreath–see **MacRae**

MacCrimmon 'Son of Rumein' a Gaelic version of Norse *Hromundr* ('famed protector'). This is a monogenetic surname, for the MacCrimmons all apparently descend from a Skye family of musical genius who were hereditary pipers to the MacLeods of Dunvegan for a period of over two hundred years–from 1595 to 1801. There are a few MacCrimmons in the Glasgow area, but the name was never common. See also **Grimmond**.

MacCrorie–see **MacRory**

MacCue–see **MacKay**

MacCulloch A Gaelic personal name, derived from *cullach* meaning a wild boar. As a surname it is first recorded in Galloway and the south west; Thomas Maculagh, later sheriff of Wigton, figures in the Ragman Roll in 1296. Another branch appeared in Ross-shire. Horatio MacCulloch was a very popular Victorian landscape painter; and J.R. MacCulloch, a graduate of Edinburgh University, a highly influential political economist.

MacCutcheon–see **Hutchinson**

MacDade / MacDaid It is strange that David, for long the most popular personal name in Scotland, should not have produced a familiar *Mac* name. *MacDaibheid*, shortened to MacDade, is an Irish name from Donegal and Derry and only recently reached Glasgow. It is not often found elsewhere; and MacDevitt is even rarer.

MacDermott / MacDiarmid Diarmid was the legendary hero of the Fingalian story of love, treachery and death from the bristle of a dead boar, and he is claimed as the progenitor of the clan **Campbell**, whose crest incorporates a boar's head. The Mac-Diarmids, although not a Scottish clan in their own right, are of the Campbell race, and were to be found in Campbell territory. The Glenlyon MacDiarmids claimed to be the aboriginal race of the district, and the name is still found in Breadalbane. It was however in Ireland that the name proliferated, and the Irish spelling (MacDermott) is now the usual one. The MacDermotts were an important clan in Connacht, Sligo and Galway, and by the 18th century the name had become one of the commonest in the country. Some of the clan emigrated to Scotland in the 1840s; and in this case the spelling of the name is some guide as to its provenance.

MacDevitt–see **MacDade**

MacDonagh–see **Duncan**

MacDonald Volumes have been written on the clan Donald and its various branches. *Domnuill* (anglicised to **Donald**) is the oldest Gaelic personal name, and at one time was almost synonymous with Highlander (just as MacDonald now has the worldwide connotation of fast food). The progenitor of the clan had a distinguished ancestry: his grandfather was Somerled, scourge of the south-west Highlands, and his grandmother was daughter of Olaf, king of Man. The first MacDonald possession was Islay; the family became Lords of the Isles, extended their possessions on the mainland by marriage (including a royal alliance), and eventually succeeded to the earldom of Ross. In the chaos which followed the forfeiture of the Lordship of the Isles in 1493, the different branches of the clan developed under their own chiefs. The main branches of Clan Donald were of Sleat in Skye, Clanranald in Moidart, Glengarry, Keppoch in Lochaber, and Glencoe. Since the original Gaelic pronunciation of *Mac Dhomnuill* would be approximately 'mak-hoonil', there have been several attempts to render this into English, including Macdonnel (the spelling favoured by the families of Glengarry and Keppoch) and MacConnell (the Irish version). Many MacDonald clansmen would originally have had ephemeral surnames which they later discarded (see Introduction): Alexander McDonald the 18th-century Gaelic poet was known by the patronymic of *Alasdair Mac Mhaighstir Alasdair* ('Alexander, son of Master Alexander'), and probably took the clan surname when he matriculated at Glasgow University. There were vast migrations from the MacDonald heartlands to North America and elsewhere in the 18th and 19th centuries; neverthless, MacDonald remains by far the commonest *Mac* name in Scotland.

MacDougall In Gaelic *dubh gall* means 'dark stranger', possibly to distinguish the darker-haired Danes from the fair-haired Norwegians. The original Dougall was the eldest son of King Somerled and heir to what was left of the Lordship of the Isles; his successors became the MacDougall lords of Argyll, a clan whose power diminished when it opposed Robert the Bruce and subsequently lost most of its possessions. Nevertheless the MacDougalls remained a power in the land, and were reckoned to be good for 500 men in the preparations for the 1715 Rising. Nor were they confined to Argyll: MacDougalls were also numerous in Galloway and Kirkcudbright, where the name sometimes became McCoull and even Cole; Sir Dugald M'Dowille was sheriff of Dumfries in 1312. In the following century several members of the clan moved to north-west Ireland as galloglasses or freebooting soldiers, and settled there; the spelling of the name became MacDowell, as evidenced by the village of Lismacdowell in Co Roscommon. The Irish name Doyle is a version of Dougall.

MacDowell–see **MacDougall**

MacDuff The name MacDuff, although very celebrated, is in fact rather rare; the historicity of Macduff, Thane of Fife, who appears in Shakespeare's *Macbeth*, is very questionable; in any case, the ancient earldom of Fife came to an end before surnames were fixed. But ordinary MacDuffs, without regal or ducal connections, were to be found as early as the mid 13th century; a M'Duif is recorded in Argyll, and there were MacIlduffs in Galloway. See also **Duff**.

MacEachern A reduced form of the Gaelic *mac each tighearna* which means 'son of the horse-lord'. Alan MacEachern was chief of the clan in 1499; the name is commemorated in the place-name Kilkerran in Kintyre, the heart of the clan-lands. The surname underwent several mutations over the centuries, including MacCochran in the 1680s, and may even occasionally have been rendered as **Cochrane**.

MacElroy–see **MacIlroy**

MacEwan Son of **Ewan**, or *Eoghann* in its Gaelic form–a favourite baptismal name in the Highlands. The origins of the clan are somewhat obscure, but the progenitor is taken to be Ewen of Otter on Lochfyneside in Argyll, whose descendants became landless and chiefless in the reign of James I. Thereafter the MacEwans seem to exist on the fringes of Highland society, holding such posts as bards, sheannachies and genealogists to the Campbells and the MacDougalls, as well as joining in some of the less reputable pursuits of the 'broken clans'. The surname is surprisingly widespread from an early date, becoming common in Lennox and Galloway; it inevitably reached Ireland also, where it became confused with the native surname MacKeon which actually means 'son of Ian'. Sir John MacEwen (1868-1948), was an unjustly neglected composer from Galloway.

MacFadyan / MacFadzean The 'z' is pronounced 'y', and the name means 'son of **Paton**'–the Scots equivalent of Paddy. The earliest recorded bearer of the surname is Malcolm Macpadene who lived in Kintyre around 1300, and the name became widespread in the Hebrides, particularly Mull and Tiree. It also became common in Ulster, with the local spelling MacFadden. MacFadyen is a good example of a *Mac* surname which is not that of a clan; it was simply a Gaelic translation of a Lowland name (see Introduction); indeed the surname Patonson was current in the 15th century along with MacFadyen but is probably now obsolete.

MacFall–see **MacPhail**

MacFarlane From the Old Irish word *Partholon*, which exists as a name in its own right but may have some connection with the Hebrew name Bartholomew. The first recorded Parlan, founder of the clan, had inherited the property of Arrochar on Loch Long, with which the MacFarlanes have ever since been associated. The last chief to reside in Scotland (he died in 1767) was a model of his kind, and earned Boswell's approval for taking exception to the fact that General Wade had addressed him as *Mr* MacFarlane : 'I and I only am MacFarlane'. A branch of the clan settled in Aberdeenshire and the name spread to Braemar and Strathspey, and eventually all over the world; but the MacFarlanes have been landless and chiefless for more than a century.

Mac Fee / MacFie–see **MacPhee**

MacGarry Originally *mac Fhearadhaigh*, an Irish personal name of unknown origin. This name is not native to Scotland, and is found in the Glasgow area as a result of immigration.

MacGarvey A Donegal name; the stem incorporates the Gaelic word *garbh*, meaning rough. Although this name was recorded in Wigtown in the 16th century, its popularity in the west of Scotland is probably due to Irish immigration. See also **Garvie**.

MacGee / MacGhee / MacGhie–see **MacKay**

MacGilchrist–see **Gilchrist**

MacGibbon–see **Gilbert**

MacGill The Gaelic word *gall* means Lowlander or stranger, and **Gall** is a familiar enough surname in Scotland. *Mac an ghoill*, 'son of the stranger', is anglicised to MacGill, a surname which appeared first in Galloway, and is still common in the south-west. It also appeared in Jura in the 18th century. (The name is however even commoner in Ireland, where it is said to derive from the personal name *Giolla*, and often takes the form Magill). James McGill, born in Glasgow in 1744, was a successful fur-trader who is remembered as the founder of the McGill University in Montreal. It was a Wigtown family who produced Donald McGill (1875—1962), 'the Leonardo of the comic postcard', a connoisseur of haggis, heather and hairy knees, who along with Harry Lauder, created the loathsome image of the music-hall Scot.

MacGillivray *Mac gille braith* means 'son of the servant of judgement'. The first Gillivray traditionally left his homeland in the West Highlands and moved east to settle in Strathnairn, ancestral territory of the clan Chattan confederation, headed by the MacIntoshes. Alexander MacGillivray, the chief, led the men of clan Chatten at Culloden, and died heroically leading a furious charge which almost annihilated Cumberland's left wing. A remnant of the original MacGillivray clan continued to preserve the surname in Mull as adherents of the MacLeans, but the Invernessshire branch lost all after the '45. The MacGillivrays emigrated in large numbers to North America where they were more than usually successful. William MacGillivray, an enterprising fur trader, became a leading Canadian politician, while Lachlan MacGillivray, the son of a Red Indian mother, negotiated with the US government after the the American Revolution in the unusual capacity of Cree Indian Chief.

MacGilp–see **MacKillop**

MacGinlay / MacGinley–see **MacKinlay**

MacGinty The name of a Donegal sept, which migrated to Glasgow in large numbers in the 19th century. It was originally *mac Fionntaigh*, from the Gaelic *fionntagh*, meaning 'follower of Fingal', the warrior-bard of Gaelic mythology: a good example of a beautiful Celtic name which with anglicization becomes faintly comical.

MacGlashan From the Gaelic *mac glasain*–'son of the grey or green man', presumably with reference to clothing. The name is found occasionaly in the West Highlands from the 16th century (and also in Derry), but with migration it underwent contraction to **Glass** or translation to **Gray**, and is much commoner in these forms.

MacGlone–see **MacLean**

MacGlynn–see **Flynn**

MacGoldrick From Irish Gaelic *mag Ualghairg*, a personal name of unknown origin. The name is not native to Scotland, and owes its frequency in the Glasgow area to Irish settlement.

MacGonagle / MacGonigall / MacGonigle From an Irish personal name Congail, meaning 'high valour'. The name is said to be notable in Ireland for the number of distinguished ecclesiastics it has produced; in Scotland, whither it migrated in large numbers, it is best known as that of the greatest (or worst) writer of unconsciously comic verse.

MacGorrie–see **Gorrie**

MacGovern An Irish name, brought to Scotland in recent times. It is an anglicized form of the (Irish) Gaelic *mag shambradhain*–'son of summer'; the name has its home in Co. Cavan, where it is embodied in the village of Ballymagauran, 'Shamrain's place'.

MacGowan From the Gaelic *mac gobhan*–'son of the smith'–see Gow. MacGowans were dispersed all over the Highlands and never formed a coherent clan. A separate Lowland tribe of M'Gowans, claiming descent from Owen the Bold, king of the Strathclyde Britons, appears in Nithsdale at the beginning of the

12th century; another flourished in Co. Cavan in Ireland: many of the Irish MacGowans changed their name to Smith, and no doubt such change was of widespread occurrence in Scotland too.

MacCraw–see **MacRae**

MacGregor The clan Gregor claims descent from the royal house of Alpin, through Griogar, the son of Kenneth MacAlpine; but there is considerable doubt and confusion about this, and the first historical chief is Iain MacGregor who died in 1390. The misfortunes of the clan began with the Wars of Independence, when the chief was captured by the English in 1296; its subsequent history is largely a struggle to retain a foothold in West Perthshire and Argyll in face of the expansionist Clan Campbell. The lawlessness of the now landless MacGregors led to the proscription of their name 'under the pain of death'. Charles II removed this penalty in recognition of the clan's services in the Royalist cause, but the luckless MacGregors were again proscribed in the reign of William III. The chief adopted the name Murray, and Rob Roy MacGregor took his mother's name of Campbell. Even in the general amnesty after the '15 Rebellion, a specific exclusion was made for the MacGregors, and it was not until 1774 that the ban was lifted. The chief then resumed the family name, and many of his adherents must have done likewise, for there are still many MacGregors in Scotland and beyond. Other dispossessed MacGregors apparently took the surnames of Stewart, Grant, Douglas, Ramsay and Cunningham: in addition the name was sometimes shortened to Gregor and **Gregory**. There is a tradition that the northern Grigors are the descendants of 300 MacGregors whom the earl of Moray transplanted there in 1624 to keep the Macintoshes in check.

MacGrory–see **MacRory**

MacGuigan An Irish name, incorporating *Eochagain,* a diminutive of Ewen–see **MacEwen**. Alternative forms are MacCougan and Geoghegan, and the name is recorded in Kintyre in 1541 in the spelling McGowgane

MacGuire A very common Irish name, anglicised from *mag Uidhir,* meaning son of Odhar–'the pale-faced'. The Maguires were the leading clan in Co Fermanagh; the name had migrated to Ayrshire by the 1740s, where it appears as M'Queir and M'Quyre, but it is to the mass immigrations a century later that the name owes its present frequency of occurrence all over Scotland. See also **MacClure**, an expanded version which is commoner in Scotland.

MacHaffie–see **MacPhee**

MacHale–see **MacCall**

MacHardy Etymologically unconnected with Hardie, the surname is from the patronymic *mac Chardaidh,* possibly related to Gaelic *ceardaich* ('a forge'–see **Caird**). The name is said to have originated in the Highland area of Aberdeenshire, and was common around Braemar in the 16th and 17th centuries. The Strathdon MacHardys counted themselves members of the clan Chattan (see **Cattanach**).

MacHugh–see **MacKay**

MacIldowie–see **Black**

MacIlraith / MacIlwraith From the Gaelic words *Mac gille riabhaich*–'son of the brindled lad'. This name, which was originally a forename and not that of a distinct clan, can have an Irish origin (with the same etymology), and this is reflected in its many variant spellings, which include a group of Reaveys and MacReavies. The name is recorded in Galloway at an early date, but is mainly associated with the Highlands and the Western Isles.

Some Skye MacIlraiths are said to have adopted the MacDonald surname from the chief of the clan which they followed.

MacIlroy From the Gaelic *mac ghille ruaidh*, son of Gilroy–'the red-haired lad'; this was an old surname in the Ballantrae district and seems to appear mainly in the Lowlands–it was not a clan surname. Michael M'Gilroy is recorded in Dumfries in 1576, and a John M'Gilroy was a lawyer in Perth about the same time. The allied surnames of Milroy and Roy are shortened version of the same name.

MacInnes 'Son of **Angus**'. Angus was the name of a Pictish king, but evidence of royal descent of the MacInneses is lacking. In fact the clan has no documented history; it appears originally in Argyll and its members adhered to the Campbells and took the government side in the Civil War and later uprisings. Nonetheless a band of MacInneses followed the Stewarts of Appin and suffered at Culloden. There is a tradition that a branch of the clan, with the abbreviated surname Neish, occupied lands in upper Strathearn until the 16th century, and the presence of Neish Island on Loch Earn seems to substantiate this. Neish is also a Lowland version of the surname, common in Dumfries and Kirkcudbright. The Gaelic spelling and pronunciation of MacInnes (*MacAonghus*) has led to its many versions (of which MacCance and MacAinsh are further examples) and its pronunciation 'eenis' to the mistaken belief that Angus is cognate with Aeneas. The name underwent further transformation when it migrated to Ireland: MacNeice, MacGinnis, Magennis and Guinness are familiar versions, the latter being the name of one of the leading septs of Ulster and that of the family of brewers.

MacInroy Properly *mac Iain ruaidh*–'son of red John'. The MacInroys were thought to be adherents of Clan Donnachie (see **Robertson**), and the name appears mainly in Atholl and Rannoch.

MacIntosh From the Gaelic *mac an toisich*–'son of the leader'–
the same word as *taoiseach*, the Irish term for their prime minister.
The clan claimed descent from the royal house of Duff, held
extensive lands in Strathspey, and assumed leadership of the Clan
Chattan confederation. The clan system largely took its form from
the imposition of feudalism on to an organisation purely tribal in
character, and the old Celtic leaders were forced to seek written
charters to lands which their ancestors had held by the sword;
the history of clan MacIntosh is of a struggle to establish a legal
title to ancestral possessions which had at one time ranged from
Lochaber to Rothiemurchus. In this they ultimately failed, but not
without winning an honourable place in Highland history. The
name later became synonymous with waterproof clothing after
Charles MacIntosh (1766-1843) patented the idea of treating cloth
with a solution of rubber; it later acquired further prestige through
Charles Rennie Mackintosh, whose reputation as an architect and
designer continues to grow; nowadays Macintosh is likely to
suggest computers. See also **Toshack**.

MacIntyre The Mac prefix here refers not to a personal name but
to a trade–that of carpenter or wright–which is explicit in the
Gaelic original *mac an-t saor*. It is therefore a polygenetic name,
with no single point of origin. MacIntyres were originally to be
found in Lorne, where they possessed the lands of Glenoe from
the 14th century until modern times. A branch of the clan were
hereditary foresters successively to the Stewarts and the Campbells;
other MacIntyres became bards to the MacIntosh chiefs, and
hereditary pipers to the MacDonalds and Menzies; another branch
attached itself to the Appin Stewarts, under whose banner they
fought at Culloden. The most famous MacIntyre of the time,
however,was Duncan Ban, who fought on the Government side
(with some reluctance and lack of efficency) but was one of the
finest of all Gaelic nature poets. Variants of the name are Macateer

and MacTier, sometimes with a further contraction to Tyrie and Teare, and occasionally translated to **Wright**.

MacIver Ivarr was a Norse chief who engaged in the siege and sack of Dumbarton in 870-1, and the name later became popular in Gaeldom in the form of *Iamhar*; the Irish spellings are McKeever and McGeever, while in the Lowlands it gives the surname **Ure**. A MacIver is recorded as early as 1219 in Arbroath Abbey; but the progenitor of the clan is traditionally the son of Duncan, lord of Lochow, a member of the Clan Campbell conglomerate who formed his own dynasty in Cowal in the 16th century. The Argyll MacIvers remained loyal to their Campbell forbears and received from them several honourable and hereditary posts such as keeper of Inveraray castle; but generally speaking the kindred dispersed at an early stage to various parts of the Highlands including Inverness-shire, the Hebrides and Caithness, and there is no particular territory associated with the clan.

Mack–see under letter **M**

McKail–see **McCall**

MacKane / MacKean / MacKeen Originally *mac Iain*, son of John (which was the commonest forename in the Highlands in the late mediaeval period). MacIan was the chiefly name of the Mac-Donalds of Glencoe, who claimed descent from one of the Lords of the Isles. The MacIans of Ardnamurchan were of the same stock; they were dispossessed of their lands and migrated east in the 17th century; MacKane and its variants then became widespread, but not frequent, in the Highlands and in Ireland.

MacKay Aiodh was a personal name which originally belonged to a pagan god associated with fire; it appears in some of the early records as Aed or Heth and is 'translated' as Hugh; the original pronunciation of the surname was something like 'ma-kee'. The

MacKays probably of Norse origin, established themselves in the north-west corner of Scotland, and by the 15th century there were reckoned to be four thousand clansmen of military age. The MacKays became staunchly Protestant, and their chief took three thousand men (including some Munros, Gunns and Sinclairs) to fight for Gustavus Adolphus in the Thirty Years War. A later chief was elevated to the peerage as Lord Reay (the name of the clan territory), but despite his having been ennobled by a Catholic Stewart sovereign the clan continued to support the Protestant succession. It was Hugh MacKay of Scourie who commanded the troops of William of Orange at Killiecrankie, and in both of the Jacobite rebellions the MacKays were in arms against the Stewarts. In the early 1800s, the MacKays, always vulnerable to their powerful neighbours the earls of Sutherland, were obliged to part with their vast possessions. The raising of the Mackay Highlanders, and the Kildonan and Strathnaver clearances, completed the dispersal of this clan, and ended the pastoral way of life so eloquently described by the 18th-century Gaelic poet Robb Don MacKay. The name, not counting its variants, is in the top ten in Scotland. The Irish MacKays, McCoys and Magees are probably of Scottish origin, the name having crossed the sea with the Ulster Plantations in the 17th century.

MacKean–see **MacKane**

MacKechnie Popularly from the Gaelic *Eachain*, a name which is 'translated' as Hector, but in fact MacKechnie is the same name as the less familiar **MacEachern**.

MacKeen–see **MacKane**

MacKellar From the Gaelic *mac Ealair*, 'son of Hilarius', a 4th century French saint. An Argyll name, first recorded in Carnasserie in 1436, it is still mainly to be found in the west of Scotland.

MacKelvie In Scotland, this name is a rendering of the Gaelic *mac Shealbhaigh*, Selbach being a hero of Celtic legend. As a surname, MacKelvie belonged to the south-west of Scotland, and is now to be found mainly in the Glasgow area. The Irish MacKelvies however derive their name from *mag giolla bhuidhe*–'son of the yellow haired lad'–equivalent to our MacAvoy.

MacKendrick In Gaelic this is *mac Eanruig*–'son of Henry' (see **Henderson**). It also appears as MacHenry and MacKenry, and is not localized in any part of the country.

MacKenna 'Son of Kenneth', from the Gaelic personal name *Cinead* (see also **MacKenzie**). As a surname MacKenna or *MacKinney* is native to the south-west of Scotland; a William MacKinney is recorded in Wigtonshire in 1544, and a John Mackyinnay in Kirkcudbright in 1546, and the name was current in Galloway. However, MacKenna is among the hundred commonest surnames in Ireland, and it is probable that it was brought to Glasgow in large numbers in the 1840s.

MacKenney–see **MacKenzie**

MacKenzie Popularly taken to be 'son of Kenneth'; but Kenneth itself is an English form of two different Celtic forenames– *Coinneach* (fair or comely), giving MacKenzie, and *Cinead* ('springing from fire'), giving **MacKenna**. The 'z' used to be pronounced 'y', as witness the alternative forms of the name, Macwhinney and MacKenney (but not MacKenna). The original Coinneach, who lived in the later 13th century, belonged to a Beauly family whose members allied themselves with the MacDougalls in opposition to Robert the Bruce and the Earls of Ross. The MacKenzies suffered ruin and dispersal, but later managed to re-establish themselves in Strathpeffer. Following their motto *Cuidich an Righ* ('help the king') they supplanted the Earls of Ross in royal favour; with the eclipse of the houses of Bruce and Ross the clan MacKenzie rose to rapid prominence in the north-west Highlands after the forfeiture of the Lordship of the Isles in 1493, only to fail again with the passing of the Stewart dynasty whom they loyally supported. The progeny of Coinneach the Fair gave their name to two earldoms, a barony and several landed proprietors, and to hundreds and thousands of ordinary Scots. They must have been a prolific clan–their fighting strength in 1745 was reckoned to be 2,500–and they later provided most of the manpower for the Seaforth Highlanders; even today MacKenzie is the commonest *Mac* name after MacDonald and MacKay.

MacKerchar– see **Farquhar**

MacKerras–see **Ferguson**

Mackie Of the same linguistic origin as **MacKay** but with a different stress: it belongs to the Lowlands, was found in Stirling in the 15th century, spread widely, and is now among the hundred commonest surnames in Scotland. It is not always recognized as a *Mac* name in the directories.

MacKillop Son of Philip. Finlaius Macpilibh is recorded as a priest of the diocese of Argyll in 1433; William Makillop, a follower of the Earl of Cassilis, was accused of murder in 1526. Traditionally the MacKillops were standard-bearers to the Campbells of Dunstaffnage, others are listed as followers of the MacDonalds of Keppoch and of Glencoe, while yet another lot are recorded, in Arran. The name also appears as **MacGilp**.

MacKimmie–see **Simon**

MacKinlay–see **Finlay**. MacKinlays, never very numerous in Scotland, were to be found most often in Glenlyon and Balquhidder in the 16th and 17th centuries. William McKinley.

25th President of the USA, was the son of an Ulster Scot, born in 1730. The name had no doubt migrated to Ireland with the Plantation, and is now common there as MacGinley.

MacKinney–see **MacKenna**

MacKinnon In Gaelic, *mac Fhionhinn* an old personal name meaning 'fair one'. From earliest times the MacKinnons were associated with the Abbey of Iona, and furnished successive abbots, the last being Iain MacKinnon who died in 1500. The clan at one time held extensive lands in Mull, which they gradually lost to the MacLeans; later they held sway in the Strathairdale district of Skye, becoming standard-bearers to the MacDonalds of Sleat, and winning the approval of Dr Samuel Johnson when he visited the island in 1773. The clan was solidly Jacobite and came out in '15 and '45 with a fighting force of 200 men; the chief was pardoned for his anti-government activities, but two generations later the clan lost its lands and its chief and the MacKinnons joined the other Skyemen in the general diaspora. It is said that before the spelling of the name became standardized, it was taken by some Gaelic-speakers to be *Mac Ionmhuinn,* 'son of the loved one', and some bearers anglicized their names to **Love**.

MacLachlan Lachlan was a favourite Celtic forename, *Lochlann* ('fjord land') being the Gaelic word for Norway. The MacLachlans, who claim descent from Niall of the Nine Hostages, High King of Ireland in 400, were granted territory in Argyllshire. Gillespoc MacLachlan's lands became part of the sheriffdom of Lorn, and his son attended the first parliament of Robert the Bruce in St Andrews in 1308. Prospering through their support of the Bruce, and keeping on good terms with their all-powerful Campbell neighbours, the clan consolidated its position in Argyll and although they participated in all the available Jacobite rebellions (and lost their chief at Culloden) they contrived to survive more or less intact. The present chief, the 24th in line, is unusual in still residing at the traditional headquarters of his clan, Castle Lachlan in Strathlachlan. A branch of the clan were hereditary physicians to the Campbells of Argyll, another provided a long succession of clerics to the local churches; and their work is preserved in the Kilbride collection of mediaeval Gaelic manuscripts. In some dialects, the first 'c' is voiced into a 'g', and in the west of Scotland the name is usually pronounced MacGloughlin–which indeed is how it is spelt in Ireland, where the name proliferates in the counties of Donegal and Derry.

MacLaren From the Gaelic *mac Labhruinn*–'son of Lawrence'. The progenitor of the clan is thought to be the 13th-century Abbot Lawrence of Balquhidder, and the MacLarens have always been associated with that area of West Perthshire; they had a more than usually turbulent existence, gaining their living by the sword and ending up as a virtually broken clan. The MacLarens were involved in a hideous and pointless massacre of the Buchanans in the 13th century, and were in turn the victims of MacGregor violence. They seem to have resorted to emigration at an early date, and were serving as mercenary soldiers in France and Italy before the end of the 15th century, and later with Gustavus Adolphus of Sweden, where some of their descendants remain. They contrived however to remain on good terms with their kinsmen the Stewarts of Appin, and it is recorded that the Appin regiment at Culloden had a MacLaren contingent, thirteen of whom were killed and fourteen wounded. In the same year there died (of natural causes) Colin MacLaurin, a mathematician thought worthy to be ranked with his contemporaries Newton and Leibniz.

MacLay / MacLeay Usually from the Gaelic *mac Dhuinnshleibhe* or son of Donleavy ('brown mountain'), only the second element having been preserved. The seat of the clan MacLay was Strathconon, and the name was widely current in Ross-shire. Some of the clan were scattered throughout the southern Hebrides, often spelling their name McOnlea. David Livingstone was a MacDonleavy of Ulva (see **Livingstone**). But there was also a Sutherland family of MacLeays which derives its name from *mac an leigha*, 'son of the physician' (see **Leitch**).

MacLean In Gaelic the name is *mac gille Eoin*, 'son of the servant of St John'; in its modern version the 'gille' bit has been gobbled up by the 'mac', leaving only the 'l' as a clue to the etymology and posing problems as to the best spelling of the name. *MacLaine* gives the current pronunciation, but the variants McClean, McGlone and MacAloon have little to commend them. The clan was known as Clan Gillean (giving rise to the Lowland surname **Gilzean**): in 1390 Donald, Lord of the Isles, granted extensive lands to his MacLean brothers-in-law, and from this stock came the two main branches of the clan–the MacLeans of Duart and the MacLaines of Lochbuie. Duart and Lochbuie are both in Mull, and Dr Johnson when visiting that island in 1773 remarked that in this country every man's name is MacLean; he might almost say the same today, for MacLean is still among the five commonest surnames in the Western Isles. Despite being heavily involved in frequent clan and dynastic wars, the MacLeans retained their influence in the West Highlands, and established power bases in other parts of the Hebrides and on the mainland in Ardgour; and the castle of Duart was itself restored to the clan in the present century. Clan Gillean has also distinguished itself in the realms of music and poetry, particularly in the person of Sorley Maclean (1911—1996) perhaps the most distinguished of 20th century Scottish poets.

MacLeish / MacLees In Gaelic, *mac gille Iosa*–'son of the devotee of Jesus'. Before the addition of the prefix the name would have been **Gillies**. MacLeish was first recorded in Dumfriesshire in 1376, and was later current in North Perthshire and Argyll. In Ireland it takes the form MacAleese.

MacLellan In Gaelic, *mac gille Fhaolain*, 'son of the servant of St Fillan', an elaborated form of the name **Gilfillan**; the names **Cleland**, Leland and **Whelan** are sometimes contractions. MacLellans were numerous in Galloway in the latter part of the 14th century, and left their linguistic fingerprint on the village of Balmaclellan in the Stewartry, an unusual example in Scotland of an ancient settlement being called after a person and not the other way round (see Introduction). The earliest mention of the surname is in 1305 when Patrick, son of Gilbert M'Lolane, captured the castle of Dumfries from the Bruce forces. The Highland bearers of the name–MacLellan was never reckoned a distinct clan–are found in Morar in the 17th century, while the Perthshire MacLellans attached themselves to the MacNabs who were lay abbots of Glendochart. MacLellans emigrated to Canada in large numbers, and their descendants are to be found on Cape Breton Island among other places. A Peter MacLellan was one of the first to receive from the Crown a grant of land after the expulsion in 1755 of the Acadians from Nova Scotia.

MacLennan In Gaelic, *mac gille Finnein*, 'son of the servant of Finnan', a personal name embodying the word *fionn* meaning white, also to be found in many place-names, including Glenfinnan. The legendary founder of the clan MacLennan is Gilligorm, leader of a tribe which flourished in Easter Ross, and whose grandson was named for St Finnan, an early Celtic saint. The clan extended its territories westward, and became standard-bearers to the MacKenzies of Seaforth; several of their number died defending the banner at the battle of Auldearn in 1645, and they remained active royalists in later Jacobite uprisings. There must however have been devotees of St Finnan in other parts of Scotland who were the founders of dynastic families, because the surname first crops up in Lennox in 1250 and is also found in the south-west Highlands at an early date.

MacLeod A clan of Scandinavian origin which takes its patronymic from an Old Norse nickname *Ljótr*, meaning ugly. The progenitor of the clan, one of the largest in the West Highlands, is supposed to be one Leod (pronounced 'lodge' in Gaelic), son of the Norse King of Man and the Hebrides, who was given lands in Lewis. Another branch of the clan acquired lands in Skye, and to these were added the island of Raasay and lands in Assynt and Strathpeffer (where they built Castle Leod, later to fall into the hands of the MacKenzies of Cromarty). The MacLeods, weary of royal ingratitude, remained as a clan on the sidelines during the Jacobite rebellions and escaped the worst consequences of the post-Culloden reprisals; had they not, Dunvegan Castle (which the MacLeods have occupied for seven hundred years) might today be in the ruinous state of Invergarry and many other castles. There were individual clansmen of a different persuasion, however, and Donald MacLeod of Skye is remembered as Bonnie Prince Charlie's henchman and pilot for seven weeks after Culloden. Another Donald MacLeod witnessed the Sutherland clearances and described them unforgettably in his book *Gloomy Memories*, published in 1857 in Canada where he settled with so many others of his kindred. Of those who stayed at home, the most notable are perhaps Iain Macleod who was a promising Tory chancellor before his early death in 1970, and Lord MacLeod of Fuinary, churchman and leader of the Iona Community dedicated to restoring the buildings of Scotland's most sacred site.

MacLure–see **MacClure**

MacMahon–see **Matheson**

MacManus 'Son of Magnus' a popular first-name in Gaeldom, deriving via Norse from the Latin *magnus* ('big, great'). MacManuses are recorded in 1506 in Dunbartonshire, where the family lived as adherents of the Colquhouns. In Ireland the clan had connections with the Maguires and the O Connors, and flourished in Fermanagh and Roscommon: in fact most MacManuses are likely to be of Irish origin. In the Lowlands the cognate name is **Main**.

MacMaster 'Son of the master', in the sense of cleric; the name has several points of origin in the Gaelic-speaking world. Colin, son of John Macmagistir, appears to have been a canon of Argyll in 1433, and there was a small clan of MacMasters in Ardgour, said to have been dispersed by the MacLeans in the 15th century. The name also flourished in Dumfries and Wigtown.

MacMichael–see **Mitchell**

MacMillan *Maolan* in Gaelic means a bald or tonsured man, and the name MacMillan has the sense of 'son of the priest'. The family of the original Maolan acquired territories in Argyll, and built the ancient fortress of Castle Sween in Knapdale. Like many another Argyll clan the MacMillans lost their land to the Campbells. One branch took refuge in Lochaber; the stewards at that time were the MacIntoshes, while the district was the hereditary domain of the clan Cameron, so that the Lochaber Macmillans lived as tenants of the MacIntoshes but as adherents of the Camerons, with the consequent conflict of loyalties which so characterised the clan system. Other Macmillans moved south to Galloway, and got into trouble as 'disorderly persons' (i.e. Covenanters); others moved to Loch Tayside, where the name is still found. The publishing MacMillans however hailed from Arran, and the site of the ancestral croft is in High Corrie. The name is very common in Antrim and Down, usually in the form Mullen or McMullen, but is not indigenous to Ireland.

MacMurchie–see **Murphy**

MacMurray–see **Murray**

MacNab 'Son of the abbot' (see **Abbott**). The MacNab clan-lands were in Glendochart in Perthshire, and the early chiefs were abbots of the great Celtic monastery which flourished there from early mediaeval times under the patronage of St Fillan. Abbacies in the Celtic church were lay and hereditary, and often became offices of great temporal as well as spiritual power. The clan's fortunes fluctuated; they were on the losing side in the Wars of Independence, and after a period of recovery they were reduced to the status of a broken clan by the end of the 16th century. Zealous royalists during the Civil War period, the Restoration brought another upturn in their fortunes, which however did not survive the thriftless dissipations of the 12th and 13th chiefs who brought ruin on their people. The MacNabs emigrated in large numbers to Canada in the early 19th century, where they were joined by the 13th chief who attempted to run a feudal society in an emergent country with predictably disastrous results.

MacNair–s e e **Weir**

MacNaughton 'Son of Neachdainn'; Nechtan was the son of the Celtic god of water, and the name of several Pictish kings: had the Angles won the battle of Nectansmere (Dunnichen) in 685, there might today be no Scotland. The MacNaughtons had been a powerful clan in Argyll before backing the losing side in Bruce's wars; they regained most of their lands in the later mediaeval period in reward for services to the king, but lost their chief at Flodden. Their subsequent history is the familiar one of misplaced loyalty to the Stewarts, resulting in forfeiture of land and fortune-seeking elsewhere: in 1677, for example, Colonel Alexander MacNaughton raised a company of 200 Highland bowmen for service in France for the relief of La Rochelle. The surname underwent many changes of form: a branch of the clan which had migrated to Antrim in the 14th century became MacNutt, and the

Ayrshire branch were MacKnights. Later versions are MacCracken (Ulster) and MacNitt (USA), while the forms Macnaught and Naughton have remained fairly common everywhere.

MacNee *Nia* ('champion') was the name of an Irish king, from whom the MacNees claim descent. The surname, in the form Maknee, is recorded in Scotland in 1594; and a few years later Donald and Gilliemoire MacNie were in trouble for involvement with the outlawed MacGregor clan. The MacNees who emigrated to Ireland took with them the tradition that they were a MacGregor sept. Some of them changed their name to Neeson, which found its way back to the Glasgow area.

MacNeil See also **Neill** for the origin of the second element. The MacNeils had been long established in Barra when Ruaraidh of that name received a crown charter in 1495. Although predominantly a Catholic clan, and as such strong supporters of the Stewarts, they remained in peaceable possession of their lands until modern times. Their kinsmen of Gigha and Colonsay (who preferred the MacNeill spelling) were not so fortunate, and lost the former island to the Campbells in the 16th century; for a period in the 1780s Colonsay was run as a model crofting community under its enlightened MacNeill chief, but it too was sold a century later. A separate Lowland family of the same name had as its founder one Gilbert McNeill, on whose son John was conferred 'five pennylands of Larganfield in the Rhinns of Galloway' by King Robert the Bruce. The Macneillys, another Galloway family, are however of different origin: their name comes from *mac an fhilidh*, meaning son of the poet.

MacNeish / MacNiece–see **MacInnes**

MacNiven–see **Niven**

MacNicol A family name found all over Scotland from the 16th century onwards, but not in great numbers and not that of a distinct clan. The MacNicols of the north-west Highlands seem to have adopted the Nicolson form of the name; others from Argyll were traditionally the progeny of one Nicol M'Phee who came from Lochaber in the 1500s. See **Nicoll**.

MacNiece–see **MacInnes**

MacNiven–see **Niven**

MacPhail 'Son of Paul', a synonym of **Polson**. The MacPhails were not a distinct clan, but a group of families who appear all over the Highlands from the 15th century onwards. The name was said to be common around Ardchattan in Argyll, and a family of MacPhails held a hereditary position as clerks and physicians to the McDougalls and the Campbells in the 17th century. Several MacPhails were among the fencible men enrolled in Glenlyon by the Duke of Atholl in 1766; another contingent regarded themselves as a branch of the MacKays, and are listed in the Reay rent books in the late 17th century. A variant spelling is MacFall, and the contraction Fyall is also found.

MacPhee A version of *mac Dhuibhshith*, literally 'son of the Black Fairy'; this has given rise to some speculation about a primeval origin of the clan (it is certainly of great antiquity), but the probability is that Duibhshith is simply a personal name. The MacPhees established themselves in South Uist and Colonsay, and were record-keepers to the Lords of the Isles. With the murder of their chief in 1623 the clan broke up and dispersed over the mainland, and the MacPhees became the classic type of the broken clan, landless and chiefless and finding protection wherever they might. Some of them followed the clan Cameron and ended their days with Lochiel's regiment on Culloden moor. Within living memory the name MacPhee was associated with bands of tinkers (or New Age Travellers as one must now call them) who roved the fringes of the Highlands; one Ewen MacPhee encamped with his family on an island in Loch Quoich, living as a sort of Victorian Rob Roy. But there have been respectable and distinguished bearers of the name, including Hugh Macphee, born in Ballachulish, the first BBC Gaelic broadcaster. MacFee and MacFie are much more rarely found; MacHaffie is another variant; and the name is sometimes further shortened to Duffie in the Lowlands.

MacPherson The Gaelic equivalent of the English surname Parsons, MacPherson dates from the time of the Celtic church with its hereditary and non-celibate priesthood. The MacPhersons originated in Lochaber, but were granted lands in Badenoch by a grateful Robert the Bruce for their services in helping to destroy his enemies the Comyns or Cummings who had previously ruled in Strathspey. Royalists and Jacobites to a man, they suffered for their political principles, but eventually it was economic forces which emptied Badenoch of MacPhersons. James 'Ossian' Macpherson, who perpetrated one of the greatest literary frauds of all time, was a Kingussie man; but others of the kindred settled in the Hebrides, one of whom, Sir John MacPherson from Skye, became Governor-General of India; another Skyeman was John MacPherson, known as the Glendale Martyr on account of his Land Agitation campaigns; and in Barra lived the famous storyteller John MacPherson, locally known as 'The Coddy'. The Anglo-American pronunciation 'mac fear son' seems merely perverse.

MacPhillips–see **MacKillop**

MacQuaid / MacQuatt / MacWatt Irish derivatives of **Watt**.

MacQuarrie Dr Johnson, on his tour of the Hebrides, described this clan as 'not powerful nor numerous, but of antiquity'. He also guessed correctly that the name is 'a depravation of some other'. It is recorded first in 1467 as M'Guaire, but has no connection with **MacGuire**: it is *mac guaire*–'son of the proud one'. The MacQuarrie chief of Ulva allied himself with the MacLeans in the 17th-century wars–with disastrous results for both clans. Lachlan Macquarie was born in 1761 in Ulva, the son of a carpenter and a poor tenant of the Duke of Argyll, but a kinsman of the last chief of his clan. His success as a soldier led to his appointment as governor of New South Wales; by encouraging public works such as road and bridge building, and by founding the first bank, he transformed a penal settlement into a flourishing colony. As a result the surname is now much better known in Australia than here.

MacQueen An anglicized form of *mac Suibhne*, from a Norse personal name Sveinn (see **Swain**). There were two Highland branches of this clan, and a Lowland family of the name. The Skye MacQueens are of Norse origin; some of them followed their chieftain's daughter to Badenoch on her marriage to a MacKintosh chief about 1410, and subsequently became a branch of Clan Chattan, sharing in the warlike exploits of that confederation. The name also appears commonly as MacSween in the Western Isles. A Hector MacSouhyn is recorded in Dumbarton in 1271, and it is possibly from this line that is descended Robert Macqueen, Lord Braxfield, the notorious hanging judge.

MacRae In Gaelic this is *mac rath*–'son of grace', originally a forename which has become a surname in many different times and places in the Highlands. It appears in a few guises, including MacCreath, McCree, MacCraw, MacGraw and Magraw, the latter being nearer to the Gaelic pronunciation. In the Lowlands the name was often connected to Reith. Alex Macrad is recorded in Lennox in 1225, and a namesake in Atholl a few years later. A Macreath of Dumfries appears in the Ragman Roll of 1296. The most celebrated bearers of the name are 'the Wild Macraes'; they held office under the MacKenzies of Kintail and were hereditary constables of Eilean Donan castle on Loch Duich, whose picturesque restoration at the beginning of the 20th century is not a little reminiscent of Disney-land. After their warlike beginnings, the 'sons of grace' lived up to their name by producing a line of clerics and scholars, bards and preachers, to whom Gaelic culture owes an incalculable debt. The name is also indigenous to Ireland, in the form of MacGraith.

MacReavie–see **MacIlraith**

MacRitchie–see **Ritchie**

MacRobb / MacRobbie / MacRobert–see **Robb**

MacRory In Gaelic *mac Ruadhri*, son of Rory, 'the ruddy one'. Rory was a personal name in its own right, unconnected with the Teutonic name Roderick (although they have often been thought to be related). One Aleyn MacRotherick of Inverness is recorded in 1296 in the Ragman Roll, and the surname was found in Galloway at the same period. The MacRorys, never a coherent clan, seem to have had a reputation for rebellion, lawlessness and general trouble-making. Although still one of the commoner names in the Western Isles, MacRory is mainly to be found (along with MacCrorie, MacGrorie and MacRury) in the Greater Glasgow area. Some of them are said to have adopted the Lowland name of **Reid**.

MacSween– see **MacQueen**

MacTaggart From the Gaelic *mac an-t sagairt*, or 'son of the priest'. The old Celtic church had a tradition of hereditary priesthood, which persisted until the Reformation. A Ferchar Mackentagar or Mackinsagart, 'son of the red priest of Applecross' was knighted by Alexander II in 1216 for his good offices in quelling an insurrection in Moray; nevertheless the name is by no means localized, and is subsequently recorded all over the land. Catharin M'Taggart was accused of witchcraft in Dunbar in 1688. William McTaggart, the painter, was the son of Gaelic-speaking parents in Macrihanish in Kintyre; his grandson Sir William McTaggart, PRSA, maintained the family prestige. In the Lowlands, the name is often contracted to Haggart or Taggart.

MacTavish 'Son of Tammas'; variants are MacThomas and Mac-Comish ('son of Thomas'); MacComb ('son of Tom'); MacCombich, MacCombie and MacComie ('son of Tommy'); all of which indicate that the surname had many points of origin. The first recording is that of Duncan M'Thomais in Glassary in 1355, where a small clan of the name had its abode; there was another family in Stratherrick who followed the Frasers, while a family of MacThomas or MacComish once held lands in Glenshee. See also **Thomson**.

MacTier–see **MacIntyre**

MacVeigh / MacVey / Mac Vie–see **MacBeth** and **MacPhee**

MacVicar 'Son of the vicar'. The MacVicars were a small Argyllshire clan, originally dependants of the MacNaughtons and later of the Campbells. The Breadalbane MacVicars claimed descent from Maurice MacNaughton and Duncan MacNaughton who were the vicars of Inchadney from 1480 to 1523.

MacVittie Probably from Gaelic *mac an bhiathaigh*–'son of the victualler or farmer'. The name seems to originate in Ayrshire and Galloway, and became a household word in Edinburgh through the achievements of a firm of bakers, confectioners and teashop proprietors. It is now relatively uncommon, with or without the double 't'.

MacVurich–see **Murphy**

MacWatt An Irish derivative of **Watt**.

MacWattie–see **Watt**

MacWhirter An Anglicization of the Gaelic *mac chruitear*–'son of the harper or fiddler'. The *crowd* was a popular mediaeval instrument, which also gives the English surname Crowther. The MacWhirters, also spelt MacWhorter, were mainly to be found in Ayrshire.

MacWilliam A 13th-century family known as *mac Uilleam*, 'the kindred of William', great-grandson of Malcolm III, were prominent as leaders of a rebellion against the throne; but there is no evidence that they took MacWilliam as their hereditary surname; more likely, the Highland MacWilliams were descended from William, son of the 5th chief of MacLeod. The name is widespread, being found variously in Aberdeen, Seaforth, Breadalbane and Wigton, and the families have no known connection one with another. Some of them used the diminutive form of MacCully ('son of Willie'), and others (notably the ones who settled in the parish of Mortlach in 1550) are said to have anglicized their name to **Williamson**.

M

Maben / Mabon From the old personal name Mabon, which is cognate with the Welsh *maponos*, the name of the sun-god, and which survives in some Border place names such as Lochmaben. The surname has been current in the Borders since the 17th century, but has never been a common one.

Mack From the old Scandinavian personal name *Makr*, of uncertain meaning and origin. It is not a vestigial *Mac* name although often treated as such, especially in directories and in the USA. A John Makke is recorded in 1424, and the name persisted in the Scottish Lowlands throughout the 16th century. It is now quite common in the Glasgow area.

Main A reduction of the forename Magnus, the Latin word for 'big' or 'great'. The name reached Scotland by way of the Norsemen, and was common on the northern seaboard, particularly on the Moray firth where Viking incursions were frequent. Magnus becomes Main when adopted as a surname in Scotland, although the more northerly forms of **Manson** and **Magnusson** are still familiar. It is said that at one time in recent history there were thirty families called Main living in the town of Nairn; Aberdeenshire also had a large number. John Mayne, a cutler in Dundee in the 1550s, was banished from the city for drawing a whinger on his employer.

Mair A *mair* was a court official whose duties were akin to those of a modern sheriff-officer (the execution of summonses and other legal writs), but the word was later applied to any delegated official function; Eustace Mare for example was collector of contributions of the sheriffdom of Perth in 1360. The surname was sometimes

Latinized by scribes, and the great scholar John Mair (1469–1550) is probably better known as Major; he was born near Haddington, wrote and lectured exclusively in Latin, advocated the union of Scotland and England, and is known as 'the last of the schoolmen'. Mair became a very common name in the fishing communities of the north-east, notably Portknockie.

Maitland The earlier spelling was *de Maltalent* which would mean 'of a quick temper', a plausible enough nickname. But 'de' in a surname context almost invariably indicates territorial origin, which has led some scholars to postulate a Norman-French place name (not, however, identified). Whatever the truth of the matter, the name reached Scotland after the Norman conquest of England. Thomas de Matalan settled in Berwickshire at the end of the 12th century. Sir Richard Maitland of Lethington (1496—1586) was a statesman, lawyer and poet; his grandson John Maitland (1616—1682), 2nd earl and 1st Duke of Lauderdale, was a favourite of Charles II and virtual ruler of Scotland until he fell from power. The Maitlands have occupied their ancestral seat of Thirlestane Castle near Lauder for over seven hundred years. The surname was also current among ordinary folk from early times; William Matalant was a retainer at Kelso Abbey in the 1200s, and Agnes Maidlen was a woman of drunken habits in Dundee in the 1560s.

Malcolm The Gaelic word *calaman* means dove, a bird which was taken to symbolise the Holy Spirit. The Latin equivalent is Columba, the name of an Irish saint who founded the monastery of Iona in 563. A follower of St Columba was termed in Gaelic *maol Chaluim,* which became the Christian name Malcolm. It was the name of four early Scottish kings, and several Maucolums appear in the Ragman Roll of 1296, from places as far apart as Berwick, Perth and Montrose. As a surname it occurred in Dunbartonshire in the 14th century, whence the family moved south to the Dumfries area. An early MacCallum chief changed his name to Malcolm; this has resulted in some confusion between the two names, which indeed have the same linguistic origin although there is no perceived kinship between the respective bearers.

Malone A reduction of an Irish patronymic *O Mal Eoin*–literally 'descendant of the devotee of St John'. Its Scottish Gaelic equivalent is **MacLean**. Malone is not found in Scotland until modern times.

Mann Either an occupational name for a servant or a nickname meaning manly. John Man was a burgess of Aberdeen in 1399; the name has been common throughout Scotland since the late mediaeval period, although it is not exclusively nor even principally Scottish.

Manson A contraction of Magnusson, a royal forename among the Norsemen. It was quite common in Caithness in the 16th century, and the Mansons were adherents of the clan Gunn. It is still one of the commonest surnames in Shetland. See **Main**.

Marr A territorial name, from the province of Mar in Aberdeenshire; most Scottish Marrs were and are to be found in the east, and particularly in the Grampian region, although the possibility remains that some are from the district of Marr in West Yorkshire. The surname occurs in the earliest Scottish historical records, and there are three Marrs who figure in the Ragman Roll of 1296, being landowners respectively in Fife, Linlithgow and Aberdeenshire.

Marshall The French word *maréchal*, originally 'horse-servant', now means farrier or shoe-smith. It arrived in Britain with the Normans, and a horse-servant became in time a hereditary office of great importance similar to constable or steward. Philip Marescallus (*fl.* 1200) married the heiress of Keith-Humbie, and became the progenitor of the Keith family who rose to great fame as Earls Marischal of Scotland. In their case *marischal* was a title and not a name: but Marshall did become the surname of many humbler folk, such as Adam Marshall who was a peasant at Coldingham priory in the 13th century. William Marshall, born in Fochabers in 1748, was an extreme example of 'the laird's Jock': in addition to being butler to the duke of Gordon for more than forty years, he was surveyor, architect, astronomer, estate factor and justice of the peace; his chief claim to fame however is that he was one of the most notable Scottish violinists and composers of his day. Marshall is among the fifty commonest Scottish surnames, is just as common in England, and has equivalents in most European languages.

Martin From Mars, the Roman god of fertility and of war; Martin of Tours was a highly-venerated 4th-century saint. As a Christian name, Martin became very popular in every European country and was well known in Scotland in the 12th century in the court of William the Lion; as a surname its growth was rapid and widespread, and it is now among the fifty commonest names in England, Scotland and Ireland. There were Martyns in Edinburgh at least as early as the 14th century. Martin Martin of Bealach in Skye, a graduate of Edinburgh and of Leyden, wrote interestingly on the Western Isles (1695), and is an invaluable source of information on contemporary Highland history. Abraham Martin (*'dit l'Ecossais'*) was the first king's pilot on the St Lawrence River; the Plains of Abraham are said to be named after lands which he was granted there in 1617. The Highland MacMartins, an offshoot of the clan Cameron, are probably named after the saint, who was revered throughout Gaeldom as elsewhere.

Mason An important and frequent occupational name, but not distinctively Scottish, except in its less usual spelling of Masson. In earlier days, the scribes frequently Latinized it to *cementarius,* but fortunately this never evolved into a surname. Richard the Mason was a burgess of Aberdeen in 1271; fifty years later the records show a William Maceoun de Berwick–a neat illustration of how a designation becomes a surname. Thomas Mason was apprenticed to the masonic craft in Coupar Angus in 1490. Stone-masonry was not a feature of Highland life, but the Gaelic term for this trade does give the infrequent surname Clacher.

Massey / Massie–see **Matthew**

Masson–see **Mason**

Masterton From a place in Fife, meaning 'master's homestead', Magister Ailricus being the title of the original owner. William de Masterton of Fife rendered homage to Edward I in 1296, and the Mastertons were a well-known family for many years in the Dunfermline area. The name is still to be found mainly in the east of Scotland.

Mathers This surname appears to have a quite different origin from its English lookalike of Mather. The latter (nowadays common in Scotland also) is an occupational name from a mower or reaper of grass or hay ('aftermath' means the residue of the mowing). Mathers on the other hand appears to derive from a place of the same name near Montrose, whose etymology is doubtful; the surname is certainly commoner in the east of the country.

Matheson/Mathieson For the Lowland version of the name, see **Matthews**. The corresponding Gaelic name would be *MacMatha* or *MacMath*, but the Highland Mathesons are really MacMahons (Gaelic *mac mhathain* 'son of the bear'), among the sixty commonest names in Ireland. The Mathesons were originally vassals of the mediaeval earls of Ross and later became supporters of the Lords of the Isles, duly sharing in their downfall. Crowded out of their Wester Ross lands by the powerful MacLeods and MacKenzies, the Mathesons nevertheless remained a force in Highland society, producing warriors, clerics and poets. Donald Matheson of Kildonan was a Gaelic poet who foresaw the Clearances fifty years before they happened and likened his clansmen to the Children of Israel; along with Nicolsons, MacLeans and MacLeods, many Mathesons were 'cleared' from Skye in the 1840s. Sir James Matheson made his fortune in the far east and was able to right some past wrongs by buying back much of Lewis, with its MacLeod castle of Stornoway.

Matthew / Matthews From a Hebrew given-name ('gift of God'), with cognates in practically every European language. In Scotland the Matthews spelling is commoner; but the characteristic forms are **Matheson** and **Mathieson**. Massey and Massie have the same derivation.

Mawhinney–see **MacKenzie**

Maxton For etymology, see **Maxwell**. A family of Maxtons owned the estate of Cultoquhey near Crieff for a reputed six centuries, and the name is still familiar in the locality. James Maxton, who died in 1946, was a Red Clydesider and a prominent member of the ILP.

Maxwell From a settlement on the River Tweed, originally 'the ville of Maccus', a Saxon lord who obtained a grant of land near Kelso from David I. **Maxton**, which also produces a surname, is probably named after the same person. The family became immensely powerful in the Borders during the Wars of Independence, and later were appointed wardens of the Marches during the reign of the Jameses. The Maxwell lords were created earls of Morton, and (after the Douglas restoration) earls of Nithsdale, and were to become one of the leading Jacobite families of southern Scotland. Another branch of the clan held the lands of Monreith in Wigtonshire from the 15th century, and from this stock came Sir Herbert Maxwell the politician and historian, and Gavin Maxwell the author. James Clerk Maxwell, the physicist, was the son of an Edinburgh lawyer. Maxwell also became very popular and prestigious as a given name, and tended to be adopted as a surname by incomers, not all of them worthy of it.

Mearns From the Gaelic term *an Mhaoirne*, the office or province of mair (see **Mair**) or steward (cf. The Stewartry); Mearns occurs as a locality name in Angus and in Renfrewshire; and the surname appears in both these districts from early times. As might be expected, it now preponderates in the Glasgow area.

Mechan / Meechan An Irish surname, *O Miadhagain*, meaning 'descendant of the honourable one'. Not native to Scotland, it first appears in the records here in the mid-19th century. In Ireland it takes the forms Mee, Meegan, Meehan and MacMeekin; in this country, the name is found mostly in the cities of Edinburgh and Glasgow, and in the spelling Meechan.

Meek This name means what it says; and since meek (*mjeikr*) is a word of Norse origin, the surname may have originated in parts of England as well as Scotland. There was traditionally a family of the name which held lands of the Abbey of Coupar Angus from the mid-15th century, and the name is still familiar in the eastern Lowlands of Scotland.

Meikle From the Scots word *mickle*, signifying big or 'muckle'; the familiar proverb correctly runs 'Mony a pickle (grain) maks a mickle (lot)'. Meikle was no doubt an ephemeral nickname to begin with, but appears as a surname all over Scotland from early times. Andrew Meikle of Dunbar was an 18th-century engineer who invented the threshing machine. John Meikle of Edinburgh made a splendid new carillon for St Giles in 1699, which for two centuries delighted a citizenry which can now hear little above the traffic noise. Meiklejohn is a Fife name, originally bestowed to distinguish between two men of the name of John.

Meldrum Originally the name of an old barony in Aberdeenshire, it comes from the Gaelic words *maol druim*, meaning 'bare ridge'. It appears first in the early records as *de Melgedrom*, which is a designation rather than a surname, but attains the latter status with William Myldrum, who was a Scots prisoner-of-war, beheaded in 1402. William Meldrum of Cleish and the Binns was a soldier of fortune in his youth and became Sheriff-Depute of Fife in 1522. Sir John Meldrum was a Scottish laird who assisted King James I with the Protestant Plantation of Ulster in 1609. The name is still frequent in the Lowlands of Scotland, and particularly in the Aberdeen area.

Melrose The name of a Border town; it was originally *maol ros*, a survival from a Celtic language spoken in the Tweed valley before the Angles arrived, and meaning 'barren moor'. As a surname it has never been very common, and is nowadays to be found mainly in Edinburgh and the Borders.

Melville From various places in Normandy called Malleville. Galfridus de Malveill or Malevin figures in several documents at the end of the 12th century, and there is more than one de Melvill in the Ragman Roll of 1296; (the other version of the place name, Malevin, gives Melvin, now commoner as a first name). The Melvilles were lairds of Raith in Fife, and one of them fought at Flodden. Sir Robert Melville of Burntisland was created a peer of Parliament in 1616 with the title of Lord Melville of Monimail; his descendants became earls of Melville in 1690, later merged with the earldom of Leven. Andrew Melville, son of an Angus laird, was a scholar and reformer who founded Scottish Presbyterianism and brought the New Learning to the Scottish universities, where he was a distinguished teacher. Herman Melville, creator of Moby Dick, was of Scots descent. The Melvilles gave their name to a parish in Midlothian and to castles, houses and streets in the eastern Lowlands, where the name has always been most frequent.

Menteith–see **Monteith**

Menzies Correctly pronounced 'mingiz', this name comes from Mesnières in Normandy, via England (where its cognate is Manners, the family name of the dukes of Rutland). Menzies is a good example of an Anglo-Norman family which received a grant of Scottish land under royal patronage and founded a clan based not so much on the idea of kindred as on feudal tenure. The clan Menzies, despite the alien origin of its aristocracy, became thoroughly Gaelicised and for a time wielded considerable power in the central Highlands. The clan heartland was in Strathtay, where the ancient Castle Menzies has recently been restored by the Clan Society. In the 1860s a Menzies family in Edinburgh established a chain of bookstalls which grew into one of Scotland's leading book and newspaper trading outlets. Sir Robert Menzies, premier of Australia in the 1950s, was the grandson of a Scot who had emigrated to Ballarat in the gold rush a century earlier.

Mercer French *mercier*, a merchant or trader, especially one who dealt in fine cloths such as satin, silk and velvet. The surname was recorded in the 13th century in Aberdeenshire, Roxburgh and Montrose. But it is Perth which seems to be the home of this family; John Mercer was a wealthy burgher of the city and became its provost in 1347, and in the later mediaeval period there were scurrilous ballads indicating that the Mercers had monopolised the commercial affairs of Perth. Another contemporary Mercer was apparently entrusted by Edward III of England with the task of raising men and horses for an expedition to Bordeaux. The name is not exclusively Scottish, and occurs sparsely in England and Wales.

Michie–see **Mitchell**

Middlemass The name of a place near Kelso; it simply means the middlemost part of a terrain (see **Middleton**). As a surname it is first recorded in 1406 in Kelso and in 1439 in Peebles. Luckie Middlemist kept a famous oyster-cellar in Edinburgh in the late 1700s–alas no longer with us. The surname is quite common in Edinburgh and the Borders but practically nowhere else.

Middleton Occurs all over the country as a farm-name; it would be situated between the Overton (the upper farm) and the Netherton (the lower farm), and is not confined to Scotland. As a surname it first appears in a grant of land in 1094 by Duncan II to Malcolm, son of Kenneth of Middleton. Umfridus de Midelton, whose name is recorded in Arbroath in 1221, probably came from the lands of Middleton near Laurencekirk, where the surname was at one time quite frequent. John Middleton, a hard-drinking Royalist soldier in the Cromwellian campaigns, was later created an earl by Charles II.

Mill / Milne / Mylne The name given to someone living or work-ing at a mill, and as such very common throughout Scotland. James Mill, the father of John Stuart Mill, was a philosopher and political scientist who came from near Montrose; his education, begun at the age of three, was completed at Edinburgh University. A.A. Milne, the creator of Winnie the Pooh, was born in Scotland. A family of Mylnes were for centuries master masons to the Scottish kings, from James III onwards; at the end of the 19th century they migrated to London where one of them engineered a large part of the city's water supply. Millan and Millen are different, see under **MacMillan**; see also **Millar**. The -n- spelling is characteristic of the north-east; the usual form of the name in England is Mills.

Millar / Miller The mill was an important centre in every mediaeval settlement, and one to which the peasantry were obliged to resort, the miller being an agent of the landowner (and often notorious for driving a hard bargain). Miller (taken with Millar) is one of the top ten surnames in Scotland, and the third commonest occupational name after Smith and Stewart. The

'Millar' spelling is probably an echo of the Latin suffix *-arius*. In 1635 Edward Millar brought out in Edinburgh an edition of the Psalms 'with their whole Tunes in foure or mo parts'. Hugh Miller, the Cromarty stonemason turned geologist and man of letters, took his own life in 1856. The English equivalent of the name, Milner, is not often found here.

Milligan From Gaelic *maolagan*, a double diminutive of the word *maol* meaning bald or tonsured. It was quite common in Galloway at an early date, and was recorded in Perth in 1468 as Milikyn, becoming fairly widespread in Scotland. The cognate forms Mullen and Mulligan, common in Ireland, are less frequent here. See also **MacMillan**.

Milroy–see **MacIlroy**

Mitchell From the Hebrew name Michael, a favourite baptismal choice throughout Christendom. The present pronunciation is from the French form Michel; the traditional Scots pronunciation is Michel, the 'ch' as in 'loch'. The surname evolved as Mitchell in many parts of Scotland, and it is now among the top twenty overall. James Michell was one of the assassins of Archbishop Sharp in 1679 and suffered the supreme penalty for his Covenanting zeal. Helen Mitchell, daughter of a Mearns farmer, was better known to posterity as Nellie Melba; James Leslie Mitchell, also from the Mearns, recently emerged from neglect under his pen name of Lewis Grassic Gibbon, author of *The Scots Quair*. A version of Mitchell in its diminutive form is found in Angus and Aberdeenshire in the name Michie, which is said to have originated in Glengairn where a Michael MacDonald of the Keppoch branch of that clan founded a family in the 16th century. Other less common derivatives are Mitchison and MacMichael.

Moffat A place near Dumfries, possibly derived from the Gaelic words *magh fada*, meaning 'long plain'. Nicholas de Moffat, the 'laughing archdeacon' of Teviotdale, was an unsuccessful postulant for the bishopric of Glasgow in 1258 and 1268. The Moffatis of the West March were reckoned among the unruly Border clans. This west-country surname is also common in the north of England. Some of the kindred emigrated to Ulster, where the name is usually spelt Moffett.

Moir *Mor* (meaning big) is one of the commonest adjectives in the Gaelic language, and gave rise to countless ephemeral nicknames in the Highlands; James Mor, the elder son of Rob Roy, is a case in point. In some instances the surname was anglicised to More, but by far the commoner spelling is Moir (the 'i' would indicate a long vowel). There is however sometimes confusion with **Moore** and **Muir**; and another possible origin for the surname is the Gaelic adjective *mordha*, meaning majestic, which is the derivation of the name of Rory O More, High King of Ireland.

Moncrieff From the place-name Moncreiffe, near Perth (probably *monadh craoibhe*–'hill of trees'), where the original family settled almost 750 years ago. In 1248 Sir Matthew de Muncrefe received a grant of land from Alexander II. By 1296, as the Ragman Roll records, other branches of the family owned lands in Angus and Kinrosshire, and a Moncreiffe laird was Chamberlain to King James III; in succeeding centuries one branch of the family was ennobled, and other bearers of the name became very distinguished in the church and the law. The name also achieved distinction in France, where a branch of the family provided archers for the Scots Guards of the Kings of France; and a Marquis de Moncrif was guillotined for his loyalty to the French crown. The name is still found mainly in the Tayside area, the common spelling being Moncrieff; it is pronounced with the accent on the 'crieff' part.

Moncur A Tayside place-name, which occurs both in the Carse of Gowrie and near Carmyllie in Angus; it is thought to mean 'moss of the pit', and the stress is on the second syllable. The family of Moncur for several generations enjoyed a high reputation as armourers to the Scottish Court. Andrew de Muncurr appears in the Ragman Roll of 1296, and the name occurs in various spellings in Angus and Fife; Andrew Moncur 'of that Ilk' (i.e. of Moncur) is recorded at Errol in 1541. In the last century a family of Moncurs were jute manufacturers in Dundee, where the name is still commoner than it is anywhere else.

Monteith From the lands of Menteith in central Scotland, the name of an old Pictish province. It is probably Brittonic *minit ted* ('Teith moor'); the etymology of Teith is unknown, but the pronunciation of the compound is in no doubt–the accent is on the second syllable. Sir John de Menteith, capturer of William Wallace was created Earl of Lennox, joined Robert the Bruce, and was present at the Declaration of Arbroath in 1320. Menteith recurs in the early records as a designation, but the first recorded bearer of the surname is Thomas Menteith in Glasgow in 1496. Robert Monteith (the change in spelling is arbitrary) graduated M.A. of Edinburgh in 1621, was a noted philosopher and historian and author of *Histoire des Troubles de la Grande Bretagne*.

Montgomery From a place in Calvados in Normandy. A Norman noble involved in the invasion of 1066 was created Earl of Arundel with large estates in Suffolk. In the late 12th century, another member of the family, Robert de Montgomerie, was granted lands in Renfrewshire by Walter, the High Steward of Scotland; his descendants became the earls of Eglinton and of Ardrossan, and owned the Island of Arran. Alexander Montgomerie, a member of the cadet branch of the family, was a brilliant poet in the court of James VI before his disgrace and dismissal. Another offshoot of the Scottish Montgomeries established itself in Donegal in 1628, and from this stock came Viscount Montgomery of Alamein.

Moodie / Moody / Mudie A nickname from the Old English word *modig*, meaning brave or proud—'moody' in the sense of mettlesome (cf. German *mutig*). A Johannes Modi is recorded in Peebles in 1262, and the name crops up in various places throughout the Lowlands including Brechin, Perth, Fife, and Orkney. Thomas Moodie was a wealthy Edinburgh citizen from whose mortification King James II financed the building of Canongate Kirk in 1688. Jonet Modye was a serving-wench in Dundee in the 1550s; the name has long been familiar in that city, nowadays in the spelling Mudie. The once-famous Mudie's Library in London was founded by the son of Thomas Mudie, a Dundee bookseller.

Moore The possible derivations are (i) locational, i.e. 'living or working at a moor' (see **Muir**); (ii) A reference to 'moorish' or swarthy complexion (see **Morris**). John Moore, a Glasgow doctor well known in the 18th century for his travelogues, was the father of Sir John Moore, hero of the Peninsular War. Moore is or was among the top forty surnames in England and Wales, and very common in Ireland and the USA as well as in Scotland.

Morgan An ancient Celtic forename, with the possible etymology of 'sea-bright'. It is most celebrated in Wales but has its own history in Scotland: the progenitor of the MacKays is traditionally Morgan, son of Magnus, and the clan has been known as *Siol Morgan*—'the race of Morgan'. The place-name Ramornie in Fife appears to mean Morgan's fort, which would indicate an early origin for the name in Scotland. It is recorded as a forename in Angus in the 13th century, and first appears as a surname in Glasgow in 1419. Morgan is however such a common surname in England and Wales (it used to be thirty-seventh) that it is probable that very many Scottish Morgans migrated from the south.

Morris / Morrison Maurice was the name of an early Christian saint (the name means 'Moorish' or swarthy), and from this is derived the surname Morris, which has been current in Scotland since at least the 14th century. Although common in Aberdeenshire (often spelt Morrice) it is not distinctively Scottish, and was indeed among the thirty-five commonest surnames in England. Michael Morris, the Dundee hangman, took on the additional duties of street-cleaner in 1591. Tom Morris, born in St Andrews in 1821, was one of the first golfing greats, only to be outshone by his son Young Tom. Morrison is among Scotland's top twenty names, occasionally appearing in the spellings Morison and Murison. The Highland Morisons are of quite different linguistic origin: their name–the third commonest in the Western Isles–is an anglicising of the Gaelic *mac gille Mhuire*, 'son of the servant of the Virgin Mary', sometimes contracted to **Gilmore** or **Gilmour**.

Morrow A version of **Murphy**

Mortimer From Mortemer ('dead sea') in Seine-Maritime. The Mortimers were a powerful Anglo-Norman family who had crossed the Channel in 1066. The name of William de Mortimer appears in charters by William the Lion c. 1165, and a family of Mortimers was granted land in Gowrie by him; they became sheriffs of Perth. A John Mortymar is recorded in Dundee in 1460, and the name was prominent in succeeding centuries as that of a landowning family in the north east. Mortimer's Deep is the name given to a channel in the Firth of Forth, said to be named for a Mortimer laird of Aberdour who (against his express wish) underwent sea-burial there.

Morton Morton means 'moor-farm' and is the name of dozens of places in England as well as in Scotland; as a surname it is not necessarily Scottish in origin, and its distribution here is fairly random. Although first recorded in Dumfries in the 13th century, it is now found more in the east. The Douglas earls of Morton took their title from the place in East Calder; no doubt many of their tenantry followed suit in respect of their surnames. The Fife Mortons are said to be of different origin: the Mortons of Cambo in Fife, whose name is first recorded in the 1300s, apparently derive from Myreton ('mire farm') near Kemback.

Mowat Of Norman origin–from the place-name Mont Hault ('high mount')–and transplanted to Wales as Mold before it became established in Scotland as Mowat. The name first appears here in the 12th century in Latinised form in the records of Arbroath and Brechin. A Mowat was sheriff of Inverness in the next century, and another was sheriff of Cromarty. Bernard Mowat, a soldier, was drowned in the Maid of Norway's ship; the lands of Kinnettles near Forfar were grabbed by Edward I from William Mowat in 1306 because of his support of the Bruce; and another Mowat signed the Declaration of Arbroath in 1320. Nowadays the name (sometimes with the spelling Mouat) is found mainly in the eastern half of Scotland, particularly the Aberdeen area, but is not nearly as popular as its early history might seem to have promised: indeed it was better-known in the Middle Ages than now.

Moyes From the French name Moise (Moses), whose meaning is unknown. It was a popular forename with mediaeval Christians, and as a surname it does not indicate Jewish descent any more than does **Salmond**. There was a tailor in Brechin in 1267 whose surname was Moyse, and a Henry Mowse is recorded in Glasgow in 1475. David Moysie was clerk to the Privy Council and king's secretary in the late 16th century. The name is said to have been common in Aberdeen over a long period, but is now rather scarce except in Edinburgh.

Mudie–see **Moodie**

Muir The Scots word *muir* means moor or wasteland, and produces thousands of place-names as well as the familiar surname

Muir, which has a long history in Scotland. King Robert II married a daughter of Sir Robert Mure of Rowallan in 1347, but the landed family became extinct in the male line in 1700. John Mur or Muyr was vicar-general of the Predicant Order in Scotland in the late 15th century. Thomas Muir of Huntershill, advocate and reformer, was transported in 1794 by a judiciary terrified lest the revolutionary enthusiasm of the French should prove catching. John Muir, born in Dunbar in 1838, one of the first conservationists, was instrumental in the creation of the Yosemite National Park in California. The poet Edwin Muir was born in Orkney, where the name is among the ten commonest.

Muirhead The name of dozens of places all over Scotland–in Angus, Ross and Bothwell–and meaning 'top of the moor' (see **Muir**). Sir William Muirhead of Lachope flourished at the end of the 14th century; the name is recorded all over the Lowlands.

Mulholland An instructive example of folk-etymology–reducing the unfamiliar to the commonplace. Mulholland is a clumsy anglicisation of the Irish name *Maolchalan*, meaning 'devotee of St Colann' (see Introduction). The family were hereditary keepers of the bell of St Patrick in Co. Derry. The name is unknown in Scotland until modern times, and is now often found in its reductive form of Callan. See also **Holland**.

Mullen–see **MacMillan**

Mulligan–see **Milligan, MacMillan**

Munro A firm tradition (supported by doubtful etymology) maintains that the Munros came originally from the mouth of the River Roe (*Bun Rotha*) in Ireland. The name is probably that of a settlement, for it is recorded as 'de Monro' in the early charters. Historically, the Munros are found in Easter Ross from the 14th century, where they held lands as vassals of the earls of Ross. The chiefs became known as the Munros of Foulis; and although as warlike as their neighbours they were among the many Protestant and Whig clans (like the Campbells, the MacKays and the Grants) who supported the Government in the Jacobite risings. Several Munro clansmen, having incurred the displeasure of Oliver Cromwell at Worcester, were transported to America in the 17th century, and the clan flourished there. Two of its members are of particular note: one of them fired the first shot in the War of Independence; another became President of the United States of America. A Munro from Kirriemuir gave his name to the group of Scottish hills of over 3000 ft, but never himself succeeded in climbing all of them. Whether the context is mountains or clansmen, the accent *must* be on the last syllable.

Murchie / Murchison–s e e **Murphy**

Murdoch The fore-names Murdac and Murdoc are found in the Doomsday Book as those of English landowners; the name is thought to have been brought to Yorkshire prior to 1066 by Norsemen of Irish descent. Certainly, its Celtic origin is not in doubt, because it comes from the Gaelic word *mur*, meaning sea. It became quite common as a forename (Murdo) in Lowland Scotland, either through the derivative *murchadh* ('sea warrior') or *muireach* ('mariner'); its Irish equivalents are **Murphy** and Moriarty. The surname appears somewhat later in Scotland and takes the form Murdoch. The primary-school teacher of the infant Robert Burns was John Murdoch; Scottish culture owes not a little to the strict educational methods of this teenage pedant. Another Ayrshire man, William Murdock, was assistant to James Watt and a considerable inventor in his own right.

Murphy The commonest Irish name by far, it has colonised large areas of Scotland, where it now occupies seventy-fifth place in order of frequency. Murphy comes from *O Murchada*, Irish Gaelic for 'descendant of the sea-warrior'; it often appears (particularly in the west of Scotland) as Morrow. A native Scottish form is Mac Murchadh, which can become MacMurchie, MacVurich, Mac-Murry, **Murchie** and **Murchieson**. See also **Murdoch**.

Murray Tradition has it that in 1130 a Fleming named Freskin obtained extensive lands in the province of Moray (which means 'sea-settlement'); in accordance with a royal fiat, his issue adopted a surname from the property, which in time became Murray, the commonest locality or territorial surname in Scotland. The senior line were ennobled as earls of Sutherland, while another branch became, by marriage, the lords of Bothwell. One of the latter, the right-hand man of William Wallace, died of wounds received at the Battle of Stirling Bridge. By means of advantageous marriages (a standard method of acquiring property) the various branches of the Murray family became possessed of the lands of Abercairney and Tullibardine in eastern Perthshire. The second Murray earl of Tullibardine married a Stewart heiress of Atholl, and in time the Murrays became dukes of Atholl. Other Murrays of the Tullibardine line founded separate dynasties, including Stormont and Ochtertyre, also in Perthshire. Large numbers of the tenantry would adopt the surname, which is now among the top dozen names in the country. John Murray, born in Edinburgh in 1745, the founder of the famous London publishing house, was originally MacMurray, indicating that at one time Murray must have been a forename as well as a territorial tag.

Mylne– see **Mill**

N

Nairn A locality name from Nairn near Inverness. The burgh (formerly called Invernairn) takes its name from the river, whose etymology has not been established and is probably pre-Celtic. The first recorded bearer of the surname was a chaplain in Inverness (1361) and the name subsequently spread throughout Scotland. The Nairn family of Kirkcaldy were pioneers in the manufacture of linoleum, and noted local philanthropists.

Naismith From the occupation of 'knife-smith'. There is no single detectable origin of this polygenetic name, which seems to crop up all over Scotland from the 15th century onwards. Alexander Nasmyth (1758-1840) was the founder of Scottish landscape painting as well as the creator of the classic portrait of Robert Burns. His son, James Nasmyth, an engineeer, made a fortune out of the invention and development of the steam hammer.

Napier Literally, a 'naperer' or person involved in the making or handling of table linen. This occupational name probably originates from a hereditary office in the English royal court, being concerned with the provision of tablecloths and linen at coronations; it first appears in Scotland in the 13th century. The Napiers were at one time earls of Lennox; a famous branch of the family produced John Napier (1550-1617) a mathematician and engineer who invented logarithms. Another branch became lords of Napier and Ettrick in 1627, with their seat at Thirlestane castle. The characteristic version of the name south of the border is Napper.

Naughton–see **MacNaughton**

Neave Virtually confined to the areas of Grampian and Tayside, Neave almost certainly comes from the Angus parish name

Nevay–a place-name which is one of a large group, found all over Scotland north of the Forth, which embodies the Old Celtic word *nemed* meaning a sacred place or shrine. Adam de Neveth was recorded in Arbroath in 1219, and Alexander de Neve was a Scots prisoner in England in 1422. Lord Neaves (1800-1870) had Neave as his family name. Neaves is also recorded at a very early date in southern England, but almost certainly with a different origin: possibly the Old French *neve* meaning nephew.

Neeson–see **MacNee**

Neil / Neill / Neilson / Nelson Niall was an Irish personal name, meaning 'champion'. The name was adopted by the Norsemen at an early stage and reached Scotland by various routes, including the Vikings, the Normans and the Irish. As a forename, Neil has enjoyed great popularity in Scotland to the present day. The surname has as many versions as it has origins. O Neill (descendant of Neil) is the most ancient; the O Neills were of the royal house of Tara, with reputedly the oldest genealogy in Christendom. O Neill is one of the commonest Irish surnames and reached Scotland by immigration. Neilson is a Lowland patronymic with many points of origin: one such is in the progeny of Neil, Earl of Carrick who died in 1256, and another is found in Caithness. Before spelling became standardised, Neilson and Nelson were more or less interchangeable, the latter form being commoner in England. **MacNeil** is probably the commonest version of the surname in Scotland, and in its truncated form can give Neill, Kneale and Nield.

Neish–see **Angus**

Nesbitt– see **Nisbet**

Ness The name of a place in the Shropshire honour of Walter fitz Alan (the Great Stewart of Scotland); it moved north, probably in the retinue of David I, and is first recorded in Scotland in the 12th century. But *ness* is also a topographical word for a headland in Norse, and the surname can originate in practically any part of Britain. In Scotland it occurs mainly in the Lothians, Fife and Perthshire.

Newlands From a barony in Kincardine or a parish in Peebles. The surname was said to have been common in the parish of Dalswinton, and later in Glasgow. Jasper Newlands of that Ilk (i.e. of Newlands) appears in the records in 1409, and Duncan Newlands was a bailie in Linlithgow in 1493. Another form of the name is Nielands, and Newland is the common English version.

Newton A common place-name element throughout the whole of Britain, Newton is one of the polygenetic surnames par excellence. In Scotland, Newton is particularly frequent as a farm name, and occurs several times in almost every Lowland parish. The surname was first documented in the 13th century.

Nicoll / Nicolson From the Christian name Nicholas, originally Greek *niko laos* ('victory people'); it became very popular in the Middle Ages through the legends attaching to St Nicolas (not all of them in his role of Santa Claus). The typical Lowland Scottish form of the surname is Nicol(l), with Nicholson as its derivative (although this name is also very popular in the north of England). The characteristic English formations of Nichols, Nicholls and Nixon (all meaning 'son of Nicholas') are found in Scotland only by importation. Nicolson originated in Skye, and the name is still frequently found in the Hebrides; the family name must have originally been **MacNicol**. Lowland Nicolsons have claimed a Norman ancestry, which an early version of the name ('fiz Nicol') might seem to support. There was an ancient family of Nicolsons in Lasswade, Midlothian, knighted in the 17th century; one of them married four times and fathered twenty-three children, thus doing his bit to perpetuate the name in that part of Scotland.

Nielands–see **Newlands**

Nield–see **Neil**

Nimmo One of the few Scottish surnames for which no satisfactory derivation has been found. The early forms Newmoch and Nemoch give little clue beyond suggesting a Gaelic basis–possibly on the lines of **Neave**; family tradition maintains that the first bearers were from the Low Countries, and adopted Nemo ('nobody') as a device for anonymity, but evidence for this improbable event is lacking. Patrick Nimmo was a tailor in the Canongate, Edinburgh, in the late 15th century: his account book survives. James Nimmo joined a rebellion against Charles II and had to flee to the Netherlands in 1680. It was at the tea-table of Miss Nimmo, an Edinburgh lady of quality, that Robert Burns was introduced to Clarinda.

Nisbet Originally a topographical name (literally 'nose-bit' or nose-shaped hill) from several settlements in the Border area; the Scottish Nisbets probably took their name from the barony of Nesbit in Berwickshire where a landed family of the name was recorded as early as the 12th century. Robert Nesbit of Lanarkshire forfeited his lands to Edward I in 1306 because of his support for the Bruce. Henry Nisbet was provost of Edinburgh in 1597. Alexander Nisbet, son of a Berwickshire laird, was an authority on heraldic matters whose Jacobite sympathies stood in the way of professional advancement.

Niven From the Gaelic *naomhin*, meaning 'little saint', and originally a forename with the spelling Nevin. As a surname it probably started life as *Mac Naomhin*, and it survives in the form of MacNiven. There were families of Nivens in Galloway and Ayrshire, and the actor David Niven claimed Scottish descent. See also **Neaves**.

Noble A nickname, meaning what it says (but possibly and occasionally with some ironic intent). The surname is not specifically Scottish, but more frequently found in this country than elsewhere. An English family called Noble settled in East Lothian in the 12th century, and the name crops up in that area throughout the Middle Ages.

Nolan An anglicised form of the Irish patronymic *O Nuallain*, comprising a personal name which contains a diminuive of *nuall*, meaning famous or noble. It does not appear in Scotland until modern times.

Norman / Normand Originally a 'Northman' (a Norwegian or a Dane), later someone from Normandy (which comes to the same thing, since that part of Gaul was colonised by the Norsemen). As a Christian name, Norman has had a great vogue in this country: the reason may be that it was erroneously thought to equate to the Gaelic forename *Tormod* (borrowed from a pagan Norse name meaning 'Thor-minded') which was particularly popular among members of the clan MacLeod. The surname usually has a terminal and accretionary '-d', a feature of Scottish phonology also found in **Lamond** and **Salmond**.

Norn–s e e **Norrie**

Norrie Norwegian visitors to Scotland in the mediaeval period included settlers as well as plunderers, and the former would be given the appelation Norrie (a reduced form of Norris, Old French *Noreis*–'Norseman'). A Norrie was sub-prior of St Andrews in 1400; Robert Norrie, a Dundee pastor opposed to the Glorious Revolution, was deprived of his charge in 1689; the name remains common in the city. Robert Norie was a celebrated Edinburgh artist in the 1780s. The old Norwegian language was known as Norn, and this has given rise to an Orkney surname, where the reference was to the incomer's language rather than his nationality. Norris (meaning a Northerner) is a common surname south of the Border but not in Scotland.

Notman A truly Scots name, whose origin is disputed, but which is probably from a west Scots dialect term *nowt man*, or cattleman. John Noteman is mentioned in 1297 as being on the king of England's service in Scotland, but there have been native Notmans in the Lothians for over 400 years. Several Notmans were recorded in 17th-century Edinburgh; the name is still surprisingly common there, but nowhere else.

Nugent In the 13th century an Anglo-Norman family from Nogent in France migrated from England to Ireland, where their kindred developed as a fully fledged Irish clan, and lent their surname to vassals who were assumed as clansmen. The Nugents were created earls of Westmeath, and the surname became prestigious and popular. The name is not recorded in Scotland until modern times, and the assumption must be that it arrived here from Normandy by way of Ireland.

O

O Brien The fifth most numerous name in Ireland, it is not recorded in Scotland before the modern era. O Brien has its origin in and derives its importance from Brian Boru, High King of Ireland. In Scotland the name is found mainly in the Glasgow area.

O Conner / O Connor–see **Conner / Connor**

O Donnell Among the fifty most frequent names in Ireland, O Donnell is that of the main Tirconnel sept, which claims descent from Niall of the Nine Hostages. The Irish O Donnells include persons of great fame and distinction. In Scotland the name is of fairly recent importation and is found mainly in the Glasgow area.

Ogg *Og* is the Gaelic word for young, and occurs countless times in Highland records as an ephemeral cognomen: for example Rob Roy's son was colloquially known as Robin Oig, and his MacGregor surname would be employed only for official purposes (usually by the arm of the law). With others however the nickname stuck (as was the case with its English equivalent **Young**). Donald Oge is recorded in Aberdeen in 1457; and the name for no very obvious reason is still commoner in the east of Scotland.

Ogilvie / Ogilvy The same Brittonic word occurs in Ochil, and it means a high plain. Ogilvie was a Pictish province in Angus (there is a Glen Ogilvie near Glamis) and the property was settled on Gillebride, second son of the earl of Angus. Gillebride normanised his name to Gilbert, and took a surname from his Ogilvie estates. The family became hereditary sheriffs of Angus, and one of them, Walter Ogilvy, the progenitor of the branches of Airlie, Inverquharity , Findlater and Inchmartin, was killed at the Red

Harlaw in 1411. His descendant was created Lord Ogilvie of Airlie in 1491, and an earldom followed a century later. Always a royalist family, the Ogilvies provided a regiment in 1745 under the command of the young son of the 4th earl; he escaped to France but was able to return in 1783 under a pardon to look after his Angus estates, as his descendants continue to do. The last Scot to be canonised (in 1976, and the first for 700 years) was the Jesuit martyr John Ogilvie, hanged at Glasgow Cross in 1615 for refusing to recognise the supremacy of James VI in spiritual matters.

O Hara A Scottish name only in the sense that it has become quite common in Glasgow in the last hundred years; it is purely Irish in origin, and native to Antrim and Sligo. Originally *O hEaghra*, it signifies 'descendant of Eagra', who was Lord of Luighne until his death in 926 (Irish pedigrees go a long way back). The actual meaning of the personal name is unknown.

Oliphant The name first appears as *Olifard* and *Olyfard*, of uncertain origin; at an early stage it seems to have become assimilated to the existing name **Oliver** and to the common noun elephant (Old French *olifant*). The adoption of an elephant as the family's heraldic symbol probably clinched the latter change; which may be why an 18th-century Edinburgh WS recorded his name as Aeneas Elephant. David Holifard, head of a French family which had settled in England after the Conquest, was of signal service to David I at the rout of Winchester in 1141, and received in reward a grant of land in the Borders; by the end of the century the family were lords of Bothwell. Another branch acquired land in the Mearns, the name having evolved through the records as Holifarth and Olifat; two Olifards distinguished themselves at the siege of Stirling Castle in 1304. The Oliphants, by now established as persons of consequence, were elevated to the peerage in 1467. The 4th lord Oliphant was the first of his line to show that fervent devotion to the Stuarts which was to be the family's undoing: Langside, Ruthven, Killiecrankie, Sheriffmuir and Culloden were the various signposts on the road to ruin; all that remained was the House of Gask minus the peerage, but it managed to produce Carolina Oliphant, Lady Nairne (1766-1845), one of the great Jacobite poetesses.

Oliver The name of one of Charlemagne's legendary knights, the faithful companion of Roland, and celebrated in various mediaeval epics. It was probably coined from the Latin *oliva* (French *olivier*), the olive branch being a biblical symbol of wisdom. Olivers are found in Scotland as early as 1180, and the name spread all over the Lowlands, becoming thoroughly confused at one stage with **Oliphant**. Auld Ringan [Ninian] Oliver, a militant Covenanter of reckless courage and hero of many a Border ballad, lived in Jedforest and died in Edinburgh in 1736. In Shetland the surname may be an assimilation of the Norse personal name Olaf.

Oman / Omand These names come from the Northern Isles, the former being the Orkney spelling and the latter the Shetland, but both are now found mostly (but still infrequently) in the Aberdeen area. The origin is the Old Norse personal name Amund, which also produces the Norwegian surname Amundsen: originally it was *Hamundr,* 'high gift'.

O Neill–see **Neill**

Ormiston Literally, 'Orm's farm', *Ormr* being a Norse personal name cognate with worm (which had the more usual meaning of snake, serpent or dragon). Ormiston is the name of various places in Roxburghshire and East Lothian. Alan de Ormiston was the ancestor of a family which settled near Roxburgh in the late 13th century; the name is now more or less confined to the Edinburgh area, although in recent years there was an outcrop in Badenoch.

Orr Two different names, one Lowland and the other Highland. (i) comes from the Old Norse personal name *Orre*, meaning 'blackcock'; it is first recorded in the person of Hew Orr who figures in the Ragman Roll of 1296. John Orr was appointed schoolmaster in Ayr in 1539. Common in Renfrewshire, it crops up frequently in Glasgow and the south west in the 16th century, and also spread to Kintyre. (ii) from the the Gaelic adjective *odhar*, meaning dun or drab. A family called Oure is recorded in Atholl in the 16th century, and there was a John Or in Moy a little later. It is now difficult to tell which Orrs are Highland and which Lowland, especially as the name was also common in Ireland.

Osborne At first sight a thoroughly English name, established there before the Conquest, and the family name of the earls of Leeds. But the derivation is Norse, from the personal name *Asbjorn*, meaning 'god-bear'. Osborne is recorded as a forename in Glasgow and the Borders in the 12th century; it was later adopted as a surname, and there are examples in John Osburn in Coylton in 1513 and Harie Osburne who was a writer to the signet in Ayr around 1648. It is now found mainly in Glasgow and Edinburgh.

Owen *Owain* is a Welsh personal name, probably cognate with the Latin/Greek *Eugenius*, and indirectly with Ewan, and with the meaning 'well-born'. Before the surname period, Owen was the name of two kings of Strathclyde in the 10th and 11th centuries. Along with Owens (the 's' indicates 'son of') the surname is frequent enough in Glasgow and Edinburgh, but is not recorded in Scotland before the modern era.

P

Pagan–see **Payne**

Page Nowadays it means a young attendant, but in the Middle Ages a page was the personal servant of a knight; the word comes from the Greek *pais*, a boy or child. John Page was a Scots prisoner captured at Dunbar Castle in 1296, Johannes Page a landowner in Strathbogie in the 14th century. The name crops up again in Fife in the 16th century, and later in Paisley.

Palmer Pilgrims returning from the Holy Land were in the habit of bringing back palm leaves by way of souvenirs and charms; the trade in these became less than scrupulous, and 'palmer' was not always a complimentary nickname. Hugh Palmer is recorded in the Borders in 1204, and Richard Palmer in Kinghorn fifty years later. There are a few more sightings in the 14th century, and the name becomes frequent in Stirling and Glasgow in the late medieval period. Although not necessarily Scottish in origin, it now tends to be an Edinburgh name.

Panton A Lincolnshire place-name, meaning 'ridge settlement'. As a surname it moved north, and appears in Fife in the 13th century in the person of Hugh de Pantona. Alisaundre de Paunton was a Lanarkshire laird who did homage to Edward I in 1296. Panton was the name of several landowners in east Scotland from the 15th century onwards, but it did not often survive into modern times; it is now known as belonging to a Scottish family of professional golfers.

Park A park in Scotland is enclosed land of any kind; in the mediaeval period it usually meant a game preserve, of some economic and social significance. Park was a surname given to persons who lived or worked at a park; it could also be a place-name in its own right, as with the lands of Park in Renfrewshire. The words 'de Park' occur as a territorial designation over and over again in the early records: not until the mid 1400s does it becomes a proper surname, with Finlaus Park of Irvine. The name was common in Glasgow in the 16th century: it cannot now be identified with any particular area, and indeed is common in England also. Mungo Park, the African explorer, was born in Selkirkshire in 1771.

Parker The occupation of park-keeper (see **Park**) was important and often hereditary. The name of William le Parker, parson of Kilmore in Perthshire, figures in the Ragman Roll of 1296. Gilcrist Parker was, appropriately enough, park-keeper at Cardross in 1329, and the name appears at an early stage in Arbroath, Dundee and Perth. Richard Parker married the daughter of a Braemar farmer, ran through her money, was impressed for debt in Perth and hanged for his leading part in the Nore mutiny of 1797; it is not however to be concluded that he was a Scot, for Parker was at that time the fortieth most frequent name in England.

Parkins / Parkinson These names incorporate a double diminutive of **Peter**. They are now frequent enough in Scotland, but are not indigenous.

Parsons In late Latin the *ecclesiae persona* was the representative of the church in the parish; this was modified to parson, and as a surname it usually refers to someone who lived or worked at a parsonage. A south-of-England name, it probably owes its presence in Scotland to immigration; but it may also come via Ireland, where **MacPherson** is sometimes rendered as Parsons.

Pate A contraction of Patrick, and a version of **Paterson** or **Paton**. Alexander Pate was a canon of St Andrews in 1528; the name is still found in Fife and Angus.

Paterson / Patterson 'Son of Patrick', a name belonging to a 5th-century Romano-Briton who became patron saint of Ireland; it means 'scion of a noble family', and it became very popular as a forename throughout Europe. In Scotland for some reason it was thought to be a more correct version of **Peter**, which it is not, and the two names for a time were almost interchangeable. William Patrison and John Patonson were 'gentillmen' in Aberdeen in 1466; Robert Patersoun was captain of a warship of Dundee in 1544; William Paterson, begetter of the Darien Scheme and founder of the Bank of England, was born in Dumfries in 1658. John Paterson, a bigoted adherent of James II, was the last archbishop of Glasgow. The name is widely recorded from the 15th century onwards, usually with a single 't' (the double 't' being more characteristic of the north of England), and is among the twenty-five most frequent in Scotland. While there were some Highland families of Patersons, notably on Loch Fyneside and in Mar, the name is essentially Lowland and with no clan affiliation.

Paton / Patton In Gaelic *Paidein*, it is a diminutive of Patrick–see **Paterson**. Paton was originally a forename–Paton Brown was given a royal pardon in 1407 for some forgotten misdeed; the name strayed across the Highland line and became **MacFadzean**. Back in the Lowlands, Thomas Patton of Aberdeen fell in the battle of Pinkie in 1547. James Paton, bishop of Dunkeld, was deprived of his office for simony in 1581; a century later another of the name was hanged in Edinburgh as a Covenanter. In happier times, the Dunfermline family of Patons (Sir Noel and his brother and sister) were notable Victorian painters. The name became strongly localised in certain fishing villages, such as Usan in Angus, almost to the exclusion of any other. It is now widespread, and to be found in huge numbers in Glasgow and Edinburgh. The Irish version is Peyton.

Pattullo There are places in Fife and Perthshire called Pittilloch, meaning 'piece of land at the little hill' (Old Gaelic, *peit tulach*). At first confined to these shires, and appearing in the early records as a territorial designation ('de Pittilo'), the surname became firmly established in Dundee, where it is now mainly to be found. Robert Pittiloch, a Dundonian on the make, raised recruits for the French service during the 1420s; he became a naturalised Frenchman and ended up as Lord of Sauveterre with the honorific title of *le petit roi de Gascogne*; in Gascony his surname was very satisfactorily rendered 'Petit-Lo'.

Paul The name of the first Christian missionary to the Gentiles and also of a number of other early saints; it consequently became a popular forename throughout Europe. As a surname, along with **Polson**, it was very frequent all over the Lowlands from the 16th century; the Highland version is **MacPhail**. John Paul from Kirkcudbright became an all-American boy and sided with the colonists in the War of Independence; as a naval commander he played havoc with the British fleet, having in the meantime amplified his surname to Paul Jones.

Paulson–see **Polson**

Paxton A place in Berwickshire, which was originally *Paecc's toun* (whoever he was). Three Paxton lairds did homage to Edward I for their lands in Berwickshire. The name spread to Edinburgh and Aberdeenshire after 1400; and in the 18th and 19th centuries was well-known as that of a family of theologians, medical writers and painters in Edinburgh.

Payne From *paien*, the French form of Latin *paganus*, 'one who lives in a village', with the extended meaning of rural and eventually barbaric. The older form of this name is Pagan, a better indication of its source. Pagan was a common forename among the Normans, applied to a rustic rather than an urban person (although the literal meaning would have been quickly forgottten). It was found in the west and south-west of Scotland, not always in its elided form of Payne. Henry Payne was a Jacobite agent and plotter, and was the last person to be put to torture in Scotland (1700). Isobel ('Tibbie') Pagan was the hostess of an Ayrshire inn at the beginning of the 19th century and the reputed author of the song *Ca the Yowes*.

Peacock By no means an exclusively Scottish name, but known all over the Lowlands for a very long time. Roger Peacock lived in Annan in the 13th century, and Andreas Pacock was a notary in the St Andrews diocese at the same time. The name appears frequently in the parish registers of Dunfermline between 1560 and 1700 in various spellings, and it was also well established in Aberdeen as that of a family of surgeons and apothecaries. It was originally applied to a vain, strutting person–or, perhaps more kindly, to a dandy.

Pearce / Pierce Piers is the Anglo-Norman form of **Peter**, and was a favourite forename with the Norsemen. Adam Pers is recorded in 1492 as tacksman in the Nethertown of Grenyng in Orkney; the name however does not belong to any one location, and was and is found all over the United Kingdom.

Pearson 'Son of Piers' (see **Pearce**). The name of the Berwickshire laird Wautier Piereson figures in the Ragman Roll of 1296. David Perisone was a Scots merchant who had safe conduct to England in 1369 (where incidentally he would find many namesakes, for it was very common in the north and midlands). Very occasionally the name is an anglicisation of **MacPherson**.

Peat / Peattie A diminutive and double diminutive of **Peter**. John Piet was a burgess of Aberdeen in 1485; the name was said to be common in Fettercairn in the 18th century. Peattie is the usual Fife version, and an alternative is **Pate**.

Peddie The Perthshire version of **Peat**. The name was commonly found in East Perthshire and Angus from the 15th century onwards, and is now thinly spread all over the country. James Peddie and his son William were noted presbyterian divines of the New Light persuasion who flourished at the beginning of the 19th century. Thomas Baldwin Peddie, the American philanthropist, was born in Edinburgh in 1808.

Peden A West of Scotland version of Paton. Alexander Peden, the Covenanter, was born in Sorn in Ayrshire in 1626 and spent his last days in a cave there: in between times this unfortunate man was hounded for his convictions and imprisoned on the Bass Rock in 1673.

Peebles A place name, exemplified principally by the town in the Tweed valley, but occurring also near Arbroath in Angus. It comes from the Brittonic word *pebyll* meaning tent or pavilion. Sir Robert de Peblis was Chamberlain of Scotland in 1328, and John de Peblys was archdeacon of St Andrews fifty years later. There were landed proprietors of the name in Ayrshire and Perthshire in the 15th and 16th centuries. David Pables was a canon of the cathedral of St Andrews and 'ane of the principale musitians in all this land in his hyme': he composed a magnificent motet for James V to sing, but the king regrettably had a voice that was 'rawky and harske'.

Pender / Pinder A *pinder* or *poinder* was an official whose duty it was to round up and impound stray animals. Known as a surname in Lanarkshire from the late mediaeval period, it occurs at least a dozen times in the records of the shire for the 17th century. William

Pender was a weaver in Glasgow at that time; much later, in the 1870s, Sir John Pender, pioneer of submarine telegraphy, was elected Liberal MP for the Wick boroughs. The name is found sparsely in Glasgow and Edinburgh.

Pendreigh Pittendreich (accented on the final syllable) is a place-name which occurs more than once in the Lowlands; it is from two Brittonic words *peit* and *drych*, and means something like 'view place'. As a place-name it is sometimes shortened to Pendreich, and this is also the case with the surname which it produces— except in Aberdeenshire where the longer version survives. William Pendreicht was at the Abbey of Deer in the mid 16th century; a hundred years later Alexander Pendrich was charged with being 'an idle and masterless man'; James Pendroch was a merchant in Edinburgh about the same time. The surname in its various versions, although nowhere frequent, is now mainly to be found in the Aberdeen area.

Penman A common Border place-name element, from the Brittonic words *penn maen*, meaning 'stone hill'. As a surname it is recorded in the Borders and Lanarkshire from the early 17th century; it is now mainly found in Fife. William Penman was a writer in Edinburgh in the 1670s; perhaps he mistakenly considered his surname to be appropriate.

Pennie / Penny The penny was a coin of some value in the later middle ages, and the surname probably indicated that its bearer was a person of substance. The obsolete Fife surname Monypenny ('many pence') certainly indicated wealth. Individuals of the name are recorded from the 14th century; Johannes Peny was in Elgin in 1343 and John Peny had a safe conduct into England a few years later. Another John Penny was prior of the Order of Preachers in Aberdeen in the 1480s; the name still belongs there.

Pennycook Penicuik is the name of a place near Edinburgh, consisting of the Brittonic words *penn y gog*, meaning 'cuckoo hill'. The surname was originally localised, and the Ragman Roll of 1296 contains the names of two Midlothian landowners Margaret de Penicoke and Hugh de Penicoke. Much later the Pennecuiks of Newhall and Romanno were a gifted family of physicians and poets; another family, spelling their name Pennycuik, won great military fame in Afghanistan, the Sikh wars, the Crimea and the Indian Mutiny.

Perrie / Perry / Pirie Usually a diminutive of Peter, through the Anglo-Norman *Pier* (see **Pearce**). Robert Pery was a tenant in Angus in the 1450s, and the name turns up in Perthshire in the following century. A family of Pyries were in Paisley about the same time. Perrie is to be found in Aberdeenshire in the 17th century, but the common form there is Pirie. The name is still mostly found in the north east.

Pert Not an adjective but a place-name element, from a Brittonic word meaning 'copse'; Perth is by no means the only name from this source. Pert appears many times in the records as a territorial designation but does not achieve surname status with any regularity. Once common among the fishing communities of Angus, it is still found mainly in that area.

Peter / Peters From the Greek *petros*, a rock, the name given by Jesus to the chief of his disciples. As a Christian name it has always enjoyed wide popularity (said to have surged in England after 1904 with the production of *Peter Pan*). As a surname it is surprisingly uncommon, except in its pet forms of Pearce, Perry and Peat. The surname Peter is found in Angus, Aberdeen and Kincardineshire: John Peter, a follower of the earl of Mar, had illegal dealings with the clan MacGregor in 1636. Andro Peiter turns up in

Kirkcaldy, and the name is found in the Borders about the same time. The terminal 's' is not traditional in Scotland, and Peterson is uncommon although it is recorded in Aberdeenshire as early as 1317.

Petrie A diminutive of Patrick (see **Paterson**) or–just as often– of **Peter**. It was a popular Christian name, particularly in Aberdeenshire (where it was apparently pronounced 'Pay-trie') and was recorded as a surname in Wick in the 1500s and in Angus a century later. Hendry Petrie ran a house of entertainment in Aberdeen in 1612; and in the same period there was a family of Petries in Montrose who were noted preachers. It has always been an east coast name, usually with the pronunciation of 'Pettrie'.

Pettigrew The accepted derivation is the French *petit cru*–'little growth' or dwarf–the name of Tristan's dog in the legend; it is difficult however to imagine circumstances in which such a politically incorrect nickname could become permanent for a human being. Another possibility is *pied de grue* ('crane's foot'), the symbol used in family trees ('pedigrees') to indicate descent. But perhaps the most likely source is an obsolete place-name. Thomas Petykreu was a Lanarkshire laird who did homage to Edward I in 1296; John Pettygrew appears in Linlithgow in1461, and the name is recorded in Glasgow many times in the next two centuries, where it is still common.

Philip / Phillips From a Greek word meaning 'lover of horses'; the name became famous in the person of Philip of Macedon, father of Alexander the Great. Rauf Philippe, a Berwickshire landowner, figures in the Ragman Roll of 1296; Robert Phillope was sheriff-clerk of Dumfries in 1629; and James Philip, an Angus laird, was author of the *Graemiad*, an epic poem in Latin on the Claverhouse campaign of 1689. In the south the name can be contracted to Phelps or Phipps: in Scotland the shortened form is Philp, which was and is particularly common in Fife (it also approximates to the local pronunciation). Stephen Philp was bailie of Newburgh in 1473, and Sir James Philp was curate at Abdie around the same time. John Philp was abbot of Lindores from 1522 to 1560. The characteristic form of the surname in England and Wales is Phillips (among the fifty commonest there), and is not by any means rare in Scotland; the terminal 's' indicates 'son of'. The pleonastic form MacPhillips is also found (showing that Mac was prefixed to an existing surname); but the commoner version is **MacKillop**.

Phimister This modern spelling is peculiarly Scottish, but the surname is widespread in England as Femister; Whimster is also found. All three versions mean 'fee-master', i.e. someone in charge of the herds and flocks. Alexander Feemaister lived in Banff in the mid-16th century; a few years later Effie and Agnes Fumester were caught practising the black arts in the same shire. The name is still most frequent in the north east.

Picken Originally an Ayrshire name, from the Norman-French personal name Picquin. Archibald Picken was a burgess of Edinburgh in the 1620s, and Andrew Picken was a tailor there at the same time. Another Scot of the name emigrated to France but was forced to leave after the revocation of the Edict of Nantes in 1685: his descendants settled in America and one of them, General Andrew Picken, rose to fame in the Revolutionary war.

Pinkerton From the former barony of the name near Dunbar (etymology obscure). Nicol de Pynkertone owned property in Berwickshire in 1296, and his name figures in the Ragman Roll; a century later a Patrick de Penkerton is recorded, and the name spread westwards in the 1500s to become localised in Glasgow. John Pinkerton was a noted historian around the turn of the 19th century; and Alan Pinkerton, founder of the famous American detective agency, was a Glasgow-born Scot.

Piper / Pyper To be taken at face value, but the instrument referred to need not not always be the Highland bagpipe: Robert and John Piper were minstrels in Aberdeen in the early 1500s. The name is subsequently found along the Lowland fringe from Wick to Perth. In Ross in 1672 a commission of fire and sword was issued against Donald and John Pyper for crimes unremembered. William Pyper, a 19th-century classicist, was professor at St Andrews.

Pittendreich–see **Pendreich**

Pollock The name of a property near Glasgow (now the home of the Burrell Collection), from the Gaelic word *poll*: Pollock means 'pool-place'. The Ragman Roll of 1296 contains the names of two persons designed 'de Pollok'–Peres from Lanarkshire and Johan from Angus. John Pollook was sheriff of Forfar at the same time. John Pullok, a merchant, had a safe conduct into England in 1453. John Bollock (unfortunate spelling) was a chaplain in Ayr in 1509. The main line of Pollock lairds is said to have died out during the wars of succession in the 1300s, but the family fortunes revived in the 19th century when John and Arthur Pollock made a fortune by importing Canadian timber–all to be lost by their land-hungry descendants. Sir Donald Pollock, born in Galashiels in 1868, combined the careers of surgeon and financial speculator; his benefactions to Edinburgh University are commemorated in the Pollock Halls of Residence. But mainly a west of Scotland name.

Polson 'Son of **Paul**', and a common surname all over the United Kingdom. It is also the name adopted by some families in Caithness, descendants of a Paul Mackay who was murdered in Dingwall Castle in 1370. In the northeast it is found with the spelling Paulson, and in Shetland as Poleson. Sir John Poilsone was cantor of Dornoch in 1500. Polsons are found in most parts of Scotland, and many will have brought their name from the south.

Poole Not a particularly Scottish name, but one with a long history in this country. William de Pol appears in the records of Dundee in 1321; John Puill was a merchant burgher in Dumfries in 1638; and Robert Poill mustered the militia in Inverness in 1684. The name was originally applied to someone who lived near a pool; it cannot be assigned to any particular location in Scotland.

Porteous A version either of 'port house' (the name would be applied to someone who lived or worked there) or a rendering of the Latin *portarius* (see **Porter**); an attempted derivation from 'Portugal' is improbable. A family of the name were lairds of Hawkshaw in Peeblesshire; and a John Porteous of Glenkirk is recorded in 1443. Sir William Portus was chaplain in Kilbucho in 1550 and James Pourtes was a glover in Edinburgh in 1670. But the most famous bearer was Captain John Porteous, who was murdered in 1736 after being unjustly reprieved by a partisan judiciary for ordering his soldiers to fire on an Edinburgh mob.

Porter From the office of doorkeeper, or alternatively carrier; in the former case the office was often hereditary (see **Dorward**). The gatekeepers of the abbey of Coupar Angus bore the surname Porter until the post became an Ogilvy perk. John the Porter of Linlithgow and Walter the Porter of Lanarkshire both figure in the Ragman Roll of 1296. Robert Porter was laird of Porterfield in Renfrewshire in the latter part of the 14th century. The name is common in England and also in Ireland, and, as well as being native to Scotland, must also have come here by both these routes.

Potter Nothing very Scottish about this name, which represents an ancient trade and has cognates in most languages. One of the Scots who were delegated to negotiate the ransom of David II in 1351 was Simon Potter of Dumbarton. The name is found in every part of the Lowlands in the succeeding centuries, and is now particularly common in Edinburgh.

Pottinger A name which at one time was almost confined to the northern islands; indeed, if such a statistic is meaningful, it is currently among the twenty commonest surnames in Shetland. It comes from the French word *potecaire*, through the Scots dialect word *pottingar*, meaning apothecary; nobody knows how it came to be localised so far north. Alexander and Thome Potyngeir were jurors on an inquest in Orkney in 1522. The name exists in small numbers. Aberdeenshire with a few exports to Edinburgh. An Irish family of Pottingers distinguished themselves in the Opium Wars and the Great Game.

Pott / Potts A reduced form of the name Philpott, which itself is an English pet form of **Philip**. Pott (the terminal 's' is a late addition) was an immigrant name, but occurs in Scotland at an early date: Richard Pott in Eskdale was charged with the theft of four cows in the same year that more important things were happening at Flodden. George Pott was merchant burgess of Edinburgh in 1694, and Charles Potts was a notary in Kelso in the 18th century. The name never became very frequent.

Pow *Pow* is an old Scots word for a ditch, cognate with the English word pool, and a familiar place-name element in the Lowlands. Thomas Pow is recorded in Glasgow in 1553, and Robert Pow in Eyemouth a century later; Robert Pow was master of the grammar school of Leith in 1697, and John Pow was minister of Coldstream about the same time. The surname still occurs mainly in the eastern half of the country.

Powell A Welsh name which has become naturalised in Glasgow and Edinburgh. It started life as a personal name *Hywil*, meaning 'eminent'; with the addition of the prefix *ap* (the Brittonic equivalent of *mac*) and with the process of aphesis it becomes Powell, a result also found in the names **Price**, Pritchard, Bevan (*apEvan*), Bowen (*apOwen*) and others. Names of this type came to Scotland in recent times and do not appear in the old records.

Powrie A place-name (it means 'pasturage') which occurs more than once in the Tayside area; as a surname it is still strongly localised there. William Powry was one of those charged with the murder of Darnley in 1567; a blameless William Powyre was schoolmaster at Linlithgow at the same period.

Pratt The Old English noun *praett* means 'trick', and is related to the adjective 'pretty'. The name Pratt was applied to a trickster or Smart Alec; it is mainly to be found in England, and is the family name of the earls of Camden. However, some Pratts apparently came north with the **Bisset**s and others; William Pratt was sheriff of Inverness at the beginning of the 13th century; and Walter Prat was a Fife laird whose name figures in the Ragman Roll of 1296. It crops up later in Aberdeenshire, but cannot be identified with any one locality.

Prentice An aphetic form of the word apprentice, with the same meaning. As a surname it is considered to belong to the south of England, but there have been sporadic Scottish examples from early times. Henry Prentice was a merchant in 18th-century Edinburgh who is credited with having introduced potato-growing into the locality. The name is now found mainly in Glasgow.

Preston Originally a north-of-England settlement name with outliers in the Lothians, Preston ('priest farm') appears as a territorial designation in Scotland from the 13th century onwards, mainly in the central belt. There is a tradition that William Preston brought from France the arm-bone of St Giles, and donated it to the church of that name in the 14th century. Sir John de Preston, taken prisoner at the battle of Durham in 1346, owned the lands of Gorton near Edinburgh; his descendant Richard Preston of Whitehill was created Lord Dingwall in 1609, but the title was lost by attainder in 1716. Sir Henry Preston of Craigmillar was provost of Edinburgh in 1434 and a descendant succeeded him in that office a century later. Prestons are now found mainly in Edinburgh and Glasgow; some may be of Lancashire stock.

Price A common Welsh surname, not native to Scotland, it was originally *ap Rhys* ('son of the fiery warrior'). Rhys was the name of the last ruler of an independent Wales. See also **Powell**.

Primrose A thoroughly Scottish name which originates in a place near Dunfermline: the Brittonic words *pren* (tree) and *rhos* (moor) combine to give a place-name which only the process of folk-etymology has associated with the flower-people. Jonne Prymros was a mason in Edinburgh in 1387, and Archibald Prymrose was a friar in the monastery of Culross in 1569; it was the Culross line which produced Archibald Primrose of Carrington who was created Viscount Primrose in 1700 and earl of Roseberry in 1703. Gilbert Primrose, a cadet of the Roseberry branch, was an eminent divine and a chaplain to King James VI and I. Another branch of the family emigrated to Sweden in the 17th century, prospered there, and were ennobled. Primroses still bloom in the south of Fife, but the surname is now mainly to be found in the Glasgow area.

Pringle A contraction of Hopringle, the old name of a place in Stow, Midlothian; it is from Old Norse *hop* ('valley') and *ringle* ('ring'), a topographical description of a circular dell. Elys de Obrinkel owned land near Edinburgh for which he did homage to Edward I in 1296; Robert Pringle was squire to the earl of Douglas and fought at Otterburn in 1388. Agnes Hoppringill was the wife of a 16th century Dundee burgess; George Pringle was a staunch Covenanter who was thought to have been involved in the Rye House Plot of 1683. Later Pringles were famous as benevolent lairds, judges, physicians and politicians; Pringle is still an important name in the Borders.

Prior A prior was a monastic official next in rank to an abbot. Ricardus Priour was sub-prior of the abbey of Dunfermline in 1448; latterly however the surname probably indicated that its bearer was a servant in a prior's household. The name (by no means exclusively Scottish) is recorded in Perth and Dundee in the 1500s, but is now rarely found outside Glasgow and Edinburgh.

Proctor A contraction of 'procurator', which means an agent of any sort, such as a tax-collector. Gavin Proctor, who worked at the smiddy of Coupar Angus in 1474, was involved in more direct labour. The name is recorded in Morayshire in the 17th century but was never associated with any particular area; indeed it is commoner south of the Border.

Proudfoot This apparently started off as a nickname for a person with a strutting, arrogant gait: there must have been a few such around, for the surname became widespread in mediaeval times in England before it came north. John Prudefote is recorded in Scotland as early as 1269; the name is said to have been common in the south west of Scotland; a John Proudfoot is recorded in Craigie in Perthshire in 1689. Most Scottish Proudfoots are now to be found in Edinburgh.

Provan The vernacular form of 'prebend', the share of the revenues of a cathedral accruing to the clergy; Provan is a place near Glasgow which was held by the prebendary of Barlanark, who was one of the canons of Glasgow cathedral. The surname would be taken by persons who lived or worked at Provan, and was to be found in the purlieus of Glasgow, particularly Strathblane and Killearn. Richard de Prebenda was clerk to William the Lion, and Robert de Probenda was bishop of Dunblane in the later 13th century. Stephen Provand was involved in the burning of Dumbarton in 1489, and Sir Robert Provane was vicar of Strathblane in the following century. Still mainly a Glasgow name.

Pryde A nickname, probably for an arrogant man; or it could conceivably have been given to someone who played the part of that particular Deadly Sin in a mediaeval morality pageant. John Pride was a Lanarkshire laird whose name figures in the Ragman Roll of 1296; Alexander Pryd was a member of the assize in Cupar in 1521. The name appears in St Andrews in the 17th century; it is still quite common in Fife, but is now associated more with Edinburgh.

Purdie Apparently a nickname originally given to someone (presumably Anglo-Norman) who habitually exclaimed *Pour Dieu!* or *Pardieu!* The existence of a French surname Pourdieu makes this theory appear somewhat less absurd; and of course the expression would have been pious rather than blasphemous. Tom Purdie was a Border poacher who became the faithful retainer and bosom friend of Sir Walter Scott. Thomas Purdie, born in Biggar in 1843, was founder of the research school of organic chemistry at St Andrews. The surname is not necessarily Scots; there is an English surname Pardoe and its variants, not to speak of a well-known make of shotgun; but the name is still familiar in Glasgow and Edinburgh.

Purves / Purvis From Middle English *purveys*, meaning provisions; the surname is metonymic, applying to the person responsible for supplying them. There were Purvises in Berwickshire, vassals of the earls of March; William Pourays appears as a laird there in the Ragman Roll of 1296, along with another Purvis laird in Peeblesshire. There was an Alan Purveys in Earlston at a later date, and the landed family of Purves of that Ilk gave their name to Purveshaugh in Berwickshire. William Purves, 'knokmaker', plied his trade of making clocks in Edinburgh in the 1540s. James Purves, the 18th-century theologian, was the son of a Berwickshire shepherd.

Q

Queen Sometimes a contraction of **MacQueen**, but more usually a variant of **Quinn**. It occurs mainly in the Glasgow area.

Quigley From the Irish patronymic *O Coiglich*, which means a descendant of an unkempt person. The name is native to Donegal and Derry, and appeared in Glasgow and Edinburgh in the last century.

Quinn One of the most frequent names in Ireland, and that of a titled family. It is an anglicisation of *O Cuinn*, 'descendant of Conn', meaning leader or chief. The name is also found in huge quantities in the central belt of Scotland, including Dundee, where it seems to have appeared for the first time in the 1850s.

R

Rae / Reay There appears to be no connection with the Caithness parish of Reay (from Gaelic *rath*, a circular fort), for the records show the surname to have been firmly based in the Borders and Central belt. It may possibly come from a lost settlement-name (such as Wrae in Tweeddale), but is much more likely to be the Scots version of roe (as in roe-deer–compare the English surnames Roe and Ray, which probably indicated a timid person). Robert Raa was a mason in Culross in 1231, and Thomas Ra's name is recorded in Glasgow fifty years later. There are Raes in Stirling and Roxburgh in the 1350s, and William Raa was bishop of Glasgow at that time. The Raes were reputed to be a troublesome Border clan, very numerous in Dumfriesshire in the 15th and 16th centuries; they had a presence in the Edinburgh area also, for another William Raa was cellarer at Newbattle Abbey in 1458, and Rae's Close off the Canongate was named after a prominent family who lived there. Dr John Rae, an Orcadian, was a distinguished Arctic explorer and ethnographer who covered vast areas of Northern Canada in the 19th century.

Raeburn From an obscure place-name, possibly Ryburn in Ayrshire, and meaning 'roe-deer stream'. It occurs as a territorial designation in the 14th century ('William of Raeburn', 1331) and emerges as a surname proper with Thomas Raburn, who was vicar in the choir of Glasgow in 1430. There were other Raburns in Lanarkshire, and David Riburn and John de Raburn are recorded as burgesses of Aberdeen, all about that time. Sir Thomas Raburn was chaplain in the cathedral of Dornoch in the 1540s. Sir Henry Raeburn, the great Scottish portrait-painter, was born in Stockbridge in 1756, the son of an Edinburgh manufacturer. The name is still found mainly in Edinburgh.

Raffan A north-eastern name, from the parish of Rathven in Banffshire. The etymology is probably the same as that of **Ruthven**.

Rafferty An Irish patronymic, originally O Rabhartaigh, from the Gaelic words *rath bheartaich* meaning 'wielder of prosperity'. Found mainly in Tyrone and Louth, it appears to have come to Scotland last century and is now reckoned to be mostly a Glasgow name.

Raitt A place-name which turns up in various parts of Scotland– Rait in Perthshire and in Nairn, Raith in Fife and Ayrshire; it is probably the Gaelic word *rath* meaning 'circular fort'. The surname has numerous points of origin also, and cannot be identifed with any particular area of Scotand. Several landowners of the name appear in the Ragman Roll of 1296, including Sir Gervase de Rate of Nairn; and John Rait was bishop of Aberdeen in the 1300s. Robert Rait was a Dundee minister who was deprived of his office by the Scottish Privy Council in 1689 for adherence to Jacobite principles.

Ralph Not a very Scottish-looking name, but with a fairly long pedigree in this country; Ralph was introduced into England by the Scandinavian settlers as Rannulfr and later Normanised as Radulf. It embodies two Germanic words *rad* ('counsel') and *ulf* ('wolf')–see Introduction . It made its way to Scotland in the mediaeval period and is recorded first as a forename, in the person of Ralph, abbot of Jedburgh. Magy and Amy Rauff were two Aberdeen quines in the early 1400s, and Henry Raife was master of a barge there in 1444. The name also appeared frequently in Nairn about then; and by the 16th century it was familiar all over Scotland (but not pronounced as 'Rafe').

Ralston The name of an estate near Paisley, meaning the toun or settlement of **Ralph**. Nicholas de Ralstoun is recorded in 1272, and another landowner, Thomas de Raulfestone of Lanarkshire, appears in the Ragman Roll of 1296. Hugh de Ralson of Ralston was killed at the battle of Pinkie in 1547, and the estate was sold to the earl of Dundonald in 1705. The surname is nowadays found mainly in the Glasgow area.

Ramage A curious nickname which comes ultimately from the Latin word *ramus*, meaning a branch. The Middle English adjective *ramage* (from the French) was used in hawking terminology to mean 'living in the branches'–i.e. wild or unpredictable. By far the earliest citation is Peter Ramage (Perth, 1304). John Rammage was curate of Blantyre in the 1550s, and the name was well-known around Haddington and Edinburgh–as it still is.

Ramsay There is a place in Huntingdonshire called Ramsey–Old English *hramsa ey*–which means 'wild garlic island'. In the 12th century, one Simund de Ramesie moved north (as did many others in the retinue of David I) and his family became established in Scotland, later acquiring the estates of Dalhousie in Midlothian. The Ramsays played a significant part in the Wars of Independence, and William of Dalhousie was a signatory of the Declaration of Arbroath in 1320. The family became earls of Dalhousie in 1633 and took the Whig side in the politics of the following century; they are still notable landowners in Angus, having inherited the Panmure estates. Another of the name, Neis de Ramsey, who was physician to Alexander II, settled with his family near Banff, and they have possessed the same lands in the direct male line for almost 700 years. Allan Ramsay, Edinburgh wig-maker turned *littérateur*, was an important contributor to the revival of vernacular Scottish poetry; he and his even more gifted son, Allan Ramsay the portrait-painter, have made the name famous in the annals of Scottish culture.

Randall One of the 'OK-words' in Germanic tribal society (see Introduction) was *rand*, the term for shield; combined with the word for wolf, it produced the forename Randolph (now virtually unknown as a surname); and with a diminutive ending it gives the name Randel or Randall. The register of the abbey of Coupar Angus contains several examples of the name in a variety of spellings, including Randall, Rendall, Randalson and Ranald (but the latter is really a mispelling, the result of a confusion with **Ronald**). There were Randalls in east Perthshire in the 15th century; Rendall took root in Orkney (where it is now the third commonest name) and although its immediate source may be the parish of that name, the etymology is identical.

Rankine Usually a diminutive of the word *rand* (see **Randall**), although the Highland Rankines may derive their name through *Mac Fhraing* ('Frenchman's son'). As a forename it was well-known in the west from the 1420s onwards, and is recorded as the surname of John Rankyne, a burgess of Glasgow in 1456, and of Peter Rankyne who lived in Kilmarnock a few years later. Thereafter it appears as a common surname in the Highlands as well as the Lowlands; Duncan Rankin was the first victim of the massacre at Glencoe in 1692 (they were not all MacDonalds), and a family of Rankins in Mull provided several generations of bagpipe-makers. The name was exported in large numbers to Derry during the Ulster Plantation. It was even Frenchified into Ranequin for use by the mercenaries serving abroad; but it is now essentially a Glasgow name.

Rattray From the old feudal barony of Rattray near Blairgowrie in Perthshire, a name consisting of the words *rath* ('fort'–see **Raitt**) and *tref* (Brittonic for 'settlement'). The first recorded member of the family is Alan de Ratheriff who lived in the late 12th century, although there is a tradition that the lands of Rattray were first granted to the family by Malcolm Canmore two hundred years earlier. Sir Adam de Rotrife took an oath of loyalty to Edward I at St Andrews in 1291, and Eustace de Retref was one of the Scots taken prisoner at Dunbar Castle in 1296. The name travelled north to Aberdeen, and west to Ayrshire, where Silvester Rettray, a follower of the earl of Cassilis, was involved in a murder charge in 1526. Two Dundee women, both called Jonet Retre, are notable because they were sisters, and illustrate the curious 15th-century practice of giving siblings the same baptismal name (see Introduction). Rattray is still rooted in the Dundee and Aberdeen areas.

Reavey–see **MacIllraith**

Redpath From a village near Earlston in Berwickshire; it means what it says, but the local pronunciation is 'Rippath'. William de Redepathe, a Berwickshire laird, did homage to Edward I in 1296; William Rypat was a friar preacher in St Andrews in 1545 and James Reydpeth is to be found at the convent of Dunfermline about the same time. The activities of George Redpath, a Whig pamphleteer who died in 1726, included bigamy and burning the Pope in effigy, for which he was imprisoned and later banished. Anne Redpath, the painter, was born in Galashiels in 1895. Jean Redpath, the Scots folk singer and musicologist, is a native of Fife.

Reid From the Old English *read* ('red'). Both the spelling and the pronunciation of the word 'red' are modern; the surname Reid therefore means red-haired or florid of complexion. Reid is among the dozen most frequent surnames in Scotland, and if one adds the English Reeds and Reades it must come even higher in the league table. Gilbert le Rede of Coul in Easter Ross died in prison in 1296; there was a John Reed in Atholl in 1362, and the name appears in Aberdeen in the spelling Red about the same time. Some Reids may have a Highland origin, for a Gaelic word for red is *ruadh*; General Reid, flautist and composer, who made a benefaction to the University of Edinburgh for the School of Music named after him, was descended from Alastair Ruadh of Strathardle. Thomas Reid, the 'common-sense' philosopher, was born in Strachan near Banchory in 1710; Robert Reid, the Edinburgh architect, is responsible for much of the best Scottish building of the early 19th century.

Reekie A version of **Ritchie**, found nowadays mainly in Fife and Dundee. John Rekie turns up in Leith in the mid 16th century at the same time as James Reky was charged with aiding the English in Dundee. Nothing to do with 'Auld Reekie', a nickname for Edinburgh.

Reilly / Riley Among the dozen most numerous names in Ireland, especially in Co. Cavan, it is a version of the patronymic *O Raghailligh*, a personal name whose meaning is unknown. The name is not native to Scotland, but became very common here in the last century, especially in Glasgow and Dundee.

Reith Of doubtful origin, in some cases possibly an abbreviation of MacReath (see **MacRae**) or perhaps a variant form of **Riach**. Lord Reith, the first Director-General of the BBC, was born in Stonehaven in 1889; the name has always been associated with the north-east.

Rendall–s e e **Randall**

Rennie A double diminutive of **Reynold**, it appears in Scotland as both a forename and a surname from the 14th century. Symon Renny was a bailie of Inverkeithing in the 1360s, and John Rayny was a burgess of Stirling seventy years later. A family named Rany or Renny were extensive landowners in Craig in Angus from the mid-15th century, and Rennie was a common name in Usan near Montrose at that period. Andro Renny, a follower of the earl of Cassilis, was implicated in a murder in 1526. George Rennie, born in 1749, was the first of a notable family of agriculturalists and engineers; his brother John, born 1761, was a famous builder of canals, docks, and harbours, and designed several bridges, including those of Waterloo, London and Southwark; Sir John

Rennie and his brother George carried on their father's work until well into the 19th century.

Renton Originally the name of a village ('Regen's toun') in the parish of Coldingham in Berwickshire; nobody knows who Regen was, but the name has the same etymology as **Reynolds**. Seldom can a surname have been more localised: the Rentons of Renton were hereditary foresters of Coldstream in the 1150s, and continued to be an important Berwick family for several centuries; Symon of Rennington was a Jedburgh laird who did homage to Edward I in 1296. Cecilia Renton of Lammerton settled in Cardross in the 18th century on her marriage to a local laird, and the village of Renton in Dunbartonshire was named after her.

Renwick A village in Cumbria called Renwick, formerly Ravens-wic ('raven village') is the origin of the Border surname, which is pronounced 'Rennick'. It is sparsely recorded in Lanarkshire and Dumfriesshire. James Renwick, the last of the Scottish Covenanting martyrs was executed at the Grassmarket in Edinburgh in 1688, shortly after preaching his final sermon in Ettrick.

Reynolds Although not native to Scotland, Reynold is the source of several other Scottish names. There was a Germanic name *Rognvaldr*, in Old English *Regenwald*, comprising two elements meaning respectively 'power' and 'rule' (see Introduction); brought to England by Scandinavian settlers in the pre-Conquest period, it survives in Scotland in approximately its original form as **Ronald**. It was reintroduced to England in its Norman form of Reginald or Reynaud, and duly evolved into the surname Reynolds (see also **Rennie**), with nowadays a considerable presence in Glasgow and Edinburgh.

Rhind / Rhynd *Rinn* in Gaelic (pronounced 'reen') means a sharp point, and is a very common place-name element with the sense of 'promontory'. Rhind is the name of a farm in Fife, and there is parish of Rhynd near Perth; the former is probably the referent for Hugh del Rynd, who was a cleric of Bishop William Lamberton of St Andrews in the early 13th century; and there are numerous individuals in the early records whose names refer to the Perth Rhynd. Thereafter, as the surname spreads, it is difficult to identify its point of origin: William Rinde appears in Edinburgh in 1426 and Henry Rynde in Caithness a year or two later; William Rynd was rector prebend of Arbuthnot in 1548; John Rind is in Elgin in 1661. Alexander Rhind, Egyptologist and expert on Theban tombs, founded the Rhind lectureship in archaeology.

Riach The Gaelic adjective *riabhach* means grizzled, brindled, singed, and was a popular epithet for the devil. As a surname Riach has no diabolical connotation, but would refer merely to hair-colouring. It is of Highland origin–and is first recorded in Inverness in 1452–but soon spread all over, appearing as Reoch in Angus, as Reauch in Aberdeen, and as Rioche in Dunfermline; it was once current in the form *Mc Awreoch*, which may be equivalent to MacIlraith, itself uncommon. Riabhach may also have produced the surname Reith. The spelling Reoch is now very unusual except in Glasgow.

Rice This relatively uncommon name, which has nothing to do with cereals, came to Scotland in modern times and by a circuitous route. It is really the Welsh name Rhys, which travelled to Munster, where it was denationalised and respelt, and made its way to Glasgow with Irish migrants. See also **Price**.

Richardson Richard is a Germanic name, popularised by the Normans, and consisting of two words which mean powerful and brave (see Introduction). Richardson is the Scottish and North Country version of Richards–'son of Richard'. In 1359 a Scottish merchant named Murdac Richardesson had his boat captured and sunk by the English during a period of truce; David Richardsone had safe passage to England in 1425 as did Robert Richardson a few years later. Master Robert Rychartsone was treasurer to Mary, Queen of Scots in the 1560s, and Thomas Richartson, a sailor, was a burgess of Dysart in 1640. These random examples serve to show that the name, in a variety of spellings, has been familiar from earliest times.

Richmond This English name comes from various places in France called Richemont ('splendid hill'). Richmond in Yorkshire is the most important example: the name was borrowed when Henry VII was earl of Richmond before he became king, and it was also transferred to Surrey. As a surname, Richmond probably comes from the Yorkshire town. It does not appear in Scotland until the 17th century, when there were one or two instances in Ayrshire; these no doubt included the ancestors of John Richmond, a friend and crony of Robert Burns.

Riddell There are two distinct sources for this name: (i) Ryedale in North Yorkshire; David I, in pursuit of his policy of normanisation, brought to Scotland in or around 1130 a Norman retainer named Walter, from Ryedale, and settled him at Whitton in Roxburghshire; the family, having taken the name Riddell, remained there until 1819. (ii) the Norman personal name Ridel; a certain Gervase Riddell, said to be of Gascon stock, also came to Scotland in the retinue of David I, and his descendants were granted lands near Edinburgh. In this instance they gave their name to the lands, and not vice-versa, and Cranstoun Riddell is their estate. Many other Riddells are on record as landowners in the 13th and 14th centuries, and the name became quite common in places as far apart as Aberdeen and Ayr, where Robert Riddel was a friend and patron of the poet Burns. The pronunciation is as in 'riddle'.

Riddoch Although found predominantly in the Aberdeen area, no local source of this name is identifiable. In the older records it appears in the alternative forms of Reddoch and Ruddoch, and is probably from the topographical term *reid heugh* ('red cliff'), which appears as a place-name in various parts of the country, e.g. Redheugh near Berwick. Redheugh was known as a surname in Linlithgow in the 13th century, and later in Stirling, and persons of the surname Riddoch appear in the shires of Aberdeen and Banff from the 16th century onwards.

Rintoul From Rentoul, an obsolete Kinross-shire place-name: although the etymology is unknown, the name suggest the Gaelic *rann an t'sabhail* ('barn part'–compare Tomintoul 'barn hill'). The surname, usually spelt Rintoul, took root in Edinburgh, and was later exported to various parts of the globe, including New Zealand, where Mt Rintoul was named after a Scottish emigrant. Robert Rintoul, born in 1787, was editor of the *Dundee Advertiser*, at that time an influential Liberal newspaper, and later of the *Spectator*.

Ritchie A diminutive of Richard (see **Richardson**); it started life as the Christian name Richie, and the intrusive 't' did not appear until modern times. Michael Richy was recorded in Inverness in the 14th century, Duncan Richie in Perth in 1505 and John Riche in Brechin in the same year. David Reche in Aberdeen had a wife who was fined for brewing ale in 1538. The founder of *The Scotsman* newspaper in 1817 was William Ritchie, who lived in Edinburgh; he was succeeded as editor by his younger brother. Ritchie is now very widespread; so is the Highland form MacRitchie, but in much smaller numbers.

Robb / Robbie / Robson Robert was a favourite Norman-French forename (from Germanic *Hrodeberht,* meaning 'fame bright' see

Introduction) and its various diminutives and derivatives have produced many surnames. One of these is Robb, which is recorded all over the Lowlands from the 16th century; Jok Robh appears in Monklands near Glasgow in 1519. The double diminutive Robbie is equally common; Beatrix Robbie and Issobell Robie were witches in Aberdeen in the late 16th century. MacRobb and MacRobbie are familiar names on the Highland borders. Robson and its earlier form Robeson were and are common in south Scotland and the North of England, and Robison was a Caithness name. The forename Bob is a late formation and does not produce a surname. See also **Robinson**.

Roberts Although a common enough name in Scotland, this is usually an import from England or Wales (where it is among the ten commonest surnames). See also **Robb**.

Robertson Robert, grandson of Donnchadh Reamhar ('Duncan the Stout'), progenitor of the clan Donnachie, had his Struan lands erected into a barony in 1509, and thereafter the chiefs of the clan styled themselves Robertson of Struan. The Robertsons were among the most ardent and persistent of Jacobites of later years; Alastair, the 17th chief, scored a hat-trick by taking up arms for the Stewarts in 1689, 1715 and 1745. Duncan Robertson of Atholl had a son from whom were descended the Robertsons of Lude, and a grandson who was the first of the Robertsons of Straloch. There was thus at one time a large network of landed Robertson families in the central Highlands; but this does not entirely explain the extraordinary number of Robertsons in Scotland, especially in the Dundee and Perth areas, where it is the commonest name after Smith and Brown. The answer must lie in the fact that apart from the well-connected, there were dozens of persons in the area who adopted the name because it was their father's forename; the first recorded Robertson was in 1371 and nobody has the remotest idea which Robert was his progenitor. So must it be with most Robertsons.

Robinson Robin is yet another diminutive of Robert (see **Robb**, **Robertson**) and one that was current in Scotland long before 'a blast o' Janwar wind blew hansel in on Robin' in 1759. But the surname Robinson has never been nearly so common here as it is in the south; it is first recorded in Irvine in 1426, in Glasgow in 1477, and in Arbroath in the 1550s, but most Scottish Robinsons must originally hail from south of the Border.

Robson–see **Robb**

Rodger/Rodgers Roger is one of the many Germanic names popularised by the Normans in England after the Conquest and re-exported to Scotland with some slight phonological variant, in this case the medial 'd'; it was originally *Hrothgar* (see Introduction) and means 'fame spear'. Roger was a popular forename from the 12th century onwards, and is first recorded as a surname in the person of William Roger in Coupar Angus in 1468. Rodgers and Rodgersons are found in Glasgow and Dundee from the 1500s; John Roger, a Black Friar, was murdered in St Andrews in 1544, reputedly on the orders of Cardinal Beaton. Rogerson is still common in Dumfries and Galloway.

Rolland Roland was Charlemagne's most famous knight, killed at the battle of Roncesvalles in 778; the name is Germanic ('fame land') and was a popular forename in many parts of Europe. The use of the term 'fitz' ('son of') is a reminder of its Norman provenance: the records of 1296 disclose that Gilbert and John fitz Roland of Ayrshire were obliged to do homage to Edward I; and Gilascope (Gillespie) Rouland of Perthshire did likewise. There were families of Rollands in Angus and Aberdeenshire from the 16th century; the surname is now mainly to be found in Edinburgh.

At some stage 'w' crept in, giving the English names Rowland and Rowley; and it is probably the common Scottish pronunciation that may have given rise to the surnames **Rowan** and Rowland.

Rollo A shortened form of Rudolf, from two Germanic terms meaning 'fame wolf' (see Introduction), by way of the pet form Rollock. Willelmus de Rollok appears in the muster roll of Berwick in 1312. In the reign of David II, John Rollo was granted a charter of Duncrub and other lands in Strathearn. The Rolloks were lairds of Wallace Craigie near Dundee in the 16th century, and there were other families of the name in the city, including that of James Rollok, an enterprising merchant who set up business in Holland in the 1530s. The Rolloch brothers of St Andrews University were noted 16th-century scholars and divines. Sir William Rollo, a major in the army of Montrose, was captured at Philiphaugh and executed in 1645. Sir Andrew Rollo was created Lord Rollo of Duncrub in 1651; the family became extensive landowners in Perthshire, Angus and Fife, where the name remains well known.

Ronald From the Old Norse *Rognvald*, corresponding to Old English *Regenweald* (see **Reynolds** and **Rennie**); it has always had much wider currency as a forename than as a surname. The chiefs of the Keppoch MacDonnels styled themselves *Mac mhic Raghnaill,* and Ronald became a Christian name which has tended to grow in popularity over the years. As a surname it first appears in Glasgow, where John Rannald was a burgess in 1463; Patrick Rannald appears in Linlithgow about the same time, and Thomas Ronnald was master of the grammar school there in 1662. The name Ronaldson is recorded in Latinised form in Glasgow in the 15th century, and Rannaldsons were known in Perth, Aberdeen and Fife in the 1500s; Cristine Reynaldsone was banished from Edinburgh in 1529 for unrecorded crimes.

Rooney The patronymic *O Ruanaidh* belonged to County Down, and spread all over Ireland in the form Rooney. It means 'descendant of the champion', and became naturalised in Glasgow during the last century.

Rose The rose is a common heraldic emblem as well as the most popular of flowers, and such is the derivation of the name as it occurs (not all that frequently) in England. In Scotland the name may be a version of **Ross**. The most likely etymology however involves a place in Normandy, whence came a family of knights who settled in England after the Conquest and took their surname (with the spelling de Roys or Royce) from their place of origin. A branch of the family, led by Hugh Rose, was re-exported to Scotland in the late 13th century and acquired by marriage the lands of Kilravock. Despite bitter feuds with the neighbouring Urquharts and Chisholms, the clan Rose were able to extend their lands in Strathnairn, and the 7th chief built Kilravock Castle which still stands on the banks of the Nairn. Although a Hanoverian supporter, the laird gave dinner to Prince Charles on the day before the battle of Culloden, and received another royal visit the next day–from Cumberland.

Ross The Gaelic word *ros* can mean either 'woodland' or 'promontory', and is a very pervasive place-name element in Scotland. A fertile headland now known as Easter Ross was one location which gave rise to this surname. The ancient Celtic earldom of Ross dated from the 12th century; it reverted to the Crown on the forfeiture of the Lordship of the Isles in 1476, became a royal dukedom under the early Stewarts but eventually died out. Meanwhile the clan Ross adopted the surname from the territory, and the chiefship devolved on the Rosses of Balnagowan near Tain. The clan carried out a prolonged feud with the Mackays to the north, culminating in a battle at the end of the 17th century at which the Ross chief and many of his clansmen were killed; the Rosses never recovered their fortunes and the lands were sold shortly thereafter. Nevertheless, Ross is still among the five most frequent names in the Highland Region. There was also a Norman family called de Ros which settled in south-west Scotland in the 11th century, producing Rosses who had no connection with either the earldom or the clan; and there may also have been confusion with the name **Rose**.

Rowan–see **Rolland**

Roy The Gaelic adjective *ruadh* refers to a fox-like shade of red and is often descriptive of personal appearance, as in Rob Roy. There was a Moritius (Maurice) Roy in Perth in the 1450s, and a Donaldus Roy in Murthly a century later. John Roy was sheriff of Inverness about the same time. William Roy, born in Carluke in 1726, was military surveyor of Scotland. Roy was a transitory surname, liable to change when the red hair became grey; and on transition to the Lowlands, it was often translated into **Reid**. See also **MacInroy**.

Runcie–see **Runciman**

Runciman An occupational name, referring to one in charge of the rouncies (Latin *runcinus*–a saddle horse) or hackneys. The surname appears in the Borders in the 15th century, moving to Moray and Aberdeenshire in the next century, and now familiar in most parts of Scotland. The brothers Alexander and John Runciman were celebrated Edinburgh painters in the 18th century; Sir Steven Runciman was a distinguished modern writer on Byzantine history. **Runcie** is a shortened form of the name.

Russell There is nothing distinctively Scottish about this name, but it is one of the first to be recorded here (Paisley and Soutra, 12th century) and is still among our top fifty surnames. It started as a nickname *rousel* ('red'), the Anglo-Norman equivalent of the Scots Reid or the Gaelic Roy. Robert Russell, a Berwickshire laird, did homage to Edward I in 1296; Andrew Russell was a bailie of Aberdeen in the 14th century. Jerome Russell was burned in the High Street of Glasgow in 1539. In England, the associations are happier: the Jack Russell terrier was named after the 'sporting parson' who rode to the Dorset hounds until he was in his eighties; and Russell is the family name of the dukes of Bedford.

Rutherford The Old English term *hryther* meant 'horned cattle', and their stream crossing-place became known as Rutherford, which was the surname adopted by a powerful landed Border family. Nicholas de Rotherford and Aymer de Rotherford were two landowners in Roxburghshire who appear in the Ragman Roll of 1296, and the term often recurs as a territorial designation before the 13th century. For a period the Rutherfords held the earldom of Teviot, which however died out in the 1750s. John Rutherford, the maternal grandfather of Sir Walter Scott, was a physician and professor in Edinburgh; his son Daniel was the discoverer of nitrogen. Samuel Rutherford, a dogmatic Covenanter from the south-west, was the author of an explosive political treatise *Lex Rex*: a scholar of international repute, his surname was rendered by his continental colleagues as Rhetorfortus and even Ritterfart. By the time of Lord Rutherford, the great physicist of the early 20th century, the name had become sufficiently well-known to escape such unintentional massacre.

Ruthven Probably from Gaelic *ruadh mhaighin* ('red place'), or possibly *ruadh abhainn* ('red river'), a settlement name which occurs widely in Scotland and Ireland; it would have been pronounced roughly as 'rivven', although the surname in Scots never has the elision. Sir Walter of Ruthven was a Perthshire laird who flourished in the early 13th century; his descendant William Ruthven was created Lord Ruthven in 1487-88; the third Lord Ruthven, although implicated in the murder of Rizzio, was made earl of Gowrie in 1581. The peerage ended with the Gowrie conspiracy of 1600 – a n unsuccessful attempt on the life of James VI which resulted in the royal fiat that the 'names, memory and dignity' of the Ruthven family were to be extinguished and their lands shared out. The name Ruthven is therefore not frequent, and its interesting history must compensate for its lack of numbers.

Ryan One of the commonest surnames in Ireland, with its roots in Tipperaray, Ryan is a shortened form of the patronymic *O Maolirian*– 'son of the servant of Irian'–possibly St Ireneus.

S

Salmon / Salmond Solomon, a biblical name from the Hebrew word *shalom*, meaning 'peace', was a popular first name in western Europe, by no means confined to Jewry; as a surname it has been on record in Scotland since at least the 16th century. The terminal 'd' is characteristic of Scottish phonology (see **Lamond**), and the name was and is common all over the Lowlands. Marion Salmond, an inhabitant of Dundee, was murdered there in 1562.

Samson From a Hebrew word *shemesh* meaning 'sun'; it was the forename of two bishops–one Welsh, the other the first incumbent of Dunkeld. It never achieved great popularity as a given name, but appears as a surname in Lanarkshire and the Borders in the 16th and 17th centuries. Agnes Sampson, born in Haddington, was a witch; interrogated by King James VI himself, she confessed to celebrating the black mass and was executed in 1592.

Samuel–see **Sorley**

Sandeman 'Servant of Alexander'; see also **Sanders**.

Sanders / Sanderson / Saunders These names are all aphetic forms of Alexander, the initial syllables having been discarded. Sanderis appears as a surname in Angus in the 1400s, and later becomes widespread. Sanderson is recorded in Perthshire about the same time, but has a separate existence in the north of England, where it is very common. Sandison is a north-east form: Thomas and Jacobus Sandesoun were servants of the bishops of Moray in the 16th and 17th centuries, and Sandison is still among the ten commonest Shetland names. Saunders, although now familiar in Glasgow and Edinburgh, tends to be of English origin.

Sangster An Aberdeen name, meaning what it says–songster or chorister. James Sankstar lived in Aberdeen in the 1450s, and Andrew Sancster was a friar preacher there a few years later. Singer is also an east coast name, although a less usual one. John Singar was 'feed to sing in the queir' for a year in St Mary's kirk, Dundee in 1474.

Saunders–see **Sanders**

Savage From the Old French *salvage*; ultimately from Latin *silva* 'a wood', and indicating wildness or uncouthness. As a surname it appears early in the records–in the person of John Sauuage in 1222. James Seavage was in Edinburgh in the 1630s and John Savadge in Dumfries about the same time. The frequency of the name in Glasgow in recent times is a reminder that Savage is also an Irish name–although one of quite different origin.

Sawers 'Son of the sawyer'; the noun has acquired an intrusive 'y', as has 'lawyer'. The surname is recorded in the west of Scotland in the 15th century, and Patrick Saware was in fact a sawer of boards in Carrick in 1529; Thomas Sawar was a friar preacher in St Andrews at about the same time. Sawyer is a much less common spelling, and was not found in Scotland until recent times.

Scally / Scolly / Scully Usually from the Irish patronymic *O Scolaidhe*, meaning 'descendant of the student'. The surname was common in Munster and Leinster, and found its way to Scotland (mainly the Glasgow area) in modern times. But the Orkney Scollay is from the place-name Skali (see **Shields**).

Scanlan / Scanlon An Irish patronymic, *O Scannail* or *O Scannlain*, meaning 'contentious one' (related to our word scandal). Most Scottish Scanlans are to be found in Glasgow.

Sclater–see **Slater**

Scobie From the Gaelic *sgolbach* meaning 'thorny', originally a place-name which cannot now be located (but probably in Perthshire). Andrew Scobie was a bailie in Perth in the 1360s, and Marcus Scobie practised a form of alternative medicine in Balhaldie in Perthshire in the 1600s.

Scorgie–see **Scroggie**

Scotland Although now to be found mainly in the Edinburgh area, the records show it to have been commonest around Kinross; this suggests that the origin is Scotlandwell–*fons Scotiae*–a famous spring and village near Loch Leven, rather than the ethnic name, which has its proper embodiment in **Scott**.

Scott Very common in the north of England, as is to be expected, for there it simply refers to someone from over the Border. Scott is however also the ninth commonest surname in Scotland, concentrated in the Border area, but familiar all over. Historically the Scots were a Gaelic-speaking race from Ireland who co-existed with the English-speaking Lowlanders and the Norse-speaking northerners. By the 'surname period', the term Scot(t) would probably apply to the language and not the ethnic origin of the referent; in other words, the Scotts would originally be Gaelic speakers living in a mainly anglophone area–and there must have been many of them, for the Ragman Roll of 1296 includes the names of six Scott lairds, all living south of the Forth. One particular family–that of Sir Richard le Scot (1249–85) produced the line which was later ennobled with the dukedoms of Buccleuch and Queensberry; Sir Walter Scott sprang from the cadet branch of Harden. Michael Scott, the wizard, probably had his origin in the Tweed Valley and was certainly buried in Melrose Abbey although he practised his diablerie in Fife.

Scouller / Scoullar Probably a student or scholar, cognate with the German names Schuler and Schiller. Henry Scoular was a 16th-century Borderer; John Scouler was a well-known Victorian naturalist and physician in Glasgow, where the name is nowadays mainly to be found.

Scrimgeour A skirmisher or scrimmager or, in the words of the historian Boece, 'ane scharp fechter'; the word later came to mean a fencing-master, but it was in the original sense that it was traditionally applied to Sir Alexander Scrymgeour, who belonged to a family who were hereditary standard-bearers of Scotland; for his services, he was granted lands in Angus in 1298 and became Constable of Dundee. His descendants became in turn viscounts of Dudhope and earls of Dundee, but the last of them died in 1688 without issue and it was not until the 20th century that the family (now Scrymgeour-Wedderburn) was restored to the title. An off-shoot of the family was Alexander Skrymcher de Aberbrothic, seneschal of the Abbot of Arbroath in the 1380s. Henry Scrimgeour (1506—72) was a St Andrews student who later converted to Protestantism and followed Calvin, Buchanan and the other Reformers.

Scroggie Said to be from a place in Perthshire, whose location and etymology are both uncertain. William Scrogie was a curate in Aberdeenshire in 1464; Robert Scrogy and William Scroggie were Aberdeenshire Jacobites involved in the '45 Rising. A David Scroghe was recorded in Edinburgh in the 16th century, but the name has always been associated with the north-east. Scorgie, also found mainly in the latter area, is possibly a variant; the 'g' is hard.

Scullion Usually from the Irish patronymic *O Scollain* (see **Scally**). There were however Scullions in Aberdeenshire whose name comes from the different Irish patronymic of *O Scallain*. Neither name has to do with the scullery.

Seath–see **Shaw**

Seaton / Seton There is no need to seek a French origin, since it occurs frequently in this country as a settlement name ('sea-farm'), notably in Seton in East Lothian and Seaton near Arbroath. Alexander Setone, who flourished in the 12th century, may have originated at the former address, while Serlove de Seton, who witnessed a deed at Arbroath around 1250, was probably of the Angus stock. The lands of Christopher Seton of Annandale (a Bruce supporter) were forfeit to Edward I of England in 1306. Sir Alexander Seton, keeper of the castle of Berwick, was obliged to surrender to the English in 1333. The Setons became a powerful family who were active supporters of Mary, Queen of Scots; their loyalty was rewarded by her son with the earldoms of Winton and Dunfermline, and the Chancellorship of Scotland. Alexander Seton, 1st earl of Dunfermline, was Lord President of the Court of Session, guardian of the young Charles I, and a commissioner for the union with England. The family later married into the houses of Gordon and Sutherland.

Sellar / Sellars The most likely derivation is from the Latin *sella* meaning a saddle; so the name corresponds to the English name Saddler or saddle-maker. Colin Sellar was a landowner in Aberdeen in 1281; John Sellar was a burgess of Aberdeen in 1407; the name was common in Glasgow in the 16th century, and is now widespread. Patrick Sellar was a lawyer from Morayshire who became factor of the Sutherland estates in the early 19th century; he was tried for his part in the clearances and acquitted, but remains a *bête noire* of Highland folk history. His two sons did something to restore the reputation of the name, becoming respectively a classical scholar and a Liberal MP.

Semple / Sempill The Scottish Semples accept a derivation from the Old French *simple*, meaning ingenuous, of humble origin. A family of the name held the hereditary post of Sheriffs of

Renfrewshire from the 13th century; a Robert Sympill is recorded in Paisley around 1317, and the name became quite frequent in the south west. The 1st Lord Sempill was raised to the nobility by James IV in 1489 and died at Flodden in 1513; his descendant, the 9th Lord, was a strong opponent of Union in 1707; the 11th Lord was colonel of Sempill's regiment which played a large part in winning the Battle of Culloden for the Government forces. A collateral branch, the Sempills of Beltrees, produced some noted poets in the 16th and 17th centuries.

Shand An Aberdeen name which probably derives from the Gaelic adjective *sean* ('old') with an excrescent terminal 'd'; the forename Sean has much the same sound. But a 15th century citation of the name as *de Shaunde* might suggest a territorial origin in the north east.

Shanks *Shank* ('leg') is a word frequently used in a topographical sense meaning part of a hill which stretches over the low ground; indeed the surname is thought to refer to a lost place-name in Midlothian, on the evidence of the existence there of a 13th century family called the Shanks of that Ilk (i.e. of Shank). Murdoch Shank, a member of this family, was granted a charter by Robert I of lands at Kinghorn in 1319. Thomas Schankes is recorded in Ayrshire in the 1420s. Although the name now belongs mainly to the west, it was an Arbroath family that produced the Shanks grass-cutting and rolling machines.

Sharkey / Sharkie An Irish patronymic originally from Co.Tyrone but which has become naturalised in Glasgow. *O Searcaigh* contains the Gaelic word *searcach* meaning 'loving'.

Sharp A nickname from the Middle English word *scharp* , meaning keen, active, quick. William Scharp was recorded in Peebles in 1376; John Scharpe was a merchant and bailie of Dumfries in 1656. James Sharp (b.1618) was archbishop of St Andrews until he was hacked to pieces by Covenanters on Magus Muir in 1679. Charles Kirkpatrick Sharpe was an artist and antiquary and a close friend of Sir Walter Scott; and William Sharp, who wrote under the name of Fiona MacLeod, was a once-fashionable novelist of the Celtic Twilight school.

Shaw The bearers of this surname divide into two groups—Lowland and Highland. The former derive their name from an Old English word *sceaga* which means a small wood or thicket and which became a common place-name element. There were three Lanarkshire landowners called Shawe or Schawe who were obliged to do homage to Edward I in 1296, and the surname became very widespread in the southern counties of Scotland. It had also been very common in the northern half of England, whence it was exported to Ireland at an early stage (and one of its bearers returned home with the given names of George Bernard). The Highland Shaws are of totally different origin, taking their name from the Gaelic name *Sithech*, meaning a wolf. This personal name underwent several transformations before becoming the surname Shaw. Early in the 13th century the clan Shaw were granted lands in Rothiemurchus which however they were unable to defend from the rapacious Cummings; although retaining their clan Chattan allegiance they became dispersed throughout the Highlands. There were Schiches and Schiochs in the Perth records in the 17th and 18th centuries, and there are still Shiachs in Aberdeenshire and Seaths in Fife.

Shearer A straightforward surname which means what it says; the only surprise is that it is hardly current outside Scotland. William Scherar was a bailie of Berwick in 1324, and Johannes Scherar was a burgess of Aberdeen fifty years later. The name was fairly common throughout the Lowlands, and is now mostly to be found in Aberdeen and Glasgow.

Shepherd This is by far the commonest spelling of the name here; Sheppard is rare in Scotland, perhaps because it involves the derivation 'sheep-ward' rather than 'sheep-herd' (see **Herd**). Henricus Scyphard held lands in Elgin in 1363; Thomas Schipherd is recorded in Angus in 1513, where the name is still at its most frequent.

Sherriff / Shirreff In the mediaeval period the 'shire reeve' was the representative of the Crown in the county, and was an officer of great importance. The surname may refer to the sheriff's household, or may be ironic in origin. Robert Schirraff was recorded in Aberdeen in 1398, and it is in that area that the name is still mainly to be found. Andrew Shirrefs, the Scots dialect poet, lived in Edinburgh in the late 18th century; George Sherriff (1898-1967) made a major contribution to the botanical exploration of Asia.

Shiach–see **Shaw**

Shields The Middle English word *schele*, Old Norse *skali*, meant a shed or hut, and has echoes in the later word shieling; *shiel* is a common place-name element here as in the south, and examples are Galashiels and Pollockshields. The surname would originally be applied to someone either from a particular place called Shiel(d)s or from any *shiel*. William Schelle was a Lothian laird who had to submit to Edward I in 1296; centuries later Alexander Sheilds was a fervent Covenanter; Alexander Sheilds went to the Darien settlement in 1699 and died of fever a year later; and Robert Shiels, a Roxburgh man, was amanuensis to Dr Johnson. The Irish Shields however claim a different etymology–from *O Siadhail*.

Sibbald From an Old English personal name *Sigebeald*, whose components mean 'victory' and 'bold' (see Introduction). The name is recorded from a very early date–David Sibald appears in the records in Carrick in 1250; Duncan Sibbaued had a charter of Lundin Mill in Fife, and Sir Duncan Sybald is recorded in Coupar Angus, all in the same century. The name of another David Sibbald, a Lanarkshire landowner, appears in the Ragman Roll of 1296. James Sibbald was a 17th-century royalist and divine; Sir Robert Sibbald (b. 1641) was president of the Edinburgh Royal College of Physicians, medical attendant to Charles II and Geographer of Scotland; a later James Sibbald was an Edinburgh bookseller and friend of Robert Burns. But despite all these sightings the name never became very popular, and is nowadays mainly to be found in and around Edinburgh.

Sievewright The making of sieves or riddles was recognised as an independent craft in mediaeval Edinburgh, and it gave rise to a surname (which, however, is very rare outside Scotland). William Suffwricht is recorded in Brechin in 1512, and Andrew Sifwricht appears in Perthshire in 1567. The somewhat illogical spelling Seivwright persists, even in Aberdeen where the name is now commonest.

Sillars / Silver Silver may have referred to the hair-colouring of the original bearer, or his financial status, or even his occupation (as a silversmith). James Silver was a *succentor* (deputy cantor) in Glasgow in 1497, and the name was recorded in the Borders and Aberdeen in the 16th century. The Scots pronunciation of silver is however 'siller', and this gives rise to the surnames Sillars and Sillers ('son of Sillar') which, despite the relentless gentrification of Scottish names, are found almost as often as Silver. John Syllar lived in Dundee in the mid-15th century, and the name became quite common in the Mearns. Silvers and Sillers are now spread fairly evenly.

Sim / Syme A shortened form of **Simon**. There was a John Sym in Banchory and an Andrew Sym in Comrie in the early 1500s; how they pronounced their surnames will never be known. John Syme was a friend of Robert Burns; James Syme, the well known Victorian surgeon, was a native of Fife. In Aberdeen the spelling 'Sim' is very common, and the spelling 'Syme' practically unknown; the same is true to a lesser extent of Glasgow, while in Dundee and Edinburgh the Sims and Symes are almost equal. The spelling 'Sime' is widespread but slightly less common than either.

Simon / Symon / Symonds Simon in its various spellings comes from the Hebrew personal name *Shim'on* , and became immensely popular as the original name of the apostle Peter, despite (apparently) meaning 'hyena'; it was also conflated with the name Simeon and later with Siegmund. In Scotland it was the traditional baptismal name of the chiefs of the clan Fraser, who were known in Gaelic as *Mac Shimidh* ('sons of Simon', and pronounced Mac-Kimmie, the modern form of the surname). Andrew Symons was vicar of Aberdeen in 1479, and Henry Symons was in Cawdor at about the same time; David Simonson turns up in Inverness in the 1530s, and George Symon lived in Huntly at the end of that century. The intrusive 'd' is merely for convenience in pronunciation and occurs in other names–for example **Lamond**.

Simpson / Simson 'Son of **Sim**'; the 'p' is an aid to pronunciation (a similar phenomenon is to be found in **Thompson**) that developed relatively recently and which implies nothing as to the provenance of the surname. William Symsoun was a burgess of Edinburgh in the early 1400s; Andro Semsoun and Jok Semssoune were petty criminals in Lanark at the end of that century–one accused of pilfering and the other of breach of the peace. To restore the balance of respectability, Sir James Young Simpson (1811—70), son of a Bath-gate baker, pioneered the use of chloroform and has a monument in Princes Street Gardens in Edinburgh. Simpson is now fortieth in the list of top Scottish surnames.

Sinclair A habitation name from Saint-Clair-sur-l'Elle in Normandy; its origin is largely obscured by the uncompromising Scottish habit of pronouncing it 'Sinkler'. The Sinclairs first came to Scotland in the wake of the influx of territorial magnates from post-Conquest England, and their name appears in the early charters relating to the abbeys of Dryburgh and Newbattle and the hospice of Soutra. Sir William de St Clair became sheriff of Edinburgh, Linlithgow and Haddington around 1263, and the family obtained the barony of Roslin in Midlothian. A later member of the family, Henry Sinclair, who had married the heiress to the earldom of Orkney, duly came into his inheritance; and his grandson was granted the earldom of Caithness by James II. The Sinclairs–a feudal family rather than a traditional clan–became great territorial magnates in the north, and the tenantry gradually adopted the feudal surname, which accounts for the huge numbers of Sinclairs, first in the north and then all over Scotland. It is now among our top seventy, and is the commonest name in Orkney by a wide margin.

Singer–see **Sangster**

Skene A picturesque legend involving knives and wolves not-withstanding, the surname probably derives from the old Aberdeenshire barony (meaning unknown). Although now a north-east name, it was never exclusively so. The Ragman Roll of 1296 contains the names of two Skene lairds, one of Edinburgh and the other of Aberdeen. The family held the estate of Skene in Aberdeenshire from father to son in almost uninterrupted succession for 500 years, but the line failed in 1828. Gilbert Skeyne, an early enthusiast for environmental health, published in 1568 a horrifying treatise on the plague in Scottish towns. Sir John Skene, Lord Curriehill, judge and zealous prosecutor of witches, prepared a revision of the Law of Scotland in 1597; his son was President of the Court of Session. Another talented family of Skenes included James, the friend of Sir Walter Scott, and his brother John who compiled *Ancient Scottish Melodies*. William Forbes Skene, born in Knoydart in 1809, was a Highland historian who towards the end of his long life became Historiographer Royal for Scotland.

Skinner An occupational name for someone who stripped the hide from animals for commercial purposes–and not a particularly Scottish name, although it is quite common in Glasgow and Fife. John Skinner was a burgess of Inverness in the mid-14th century, and Stephan Skynnar was a fellow resident; another John Skinner was a burgess of Aberdeen in the following century. A later family of Skinners produced John (born 1721), who was a collaborator of Burns and a song writer whose compositions included the famous *Tullochgorum*; his son John became Dean of Dunkeld and another son William became bishop of Aberdeen. Scott Skinner, 'the Strathspey King', was a famous violinist born on Deeside one hundred and sixty years ago.

Slater An occupational name whose meaning is obvious; the older spellings were Sclater, Sklaitter and Slatter, but most bearers have modernised their names–except in the north east, where Sclaters are still found. Henry Sclatur was involved in a breach of the peace in Aberdeen in 1399; Robert Sklatere was recorded in Glasgow in the 1430s, at about the time that John Sclater was a burgess in Arbroath. The most satisfying examples however are John Sklaitter, who in 1514 was employed in the palace and church of Dunkeld in the capacity of slater, and his contemporary Will Sklaitter who followed the same trade in Dundee. The name is still most often found in the Aberdeen area.

Sleigh Probably from the Gaelic place-name element *sliabhach*– 'moory place' which occurs widely, e.g. in Glen Gairn on Deeside.

The surname is also found in this area, the first recording being that of John and Andrew Sleth in Aberdeen in the 1270s. The name (pronounced 'slee') now occurs sporadically all over Scotland.

Slessor An Aberdeenshire name of mysterious origin; it has been suggested that it might originally be from the Netherlands, and it is tempting to link it with Slezer, the name of a Dutch landscape artist of the 17th century who produced a series of Scottish scenes entitled *Theatrum Scotiae*. Robert Slesser was a burgess of Aberdeen in 1487, and several occurrences of the name were noted in Peterhead in the late 17th century. The most celebrated bearer is Mary Slessor (1848-1915), a self-educated Dundee jute worker who became a missionary in Old Calabar.

Sloan The Gaelic personal name *Sluaghadhan* is pronounced (approximately) as 'Slo-oan', and is the source of the surname; it embodies the word *sluaghadh*, which means a 'hosting' or raid. William Slowane is recorded in Dalkeith and Johnne Slowane in Kirkcudbright, both in the early 1500s, and the name was relatively common in the Lowlands and Borders. A family of the name emigrated to Ireland in the reign of James I, and its offspring included Sir Hans Sloane (1660-1753) whose collections were the foundation of the British Museum and in whose memory Sloane Square was named. (The prototype of the Sloane Ranger may therefore have been a Gaelic-speaking raider). Irish name *O Sluaghain*, of similar origin, was anglicised to Sloan, and many of the Glasgow bearers of the name may be of this descent.

Slorach The etymology of this name is obscure; a Scottish dialect word *slorach* means 'slobberer', but such an uncomplimentary term would be most unlikely to be perpetuated as a surname. It appears in various spellings in the north-east from the 16th century, but is now rare except in Edinburgh.

Small / Smail 'Of slender build or diminutive stature' would be a likely description of the original bearers of this name. There is no reason why it should be Scottish, but the fact remains that it is rather unusual south of the Border, while being quite common in Edinburgh, Glasgow and Tayside. Richard Smale or Small was a canon of Glasgow in the 14th century, and the name was recorded in the Borders and Aberdeenshire. James Small was a Berwickshire farmer who invented the iron plough in the late 18th century. Tom Smail, an Ecclefechan lad, befriended the thirteen-year-old Thomas Carlyle when he enrolled at Edinburgh University. In Ireland, where names were translated as well as anglicised, Small was said to be a frequent rendering of **Begg**, and this may obtain in the Highlands also.

Smart The Old English word *smeart* originally meant 'stinging', 'painful', and still has this sense when used as a verb; as an adjective it came to mean 'quick', 'brisk', which is how the surname originated. Although not essentially Scottish, the name has always been frequent here, often in its earlier spelling (and pronunciation) of 'Smert'. William Smert is recorded in Fife in 1376, John Smert in Brechin in 1452, and Johannes Smert in Kintore in 1488. William Smart, a burgess of Tain in the early 1600s, was in trouble for unlawful dealings with the outlawed clan MacGregor. Smarts are now in Glasgow in large numbers.

Smeaton There are two places in Lothian so-called; the name means 'smith settlement'. The name of Henry de Smithetone figures in the Ragman Roll of 1296 as a landowner in the area; the name migrated to Shetland in the 16th century, but remains most common in the central belt. Thomas Smeton or Smeaton, educated at St Andrews, was principal of Glasgow University in the 16th century; and John Smeaton was the man who in the 18th century built the bridges of Perth, Banff and Coldstream, and created the Forth-Clyde canal.

312

Smellie / Smillie The Scots dialect word *smallie* (meaning undersized person and pronounced to rhyme with 'ballet') is claimed to be the origin of this name–and not only by the bearers, who might legitimately object to the proposal that the name means what it says. And it is indeed true that uncomplimentary nicknames seldom outlast the original bearer. Thomas Smellie was a merchant and guild brother in Glasgow in 1612; William Smellie was a man-midwife who left Lanark for London in the early 1700s and built up a large practice in London. William Smellie, printer and naturalist in Edinburgh, contributed to and produced the first *Encyclopaedia Britannica* in 1771. Robert Smillie was a pre-war Labour MP, with Keir Hardie a founder member of the ILP.

Smith The problem about this name is its universality: it is easily the most common occupational name in Europe, and the commonest surname in the USA and all parts of Great Britain except Wales (see **Jones**). In Scotland it heads the list in eight out of the twelve former Regions–its only rivals being Scott in Border, MacDonald in Highland, Sinclair in Orkney and MacLeod in the Western Isles. So common has the name become that differentiation is often sought through hyphenation or through fancy spellings such as Smythe. One explanation for the popularity of Smith is that metal-working was one of the earliest skilled occupations, with applications in industry, weaponry, agriculture and transport; if the name Smith were to be given to everyone employed in the modern equivalents of these activities (including the motor industry) the frequency of the name would begin to be under-standable. There is also the fact that in Scotland Smith is sometimes a translation of a Gaelic equivalent such as **MacGowan** or even more often a 'convenience' surname to conceal a clan affiliation post-1746. Occurring frequently as an occupational designation in the early Scottish records, the first appearance of Smith as a hereditary surname is in Aberdeen in 1398. The most celebrated Smith of any time or place must be Adam Smith, the Kirkcaldy-born political economist, whose *Wealth of Nations* (1776) revolutionised the economic theory of the day.

Smollett Although the etymology is Anglo-Saxon–'small head', and the name is not exclusively Scottish, it has a fairly long history in this country. John Smolet was a sheriff in Lennox in the 16th century, and there is a local legend that a Smallet of Dunbartonshire was successful in blowing up one of the vessels of the Spanish armada in 1588. Tobias Smallet, a bailie of Dumbarton, died at the hands of some murderous MacGregors in 1604; more fortunate was the bailie's descendant Tobias Smollett, the surgeon's mate turned novelist and polemicist, who left his native Dunbartonshire after graduating from Glasgow University, revisited Scotland only once, and died in Italy in 1771.

Sneddon This surname, now relatively common in the central belt of Scotland, is unaccountably absent from the early records; it probably comes from the Old English *snaed dun* ('wooded hill'). There was a settlement called Snawdon in East Lothian; and John Snadoune was recorded in Dumfriesshire in 1659. Snaddon was an earlier spelling which is still found.

Snodgrass The name originated in Ayrshire, where there was a parish called Snodgrass or Snodgers in Irvine; it probably comes from the Scots word *snod* meaning 'smooth' or 'trim'. Adam Snorgyrs is recorded in Ayr in 1372, and several Snodgers appear in the Glasgow records of the 15th and 16th centuries. Nowadays the name occurs sparsely, and mainly in the big cities.

Somerville The Germanic personal name Sigimar produced several place-names, including Semerville in Normandy. A Norman knight brought the name to Scotland in the 12th century in the train of David I, and was granted 29,000 acres of land in Lanarkshire; the family continued to possess the lands of Carnwath until the 17th century. Five successive William de Somervilles appear as charter-witnesses for the great religious houses in southern Scotland, the last in 1282. Thomas and John Somerville forfeited their lands in the Borders and Lothian to Edward I in 1306. John Semrell was recorded in Kelso in 1527, and John Symmerwill was a burgess-freeman of Glasgow in 1614. The name is still common in Glasgow and Edinburgh, frequently spelt with a double 'm'.

Sorley From the Gaelic personal name *Somhairle*, which in turn was borrowed from an Old Norse name *Somerled* meaning 'summer warrior'. As a surname it has always been sparse and scattered, and sometimes appears in Edinburgh as Sorrie. For some reason Sorley was taken to be the Gaelic equivalent of Samuel, which it is not: Samuel is an Old Testament name which has however had some currency in Scotland since the 17th century.

Soutar / Souter This common Scottish surname is virtually unknown in England, except in the very unusual form of Souster. It comes from the Old English *sutere* ('cobbler') and was the ordinary Scots word for shoemaker. Roger Sutor lived in Dumfries in the early 13th century; Reginald Souter was a burgess of Glasgow in the 1400s, and from then on the name is frequently recorded in Stirling, Lanarkshire, Perthshire, and (particularly) Aberdeenshire. Androw Soutar elder and Andro Soutar younger, who flourished in Dundee in the 1520s, were not father and son but brothers. 'The Soutars of Cromarty', two notable promontories on the Firth, were supposed to be the workstools of two giants who supplied their comrades with shoes and buskins. In real life, William Soutar, the Perth poet (1898—1943), supplied his fellow-men with a delightful body of Scots verse.

Spalding The name of a town in Lincolnshire, meaning 'place of ditch-dwellers'; the surname was brought to prominence in Scotland in the 13th century by Peter of Spalding, the English burgess of Berwick-on-Tweed, who traitorously aided in its capitulation to the Scots in 1318; he was awarded lands in Angus for his transfer of loyalty. Earlier Spaldings had been recorded in Kincardineshire and Elgin, and the Ragman Roll contains the name of one Symon de Spalding who was parson of Ochiltree in Ayrshire. The name turns up in Aberdeen, where George Spalding was provost in 1479; there was also a notable family in Dundee at the time, commemorated in Spalding's Wynd. A 17th-century Spalding laird brought a curse on his family when he hanged a retainer from a tree near his castle in Strathardle; the curse was that no male heir would ever be born at Ashintully–and it seems to have been effective for there have been no Spaldings in that area for some time. A more civilised contemporary was a historian and antiquary, for whom the Spalding Club is named. Generations of Spaldings were golf club makers in St Andrews.

Speed / Speedie The Middle English word *sped* meant 'good fortune' (as in Godspeed); the swiftness element is modern. The original Speed would be a fortunate person: and Speedie is the diminutive. Nicholas Speed is recorded in Angus in 1410; Thomas Speedy lived in Edinburgh and John Spidie in Dunfermline in the mid 1500s; George Speed and William Speed were ministers in the 17th century of Aberlour and Ednam respectively. Despite its auspicious meaning, the name was never common.

Speirs / Spiers In the second spelling the name is from the Old French *espier*; it means 'spy-er', and most bearers will prefer to interpret the derivation in the sense of watchman rather than nosey-parker. In the Speirs spelling (which is commoner, especially in Glasgow), the origin may be spear, the weapon. Willelmus Sper is recorded in Perth in the early 13th century; Gilbert and Roger Spere in Irvine in the early 1400s, and David Spere in Glasgow a little later. Thomas Speir was a merchant burgess in Edinburgh in 1626. The terminal 's' means 'son of': George Speris, who lived in Stirling in the 1540s, may have had a watchman or spearsman as ancestor.

Spence An occupational name for someone who worked in a larder or store; the word is a reduced form of 'dispenser', and the early records refer to an official known variously as *spensa, dispensa* and *dispensator*. The surname was originally Spens, and the brave Sir Patrick of the ballad was a historical person. John Spens was a bailie of Irvine in 1260. Henry de Spens, a Perthshire laird, was obliged to do homage to Edward I in 1296; his descendants settled in Gascony and married into the Estignols family, and his name appears there as d'Espences. A ship in which Laurence de Spense had a share was wrecked off the Northumberland coast in 1365. Thomas Spence was bishop of Aberdeen in the late 15th century; Sir James Spens was sent to Sweden by James I, where the family still thrives. The English form of the agency-noun–Spencer–is rare as a name in Scotland.

Spottiswoode Originally a place-name, from an old barony in the parish of Gordon in Berwickshire; Spott would be a personal name, but the reference appears to be unknown. The founder of the family was Robert de Spotteswoode of Berwickshire, who was obliged to submit to Edward I in 1296. John Spottiswood (1565—1639) was archbishop of St Andrews and a noted historian. A descendant, Alexander Spottiswood became governor of Virginia in the 18th century, and was one of the chief promoters of the Glasgow tobacco trade. The surname is now relatively uncommon in Scotland.

Spreull / Sproule The origin of this name is quite uncertain; it may be connected with the Old English personal name *Sprow*. The surname is recorded in Dunbartonshire as early as the 13th century, and was current in Donegal and Derry from the 1600s, but is entirely absent from the English records. Walter Spreul was steward to the earl of Lennox in the 1280s, and the name of Wautier Spreule, a Lanarkshire landowner, appears in the Ragman Roll of 1296. John Spreull (1646—1722), a nonconformist merchant of Glasgow, was tortured and imprisoned on the Bass rock for six years. The name is still found mostly in Glasgow.

Stalker The word stalker is derived from Old English *stelan* (to steal, hence 'stealth'); the surname however is to be taken in the occupational sense. It first appears in the 15th century records in the persons of Patrick and John Stalcare. James Stalcare is recorded in Tweeddale in the mid 15th century, and Donald Stalker in Glenisla about the same time. John Stalker was a 17th-century lansdcape painter in Edinburgh.

Stark The Middle English adjective *stark* meant firm, unyielding– i.e. a strong person. Richard Starke is recorded in 1376 in 'Estirbalbretane' (which is probably a forgotten estate in Strathclyde); William Stark was in Carstairs in the 1540s and Beatrix Sterk lived in Glasgow at the same time; another Glaswegian, Archibald Stark (b. 1677), had a son, General John Stark, who fought in the American Revolution. It is still a Glasgow name.

Steedman / Steadman In Anglo-Saxon times *stede* meant an estate or farm (cf. our word 'steading'), and the stead-man would be a farm servant or overseer. Symon le Stedman is recorded in 1321, and the name crops up again in Angus in the early 16th century. Alexander Steedman appears in Kinross in 1621; the name is now found mainly around Edinburgh. The form Studeman, current in Edinburgh in the 16th and 17th centuries, may be from 'studman'–the keeper of the stallions; indeed, the old word for stallion was 'steed', and it is possible that some Steedmans may derive their name from cavalry.

Steele Usually from the Old English word *stigel*, a stile, a word which appears in several place-names such as Ashiestiel. But there are many English Steeles in the midlands and north whose name will have a metallic origin, either as steelworker or 'true as steel'. The name is first recorded in Scotland in 1259 in the person of Henry Stel, about whom nothing is known. William Stele was a burgess of Edinburgh in 1423, and John Steyll turns up in Coupar Angus in 1486; John Steill, a Borderer, was hanged for theft in 1524. Steeles are very numerous in Glasgow.

Steen / Stein A contraction of **Steven**. The terminal 's' (now uncommon) indicates 'son of Steven': John Stenes was King James I's ambassador in 1425; Andrew Stanes was king's bailie in Fife a century later, and Robert Stanes was a bedesman in Edinburgh in the 1580s. Alan Steyn was a monk of Kilwinning Abbey in the 1550s, and John Steyne and James Stein were burgess freemen of Glasgow at the same time. Jock Stein, Celtic boss and later Scotland's national manager, died in Cardiff in 1985 just as his side was about to qualify for a World Cup play-off. See also **Stone**.

Stenhouse From the former barony near Falkirk; it means 'stone house'. John de Stanhus is recorded as early as 1200, and Adam de Stanus of Dunipace flourished about the same time. Sir Robert Stanhus was chaplain in the diocese of Brechin in the 1440s; John Stainehous was merchant burgess of Edinburgh in the 17th century; the name is still commonest there.

Stephen / Stephenson–see **Stevenson**

Stevenson Stephen (which means 'crown' or 'wreath' or 'garland') has been a popular Christian name since the martyrdom of the eponymous saint; as a surname, especially in the form and spelling Stevenson, it is peculiarly Scottish; indeed, Stevenson is among the fifty top Scottish surnames, and among the top twenty-five in central Scotland in order of popularity. John Steywynson is recorded in Banff in 1388, and Alexander Stephenson in Coupar Angus in 1446; John Steuin was in Aberdeen early in the 16th century, and Alexander Stevyn was in Glasgow at the same time. Thereafter the name is frequent all over the Lowlands, but there is no common *Mac* name derived from Stephen. Stiven seems to be a 19th century variant; and the contraction **Stein** has been discussed. George Stephenson, the inventor of the locomotive, was of Scottish parentage; but the most famous is Robert Louis, whose lighthouse-building forebears had made the name known in Scotland before his literary genius caused it to resound throughout the world.

Stewart The most famous occupational name in Scotland, it comes from the office of steward, which in the early mediaeval period was a position under the Crown of great importance and honour, both in the administrative and the military sphere. Walter FitzAlain, a Norman knight, was created Great Steward of Scotland by David I; during the 13th century his kinsmen, by now bearing the surname Stewart, acquired vast territories in Kintyre, Arran, Cowal and the whole of Bute, together with fleets of galleys and large numbers of Gaelic-speaking clansmen. A descendant of the Great Steward married Marjorie, daughter of Robert I, and begot the dynasty of Scottish kings and queens who reigned until 1714. The numerous royal descendants founded other branches of the family in such places as Atholl and Strathearn in Perthshire, Appin in Argyll, Menteith and Strathspey. And there were earlier and lesser stewards who had adopted the surname, such as Phillippe Styward of Roxburghshire and William le fiz de Stywarde of Berwickshire, whose names figure in the Ragman Roll of 1296. Even lowlier subjects may have taken the royal surname from their stewarding occupation (see Introduction). The spelling 'Stuart' occurs because there is no letter 'w' indigenous to the French language.

Stirling From the town, which was earlier known as Strevelin, and which is probably a river-name. Gilbertus de Struelin is recorded in 1136, and the surname occurs regularly in the records in this form until the late 14th century. Thereafter it becomes very frequent in its present spelling, especially in Glasgow and Edinburgh. A Stirling family settled in Nairn at an early date; and the Stirlings of Keir have held their lands from 1160 (although spelling their surname in no fewer than sixty-four different ways).

Stobie / Stobo The name of the village of Stobo near Peebles, in Old English *stubb-holh*, means 'stob or post-hollow'. David de Stubhou or Stobhou appears in the records in the late 12th century and Adam de Stobhou was in Peebles a hundred years later. William Stobbe was a burgess of Berwick in the early 1300s. The name became familiar throughout the Lowlands, especially Lanarkshire, and it was a Glaswegian, Major Robert Stobo, who led the Fraser Highlanders up the Heights of Abraham in Quebec in 1757.

Stoddart From the Old English word *stod*, followed by *herd* or *ward*; the original Stoddart was in charge of a stud of horses. David Stothirde, John Studehird and William Studhirde were all Douglas tenants in Dumfriessire in the 16th century; Sir James Stodart was chaplain in Methven around the same time. Thomas Stoddart wrote on angling topics in the Victorian period, and R. Stodart published a book on Scottish arms, heraldry and genealogy in Edinburgh in 1881. The name is nowadays found mainly in Glasgow and Edinburgh.

Stone This name occurs mainly in the big cities in Scotland, and many bearers will be of English origin. However, it does appear sparsely in the early records: Thomas de Stone was a landowner in Roxburghshire in the 1290s, and the name occurs in Aberdeen in the following century. Stone is a common place-name element, which is probably the origin of the surname. The German and

Jewish name *Stein* of course has the same meaning, and in some cases underwent translation.

Storrey / Storrie The Old Norse personal name *Stori* comes from a word meaning big or large. William Stori is recorded in Dundee in 1281, and Walter Stori was in Aberdeen a few years later, where the name became quite common. Johannis Stury turns up in Edinburgh in 1389. Robert Story was a 19th-century Principal of Glasgow University.

Stott A Scots dialect word for a bullock; the surname, frequently found in Aberdeen, may be either a nickname or occupational in origin. Stott is also a common surname in Lancashire and Somerset, where the word can also mean heifer or nag. Gilbert Stute was born in Aberdeen in 1212, and Andrew Stott was a burgess of the city in 1490. Margaret Stote lived in Lanarkshire in the 1670s.

Stout Stout on the face of it means what it says, but in a comp-limentary sense, as in 'stout fellow'. There was however an Old Norse by-name *Stutr* which meant the opposite–a gnat or under-sized person. The name was found mostly in the Northern Isles, and said to be the commonest name on Fair Isle. It is now scattered fairly evenly throughout Scotland.

Strachan The name of a village near Banchory on Deeside, probably from the Gaelic *srath eachain* , meaning 'foal valley'. As a place-name it is correctly pronounced 'stra-an', and 'Straughan' tends to be the 'posh' pronunciation of the surname also; indeed some bearers spell it in this manner. Waldeuus and Ranulph de Stratheihan appear in the records of the early 13th century, and the name is frequently recorded in this form for the next hundred years. Abraham Stratheykyn and William Stradachin lived in Aberdeen in the 15th century, the name becoming and remaining common in that city. Alis Strathachine was a Dundee 'wifie' of the 1520s; a contemporary family of Strachans were lairds of nearby Carmyllie. John Strachan, who was born in Aberdeen in the late 18th century, became the first bishop of Toronto and founded the university there. Strachans were also well-known in the armed services: Archibald Strachan, a supporter of Cromwell, defeated the Marquess of Montrose at Carbisdale in 1650; and a family of Strachan baronets were naval captains in the wars against Revolutionary France.

Strang / Strange These names are of two different origins, one English and one French, and are not now readily distinguishable. The first is from Old English *strang,* preserved in Scots and meaning 'strong'. It is common enough in Scotland, but not found in the south. The second comes from the Old French *estrange* meaning 'foreign', and as a surname belongs to the group which refers to bearers of different national or ethnic origin–like **Scott, Inglis, Norrie, Wallace** and **Galbraith**. William Strange, a burgess of Montrose, figures in the Ragman Roll of 1296; John Strang lived in Aberdeen in the 1390s and Walter Strang was in Forfar a little later. The Strangs of Balcaskie were at one time a well-known Fife family. Alexander Strang was a merchant in Kirkwall in the 1520s; two hundred years later another another Kirkwall native, having added an 'e' to the end of his name, became well-known as Sir Robert Strange, engraver, art-collector and fervent Jacobite. John Strang had to resign his post as Principal of Glasgow University in 1650 when accused of heresy.

Stronach An Aberdeenshire surname, from the Gaelic word *sronach*, meaning 'having a prominent nose'. Duncan Stronoch appears in the records in 1447; James Stronach was chaplain at Kilravock in 1524, and Andro Stronach was in Dipple 50 years later. The name never became common elsewhere.

Struther / Struthers The Old English word *strod*, meaning 'marsh land' (as in Stroud) did not pass into modern English, but it did form a Scots dialect word *strother*. This word is the basis of many place-name elements in Lanarkshire and Fife; but it is an estate in Northumbria which is thought to have been the origin of the surname Struther (and this is preferable to the usual derivation from the Gaelic *sruth* meaning stream). Thomas Strothers was recorded in Kelso in the mid-16th century, and John Stwtheris was in Glasgow about the same time; it is in the latter area that the name is now most frequent. John Struthers is a good example of an early Victorian 'lad o' pairts': he was a cowherd turned successively shoemaker, poet and librarian.

Stuart–s e e **Stewart**

Sturgeon Probably a metonymic occupational name for a fish-monger, but possibly a nickname based on some perceived characteristic of the fish. It is not exclusively Scottish, but has a long history here having been recorded in the south-west from the 16th century.

Sturrock An Angus name, although the first sighting is in Aberdeen in 1488, where Laurentius Sturrok was a chaplain. Alexander Storrok lived in Angus in the late 15th century; and John Storrock caused a breach of the peace in Dundee in 1676. Nobody knows the derivation of the name; it could well be the Gaelic adjective *storach*–'having broken teeth', but evidence is entirely lacking.

Sullivan This is or used to be the third commonest name in Ireland, and is now found fairly frequently in Glasgow. It is from the patronymic O Suileabhain, which comes from *suil dubhan*–'little black-eyed one'.

Summers While a reference to the season is possible, the derivation is more likely to be the old occupation of sumpter or 'driver of pack-animals' (Old French *sommier*, *sommetier*, a pack-horse). The name of William Sumer is recorded in connection with the hospice of Soutra in the early 13th century. Johannes Soumer was a burgess of Perth in 1365, and Adam Summer lived in Glasgow in the mid-16th century. David Sommer was in Ancrum in 1633 and John Symer was a burgess of Aberdeen about the same time. A family named Symmer or Somyr, who held their Angus lands from 1450 to 1750, are said to have changed their name to Seymour.

Sutherland The 'southern land' of the Vikings–that is to say, south of their colonies of Orkney and Shetland. With the eclipse of Norse power in the 13th century, Sutherland became a Scottish earldom and evolved into a clannishly feudal society at constant strife with the land-hungry Gordons to the south. The Gordons indeed usurped the Sutherland earldom, and when the title was finally restored to the rightful claimants the evil days of the Clearances were about to begin. In the interim, many of the ordinary tenants had adopted the chiefly name, and in Victorian times Sutherland was among the top fifty Scottish surnames. Depopulation changed that, but Sutherland continues to be among the commonest names in Orkney and Shetland, and is seventh in the Highland Region.

Swain From *Sveinn*, an Old Norse by-name, involving the concept of swain or servant; it is said to have been one of the most usual Scandinavian names in England during the mediaeval and early modern periods. As a surname it has a long history in Scotland: Elyas Sweyn was constable of Leuchars in 1250 (a very early appearance of a surname); James Swayne was in Kilbucho, Peebles, in 1376, and Patrick Swane in Glasgow in the 1470s. The name is now much less common than **Swan**, of which it is sometimes a variant. See also **MacQueen**.

Swan Taken at its face-value it refers to one or other of the attributes of the bird, which included purity and elegance. Very often however it is a variant of **Swain**. Swan became a common surname all over, and is now found mainly in Edinburgh; Annie S. Swan, once a best-selling novelist with a mainly female readership, was born in Coldingham in Berwickshire. Swanson is found in Highland Region, particularly Caithness, and Swanney (the diminutive form) is current in Orkney.

Sweeney Originally a Highland name, *MacSuibhne* means 'son of the pleasant man'. It was carried to Ireland in mediaeval times by the galloglass soldiers of fortune, and re-exported to Scotland (mainly Glasgow) in the modern period. It also forms the basis for one of the two versions of the surname **MacQueen**.

Syme See **Sim**

T

Taggart A contraction of **MacTaggart**. Patrick Taggart is recorded in Dumfries in 1544, and about that time the name occurs several times also in Kirkcudbright. In general, Taggart is the west-country version while the aspirated form **Haggart** is current in the east of Scotland.

Tait The Old Norse word *teitr*, which means 'cheerful', had a certain currency as a personal name; it achieved surname status in Scotland in the early 14th century, the first recorded example being that of Thomas Tayt. In the 1360s John Tayt was a clerk at the hospital of Montrose, and Alexander Tayt was a burgess of Edinburgh. Adam Tayt is recorded in Paisley in 1432; the name migrated to Orkney, and also became numerous in Ulster. It was a Scot, Archibald Campbell Tait, who became a very influential Archbishop of Canterbury in 1869; and Freddie Tait, son of an Edinburgh mathematician, was amateur golf champion before his untimely death in the Boer War.

Tasker A tasker was a piece-worker, usually engaged in threshing or reaping; the term is from Middle English and survives in Scots dialect. The surname, not frequent, is commonest in Tayside; William Tasker was sergeant of the guard in Dundee in 1643.

Tawse A phonetic rendering of *Tamhas*, the Gaelic form of Thomas. It is recorded as a surname in Perthshire and Aberdeenshire in the 17th century. See **MacTavish**.

Taylor A tailor was originally a cutter-out of cloth (from Old French *tailler*, to cut). The name occurs as an occupational designation in Scots records from the earliest times (occasionally alternating with its Latinised version, Scissor–now alas unknown), and is among the twenty commonest in Scotland; it is however even commoner south of the Border. Alexander le Taillur was valet of Alexander III around 1276; John le Taillur was in charge of the mill of Selkirk in 1292, and Brice le Taillur was taken prisoner at Dunbar in 1296. William Leslie alias Tailzour was a tailor in Dundee in the 1520s who was obviously in process of changing his surname; Brunan Talzor, another tailor, had already done so. The word tailor passed into Gaelic as *taillear,* and gave rise to a Highland version of the surname, Macantaillear, which however did not successfully transplant in the Lowlands and reverted to its original form of Taylor. Based on the flimsy evidence of one *Taillear dubh*, who was a follower of Cameron of Lochiel, it has been maintained that the Taylors are a 'sept' of the clan Cameron. This will not stand up to examination, and the truth is that most Scottish Taylors are descended from one or other of the many practitioners of the trade of tailoring, whether in the Highlands or the Lowlands or even in England.

Teare–see **MacIntyre**

Telfer / Telford From Old French *taille fer*–'cut iron', probably in the sense of armourer. The name of Willelmus Tailfer is recorded in Angus at the beginning of the 13th century; the Tailferes of Haircleugh in Lanarkshire are said to have held their land there for over three hundred years; Andrea Taillefere is recorded in Inverkeithing in 1413; and by the mid-17th century the name appears in most of the records of Lowland Scotland. Telfer and Telford are one and the same surname, the terminal 'd' being a formation analogical with the very common place-name element of ford. Thomas Telford, 'the Colossus of Roads', who built over 1000 miles of highway in Britain, plus innumerable bridges and the Caledonian Canal, used the Telfer form to begin with.

Temple The Knights Templar were a mediaeval chivalric order who took their name from Solomon's temple in Jerusalem, the site of which they at one time claimed to occupy. The Scottish branch of the order had its HQ in a village in Midlothian, to which it gave the name of Temple. The surname in Scotland comes from the village; although it has a long history it never became frequent. Agnes de Tempill held lands in Haddington in 1429; Johannes Tempill took part in the burning of Dumbarton in 1489. Much later, William Temple was a friend of Boswell, and grandfather of Dr Frederick Temple, Archbishop of Canterbury.

Templeton From a settlement near Dundonald in Ayrshire, said to have been on the site of a Knights Templar house–see **Temple**. Gilbert de Templeton was an Ayrshire laird whose name figures in the Ragman Roll of 1296; his contemporary Gilbertus de Templeton was rector of the church of Rothesay. The name is still commonest in the west of Scotland.

Tennant Despite its various spellings, it is to be understood in its literal sense. William Tennant was recorded in Linlithgow in the 14th century, and John Tenant was one of the garrison of Edinburgh Castle in 1339-40. John Tennand was burgess of Stirling in 1366; and thereafter the name occurs frequently in the registers of Glasgow, Ayrshire and Fife. William Tennant, Professor of Hebrew at St Andrews University, was the author of the poem *Anster Fair*, published in 1812. Charles Tennant established the chemical works at St Rollox, Glasgow, in 1800; his grandson, Sir Charles, a noted art collector, became 1st Baron Glenconner. But the name is not exclusively Scottish, being also native to Yorkshire.

Teunion / Tewnion–s e e **Younie**

Thain The Old English word *thegn* (thane) means in general a noble retainer or attendant, and in Scotland it was a legal term denoting someone who held land direct of the Crown. It is a frequent occupational designation in the records of the 12th and 13th centuries, by which time it must have lost the exalted status that it has in, say, Shakespeare's *Macbeth*. Patone Thane is recorded in Arbroath in 1493, and David Thane in Strathmartine near Dundee some years later. Richard and James Thayne were burgesses of Dundee in 1563, and in the next century Patrick Thain was in charge of the gibbet in Aberdeen. The name is still commonest there.

Thaw–see **Thow**

Third Tripartite land-division was very common, particularly in farm tenancies, and there are several Lowland place-names embodying the term 'third'. Adam Third was a burgess of Aberdeen in 1596; and for no very obvious reason the name has always been commonest in the north-east.

Thom / Thoms A pet form of **Thomas**. Alexander Thome was vicar of Stracathro in 1433; Jok Tom is recorded in Coupar Angus in 1473; and Andrew Thome lived in Glasgow in the 1490s. Much later, James Thom was an early 19th-century sculptor noted for his modelling of the characters in Burns' poem *Tam o Shanter.* The genitive form Thoms is sometimes a reduction of MacThomas.

Thomas A Hebrew name, meaning 'the twin', that of a disciple of Christ renowned for his intellectual caution. Very popular as a Christian name through the martyrdom of Thomas Becket, and at one time among the top ten surnames in England and Wales. It is not found in Scotland as a surname before the modern period, but is now quite common in the larger cities.

Thompson / Thomson As a rough guide, Thomas as a surname is native to Wales, Thompson to the north of England and Thomson to Scotland. (The medial 'p' is a glide consonant typical of English phonology). A John Thomson is recorded in Ayrshire in 1318, and an Adam Thomson in the same county a generation later. A family of Thomsons possessed the estate of Duddingston near Edinburgh for five generations, until it was sold in 1668. The name appears frequently in records all over the Lowlands, and it has only recently relinquished third place in the league table of commonest Scottish surnames (it is now fifth). Thomson is a polygenetic name par excellence, in that it has many points of origin, does not belong to any particular area of Scotland, and its bearers (despite the existence of a Clan Thomas Society) do not claim descent from a common ancestor. But Thomson does have its Gaelic equivalent in MacThomas; and there are other derivatives such as **MacTavish** ('son of Tammas') and MacCombie ('son of Tommy'). MacLehose is Gaelic *mac gille Thoimis*, 'son of the devotee of St Thomas'. A small clan called MacThomais or MacComish had lands in Glenshee until ousted by a series of clan feuds and lawsuits in the 17th century; some of them would have anglicised their names to Thomson on leaving their native Perthshire.

Thorburn From one or other of the Old Norse names Thorbjorn or Thorbrand; (Thor was the Norse god of thunder, *bjorn* meant bear, and *brand* meant sword). Ricardus Torbrand was provost of Aberdeen in 1330; Thomas Thurbrande was a notary in Glasgow a century later; John Thorbrand is recorded in Selkirk around the same time, and there are many other instances in the Borders. William Thorburn of Leith emigrated to Sweden in 1823, and the name proliferated there; it remains quite common in the Edinburgh area.

Thornton Any settlement with a hedge round it could have become known as Thornton, and there are over thirty such places in the United Kingdom. The surname can come from any of them; but the Scottish Thorntons are thought to hail from the Mearns.

Laurence de Thorneton is recorded in Arbroath in the early 13th century, and two landowners with the designation 'de Thorntone', from Montrose and Kincardineshire respectively, figure in the Ragman Roll of 1296. Valentine de Thorneton held lands in the Mearns in the reign of Robert I; the name turns up in Glasgow in the 15th century. Some Scottish Thorntons settled in Prussia in 1644, and their name was translated to Dornthon. The reverse process happened in Ireland, where several native names such as Drennan, Skehan and Tarrant (all containing a 'thorny' element) were assimilated to Thornton.

Thow This name (pronounced to rhyme with 'how') is quite common in Angus and Aberdeenshire, along with its variant Thaw; no convincing derivation has been suggested, but it could be from a place-name. The name of James Thaw was recorded in Aberdeen in 1789.

Tierney From an Irish patronymic *O Tighearnaich*–'descendant of the lord', and one of the words used for God in the Gaelic liturgy; it is the name of three separate Irish septs, and is found frequently in Glasgow, and also in Edinburgh.

Timmins / Timms Usually from the Irish *MacToimin*–'son of Tommy'; but if the name is of English origin it will be 'son of Timothy'. In Scotland the name is found in Edinburgh and Glasgow.

Tindall 'Valley of the Tyne'; and although there are several rivers Tyne, the Cumbrian one is the most likely source of the surname. William de Tindal is recorded in Glasgow early in the 13th century, and there were families of the name in Angus. John Tendall was a burgess of Dundee in the 1520s; it may have been his family who gave their name to Tendall's Wynd in the city. By the 16th century the name is found all over Scotland, but not in any great quantity.

Toal–see **Tollin**

Togher / Tocher In its second spelling it is from Tocher, a place-name in Aberdeenshire, whose derivation is Old Gaelic *tochar* (a causeway). Taucher in Banffshire is another possibility. The surname was and is current in both these shires. The spelling Togher may indicate an Irish origin, from *O Tuathchair,* which is thought to incorporate the words *tuath*–'people, land', and *caraid*–'friend'. Toghers are found in Glasgow, but only relatively recently and not in large numbers.

Tod / Todd Tod is the Scots word for fox, and like very many other such words was also current in the North of England, first as a nickname-forename and later as a surname. The former spelling is reckoned to be the Scottish one, but either way the name referred to some characteristic of the bearer–sly, foxy-faced, red-haired or whatever. There is a reference in the 1270s to a Baldwin Tod of Lamberton in Berwickshire, and the name appears to have been current in the eastern Borderland from that time onward. By the 16th century it was widely established in the Lowlands.

Tollan / Tollin An Irish name, usually spelt Toole, but sometimes appearing in Glasgow as Toal. It is from the patronymic *O Tuathalain,* involving the Gaelic word *tuath*, which means people, tribe or country.

Toner A surname which came to Scotland via Ulster, it incorporates the Old Norse personal name *Tomhrair,* meaning 'protection'. It is virtually confined to the Glasgow area.

Torrance The word *torr* in Gaelic means 'heap'–sometimes in the literal sense of a mound (English 'tor'), sometimes in the figurative one of a 'lot'; in place-name parlance, *torran* is 'little mound', and there are two places called Torrance, one near Glasgow and the other at East Kilbride. In the mid-17th century there was a John

Torrance in Glasgow, and another of the name at Newbattle; at the same time the name is recorded in Edinburgh in the spelling Torrens, and is thought to have migrated to Sweden whence it returned home via an officer of King William in 1690. The name was that of several early Australian pioneers who gave it to a lake and a river in the Antipodes. Torrance, still the usual spelling, is nowadays found mainly in Glasgow and Edinburgh.

Tosh / Toshack Tosh is nearly always a contraction of **MacIntosh**, and is found mainly in the Tayside and Grampian areas. Alexander Toshe was a burgess of Aberdeen in the early 1600s, and Margaret Toash was recorded in that city in 1794. Toshack has the same etymology, but a slightly different origin: in the 14th century the Toschachs of Monzievaird in Perthshire were thanes (in Gaelic *toiseachan*) of Glen Tilt, having adopted the surname from their rank. They were later known as MacIntoshes, but the earlier form of the name persisted in Perthshire until the 17th century; it is now found mainly in Edinburgh.

Tough Correctly, but increasingly seldom, pronounced 'tooch' (the 'ch' as in 'loch'). Like **Tulloch**, this surname has its basis in the Gaelic word *tulach,* which means 'hillock' and is a recurrent place-name element. The parish of Tough near Alford in Aberdeenshire gave a local surname with the same spelling but pronounced 'teuch'. The Aberdeen records abound in mentions of the name: Isabel and Henry Toulch are recorded in 1361, Sande Touch two hundred years later; John Towicht was a baker in the city in the 1580s, and there are many other examples. The name soon spread to Fife, one of the first sightings being Sir James Toucht who was a notary there in the 1540s. Tough is however still reckoned to be an Aberdeenshire name.

Tracey In Irish Gaelic the word *treasach* means 'warlike', and it produced the patronymic *O Treasaigh* which became a common surname with the spelling Tracey. It began to appear in Glasgow and Edinburgh in the last century, and is now a popular girl's forename (its etymology having presumably been ignored).

Traill The source is probably a place-name from south west Scotland, and likely candidates are Trailtrow and Trailflat in Dumfries, not excluding Treales in Lancashire; all embody the Brittonic word *tref* meaning homestead. The Traills of Blebo in Fife were a notable family; one of them was bishop of St Andrews in 1385, and presided over the coronation of Robert III in the cathdral there in 1390; another, Magister Thomas Trayl, held office in the priory of St Andrews; they are said to have provided off-shoots in Orkney in the 16th century, and the name still appears there and in Caithness. Thomas Trayle was a canon of Aberdeen in 1366, and others of the name continue to figure in the burghal records in the next two centuries. Another Thomas Trail is recorded in Glasgow in the 1450s; and a 17th-century Robert Traill, a graduate of Edinburgh, had to take refuge in Holland on account of his radical presbyterian views. The surname is now strongest in Aberdeen.

Trainer / Trayner / Traynor In England the surname means what it says, and has the additional sense of 'trapper'. But in Glasgow, where the name is chiefly located in Scotland, it is much more likely to be a reduction of the Irish patronyic *Mac Threinfhir*–'son of the strong man or champion'.

Trotter The name of a Border clan, whose progenitor must have been a runner or messenger. The name was current in Durham also; but the leading family seems to have been the Trotters of Mortonhall near Edinburgh, who date back to the late 14th century. John Trotter apppears in Berwick-on-Tweed in 1370, and the name continues to be prominent in the Borders and in Edinburgh and Glasgow.

Troup There seem to be two separate places called Troup which are the source of the surname: one is in the parish of Gamrie near Banff and the other in Ayrshire, and the early records broadly confirm this. Finlay Troup is recorded in Kincardineshire in 1481, and Normond Trupt was a burgess of Aberdeen in the 17th century. The southern branch is represented by Hamelin of Troup whose lands were forfeit to Edward I in 1306, and by Thomas Troup, a burgess of Linlithgow in the 1530s.

Tulloch There are dozens of place-names which embody the Gaelic word *tulach,* meaning a knoll or hillock, a topographical feature which occurs with peculiar frequency in the Grampian area; any or all of these knolls could have given rise to the surname Tulloch, which is nowadays at its commonest in Aberdeenshire. Nicholas de Tolach and Fergus de Tulache are recorded in Brechin in the 14th century, and many others appear in Angus and Kincardineshire at the same time. John Tulach was a burgess of Aberdeen in 1411, and Thomas Tulloch became bishop of Orkney shortly thereafter; the name seems to have taken root in the island, with several more contemporary mentions in the records. John Tulloch, a leading Victorian churchman and authority on sin, was Principal of the University of St Andrews. Tullo and Tully are both contractions, but Tullis is different—a Fife name of Irish provenance. See also **Tough**.

Turnbull A surname belonging to what was reckoned to be one of the more turbulent clans on both sides of the Border. At one time thought to be from the Old English adjective *trumbald,* which means 'strongly bold', later scholarship derives it from the Norman name de Tremblay (see however the Introduction for a picturesque legendary origin). There was a Robert de Tremblay in Fife in the late 13th century, and others of the name crop up in in Angus a few years later. But the chief representative of the family was

Walter Turnbull, who in the 14th century had a charter from David II of the lands of Minto, where his family held sway for several generations. The Turnbulls began to migrate from their native Teviotdale at an early stage: Walter Tornbole is recorded in Stirling in the 1350s, Patrick Turnbull was a bailie of Edinburgh a little later, and William Turnbull, founder of Glasgow University, was bishop of the diocese until his death in 1454. Nowadays Turnbulls, while still commonest in Edinburgh, are scattered all over Scotland and beyond.

Turner An occupational name, usually from lathe-working, but sometimes involving other senses of the word 'turn'. It was very much commoner south of the Border, and has been widely distributed in Ireland since the 16th century, but the name has a long enough history in Scotland. Thomas Turner was in Aberdeen in 1382; a century later there was a John Turnoure in Irvine and a William Turnoure in Edinburgh. James Turner, soldier, author, royalist and Glasgow graduate, served under Gustavus Adolphus in 1630 and was knighted at the Restoration.

Turpie The Old Norse name Thorfinn was frenchified by the Normans to Turpin, and is the name of the legendary Archbishop in the *Chanson de Roland* (c.1100). It appears in Scotland later in the same century in the person of Turpin, bishop of Brechin. The name took on the familiar form of Turpie, and became in due course a surname, occurring mainly in Fife. John and William Turpy are mentioned in the late 16th century, William Turpie appears in Kirkcaldy in 1641 and Alexander Turpie in Leven in 1688. The notorious highwayman had no Scottish connection, and his particular version of the surname appears to be obsolete even in England.

Tweddle A corruption of Tweed-dale, and a surname originally taken by someone from that valley. John and William Twedale appear in the records as Border archers in the early 1400s, and the name was said to have been common in Lanarkshire in the following century. The spelling Tweddell tends to be found in the north of England.

Tweedie From the lands of Tweedie in the parish of Stonehouse in Lanarkshire. The Ragman Roll of 1296 records the name of Finlay de Twydyn of Lanarkshire; but the main family was that of Drummelzier, near Peebles, who owned the barony for three hundred years from 1320 and imposed their will on the surrounding district. It was the habit of Sir James Tweedy, from his vantage-point in Drummelzier castle, to exact a toll from passing travellers, usually by violent means; the legend goes that he did it once too often, the intended victim being James V. Thomas Twedye is recorded in Irvine in 1542, Elizabeth Twedy in Glasgow in 1550 and Thomas Tweadie in Aberdeen in 1583. The name is still strong in Edinburgh.

e painter named William Vallance who studied
name also turns up in Aberdeen, but is now
asgow.

rsion of the French place-name element *vaux*,
valley'); it appears in the early records in the
llibus. The ruined castle at Dirleton is a Vaux
early 13th century (but Vauxhall is from a
'illiam de Vas was a charter-witness at that time,
us was an Edinburgh knight who did homage
6. The name occurs in Elgin a hundred years
Inverness. It may sometimes have become
ther Old French word for servant, related to
appears in Aberdeen in the 15th century and
th–it is still commonest in the north–by which
which of the two possible origins is the correct

name, from the word for small. It is found
d, where it has occurred sporadically since the
ost Vaughans will be recent imports. Another
n is the Irish patronymic *O Mohan*, which
erates as Vaughan.

n origin, first recorded in 1200 in the person of
and shortly to become Vacca. These forms
er a corruption of the personal name *Ucca* or
ning a cow. Alexander de Vacca is recorded in
n the 13th century, and William le Wache figures
of 1296 as a Peeblesshire laird. William Veitch
mmelzier in 1331, and the nearby lands of
ined by the powerful family of Veitch in the
ame, historically associated with the shire of
to appear in the Edinburgh and Border records

U

Ure A variant of Iver–see **MacIver**. There have been a few notable Glasgow Ures: David Ure was a weaver who became a cleric and later a geologist, and died in 1798; Andrew Ure was an early 19th-century chemist, and professor in Anderson's College; Alexander Ure was Lord President of the Court of Session from 1913 to 1920 with the judicial title of Baron Strathclyde. Although a John MacUre was recorded as a lawyer in Glasgow at the beginning of the 18th century, the name appears no longer to survive in this form.

Urie A much less common name than Ure but with a longer history; it usually comes from a river-name in Aberdeenshire (giving rise to Inverurie), or possibly from a place-name in Kincardine (involving *iubhar*, the Gaelic word for yew). Adam Urri was a burgess of Irvine in 1260, and two more of the name figure in the Ragman Roll of 1296–Huive Urry of Ayrshire and Hugh Urry of Forfarshire. The Urries of Pitfichie in Aberdeenshire produced an officer in the Civil War who became known as Sir John Hurry–an alternative spelling which is still to be found. See also under **Barclay**.

Urquhart From two Brittonic words *air* and *cairdean*, meaning 'at the woods', Urquhart is the name of a district on the north-west shore of Loch Ness, dominated by the spectacular Castle Urquhart. The vernacular pronunciation of the name was Orchar, and the somewhat odd spelling simply preserves the old Scots use of the letters 'quh' to represent the sound 'wh'; other spelling variants included Urcart and Hurcar. The earliest known bearer of the surname was William de Urchard, who fought for Robert the Bruce between 1297 and 1328, and became the first of the hereditary sheriffs of Cromarty. The family and its adherents became established as a clan, and the chief was knighted under Charles II. Sir Thomas Urquhart (1611-60) an eccentric scholar who claimed to trace his descent from Adam, and was a brilliant translator of Rabelais, was reported to have died of convulsive laughter on hearing of the Restoration. The line of the Urquharts of Cromarty died out in the 18th century, and the lands were sold; but the name is still very common in its place of origin and throughout Scotland–indeed, all over the world.

19th century m
in Edinburgh.
mainly found

Valentine The Latin word *v*
produced the forename Vale
popular saint whose festival
day of Spring. A knight call
Robert the Bruce of the lands
the landed family died out,
area and in Perthshire. Tho
1561; John Wallentyne was
the end of that century. Jan
studio in Dundee in 185?
establishments of its kind i
of the whole of Britain. T
spelling Weland (John We
1550s); the spellings Wil
Valentine, not exclusive
languages, and was also
version, Valente, has a str

Vallance The Vallances we
family in Scotland, but the
to have come from Valog
who came to Scotland in
of the baronies of Panmu
court of William the Lior
the 13th century with an
the Maules. Simon Waler
in the Carse of Gowrie i
landowner whose nam
Andrew Valance was a I

Vass Probably
the plural of *v*
Latin form of *v*
stronghold of
different source
and Sir John de
to Edward I in
later, and then
confused with
'vassal'. The na
in Orkney in the
time it is hard to
one.

Vaughan A We
throughout Scot
17th century, bu
possible deriva
sometimes trans

Veitch Of uncert
Radulphus Uac
would suggest e
the Latin *vacca*, n
the Soutra record
in the Ragman R
is recorded in D
Dawick were ob
15th century. The
Peebles, continue

of the next century, often in connection with a bloody feud with the neighbouring Tweedies, which persisted until the 17th century and beyond. William Veitch, a fervent Covenanter, was outlawed in 1667 and imprisoned on the Bass Rock in 1679; James Veitch, lawyer and correspondent of Frederick the Great, took the judicial title of Lord Eliock.

W

Waddell Wedale is an obsolete place-name in Midlothian whose origin is obscure but whose final syllable means 'valley'. The surname is all too often pronounced with the accent on the second syllable–presumably to avoid any association with the word 'waddle'–but the fans of the famous footballer Willie Waddell made no such mistake. Adam de Wedale is recorded as early as 1204; Thomas de Wedal was a canon of St Andrews in 1280, the first of a series of clerics of that name in the diocese. William Waldale crops up in Musselburgh in 1359, and Thomas Vadle was a merchant in Edinburgh in 1555. Wedell is another spelling which is still current. Betha Waddell, a pioneer in children's theatre in the 1920s and 30s, came from near Glasgow, where the name is now found mainly to be found.

Wade Not native to Scotland; most Scottish Wades probably originated in Ireland, where the name has been current since the 13th century, often as a contraction of McQuaid ('son of Wat'–see **Walter**). Field Marshal George Wade, who started Scotland's road-building programme in the 18th century, was an Irishman. In England the name can come either from the Old English personal name *Wada*, or from a noun in that language meaning 'ford'. Most Scottish Wades are to be found in Glasgow.

Wales A spelling variant of **Wallace** and **Walls**–the name need not imply Welshness. Ibbote Wales was a tenant of the Douglas lords in the 14th century; John Wales was recorded in Dumfries in 1659; there is little trace of the name in between times, but it is still quite common in Glasgow.

Walker Not somebody who walks, but who 'waulks', i.e. treads cloth in the process known as fulling. This obsolete trade was very important at one time: a Craft of Waulkers was founded in Edinburgh in 1500; and Walker is among the twenty commonest surnames (it is also very frequent in England, particularly around Leeds). Thomas *dictus* Walker is recorded in Berwickshire in 1324, and a William Walk turns up in Inverness a generation later. Johnanes Walkerr was a juror in Elgin in 1393, and Donald Walcare appears in Edinburgh in 1457. Johnnie Walker whose motto 'Still Going Strong' has been translated into most of the world's languages, was the name of the founder of a family firm of whisky distillers and blenders in the west of Scotland.

Walkinshaw Lands of this name in Renfrewshire have the probable meaning of 'Walker's copse', and this is the origin of the surname. The Walkinshaws of that Ilk, who obtained the lands in the 13th century, were hereditary foresters to the High Stewards of the Barony of Renfrew; Robert Walkyngschaw appears in Glasgow in 1551, and Adam Walkinschaw in Lauder in 1679. Clementina Walkinshaw, daughter of a Jacobite merchant in Glasgow, became for a time the mistress and companion in misery of the exiled Charles Edward Stuart.

Wallace The Old English word *waelis* and the Anglo-Norman word *waleis* both mean 'foreign'; the former gives the names **Walsh** and **Welsh,** and the latter **Wallace** (together with the English surname Wallis). The concept could refer to any minority group; the English applied it to Cymru, thus coining the term Wales. In Scotland it was used with reference to the inhabitants of the ancient kingdom of Strathclyde, who were of the Brittonic or Welsh race; those of them who survived into the mediaeval period came to have the surname Wallace. The first recorded bearer is Richard Wallensis (the name is in its Latinised form), a knight of Shropshire origin who came to Paisley in the 12th century; he was very probably a forebear of Sir William Wallace the great Scottish patriot and *terror Anglorum* who was executed in 1305. The lands of Elderslie in Renfrewshire, not Ayrshire as used to be thought, were held by Wallaces until the mid-15th century, and there were other important branches of the family, in Craigie near Dundee and in Fife. The name became quite common, particularly in the west; a 17th-century William Wallace was the master mason responsible for Heriot's Hopital, for the King's Lodging in Edinburgh Castle and for Linlithgow Palace.

Walls In England it means 'living near the wall'; in Lowland Scotland it is usually a version of **Wallace**. In the Northern Isles it is from the Orkney island of that name, which derives from Old Norse *vagr*–'a bay'–as in Kirkwall.

Walsh A variant of the English name Wallis, directly derived from Old English *waelise* (see **Wallace**); it was exported to Ireland, where at one time it and its variants Welsh and Welch were fourth most numerous of all surnames in that country. (Walsh is the noun, and Welsh the adjectival form). The name is present in the early Scottish records (John Walshe, Roxburgh 1360; John Welch, Peebles, 1376); but mostly the provenance will have been Irish.

Walter / Walters Not by origin Scottish, but the basis of several other Scottish names–see **Watson** and **Watt**. Walter is a Germanic forename consisting of the elements *wald* ('rule') and *heri* ('army')– see Introduction. The Normans brought the name to these islands, and usually elided the 'l', giving the abbreviation Wat. Patrick Walter is recorded in Kirkcudbright in 1376, but thereafter the name is fairly thin on the ground. Walterson is found in Orkney and Shetland.

Ward The name, referring to the occupation of watchman or guard, appears very sporadically in the Scottish records but is now quite common in all parts of the country. There was a John de Warde in Peebles in 1366, and Robert Waird was a burgess of Stirling in 1601. David Ward, the operatic bass, was born in Dumbarton in 1922. The name is common in Ireland, where it is usually a rendering of *mac an bhaird* ('son of the poet'); no doubt some Scottish Wards are so descended.

Warden Sometimes an occupational name (see **Ward**), but more likely to be from a place name which occurs in several locations in England and involves the words *ward dun* ('watch hill'). John Wardein and David Wardine were 17th-century Glaswegians, and John Warden turns up in Perthshire in the 1680s; the name is now relatively common there and in Fife and Angus.

Wardlaw The place name means 'watch hill' and occurs more than once in Scotland. Henricus de Wardlaw received from Robert the Bruce a charter of half the barony of Wilton in Roxburghshire. Master Walter de Wardlaw was canon of Aberdeen in the 1350s; another Walter de Wardlaw was bishop of Glasgow and later a cardinal and ambassador to England. It was his nephew Henry who became bishop of St Andrews in 1403, restored the cathedral, founded the University and became its first chancellor. Henry's brother William was progenitor of the Wardlaws of Pitreavie in Fife. Marion Wardlaw is described as 'Lady of Dudhope' in Dundee in 1554.

Wardrope The original bearer of this surname was keeper of the garments of a feudal household; the post was often hereditary, and 'wardrobe' in the 13th century included not only clothes but domestic chattels of many kinds. Robertus de Warderob figures in the annals of Arbroath Abbey in 1210; there was a John de

Wardroba in Dunbartonshire sixty years later, and a Randinus de Warderoba in Fife at the same time. Alisaundre and David de la Garderobe, landowners in Lothian and Fife respectively, were obliged to do homage to Edward I in 1296. Later the name appears in Aberdeen as Gardropa, in Perthshire as Gardroper and in Govan as Wedderop. Nowadays it is found mainly in Glasgow and Edinburgh.

Wark A place on the Northumberland side of the Tweed, it means 'earthworks' in the sense of fortifications. Johne of Wark is recorded in Lanarkshire in 1520; Robert Wark was a fugitive from justice in 1686; and the name is said to have been quite common in Ireland. The variant Work can be of the same origin, but in Orkney (where it has been found since the 16th century) it comes from the lands of that name in St Ola.

Warnock The Gaelic patronymic *Mac gille Mhearnaig* was sometimes anglicised to MacIlvernock. It means 'son of the servant of St Mearnag', and had a separate existence in County Down. In Scotland it was even more drastically reduced to Warnock, which however retains at least a vestige of the Gaelic pronunciation. Andree Warnock was recorded in Lanark, John Warnok in Glasgow and James Warnock in Ayrshire, all in the 1500s. The modern distribution of the name is similar.

Warren / Warrender La Varenne is a place near Dieppe, with the original meaning of 'warren' or game-park. There was a very important Norman family called Warrenne, some of whom settled in England after the Conquest; Ada de Warenne, mother of Malcolm IV and William I, was of this stock, as was Reginald de Warenne, who in the 13th century was granted a charter of the lands of Forgandenny and Culross. But there were other hunting grounds in Scotland whose inhabitants would take the name Warren; and the version Warrender almost certainly indicates employment of this kind, i.e. one who looks after a warren. John Warrender is recorded in Fife in 1601, and George Warrender was Dean of Guild in Aberdeen in the 1700s. Sir George Warrender of Lochend was Lord Provost of Edinburgh during the '15, and his Whiggish activities in the city hastened the failure of that botched enterprise.

Waters / Watters Most probably a variant of **Walters**, but also very common in Ireland, where it is thought to be a translation of one of several names involving the word *uisce*, Irish Gaelic for 'water'. The name has been recorded in Scotland since the 14th century (John Water, Newlands, 1376); Patrick Watter was in Aberdeen in 1598 and Adam Watter in Lauder in 1667. Sir George Waters was editor of *The Scotsman* in the inter-war period.

Waterson / Waterstone In either spelling the name means 'Walter's homestead', and can refer to one of a number of places in Scotland, some of them no longer on the map. William de Walteristoun and David de Walterstoun are recorded in the Mearns in the 14th century, and at the end of the 15th they are styling themselves Watterstone of that Ilk; the family did not survive into modern times. The lands of Waterstoun in Kilbarchan parish were alienated by William Waterstoun in the reign of Robert II; the name keeps cropping up in Glasgow in the 16th century. There were also Waterstons of that Ilk in Midlothian who were appointed surgeons to the royal household in the 14th century; Waltherston and Watherston were reputed to be common in Lauderdale, and the name in its modern form is well known in Edinburgh.

Watson By far the commonest of the Walter derivatives (see **Walters**), this surname is among Scotland's top twenty; in England it has to share the honours with Watts, Watkins and Watkinson, forms not native to this country. John Watson was a citizen of Edinburgh in the late 14th century; Robert Watsoun appears in Aberdeen in 1402, Thomas Watson in Dunipace in 1426, and Sir Donald Watsone in Moray in 1493. By the 16th century the name was becoming very common in the Lowlands, particularly in the north-east. George Watson, born in Edinburgh in 1654, made a fortune as a merchant banker; he endowed a hospital for children, which became George Watson's College in 1870.

Watt Another of the Walter-derivatives (see **Walters** and **Watson**), this surname is common throughout Scotland but particularly in the north-east where in some rural districts it used to flourish almost to the exclusion of all others. It was also common in Ulster, and may have been re-imported thence in recent years. Alexander Wat is recorded in Panmure in Angus in 1512, Walter Wat was in Brechin in 1586, and Patrick Watt in Turriff in 1609. The double-diminutive version Wattie is still current in Aberdeen. James Watt, engineer, inventor and pioneer of steam power, was born in Greenock in 1736: the unit of power known as the watt was named after him. Sir Robert Watson-Watt, born in Brechin in 1892, played a major part in the development of radar.

Waugh Traditionally a Border surname, found both on the English and the Scottish sides, its derivation is the Old English *wealh* ('a foreigner'–see also **Wallace**). Three Border lairds, David de Waughe of Lanarkshire, Robert Walgh of Roxburgh and Thomas Walghe of Peebles all figure in the Ragman Roll of 1296. William Waugh had a safe conduct in 1436, and John Wach was a notary in Peebles in 1448; John Walcht was a monk of Newbattle in 1467, and the Waughs of Heip in Roxburghshire were a landed family for four hundred years. Alexander Wauche bought a silken hat from Thomas Hodge in Dundee in 1560. The name is now found mainly in Glasgow and Edinburgh.

Webb The non-Scottish version of **Webster**, Webbs were numerous in the midlands and south of England, as well as in Belfast and Dublin. Most Scottish Webbs will be of fairly recent weaving.

Webster The first Webster worked at the weaver's trade, not necessarily in Scotland. The form '-ster' was an agency suffix in Middle English which underwent linguistic devaluation (see Introduction); it appears to have survived longer north of the Border, for Webster is a common name in Scotland, while Weaver is not. Nicholas Webster was a bankrupt in Berwick in 1251, Malcolm Webstare a burgess of Stirling in the 1430s, William Webster a baker and burgess of Dundee in 1688. The name is common in Angus and Aberdeenshire.

Wedderburn An obscure place in Berwickshire referring to a stream frequented by 'wethers' (sheep), and which gives a better-known surname. Walter de Wederburne, a Lothian laird, had to submit to Edward I in 1296. The name continues to be recorded in Berwickshire up to the 15th century, after which it re-surfaces in Dundee where a family of Wedderburns were town clerks and notaries from the 16th to the 18th centuries. Robert Wedderburn, a member of this gifted family, was the putative author in 1548 of the allegory *The Complaynt of Scotland* in which Dame Scotia denounces the English for their recent misdeeds. The family had been intermarrying with the **Scrimgeours**, another notable Dundee family, since at least the 16th century. The name is still current in Dundee, and also Fife and Aberdeenshire.

Wedell–see **Waddell**

Weir The Weirs of Blackwood in Lanarkshire claimed descent from one Radulph de Vere; it is probably this circumstance which has encouraged the tempting derivation from the French place-name Vere, which brings with it an association with the blue-blooded de Veres from Normandy (the Vere form is now virtually obsolete here). Other possible etymologies are the Gaelic patronymics *mac a mhaoir* ('son of the steward') or *mac an fluibhar* ('son of the smith'), both of which appear in modern dress as **MacNair**. But on the whole, a more prosaic origin of the name seems most probable, to wit the Old English word *waer*, modern English weir, meaning dam or 'fish-trap', and which gave rise to several place names both north and south of the border (e.g. Bridge of Weir). Most Scottish bearers of the name will therefore be descended from someone who lived by a dam. Major Weir, the celebrated warlock, was burned for witchcraft in 1670; but the name is otherwise respectable and figures in the peerage as that of the Barons Inverforth. It is now widespread throughout the country.

Welch / Welsh Welsh is very common in Glasgow; both names are variants of **Walsh**. John Welsh, a Presbyterian clergyman born in Dumfries in 1568, fell foul of both James I and Louis XIII and was banished from their respective countries; one of his descendants however returned to beget Jane Welsh, the sprightly wife of Thomas Carlyle.

Wells Someone who lived by a spring or a well might have received this surname; or it could come from one of the many places in England which incorporate the word Wells–the surname is by no means exclusively Scottish. In the early records it is Latinised to *de Fontibus*, and 'de Welles' is also used as a territorial designation from the 13th century onwards, mainly in north-east Scotland. Patrick Wells was a canon of Scone in the 1490s and Gilbert Wellis a burgess of Aberdeen at the same time; John Wellis was a presbyter in the diocese of Brechin and Patrick Wellis was prior of Perth, while James Wells had a merchant's booth in Dundee in the 1520s. The name is among the top twenty in the Dumfries and Galloway region.

Wemyss From *uamh*, earlier *uaim*, the Gaelic word for cave, with the locative ending *ais*; there are instances of the place name in Ayrshire and Fife, together with Weem in Perthshire; the received pronunciation of the surname is 'weems'. De Wemyss is used as a territorial designation from the beginning of the 13th century, and Wemyss became the surname of a branch of the royal house of Duff, the hereditary earls of Fife. Sir David Wemyss was ambassador to Norway in 1286; Sir Michael Wemyss was a Fife laird who, although he had submitted to Edward I in 1296, nevertheless suffered persecution at the hands of that relentless monarch. After the Wars of Independence the family reaped the reward for their support of the Bruce, and the senior branch received from Charles I the earldom of Wemyss. Lord Elcho, heir to the earldom, was attainted after the 1745 Rising, but the line continues (with some change of surname) to the present time. Most frequently found in Fife and Lothian.

West Someone who came from the west; the name occurred all over the Lowlands, and in the 17th century, and for no apparent reason became very frequent in parts of Aberdeenshire and Perthshire–where it still is mainly to be found. It also has dozens of compound forms including Weston ('west farm'), Westwood (places in Fife and Perthshire) and Westwater (John Westwater was a friar at Culross in 1565). West was a very common surname in Co. Limerick, and some of the city-dwelling Wests in Scotland may be of Irish origin.

Whelan The Irish patronymic *O Faolain* means 'descendant of the wolf' and evolved into the surname MacWhellan. Some of the MacWhellans of Antrim are reputed to have taken refuge in Argyll after persecution by the Macdonnells. The surname arrived in Glasgow–whether by way of Argyll or Ulster–in the spellings Whelan, Wheelan and occasionally Whelehan. The *Mac* form seems now to be obsolete.

White / Whyte Over the years, White has occupied around fiftieth place in the list of leading Scottish surnames; it is particularly common in the Tayside region, where the 'y' spelling is twice as frequent as the 'i'. (Whyte is apparently not an affectation like Smythe, merely a spelling variant). Both forms started off as nicknames, referring to the hair, complexion or even clothing of the bearer. Adam Quhyt received from Robert the Bruce a charter of land at Barskimming in Ayrshire; Gilbert Qwhytt was bailie of Rutherglen in 1376; Thome White was in Irvine in 1426, and Andrew Qwhit in Brechin in 1472; Robert Whyte was provost of Kirkcaldy in 1658. Ian Whyte, the composer and conductor, was born in Dunfermline in 1901.

Whiteford From the lands of Whiteford on the River Cart near Paisley. There are references to Whiteford of that Ilk from the 13th century, but the family seems to have died out around 1688. Walter Whiteford is recorded in Renfrewshire in 1263, and Johannes Quhitefurd was involved in the sack of Dumbarton in 1489; Robert Quhytfurd was cellarer of Crossraguel around the same time, and there are references to a family of Quhitefurde of Milton in 1558. The surname is still localised in that area.

Whitehead A development of **White.** Whitehead appears first in Berwickshire in 1300; it turns up in Dundee two hundred years later in the egregious spelling Quhithed.

Whitelaw *Law* is the characteristic word for hill in the eastern Lowlands, and Whitelaw means 'white hill'; as a place-name it has several instances, but the surname probably comes from Berwickshire. The Whitelaws of that Ilk lived near Dunbar, and their progenitor John de Wytelowe figures in the Ragman Roll of 1296. Archibald de Quhitelaw, eminent cleric and secretary of state to James III, was archdeacon of St Andrews in the 1470s. Patrick Quhitlaw is recorded in Angus in the 1560s. The late Viscount Whitelaw had a family estate at Gartmore in Perthshire.

Whitten / Whitton A common place-name, occurring all over the United Kingdom; it was originally either 'white *tun*' ('white homestead') or Hwita's *tun'*. The surname in Scotland comes from the lands of Whitton in Morebattle, Roxburgh. Magister R. de Wytton was a charter witness in Newbattle in 1285; Michael de Witton and Adam de Witton, both Selkirk landowners, and Richard de Wyttone, parson of Hawick, all had to do homage to Edward I in 1296. Two thirds of the bearers of the name now live in Dundee and district.

Wight / Wightman The Old English adjective *wight* meant valiant or stalwart, and the surname is common in the north of England as well as in Edinburgh (its main Scottish location). Thomas Whight of Perthshire figures in the Ragman Roll of 1296; James Wicht was prebendary ot the College Church of Holy Trinity, Edinburgh in 1554; and Alexander Wycht was a monk of Inchaffray at about the same time. The surname Wightman is of the same derivation and has a similar distribution. Gilbert Wichtmann was rector of Lyne near Peebles in 1527, and John Wychtman lived in that area a few years later; Thomas Vychtman appears in Perthshire in the 1540s, and John Waichtman lived in Melrose in 1606. The surname Wighton, found mainly in Dundee, has a different derivation; it probably just means 'dwelling place'.

Wilkie The Scottish version of Wilkins (a name not native to this country), and a double diminutive of William (see **Williamson**). It is an east-of-Scotland surname, found in large numbers in Midlothian, Fife and Angus from the beginning of the 14th century. David Wilkie is recorded in Pitcairn, Fife in 1495. James Wilkie was principal of St Salvator's College, St Andrews in the 1570s, and Robert Wilkie was principal of the sister college of St Leonards from 1589—1611; in the 1750s, William Wilkie was professor of Natural Philosophy in the University. The most famous however was Sir David Wilkie, a son of the manse of Cults in Fife, and one of the finest Scottish genre painters of the early 19th century.

Another Sir David Wilkie, born in Kirriemuir in 1882, became a pioneer in abdominal surgery and endowed the laboratories in Edinburgh University which bear his name.

Wilkinson A North-of England surname, much less common in Scotland. More frequently found was Wilkieson (son of **Wilkie**) which appears in the records from the 14th to the 17th centuries. However, Wilkinson has been recorded here sporadically for a long time, and now has a strong presence in the major cities. John Wylkynson or Wilkinsoune lived in Uddingston in 1498, and a cleric called William Wilkinsone appears in the records at the same time. Robert Wylkynsone was vicar of Ardrossan in 1537–perhaps a surprising name to find in a solidly Gaelic-speaking community.

Will This surname, although an obvious contraction of William (see **Williamson**) scarcely exists outside Scotland; conversely the patronymic Wills, common in England, is rare north of the Border. The records disclose a Robertus Will, a councillor of Aberdeen in 1435; John Will lived in Partick in 1577; Andro Will was a butcher in Aberdeen in the 1530s, and the name is still most often to be found in that city.

Williamson The Christian name William was common all over the Western world, rivalling John in popularity. In origin it is Germanic, consisting like so many others of two unconnected but warlike words, in this instance 'will' and 'helmet' (see Introduction). If the popularity in England of the name William is due to the Conqueror, in Scotland it is because of William the Lion (1165—1214). Like every common forename, William gave rise to a wide variety of surnames. Williamson is a common enough form in Scotland: it first appears in the records in the 14th century (quite late for a patronymic of this kind), and is surprisingly common in the Highland region (taking twenty-ninth place). Ion Willameson was an Angus man of the 1380s; Alexander Willyamsone appears in Aberdeen and John Williamson in Perth late in the following century. Peter Williamson, born in Aberdeenshire in 1730, had a varied career: successively a slave in the Americas, prisoner of the Cherokee Indians and then of the French, he later became an author and finally instituted the penny post in Edinburgh and published the city's first street directory. Williams, the third commonest name in England and Wales, is not native to Scotland.

Willis / Willison Both these names are 'son of Willie', a diminutive of William (see **Williamson**). Walter *filius* Wille held lands in Dumfries around 1214; John Willieson was commissioner to the Convention for Stirling in 1573. The names were current in Stirling and Lanarkshire, and are now found mainly in Glasgow and Edinburgh.

Willock / Willocks / Wilox 'Little Will', a double diminutive of William (see **Williamson**), this group of surnames is almost entirely confined to the north-east. John Willok is recorded in Aberdeen in 1506, Gilbert Willox in 1584; James Willox was a burgess there in 1611, and John Wiliks was a citizen in 1727. John Willok was vicar of Stracathro in the 1520s and there was another John Willok recorded in Brechin later in the century. Outliers are found in Ayr and Orkney; the spelling Wilox is still surprisingly common in Aberdeen.

Wilson By far the most popular of the William derivatives (see **Williamson**), Wilson is now the third commonest surname in Scotland. It is so widespread as to defy categorisation, but is noticeably frequent in Fife and Dundee where it presents something of a hazard in the telephone directories. The name is also very common in England and in Ireland, and no Scottish origin can be assumed without additional evidence. It has been steadily exported to America for over two centuries: notable bearers were James Wilson, born on a farm near Ceres in Fife, who became a political ideologist and one of the framers of the Constitution of the USA; and Alexander Wilson, born in Paisley in 1766, known as the father of American ornithology. George Washington Wilson, despite the translatlantic echoes in his name, was a stay-at-home: born near Banff, he spent most of his life behind a camera and from the 1850s until his death in 1893 published the world's largest collection of photographic views.

Winning This Galloway surname is a shortened version of *Mac gille Winning*–'son of the servant of St Winnan'. Winnan is the Cumbric form of Finnan (c.f. Glenfinnan), and is celebrated in the name Kilwinning in Ayrshire. The *Mac* form of the surname is recorded in south-west Scotland in the 13th century, but is now obsolete. John Wynning, cordiner, was a burgess freeman of Glasgow in 1591; a century later Robert Winnie was a bookseller and stationer in Dumfries. The name is now seldom found outside Glasgow and the south west.

Winter / Winters A wintry reference is meant, whether to the original bearers' temperament or appearance or season of birth. Jop Wyntyr is recorded in Yester, East Lothian in 1374; Thomas Wyntir was a baillie of Glasgow in 1447, and John Wyntyr a burgess of Arbroath at the same period. Robert Wynter was a monk at Culross in the mid 16th century. The name has always been common in Dundee and Angus.

Winton In the country around Edinburgh there are several settlement-names of this type, from the Old English personal name *Wine*, meaning friend; thus 'friend's homestead'. The place-name is the same as Winston, and also occurs all over England. Alan de Wyntoun's name appears in the Soutra records, and Henry de Wynton's in those of Newbattle at the end of the 12th century. Alan and Gode de Wyntone were landowners in this district who had to submit to Edward I in 1296, and Thomas de Winton of Ayrshire was under the same compulsion. Andrew de Wynton, prior of St Serf's on Loch Leven in the late 14th century (he who compiled a chronicle of Scotland from the beginning of the world until the reign of James I) was probably of Aberdeen stock, as were certainly George de Venton, Andrew Wentoune and James Wentoun in the following century. The name remains most frequent in the Dundee and Aberdeen areas.

Wise / Wiseman The original bearers of these names must have been thought learned or sage. William Wyse was a canon of Moray in 1358; the name of Thomas Wyse is recorded in Caithness in 1381. Wiseman has an even older pedigree: Andrew Wysman was recorded in Dallas, Moray, in 1232, Thomas Wisman in Elgin in 1261 and William Wysman in Forres in 1266. William Wiseman obtained from David II the barony of Don in the late 14th century. The north-east however had no monopoly of wisdom, and the name also occurred in Berwickshire in the 13th century, and thereafter is found sparingly all over the Lowlands. Wiseman is still mostly to be found in Aberdeen and district.

Wishart From the Norman Wischard (Old Norse *visk hard*–'wise and bold'. It became Wishart when it reached Scotland (still in the form of a forename) and in England was sometimes corrupted to Wisker. The Central French form is Guiscard. As a surname it truly belongs to Scotland; William Wischard is recorded in Cambuskenneth around 1200; John Wischard was in Ross fifty years later; and William Wischard was a Culdee monk at St Andrews during the same period. John Wychard, a Mearns laird, figures in the Ragman Roll of 1296; Johnett Wischart was burnt for witchcraft in Aberdeen in 1596. The most famous, George Wishart, a good Christian and a charismatic preacher, was burned for heresy at St Andrews in 1545; the contemporary rumour that he was plotting the death of Cardinal Beaton is almost certainly a case of mistaken identity, for Wishart came of a large and influential Angus family, at least one of whose members shared his forename. A later George Wishart, unrelated, was private chaplain to the great Montrose and wrote his biography; he became the first bishop of Edinburgh after the Restoration.

Witherspoon–see **Wotherspoon**

Wood / Woods Much commoner without the terminal 's', Wood occupies fifty-fifth place in order of frequency of surnames in Scotland; in England it would be much higher. The name referred originally to someone who lived or worked by a wood. William Wod is recorded in Kilravock in Moray in 1295; Ade Wood and Rogers Wode were Douglas tenants in East Lothian; Thomas Wod features in the Newbattle records of 1458, and John Vode was a friar preacher in Aberdeen in 1486. Sir Andrew Wood, the naval commander, born in Largo, defended the Firth of Forth against English raiding vessels in the early 1500s. Alexander Wood ('Lang Sandy') was a celebrated Edinburgh surgeon in the late 18th century, and the first man in the city to carry an umbrella. The form Woods is very common in Ulster, where it was reputedly a translation of half a dozen different names which contain an element resembling *coille*, the Irish Gaelic word for wood or copse.

Work–see **Wark**

Wotherspoon Of doubtful etymology, this probably originated as a place-name with some such meaning as 'sheepfold' (? 'wethers' pound'). Roger Wythirspon is recorded in Renfrewshire in the late 13th century, and John Wydderspwn in Coupar Angus in 1518; Nicholas Withirspwne appears in Glasgow in 1548 and Sir Thomas Vadderspoun in Falkland in the same year. The Rev. John Witherspoon, born in Gifford in 1722, became president of the college that is now Princeton University in 1768, and took an active part on the side of the colonists in the American Revolution. Although the Witherspoon spelling is probably more correct, the 'o' form is commoner, especially in Glasgow.

Wright A person who made things, or 'wrought', was liable to be known as a wright (from Old English *wyrhta*, related to *wyrcan*, 'to work'). The word not only caught on as a surname but survived longer in general use in Scotland than in the south; it came to have the restricted meaning of joiner–which it still does in some areas. The records of Coupar Angus abbey for 1468 contain the names of Robert and Thomas Wrycht, who were carpenters. There is no other Scottish surname which embodies the woodworker's trade: Carpenter and Joiner are both very rare in Scotland (but see **MacIntyre**). Rauf le Wrighte of Stirling and Wiliam Wrycht of Lanarkshire were men of substance whose names figure in the Ragman Roll of 1296. The name was common in Aberdeen in the 14th century, and there are references in the Brechin episcopal records to a William Wrycht who was 'lord of Glenesk' in the 1430s. The compound forms of Cartwright, Wainwright and Sievewright tend to be commoner south of the Border.

Wylie Very likely from the adjective 'wily' or crafty; it was often used as a standing epithet for the fox, as in Tod Wylie in Henryson's *Fables*. It was common as a forename in Scotland, and as a surname it is found hardly anywhere else. Donald Wyly lived in Thornhill, Dumfriesshire in 1376, and John Wili in Montrose in 1431; Robert Wylye was vicar of Kincaldrum near Forfar in 1434, and William Wyly appears in Ayrshire a few years later. Richard Wyly was vicar of St Mary's, Dundee in the 1450s. The name is common all over, more particularly in the west of Scotland.

Y

Yates Literally, 'at the gate or gap', an Old English usage; so the surname is not confined to Scotland. It is the same name as Yeats, the poet's forebears having been Dubliners of Anglo-Saxon stock. Adam del Yate is recorded in Lochmaben in 1347, John Yet in Arbroath in 1425, William Yet in Banff in 1607 and Agnes Yatts in Falkirk in 1681. A landed family of Yetts were established in Teviotdale, and gave their name to the hamlet of Yetton. Yeats is now found mainly in the north-east, Yates in Glasgow.

Yeaman The Scottish version of yeoman, which originally meant 'young man', but in the late mediaeval period came to signify a freeholder. The surname does not appear in Scotland until the 16th century; there was a George Zeman in Moray in 1565, and an Archibald Yemen in Berwickshire a century later. But the name for some reason has long been associated with Dundee: David Yeamen was a merchant there in 1592 and Christina Yemane appears in the next century; a thoroughfare leading from the Nethergate to the docks was called Yeamen Shore.

Young A surname originally given to a son who had the same forename as his father, Young exactly corresponded to the use of the term Jr. in the USA–and, indeed, to the use of *Mac* in early Highland history. Young is the commonest nickname-surname in Scotland after Brown and Reid, and at the present time is fifteenth in the list of leading Scottish surnames. Young cannot be assigned to any particular area of Scotland, but the earliest documented occurrences are in the north: there was a John Young in Dingwall in the 1340s and Symone Yong was a burgess of Elgin at the same time. Peter Young, born in Dundee in 1544, was tutor to King James

VI; Thomas Young, born in Perthshire a generation later, performed a similar function in relation to the poet Milton.

Younger Probably of the same derivation as Young, although the prevalence of the name in Fife, especially in the trade of salt-making which came from Flanders, has given rise to the theory that Younger is from Youncker, a common Flemish name (*jongh herr* means 'young master', cf. *Junker*). William Yhunger is recorded in Aberdour in 1376; Fynlaw Ywnger was in Banff in 1388, and Jhone Zounger in Perth in 1474. The Youngers were a landed family in Clackmannan from the 16th century; an offshoot made the name famous as brewers. The name, much less common than Young, is now found mainly in Glasgow and Edinburgh.

Youngson An Aberdeenshire name, meaning what it says, and much less frequent than **Young** of which it can be said to be the next stage. Patrick Zongsone is recorded in Aberdeen in 1511; Alexander Yowngsone was recorded Strathdee in 1558, and the Rev. Robert Youngson was minister of Aboyne a generation later.

Younie This name, pronounced 'yoo-nie', is possibly a variant of *Eunon*, the Gaelic form of Adamnan. St Adamnan was ninth abbot of Iona, one of the leading ecclesiastics in early Scottish and Irish history, and now best-known for his biography of St Columba, written towards the end of of the 7th century. John Eunie appears in Rothes in 1692, and John Yunie in Moray a year or two later. It is still relatively frequent in the Aberdeen area, sometimes in the versions Tewnion or Teunion, where the 't' was either carried over from 'saint', reflecting vernacular usage, or developed as an aid to pronunciation.

Yule Originally given as a Christian name to a child born or baptised during the twelve-day season of Yule or Christmastide. Johannes Yhole appears in Haddington in 1374, and another of the same name was chaplain in Aberdeen in the 1390s. John Youll was in Stirling in 1525, Robert Ywle in Glasgow in 1551, and James Yuill was minister of Dairsie in Fife in 1585. There were also Yules in Orkney in the 16th century; they seem to have died out there, but retain a presence in Aberdeenshire, and also in Glasgow.